THE WARRIOR QUEENS

THE
WARRIOR
QUEENS

ANTONIA
FRASER

ALFRED A. KNOPF
NEW YORK
1989

THIS IS A BORZOI BOOK
PUBLISHED BY ALFRED A. KNOPF, INC.

Copyright © 1988 by Antonia Fraser

Library of Congress Cataloging-in-Publication Data
Fraser, Antonia, [*date*]
The warrior queens / Antonia Fraser.
p.   cm.
Bibliography: p.
Includes index.
ISBN 0-394-54939-2
1. Women – Biography.   2. Queens – Biography.   3. Women in
politics.   4. Women soldiers.   I. Title.
D109.F72   1989
920.72 – dc19   88-45778   CIP

Manufactured in the United States of America
First American Edition

For my daughters Rebecca and Flora
Who drive their own literary chariots
With love

CONTENTS

List of Illustrations   ix
Author's Note   xi

PART ONE

1   A Singular Exception   3
2   Antique Glories   14
3   The Queen of War   27
4   Iceni: This Powerful Tribe   43
5   Ruin by a Woman   58
6   The Red Layer   77
7   Eighty Thousand Dead   90
8   O Zenobia!   107

PART TWO

9   Matilda, Daughter of Peter   131
10   England's Domina   151
11   Lion of the Caucasus   167
12   Isabella with her Prayers   182
13   Elizabetha Triumphans   203
14   Jinga at the Gates   226
15   Queen versus Monster   247
16   The Valiant Rani   272
17   Iron Ladies   297
18   Unbecoming in a Woman?   323

Reference Notes   337
Index   363

ILLUSTRATIONS

Between pages 96 and 97

Thomas Thornycroft's statue of Boadicea and her daughters (photograph by Sue Lanzon)
Boadicea, from Thomas Heywood's *Exemplary Lives* (British Library)
Boadicea, from Aylett Sammes' *Britannia Antiqua Illustrata* (British Library)
'Boadicea haranguing the Britons', by H. C. Selous (Mansell Collection)
Boadicea, from H. E. Marshall's *Our Island Story*
The Boudican firing of Londinium, by Richard Sorrell (Museum of London)
Boadicea and her ladies, from Holinshed's *Chronicles* (British Library)
The Britons' last battle against the Romans, by Alan Sorrell (Museum of London)
Crater depicting Amazons fighting Greeks (Mansell Collection)
Engraving of Cleopatra (Mary Evans Picture Library)
Ptolemaic plaque showing Cleopatra (Werner Forman Archive/Schindler Collection, New York)
Judith and Holofernes (Ronald Sheridan/Ancient Art and Architecture Collection)
Engraving of Zenobia (Hulton Picture Library)
Semiramis (Mansell Collection)
The Trung sisters (print kindly supplied by Dr Ralph Smith)
Trieu Au (Maurice Durand Collection of Vietnamese Art, Yale University Library)

Between pages 256 and 257

Countess Matilda of Tuscany (Biblioteca Apostolica Vaticana)
The Empress Maud (British Library)
Countess Matilda at Canossa, by Alfred Cluysenaar (Roger-Viollet)
Queen Tamara (Mary Evans Picture Library)
Monogram of Queen Tamara
Queen Isabella, a detail from *The Madonna of the Catholic Kings* (Oronoz, Madrid)
Medal showing Caterina Sforza (Victoria and Albert Museum)
Triumphal entry of Ferdinand and Isabella into Granada (Foto Mas, Barcelona)
William Rogers' *Eliza, Triumphans* (Weidenfeld and Nicolson Archive)
Joris Hoefnagel (attrib.), *Queen Elizabeth and the Three Goddesses* (reproduced by gracious permission of Her Majesty Queen Elizabeth II)
Queen Elizabeth I at Tilbury (National Maritime Museum, Greenwich)

Illustrations

Queen Jinga being received by the Portuguese Governor (photograph supplied by the School of Oriental and African Studies, London University)

Queen Jinga receiving Christian baptism (photograph supplied by SOAS, London University)

Queen Jinga venerating her brother's bones (photograph supplied by SOAS, London University)

Statue of Queen Anne by Rysbrack (photograph by Edwin Smith)

Catherine the Great (Novosti Press Agency)

The Empress Maria Theresa of Austria (Archiv Gerstenberg)

Monument to Maria Theresa in Vienna (Roger-Viollet)

Queen Louise of Prussia, a portrait by Joseph Grassi (Bildarchiv Preussischer Kulturbesitz)

Queen Louise, King Frederick William III of Prussia and Tsar Alexander I at the tomb of Frederick the Great (Ullstein Bilderdienst)

Napoleon receiving Queen Louise at Tilsit, by N. L. F. Gosse (Ullstein Bilderdienst)

Kalighat watercolour of the Rani of Jhansi (Victoria and Albert Museum)

Contemporary painting of the Rani of Jhansi (photograph supplied by the Royal Commonwealth Society)

Site of the massacre at Jhansi (British Library)

Durga (Victoria and Albert Museum)

Statue of the Rani of Jhansi at Gwalior (photograph by Sophie Baker)

Golda Meir (Camera Press – Goldman/Setton, London)

Indira Gandhi (photograph by N. V. Edwards, Camera Press, London)

Margaret Thatcher (Press Association)

Queen Elizabeth II at the Trooping of the Colour (Hulton Picture Library)

Mrs Thatcher with members of her Cabinet (Associated Press)

Cartoon of Mrs Thatcher driving a chariot, by Griffin (Express Newspapers)

AUTHOR'S NOTE

'That's the Romans for you – four hundred years of occupying *our* country': these indignant words were spoken in 1986 by one who, like myself, was gazing down from an observer's platform into some archaeological excavations in the City of London. Such robust patriotism, undaunted by the passage of quite a lot of time, reminded me of my earliest involvement with Queen Boadicea, via H. E. Marshall's inimitable *Our Island Story*, a work enjoyed by me with passion as a child in the 1930s. It was Boadicea the patriotic heroine whose story first thrilled me; I wept for her treatment – and that of her daughters – and wept again, but this time in admiration, for her death.

The word heroine, as opposed to hero, is important in all this: for there is no doubt in my mind that a part – indeed a large part – of Boadicea's appeal to me then lay in her female sex (the early feminism of those who have brothers close in age should never be underestimated). Half a century later in exploring both the history and the subsequent reputation of Queen Boadicea, those two interwoven themes of her patriotism and her femininity have not seemed to me either irrelevant or outmoded. I suppose therefore I can claim a lifetime's preoccupation with the subject of Boadicea, even if my early feelings of dislike for the misogynist Romans have waned – just a little.

In recounting the stories of other Warrior Queens, as indeed in investigating that of Boadicea herself, I have obviously been dependent on the works of many scholars and experts in their field, to which detailed acknowledgement is made in the Reference Notes, but I should like to express my deep overall gratitude here. The spelling of proper names in a book crossing so many civilizations and cultures has obviously constituted a real problem; I have attempted to solve it by choosing that spelling I have judged most intelligible to the English-speaking world at the present date; but I should emphasize that ultimately these various choices have been mine, not those of the experts acknowledged above.

In particular I should like to thank the following: HM the Queen for gracious permission to quote from the Royal Archives at Windsor and Miss Jane Langton, late of the Royal Archives, for her assistance; Dr Chaim Herzog, President of Israel, for conversation on the subject of Golda Meir and permission to quote from material unpublished in this country; Dr Michael Grant for help and encouragement at many stages; Rana Kabbani for stimulating discussions and advice concerning the Arab world in general and Zenobia in particular, and General Moustapha Tlass, the Syrian Minister of Defence; my 'Georgian' consultants, the late Sir Charles Johnston (who first called Queen Tamara of Georgia to my attention), Mr Laurence Kelly, Professor Nico Kiasashvili of Tbilisi, and Mrs Katharine (Vivian) Ashton; and Dr Graham Webster and his wife Diana, not only for his help but for their hospitality. Mrs Maria Fairweather provided me with fascinating information concerning the reputation of Queen Jinga (Nzinga) in modern Angola; lastly the help of Angus Clarke and Daniel Johnson, who acted as my *occhi* and my *Augen* respectively, translating references to Matilda of Tuscany and Louise of Prussia, was invaluable.

I wish to thank the following for advice and/or support in many different ways: Dr R. J. Bingle of the India Office Library and Records; Dr Philip Crummy, Director of the Colchester Archaeological Trust; Mr Frank Delaney with whom I discussed the title at an early stage; Mr Donald Freed; Mr Tony Garratt who reminded me of Charles Doughty; Mr Tony Gregory of the Norfolk Archaeological Unit; Gale of the *Daily Telegraph* (Mr George Gale); Earl Gowrie; Mr Henry Grunwald, former Editor-in-Chief of Time Inc. for references to early Vietnamese heroines, and Ms Judy Stowe of BBC External Services for information concerning their reputation in modern Vietnam; Sir John Hale; Lady Selina Hastings; Mr Christopher Hibbert; Princess Antoinette Hohenlohe; Dr Lisa

Jardine; Mr John Keegan; Lady Pansy Lamb; Professor Joyce Lebra-Chapman for illustrative material concerning the Rani of Jhansi; Professor Karl Leyser; Ms Sharon Macdonald; Miss Elizabeth Owles of the Moyses Hall Museum, Bury St Edmunds; Dame Felicity (Hanbury) Peake for recollections of her wartime service; Diana Phipps; Mr C. A. Price; Mr Denis Richards; the Hon. Hannah Rothschild; Mr David Spanier; Ms Dale Spender; Emma Tennant; Mr Michael Trend; Mr Paul Usherwood; Ms Kaari Utrio; Marina Warner; and Simone Warner who was my wonderful charioteer in the summer of 1985 when we explored East Anglia.

I have received editorial suggestions and advice from a galaxy of stars in the firmament of publishing, including Robert Gottlieb; Christopher Falkus, Juliet Gardiner and Linden Lawson, all of Weidenfeld's; Sonny Mehta of Knopf; and my agent Michael Shaw of Curtis Brown; Mr John Gillingham and Mr Alan Palmer provided helpful comments on the text; Ms Jane Blumberg checked the references and Mr Douglas Matthews of the London Library did the index: to each and all of these I have good reason to be profoundly grateful. As for Richard Bates, who created out of my unruly manuscript, with the aid of his word processor, the disks from which this book was set, it seems appropriate to quote the words of Henry James concerning art itself to express my thanks: 'I know of no substitute whatever for the force and beauty of its process'. Finally I must not forget the Home Team: from my son Orlando Fraser who did research for me at the Colindale Newspaper Library and elsewhere, and my daughter Flora Fraser Powell-Jones, always prepared to discuss the Classical world with energy, to my mother Elizabeth Longford, who may never have realized what an editorial burden lay ahead when she first encouraged me to read history. My husband Harold Pinter, although coming last in these acknowledgements, is always the first to read my work: no words of mine can express my debt to him sufficiently, so I will use his to thank him for his support when I ventured into 'quite remote ... utterly foreign ... territories'.

ANTONIA FRASER

St Cecilia's Day 1986 –
Feast of St Joseph 1988

PART ONE

CHAPTER ONE

A SINGULAR
EXCEPTION

A singular exception . . . a woman is often acknowledged the absolute sovereign of a great kingdom, in which she would be deemed incapable of exercising the smallest employment, civil or military.

Gibbon, *Decline and Fall of the Roman Empire*

The stark tale of Boadicea's stand against the Romans 'flashes afresh to hold and horrify' with each generation. Every British school-child learns her story. And lest for a moment we forget her, on the banks of the Thames, not far from the Houses of Parliament, she stands aloft in her chariot, knives sprouting from its wheels; and it is in fact those murderous knives which stamp our perception of her indelibly. Hers is a gallant – and a savage – story. Even as we bow the knee, we shudder and step back as the Warrior Queen rides by.

For all the strength of this image – depictions of Boadicea be they in art or caricature are made instantly recognizable by use of this detail – Boadicea's chariot did *not* actually have knives (or scythes) affixed to its wheels. This is one of the very few statements which can be made with any certainty concerning her.

Thus one of the most powerful figures in our history in terms of popular imagination, one who did unquestionably exist in that period assigned to her, unlike 'King' Arthur – no chivalric monarch if he did exist but a sixth-century Romano-British commander –

3

survives by virtue of an image which is in itself spurious. This is an apt illustration of the paradox which lies at the heart of the subject of Queen Boadicea, and by extension that of the Warrior Queen in general.

Of course the name Boadicea itself is not genuine either. That is the name generally employed in the prolific allusions made to her in contemporary society: it would be a rare day which did not produce at least one in the British Press.[1] This is something which is only partly dependent on the emergence of a female Prime Minister (although, as we shall see, certain specific military situations such as the Falklands War can produce a bristling harvest of such comparisons) since Boadicea's name can be and is invoked in a variety of different contexts. Nor is our own age unique in this respect, the unwithered 'infinite variety' of Queen Boadicea's images as perceived down our history being one of the themes of this book.

While Boadicea remains therefore the convenient name for what may be termed the fabulous Queen, driving her cruelly accoutred carriage (and it will be used for that Queen in this book), a clutch of other names have been proposed as being more plausible in relation to the woman herself. 'Our own honour, VOADICEA, or BOODICIA, by some BUNDUICA and BUNDUCA, Queene of the Iceni' was Ben Jonson's somewhat despairing description in *The Masque of Queenes*.[2] It is a desperation that a modern chronicler of Queen Boadicea's fortunes can share (although Ben Jonson cited only a few of the possible variants).

This uncertainty jostling the Warrior Queen's actual name, its spelling and derivation, may also be seen as part of the paradox: the extreme fame of Boadicea contrasts with the extreme ignorance and, in many instances, actual misapprehension about her. It is 'Boudicca', given by Tacitus, which is in fact the only contemporary rendering of the name which has come down to us. As a result it has been in the past 'relished by the learned' as Winston Churchill felicitously phrased it. 'Boadicea', sounding so different to our ears, is actually only two letters apart from Boudicca and the famous name is thus probably based on inaccurate transcriptions of Tacitus' Boudicca.[3]

In recent years however the learned have lost some of their relish for Boudicca. It is suggested, on philological evidence, that Tacitus too was in error: 'Boudica' must have been the correct spelling.

This brings the British Warrior Queen's name in line with the various Celtic words for victory, notably the Old Welsh *bouda*. It also means, happily, that Boadicea too can claim to be described as Queen Victoria (as was not infrequently noted in the late nineteenth century): for these two reasons, scholarly and sentimental, Boudica will be the name adopted for the historic figure who led the AD 60/61 rebellion against the Romans,* whereas Boadicea will be used for the legendary character.[4]

Other variants will be encountered and their origins traced in the course of Boadicea's latter-day history. At the moment it is enough to point out that this ambivalence towards Boadicea's name, like the misapprehensions concerning her career and circumstances, is also part of her aura: it has even allowed her at times to flourish under two separate identities.

In the late sixteenth century for example, an enterprising Florentine scholar–courtier named Petruccio Ubaldini, seeking royal patronage in England, wrote two volumes about the lives of illustrious ladies of yore and dedicated them to Queen Elizabeth. 'To satisfy the most pedantic readers', as he put it, he decided to divide the characters of Bonduica and Voadicia (although the distinction was of course a mistaken one arising out of the confusions produced by these endless variations of spelling). Faced with the stories of two queens which were, as he honestly admitted, astonishingly similar, Ubaldini boldly decided to derive a different moral from each. The moral of Bonduica's story is thus that 'Cruelty destroys any praise for honourable courage...'; that of Voadicia: 'Tyranny often brings intolerable wickedness which provokes in its victims a thirst for revenge...'.[5]

As a matter of fact, both these morals can be derived quite correctly from Boadicea's story, although in modern parlance we might prefer to transform Ubaldini's 'morals' into questions. Was Boadicea a savage attempting to destroy a superior civilization in a series of atrocities (and a *female* savage to boot...)? Or was she a patriotic leader rising up against an alien and brutal occupying

---

* The date of Boudica's rebellion – AD 60 or 61 – is another matter in dispute. As to how Boudica is or was to be pronounced, one can only observe that an expedition of archaeological enquiry by the author to East Anglia in 1985 produced three separate pronunciations from the first three experts encountered: i.e. Bōudica, Boudīca and Boudicā.

power? Suffice it to say for the moment that in this respect the existence of so many variations of her name has evidently been a positive advantage in the promotion of her legend.

Thus the learneds' Boudica can easily possess quite different characteristics from the chariot-driving heroine aloft on London's Embankment without troubling the national consciousness too much. This celebrated Warrior Queen turns out to be like Proteus, he who could assume different shapes at will, beginning with her very name. Returning to Warrior Queens in general and the paradox which they present, it will be found that the protean quality is something which many of them have in common with Boadicea.

The central nature of this paradox can be stated as follows: whereas woman has on the whole, taking the rough with the smooth, the good epochs with the bad, been considered inferior to man throughout history, the arrival of a Warrior Queen, by whatever accident of fate, descent or sheer character, has been the signal for a remarkable outburst of excitement and even awe, sometimes accompanied by admiration and enthusiasm for her cause, beyond the ability of a mere male to arouse.

'In man's apparel ... hanging about her the skins of beasts, before and behind, with a Sword about her neck, an Axe at her girdle, and a Bow and Arrows in her hand, leaping according to the custom, now here, now there, as nimbly as the most active among her attendants, all the while striking her Engema, that is, two Iron Bells, which serve her instead of Drums ...'. Thus the Dutch Captain Fuller, commander of her personal bodyguard, admiringly described the seventeenth-century Queen Jinga of Angola, in her long battles against the Portuguese invaders. To Fuller, Jinga was 'A Cunning and Prudent Virago', despite or even because of her habit of keeping fifty or sixty young men as husbands (and another habit of human sacrifice); he served her faithfully for many years.[6]

Conversely, the emergence of a Warrior Queen has at other times been accompanied by disgust and fear at her very existence, emotions which would never be aroused by a male leader occupying the same position: Queen Jinga, the nightmare of the armed and voracious Amazon come to life, was viewed quite differently by her Portuguese enemies. To those on the other side, the actual atrocities committed or instigated by a woman leader bring about a special shudder, which recalls our reaction to the knives on Boadicea's chariot: it is not so much the mythical weapons themselves as the woman driving the chariot which gives us surely that special *frisson*.

Part of this *frisson* – of fear or admiration – is undoubtedly due to the fact that woman as a whole has been seen as a pacifying influence throughout history, this pacifying role being perceived as hers by nature and hers in duty. The whole question whether women actually *are* more pacific by nature is not the subject of the present book. For our purposes, it is however highly relevant that they have been perceived as such.

Some feminist writers have recently promulgated strongly the notion that a matriarchal society would or did lack the aggression that does and did characterize a patriarchal one. (Evidently non-pacific types such as Mrs Gandhi, Mrs Meir and Mrs Thatcher count as honorary men for the purposes of this argument because they have adopted masculine values in order to succeed in the patriarchal world.) 'And I know, in the depth of my being and in all my knowledge of history and humanity, I know women will struggle for a social order of peace, equality and joy' wrote the distinguished historian of women Joan Kelly in 1982, on the eve of her death. On the other hand, Lynne Segal, author of *Is the Future Female?*, expressed another view in an interview in 1987: 'I accept that women are gentler at the moment', but 'if they had the same amount of power as men, they wouldn't be more virtuous.'[7]

But the argument is not a novel one. The writings of Christine de Pisan in the fourteenth century drew attention to the pacifying potential of 'the good princess'. 'Supposed weakness is in fact often a moral strength,' she wrote, 'as when women, who are physically weak and timid, are therefore more inclined to make peace and avert wars.' She added, citing the work of Queen Blanche, mother of St Louis: 'O God, how many great blessings in the world have often been caused by queens and princesses making peace between enemies.'[8] Thus in a sense the concept of the Warrior Queen cuts across not only man's view of woman's traditional weakness but also woman's view of her own ordained role as a peacemaker.

Nevertheless almost every culture throughout history has had its Warrior Queen or Queens either in fact or in fiction, or in some combination of them both. The United States of America is so far one of the significant exceptions in spite of 'the singular address and happy boldness' which Alexis de Tocqueville discovered in its unmarried young ladies as long ago as 1835. When a possible future Warrior Queen was presented in the 1984 Vice-Presidential Candidate Geraldine Ferraro, the reaction was, as will be seen, extremely uneasy. The Roman Empire, for all the host of noteworthy Empresses, those celebrated, strong-minded and sometimes disreputable women, was another *imperium* where an actual female reign would, as Gibbon pointed out, have appeared 'an inexpiable prodigy'.[9]

It is certainly of importance to the story of Boudica and her uprising against the Roman regime in Britain that she herself, in her gender as well as in her independence, bore something at least of the appearance of a prodigy, and an unwelcome one, to the occupying power. But of course both Rome then and the United States now have experience of dealings with foreign 'Warrior Queens'.

The opportunity should be taken to define the way in which the term will be understood in the present study. A potential Warrior Queen, in the modern sense, is one who might under certain circumstances have to take the decision to deploy her country's military resources. Thus for these purposes Mrs Thatcher at the time of the Falklands War played the Warrior Queen while Queen Elizabeth II was merely the reigning monarch. In the historical sense on the other hand, a Warrior Queen will be regarded as one who combined both elements of rule and martial leadership. It must therefore be emphasized that Joan of Arc (although admittedly a frequent source of inspiration to many Warrior Queens) was not actually one herself in our terms. Since she led but did not rule, like the heroic 'General' Harriet Tubman, who commanded an action in the American Civil War, Joan of Arc belongs to that other wider category of Women Warriors, a fascinating but more diffuse subject than that of the present study: women having fought, literally fought, as a normal part of the army in far more epochs and far more civilizations than is generally appreciated.[10] Similarly Judith, the pious assassin of Holofernes (another frequently cited comparison) belongs to the category of Warrior Woman, or maid – although as a matter of fact the historical Judith was a widow.

If one examines a saying of Muhammad: 'The men perish if they obey the women', or another of his alleged quips regarding a princess on the Persian throne: 'No people who place a woman over their affairs prosper', the lesson of history does not exactly confirm the truth of this notion.[11] On the contrary a Warrior Queen – or female ruler – has often provided the focus for what a country afterwards perceived to have been its golden age; beyond the obvious example (to the English) of Queen Elizabeth I, one might cite the twelfth-century Queen Tamara of Georgia, or the fifteenth-century Isabella of Spain. The extra value of a Warrior Queen as a rallying point for the chivalric feelings of her nation will be one of the recurring themes of this book.

Returning to America and its present culture, the United States does of course lack a hereditary monarchy, which for better or for worse is a system inclined to throw up such things as queens, and thus by implication Warrior Queens, from time to time. The irony of this situation was summed up by Gibbon:

> In every age and country, the wiser, or at least the stronger, of the two sexes has usurped the powers of the State, and confined the other to the cares and pleasures of domestic life. In hereditary monarchies, however, and especially in those of modern Europe, the gallant spirit of chivalry, and the law of succession, have accustomed us to allow a singular exception; and a woman is often acknowledged the absolute sovereign of a great kingdom, in which she would be deemed incapable of exercising the smallest employment, civil or military.[12]

So we have an extension to the paradox of the Warrior Queen: the phenomenon is found almost everywhere (if not within a culture, by conflict with another culture); yet the person concerned is generally regarded as the 'singular exception' and that very singularity for better or for worse provides her aura.

There is after all a good deal to be said – in purely practical terms – for General de Gaulle's view of the omnipresence of force in history: 'Is it possible to conceive of life without force?' he wrote in *The Edge of the Sword*. 'Force has watched over civilization in the cradle: force has ruled empires, and dug the grave of decadence ... It is true to say that the fighting spirit, the art of war, the virtues of the soldier are an integral part of man's inheritance. They have been part and parcel of history in all its phases, the medium through which it has expressed itself.' He concluded that 'the noblest teachings of philosophy and religion have found no higher ideals' than

9

those of 'self-sacrifice for the sake of the community, suffering made glorious – these two things which are the basic elements of the profession of arms'.[13]

One can gainsay de Gaulle's conclusion, or at least his overall description of the profession of arms, without contradicting his general – and even obvious – point that history can be interpreted at one level as the history of 'force'. If this be true, and, more importantly, society itself has believed it to be true, then on the one hand the traditional lack of involvement of woman in the world of 'force' will add to her air of inferiority; on the other hand her involvement in that world, when it occurs, stands a good chance of raising her status. As Tacitus wrote of the warlike Germans: 'Renown is easiest won among perils.'[14] To put it another way, many women leaders have found in the crucible of war – if successfully survived – the fiery process which has guaranteed them passage into the realms of honorary men.

It is because 'all history has been made by men' and 'it is still a world that belongs to men', in the words of Simone de Beauvoir, that the characters and careers of those women who have been the singular exceptions become crucial.[15] Such careers have always afforded much of interest to both sexes, not just because a tradition of independent womanhood is kept alive for the female sex in darker days. The same names will be found recited over and over again like an encouraging (or admonitory) litany the moment a new Warrior Queen appears. Not merely Boadicea herself, but Penthesilea, Judith, Semiramis and Zenobia from ancient times are invoked in this roll-call of the armed and female faithful. Zenobia drew upon comparisons to Cleopatra, from whom she claimed to be descended. Dio Cassius compared Boadicea to Semiramis. Elizabeth I and Catherine the Great, frequently compared in their own time to the above (Catherine to her admiring correspondent Voltaire was his 'Semiramis of the North'), themselves provided the rich sources of historical comparison.[16]

An appeal to bygone 'heroines' as a source of strength and above all validity would indeed appear to be exceptionally important where female leaders are concerned, down to our own day. The unnatural, even bizarre aspect of a woman in such a role – 'that boisterousness with which she terrifies us', in the words of an eighteenth-century commentator on Boadicea – is thus tacitly admitted, before being justified by this sonorous appeal to the past. The names of the 'heroines' cited do of course vary to a certain degree – but not nearly as much as the character and circumstances of the women citing them. At the time of the Falklands War, Mrs Thatcher as Prime Minister neatly recalled Queen Victoria by quoting her in a television broadcast: 'Failure? The possibilities do not exist.'[17] The evocation of the strong and successful female image was surely as important as the sentiment, although inspection reveals little in common between the nineteenth-century hereditary monarch and the late-twentieth-century democratically elected leader – except their sex.

It is also true that exactly the same names from this important but limited female pantheon can be used to insult, while the nature of the insult can also vary. When Denis Healey, as a senior Labour statesman, reflected that Mrs Thatcher reminded him 'very much' of Catherine the Great, he was not of course referring to the former's impeccable private life, but to the imperiousness 'allied to a temperament which is in many ways very masculine' which he considered both ladies had in common.[18] Yet the allusion to Catherine the Great, Voltaire's 'Semiramis of the North', like that to Semiramis herself, is one which could in different circumstances bear a sexual connotation, since both the ninth-century BC Semiramis and the eighteenth-century AD Catherine the Great might be described, at least in popular terms, as 'a great sovereign and a great lover'. Boccaccio in the fourteenth century delineated Semiramis as one who on the one hand showed 'that in order to govern it is not necessary to be a man, but to have courage', and on the other hand 'gave herself to many men' along the way.[19]

The presumed sexual voracity of a Warrior Queen, at least up till the twentieth century, will be found to be one of the recurring themes of her treatment at the hands of her contemporaries and of history. Conversely, but not contradictorily, another theme will be found to be her chastity: on occasion maintained, according to the myth, under the most remarkable circumstances – against all the available evidence. Sometimes the same woman – such as Matilda of Tuscany, whom we shall find leading her men in the cause of the eleventh-century Pope Gregory VII – bears both accusations. This treatment of the Warrior Queen as a supernaturally chaste creature, put against that other image of her as preternaturally lustful (the

Voracity Syndrome), seems to indicate that, because her sex is first and foremost what makes the Warrior Queen remarkable, her sexuality must always be called into question as well.

Other themes will be found to occur and recur: that of the Holy (and sometimes Armed) Figurehead is one of them, from the Arab Lady of Victory to Isabella the Catholic, scourge of the Spanish Moors (such characters frequently also forming part of the Chaste Syndrome). Then the Appendage Syndrome runs through the whole book: the stressed connection of so many Warrior Queens to the nearest strong masculine figure. In turn the Shame Syndrome, whereby all the surrounding masculine figures are described as failing in courage compared to the Warrior Queen herself, under-lines in another way the purely masculine context in which most Warrior Queens have operated. It is this context which has enabled many a Warrior Queen, endowed with a partner, to be hailed as the 'Better-Man' (of the two). Conversely, the 'Only-a-Weak-Woman' Syndrome has the normally robust female leader indulging in a sudden diplomatic outbreak of modesty, pleading the notorious weakness of her sex, generally for good practical reasons of self-interest.

It is indeed this recurrence of themes which gives the Warrior Queens chosen for discussion here their special significance. As has been stated, this is not intended to be an encyclopaedic work on a vast subject, and even such compelling figures as the real, not the operatic, Brünnhilde, a sixth-century Visigothic Queen of Austrasia, or the ferocious Nanny, wife of Old Cudjoe, chief of the Maroons, who led a seventeenth-century uprising in Jamaica, do not necess-arily find a place in it.[20]

One important theme may be termed the Tomboy Syndrome, whereby the Warrior Queen in youth, all unknowing of her martial destiny, is depicted as unconsciously eschewing dolls in favour of soldiers, domestic pursuits in favour of hunting.[21] The Tomboy Syndrome in particular demonstrates the perpetual need for reassur-ance which the emergence of a Warrior Queen seems to evoke: this woman is not like other women, runs the refrain; this being so, her strangeness should be established from the start. A quotation from the start of one of the many historical romances in English on the subject of Boadicea shows that the British Queen is certainly not immune from the syndrome: 'Wait for us, Boadicea! That horse of yours must have invisible wings to carry you at such speed.' So runs *Boadicea* by Betty King, published in 1975.[22] (Absolutely nothing is in fact known about the childhood of Boadicea.)

Boadicea is selected as the pivot of this book partly for the fascinating combination of fame and ambiguity which her career provides, partly because so many of the themes which recur in the treatment of other Warrior Queens are raised in her story and its subsequent treatment. Stories of these other historic Warrior Queens are brought forward where relevant not only to supplement hers but also to illustrate the universality of the subject. But it is Boadicea who is a convenient starting-point, and Boadicea who is the engrossing exemplar.

Nevertheless the first task, before turning to the true story of Boudica in her own time, in so far as it can be established, must be to look back into the depths of time and culture. Is there something primitive in the human heart which can be held accountable for the mingled awe, horror, and ecstasy which so often attends the manifestation of a Warrior Queen in our midst? Is it the deep-rooted allegiance which we owe to the idea of woman-as-goddess which makes her fleshly apparition before us, fully armed, in the guise of the Warrior Queen so thrillingly traumatic?

Let us begin with the Celtic goddess and see how far chariot-driving Boadicea descends from her: for it is to her, if anyone, that Boudica must have been related in the perception of her British contemporaries, those who teemed after her.

CHAPTER TWO

ANTIQUE
GLORIES

Where is the antique glory now become
That whilom wont in women to appear?

Spenser, *The Faerie Queene*

Goddesses stalk the land in the Celtic mythology, ride their chargers, drive their chariots, fight their battles, are vanquished – sometimes – and more often than not emerge victorious. Nor was the sexuality of these deities ignored, as was appropriate in goddesses who were connected with birth (and the fertility of the earth and crops) as well as with war and its companion death. The concept of the Celtic Great Mother, overlording the other lesser tribal deities, may or may not have been universally known (although it was certainly known); what is evident is the rampant and rich nature of the female deities who paraded through the Celtic world. The precise relationship of goddess to goddess may also be impossible to deter-mine – these were after all deities of a non-literate society, whose tales were finally written down hundreds of years after they had first been sung, chanted and spoken to Celtic audiences. What is evident is that a series of female 'High Ones' were celebrated in the epics.[1]

Furthermore, in the Celtic world, again and again it is the magic intervention in the course of battle of a female, goddess, queen or a combination of the two, which provides the focus or climax of the story. Such a female may be a hag or a beauty (or one disguised as the other). She may be as Rhiannon, the horse goddess of the Welsh *Mabinogion*, 'a woman dressed in shining gold brocade and riding a great pale horse' or the nine sorceresses of Gloucester encountered in the same sequence of tales who laid waste the country in their helmets and headpieces before the champion Peredur finally smote them.[2]

The name of the Welsh Rhiannon connects to the Celtic Rigantona, great queen or 'Queen of the Demons'; she in turn links to the Morrigan, sometimes merely a sinister (and sexually active) raven-goddess of war and sometimes used as a composite name to denote a trio, Badbh, Nemain and Macha, all with strong connections to both fertility and battle.[3] Above all there is the character of Queen Medb (or Maeve) who is to the great Celtic cycle of *The Tain* what the Greek goddesses are to *The Iliad*, the physique and appetites of a woman, the magic powers of a goddess.

It can indeed be argued that Queen Medb is the true heroine of *The Tain*; for although the champion Cúchulainn, the Hound of Ulster, is unarguably its hero, Medb, his adversary, is the female protagonist, a vivid character in her own right, both glamorous and ferocious, and it is her ardent desire to secure the Brown Bull of Ulster which sets the whole cycle in train. Like the *Mabinogion*, *The Tain* first emerges in written form long after its stories must first have been current, in the case of *The Tain* Christianized by monks in the eighth century AD (as it was later to be bowdlerized by Lady Gregory). But the society which *The Tain* actually reflects is thought to be placed around the time of the birth of Christ – that is to say some sixty years before the Boudican revolt.[4]

At the start of *The Tain*, Medb is having 'pillow talk' with her husband Ailill, her theme being her superior state before she got married – not an unusual theme for such conversations, perhaps, but Medb is able to back her claim by pointing out that she was the daughter of the High King of Ireland, the 'last and haughtiest' of his six daughters: 'I outdid them in grace and giving and battle and warlike combat', she boasts; moreover she controlled fifteen hundred soldiers and as many freeborn native men.

Ailill responds that he too is a king, by descent from his mother (a queen). It is however as they wrangle on the subject of possessions, the pair matching bull for bull, that Medb has to admit that one of Ailill's bulls is finer than all of hers, since her own star animal, Finnbennach, has deserted to the King's herd, after refusing to be led by a woman. Since the finest bull in all Ulster is known to be the Donn Cuailnge – the Brown Bull of Ulster – Medb determines to secure him with her Connaughtian army, and vanquish her husband's claims. In this fashion begins the long epic of *The Tain*, glorious and bloodstained, the most magnificent cattle raid in literature, with Medb leading the attack and Cúchulainn as the champion of Ulster attempting to defend the Brown Bull from her rapacity.

Where Medb's character is concerned, she is certainly both cunning and imperious as well as lustful (her behaviour in that respect certainly forms part of the Voracity Syndrome). It is also noticeable that when she does suggest breaking the rules of fair fight, this deviousness is ascribed to her sex. On one occasion Medb suggests, from the vantage point of her chariot, that certain people, currently friendly but potentially hostile, be killed as a safeguard. Ailill condemns this as 'a woman's thinking' – and wicked. When Medb sleeps with the warrior Fergus in order to seduce him to her side, Ailill forgives Fergus with the consoling words: 'I know all about queens and women, I lay first fault straight at women's own sweet swellings and loving lust'.

Cúchulainn is the persistent target of the Queen's attempted treachery. Medb first suggests a truce and then secretly sends six soldiers against the champion, all of royal blood (fortunately Cúchulainn is able to slay all six). Medb then suggests a private meeting between Cúchulainn and herself, promising to be attended only by her unarmed women. Cúchulainn's own charioteer warns him against such a dangerous rendezvous: 'Medb is a forceful woman. I'd watch out for her hand at my back.' So Cúchulainn does at least take along his sword – which is just as well, because he finds the rendezvous has actually turned into an encounter with fourteen armed warriors. (Fortunately Cúchulainn is able once again to despatch the whole lot.)

Queen Medb, with the magical birds or squirrels on her shoulders, is not the only strong goddess–woman in the Celtic legends. Part of Cúchulainn's training as a fighter consists of his encounter with Aife, 'the hardest woman warrior in the world', while Cúchulainn himself is being trained in arms by another woman named Scathach. But it is the physical description of Queen Medb which seems to sum up the type of the Celtic goddess-cum-warrior. This is the fighting Queen Medb, as described to Cúchulainn by his fellow warrior Cethern, grievously wounded by an unknown assailant. 'A tall, fair, long-faced woman with soft features came at me ... She had a head of yellow hair and two gold birds on her shoulders. She wore a purple cloak folded about her, with five hands' breadth of gold on her back. She carried a light, stinging, sharp-edged lance in her hand, and she held an iron sword with a woman's grip over her head – a massive figure. It was she who came against me first.'

'Then I'm sorry for you,' is Cúchulainn's comment. 'That was Medb of Cruachan.'

The connection between the insubstantial if vigorous goddess and the historic figure of the Warrior Queen remains for all this an elusive if fascinating one. If we take a character like Semiramis, the ninth-century BC Queen of Babylon who did exist but whose legend far outstrips her historical reality, it is clear that her identification with the goddess Astarte formed a valuable part of that legend in the mind of posterity. Eight centuries later we find the Hellenistic Queen Cleopatra deliberately donning the mantle of the goddess Isis for sound political reasons. The reporting of Boudica by Dio Cassius, which will be discussed later, suggests that she was herself conforming to some kind of stereotype of the Celtic warrior–woman; this in turn derived from the infinitely powerful character of the Celtic mother-cum-war-goddess, like Medb.

Such attempts on the part of the ancient Warrior Queens to assume the mystical authority of the War Goddess were obviously linked with the prevalence of these martial goddess figures. Let us suppose that together they constitute proof that there is something deep in the human spirit which finds in the image of the strong and armed woman a figure of awe. If that be so, then the next step is to consider whether such awe springs not so much from the human subconscious as from some real state of society in the remote past. Is it possible that the aggressive goddess, far from being a surprising figure, in terms of the patriarchal attitudes which have generally prevailed, is actually a reflection of the preceding *matriarchal* age when women as a whole were the dominant sex? Thus the Warrior Queen herself might appear as a kind of vestigial relic of that distant epoch: hence her encouraging or terrifying aspect according to the contemporary view taken of women's rightful role in society.

It is certainly tempting to regard the chariot-driving Warrior Queen as owing her authority to deep memories of a matriarchal society where women either held the reins of the chariot or gave the men the orders which enabled them to do so. Matriarchy has always been an attractive concept (to some). On the one hand a nostalgic conviction that there was a golden age when women enjoyed a now vanished prestige is comforting to the oppressed. This is the age whose passing Spenser mourned in *The Faerie Queene*:

> Where is the antique glory now become
> That whilom wont in women to appear?[5]

On the other hand, more vigorously, a remedy for the future is suggested by this nostalgia, to restore what was evidently Nature's intended ordering.

Interest in the notion of matriarchy, keen in our own day as an obvious development of the rise of feminism, is nevertheless not exclusive to it. In particular, the influential work of J. S. Bachofen, first published in 1861, supposed the existence of 'mother right', a pre-Classical and pre-Biblical culture of the Bronze Age. Ending around 1200 BC, this was a culture in which the male role in procreation was ignored, and descent was traced only in the female line. Bachofen found examples of such matriarchal societies in places as diverse as Lycia, Athens, Crete, Lemnos, Egypt, Tibet, Central Asia and India.[6]

More recently, however, scholars have been stepping warily where such positive statements concerning historical matriarchies are concerned. It is suggested that the archaeological discoveries of women buried with horses and spears – for example the Sarmatian graves of the fourth century BC – may point to the presence of women in the fighting force, but that in itself does not necessarily suppose a matriarchy.* [7] After all, if the graves of females who have served in the Israeli army were to be discovered in a thousand years' time, it would be a mistake on the part of scholars to regard this as proof of a matriarchal organization in the Israeli state. In 1986 shortage of recruits in the prolonged Iraq–Iran war led to girls

---

* The *Oxford English Dictionary* (1933) definition of 'matriarchy' is: 'That form of social organization where the mother, not the father, is the head of the family, and in which descent and relationships are reckoned through mothers not fathers.' The *Concise Oxford Dictionary of Current English Usage* (1963), in its entry for the word 'matriarch', adds: 'usually jocular'.

being sent into battle, pictured in the newspapers dressed in the chador and carrying a gun: their skeletons, surviving by chance alongside their guns, would give an even more distorted picture of the Muslim state if some kind of 'matriarchal' conclusion were drawn.

Replacing the belief in actual matriarchies, it is now supposed that while certain strong-minded Bronze Age queens did exist, just as individual women in certain societies of the past did display at least something of Spenser's 'antique glory', the status of women as a whole was not superior to that of men. The existence of these spirited and respected individuals represents a state of affairs which is a far cry from the dreams of true matriarchy and matrilineal succession, the evidence for which has been described, even in the free Celtic world from which Boudica sprang, as being 'very dubious' and 'best consigned to the large corpus of myths surrounding Celtic society'.[8] It seems, as with the clearly legendary goddesses of war, that it is the continued tradition of pre-Classical matriarchies which is important here, rather than the fact of their existence.

The question of historical truth becomes even more acute in the case of the Amazons and their leaders, including most prominently Penthesilea and Hippolyta. Like the alleged early pre-Classical matriarchies, the Amazons have sometimes been granted a proper historical existence; however in their case the evidence actually comes from the Classical writers, most notably Herodotus.[9] If true, this would be another interesting possibility to explore with regard to the nature of the Warrior Queen's origins: should we look to these colonies of armed and self-mutilated women for inspiration? (They were supposed to remove one breast for the sake of drawing the bow: the name Amazon itself was once thought to derive from the Greek 'without breast'.) Many of the ancient writers site the Amazons in an area around the Black Sea, and indeed if they are allowed a historical existence, what is now Northern Anatolia seems the likeliest place for the cradle; coincidentally or not, the lands contiguous to the Black Sea will also provide a number of indisputably authentic Warrior Queens. Scythia to the north however also has its claims. Herodotus, on the other hand, supported by Diodorus Siculus, places his armed maidens on the shores of the Mediterranean in Libya, the significant point being that the Classical writers in general situated the Amazons on the outskirts of their known world, and as this world expanded, so the kingdoms of the Amazons receded into more distant territories.

Outside the known world of the Greeks lay the barbarians – those rude and unfortunate strangers who lacked the brilliant order of the Greek state, and it is to this realm of disorderliness and unnaturalness that the Greek tradition of the Amazons belonged.[10] Thus the Greek heroes of legend are frequently found undergoing a kind of ritual encounter with an Amazon, from which the Greek emerges the victor – the point being less the victory of one sex over the other (since the superiority of the male sex would be taken for granted by the Greeks) than the subjugation of the barbarians by the forces of civilization: it was one of the labours of Hercules to secure the girdle of the Amazon Queen Hippolyta. Similarly in art, Amazonomachy was a popular theme for many temple friezes and vases: but the defeated women there depicted actually stood for the Greeks' victories over their male enemies – such as the Persians.

Diodorus Siculus, writing in about 40 BC, has, like Homer, Penthesilea involving her Amazons in the Trojan War, in support of Priam, and being killed as a result by Achilles: after that the power and prestige of the Amazons declined. And it was the defeat and death of the 'Amazonian' Camilla of the Volscians, described by Virgil in *The Aeneid*, which presaged the establishment of the new Roman Empire under Aeneas.[11]

Camilla is introduced to us at the head of 'her cavalcade of squadrons a-flower with bronze'. She is among the Italian leaders who have gathered together, hoping to expel the invading Trojans led by Aeneas from their native land: a maiden warrior so fleet of foot that she could run across a field of corn without damaging the blades, across the sea without wetting the soles of her feet. Her description also provides an excellent Classical example of the Tomboy Syndrome: 'She was a warrior; her girl's hands had never been trained to Minerva's distaff and her baskets of wool, but rather, though a maid, she was one to face out grim fights and in speed of foot to out-distance the winds...'. As Camilla passed, wayfarers gaped 'to see how regal splendour clothed her smooth shoulders in purple, how her brooch clasped her hair in its gold, and how she wore on her a Lycian quiver and carried a shepherd's myrtle staff with a lance's head'.

In the final military confrontation with Aeneas Camilla rides 'armed with her quiver, exulting like an Amazon, through the midst of the slaughter, having one breast exposed for freedom in the fight. Sometimes with all her strength she would be casting her tough spear-shafts in dense showers, and sometimes without pause for rest her hand would wield a stout battle-axe.' Camilla is surrounded by her faithful female attendants ('daughters of Italy') equally bold in the affray, Larina, Tulla and Tarpeia 'wielding her bronze axe'; Virgil compares them directly to the Amazons of Thrace, 'who, warring in their brilliant accoutrements, make Thermodon's streams echo to the hoof-beats, as they ride, it may be with Hippolyta, or else when martial Penthesilea drives back in her chariot from war, and her soldier-women, shrieking wild battle-cries, exult as they wave their crescent shields'.

Camilla's previous exploits – man-killing on a vicious scale – are related in gory detail ('She battered through his unguarded breast with her long firwood-shafted spear', etc., etc.), as is Camilla's pride in her achievements. Here she addresses the mighty hunter Ornytus, whom she has pierced through: 'Etruscan, did you imagine that you were chasing wild beasts in a forest? Well, the day will come which will prove that you and your fellows imagined wrongly; and it will be proved through a woman's weapons. Yet you shall carry to the spirits of your fathers no mean fame – the fame of falling by Camilla's spear.'

In the end Camilla does fall to a man: it is the javelin of Arruns, whistling out of the blue which smites her down, signalling the defeat of the Italian cause. But Arruns only succeeds with the direct intervention of Phoebus Apollo; and subsequently Diana, the goddess Camilla serves, sees to it that her sentinel Opis avenges the Volscian's death: 'Your passing shall not be without fame throughout the world.'

It is indeed the fame of the Amazons, and prototypes such as Camilla, which foreshadows the Warrior Queen, rather than the historical truth of their existence. Again and again we shall find a Warrior Queen acting out her life voluntarily or involuntarily as an example of the Appendage Syndrome: that is to say, she will either be regarded officially as an appendage to her father, husband or even son (as in the case of Cleopatra) or stress the relationship to give herself validity (as in Elizabeth I's frequent stress upon her father Henry VIII). The Amazons of legend, however, specifically derived their exotic quality from the fact that they were nobody's appendage.

The latter-day reputation of the Amazons and their imitators was expressed by Thomas Heywood in his popular *Gynaekeion or Nine Bookes of Various History Concerning Women*, first printed in 1624. He praised Camilla for being the product of a tomboy upbringing by her father: for taking a vow of chastity to concentrate on the hunting and killing of wild beasts. Heywood translated Virgil's account of Camilla in battle array with verve if not melody:

> To their supply Camilla came
> The gallant Volscian lass
> Who bravely did command the horse
> With troops that shin'd in brass.[12]

The fact that the Classical writers described the Amazons originally as an example of how badly things would turn out if the world was turned upside down and women ruled was disregarded. Ironically, John Knox, approvingly citing Aristotle on the 'monstrousness' of the Amazons, as he thundered against female rule in the mid-sixteenth century ('their strength weakness, the counsel foolishness and judgment frenzy') was in fact on firm historical ground.[13] It could even be argued that the perversity with which the French King Henri III had male *mignons* dress up as (female) Amazons at the court of the 1570s had something to be said for it historically: for it reflected the original concept of the Amazon kingdom as a place in which the natural order had been turned upside down.

The Warrior Queens cheerfully ignored all this. In any situation in which a female ruler had perforce to involve herself in war, an allusion to the Amazons was an appeal to history for the verification of her role. Queen Louise of Prussia, the exquisite fragile butterfly whom Napoleon would break on the wheel despite her valiant spirit, was contemptuously described by him as appearing on the battlefield 'dressed as an Amazon in the uniform of her regiment of dragoons'.[14] Napoleon did not want pretty women on the battlefield dressed as Amazons or anything else; but to the Prussian soldiers who cheered the straightforward patriotism of their lovely queen (in contrast to the vacillation of her husband) the deliberate assumption of male uniform by a highly feminine woman was an inspiring symbol.

Eleanor of Aquitaine was the great feudal heiress whose marriage to Louis VII of France in 1137, shortly after the death of her father, brought him vast possessions. At the time of her marriage Eleanor was only fifteen and the complicated future which awaited her, gifted as she was with beauty, riches and the intelligence to make use of her gifts, could hardly have been foreseen: the marriage itself would end in divorce, following which the heiress Eleanor would wed the rival monarch across the water, Henry II of England. Eleanor therefore was still a comparatively young woman on that Easter Day 1146 when she knelt before the celebrated orator, the Abbé Bernard of Clairvaux at Vézelay, and, moved by his eloquence, offered him her thousands of vassals for what was to become the Second Crusade.[15] She was attended by numerous 'ladies of quality' as she knelt, bearers of such heraldic names as Sybille Countess of Flanders, Mamille of Roucy, Florine of Bourgogne, Torqueri of Bouillon and Faydide of Toulouse.

It was one thing for a great lady to pledge her vassals, quite another for her to go on the crusade herself. This however was what Queen Eleanor proceeded to do, and opinions have varied concerning the reason. Did chivalry demand the presence of a woman at the centre of this pious procession? More humanly, did King Louis himself fear for the consequences of leaving his fascinating young wife at home? Whatever the reason, the chronicler who related the episode considered that the Queen's departure, surrounded by her ladies, set an extremely bad example to the female sex as a whole. Furthermore the papal bull which promulgated the Crusade, and which was read aloud at Vézelay, expressly forbade the attendance of concubines on the expedition.

It was at this point, according to legend, that Queen Eleanor suddenly appeared among the crowds at Vézelay 'taking the cross', riding a white horse and herself dressed in the guise of an Amazon, with gilded buskins on her feet and plumes in her hair. Surrounded by her ladies, similarly if less gorgeously attired, the Queen galloped through crowds, urging on the faithful to join the Crusade in a deliberate imitation of Penthesilea and her 'soldier–women'. Her squadron of ladies also distributed white distaffs to the fainthearted – an early form of the First World War's white feather.

According to Nicetas, the Queen kept up her enjoyable Classical charade along the route to the Holy Land. The Greek historian wrote of the 'women dressed as men, mounted on horses and armed with lance and battle axe' that they 'kept a martial mien, bold as Amazons'. And he mentioned that at the head, 'one in particular [presumably Eleanor] richly dressed ... went by the name of the "lady of the golden boot", the elegance of her bearing and the freedom of her movements recalling the celebrated leader of the Amazons'.[16]

In a bold gesture, Queen Eleanor had thus separated herself from the category of mortal women, mere concubines (albeit royal) and other female companions; by her plumes and her bold buskins she had appealed ostentatiously to the past, and declared in so doing her right to accompany the Crusade. It should perhaps be noted in conclusion that the bull for the next Crusade – the Third Crusade of 1189 – expressly forbade women of all sorts to join the expedition by general agreement of all the Christian monarchs including King Louis. But by this time Queen Eleanor had been married to King Henry II of England for nearly forty years.

The problem which faced Eleanor's descendant, Anne, Queen of England from 1702 and of Great Britain from 1707, was one not so much of action as of image. Unlike her sister Mary, in the preceding reign, Queen Anne had no William III at her side as consort, co-ruler and in effect sole controller of the destinies of the country. It was clear that William after Queen Mary's death in 1694 was as much a *de facto* ruler by right of his male sex as a *de jure* monarch. Queen Anne on the other hand had as her consort the dim Danish Prince George who had no claims to the English throne, and whom no one considered making *de facto* ruler. Yet Anne reigned throughout a period of extraordinary military activity in the history of her country, ending gloriously with the victorious Marlborough campaigns, but coming perilously close to defeat before that happy outcome was achieved.

Across the Channel, Anne's cousin, Louis XIV, the Sun King, had long dazzled his compatriots with his martial exploits. How was Queen Anne, a middle-aged lady in poor health at the time of her accession, to present an image which was both imposing and opposing? As a younger woman she had had recourse to the traditional training of many Warrior Queens and loved to ride, as though to emulate some legendary goddess of the chase. Swift described Queen Anne out hunting, attired in dark cloak and hood, driving her one-horsed chaise 'furiously like Jehu, and as a mighty hunter like Nimrod' (a Boadicean as well as a biblical image). Later the Queen's enormous weight, following seventeen ill-fated pregnancies, caused her to take to a 'chariot' with huge wheels.[17]

The age of the active warrior monarch was drawing to a close (George II, in the next reign but one, was the last British monarch to lead his own army in battle) but was not yet concluded. Since Queen Anne, for all her command, both titular and actual, of the army and navy, could scarcely fulfil the practical obligations of a commander-in-chief, art and fantasy had to be called into play. Verrio painted the Queen as Justice for the ceiling of Hampton Court Palace, armed with a sword and holding a pair of scales. At a state visit to Bath, for example, Queen Anne was surrounded by a guard of honour of virgins 'richly attired like Amazons with bows and arrows', and others who danced beside her coach. Verses solemnizing the Vigo Bay thanksgiving at St Paul's in 1702 thundered a sonorous message:

> As threat-ning Spain did to Eliza bow
> So France and Spain shall do to Anna now...

The reality was very different as Sir John Clerk, one of the Scots commissioners, wrote in his memoirs: a gouty old woman with a red spotted face, some nasty bandages and a poultice.[18]

Nor has the allusion to the Amazons been deemed to lose its usefulness in the modern age: in 1986, for example, the women surrounding Benazir Bhutto, bold female claimant to the leadership of Pakistan, are colloquially known as 'The Amazons'.[19] Yet no appeal to the (incorrectly interpreted) past for validation seems more touching and more paradoxical than that made on the magnificent tombstone of Matilda of Tuscany, constructed on a significantly heroic scale following her death in 1115.

It was held to be appropriate that some allusion to her career on the battlefield should be made, apart from the four huge female figures of Prudence, Justice, Fortitude and Temperance which supported the tomb. So Penthesilea was called into play: *Et tunc disposuit turmes invicta Virago Qualis Amazonide Penthesilea solet* (And then this warrior–woman disposed her troops as the Amazonian Penthesilea is accustomed to do).[20] Thus the deeply religious, Christian Countess

Matilda, whose personal crusade was on behalf of the Pope, for the empire of Christ, needed the imprimatur of the savage pagan Queen to justify her unwomanly role.

CHAPTER THREE

THE QUEEN
OF WAR

I am the queen of war. I am the queen of the thunderbolt.
I stir up the sea and calm it. I am the rays of the Sun.

Ptolemaic creed of the goddess Isis

Flesh-and-blood Warrior Queens – stepping out from behind the image of the war goddess – were not unknown to the ancient world; in general their activities were zestfully chronicled, particularly if some lesson could be derived to the detriment of the contemporary male, whether as leader or soldier. For there is a new element introduced by the reality of reported history – or what passes for such – and one which will emerge significantly with many a Warrior Queen including Boudica herself when she proposed the alternative of victory or death: 'This is what I, as a woman, plan to do: – let the men live in slavery if they will.'[1]

This is what might be termed the Shame Syndrome: not only is it wondrous to find a mere woman acting in a martial manner, but in so doing the woman concerned shows up, positively *shames* the weaker males who surround her. The earlier goddess–women were in a sense not able to shame the males they encountered since their supernatural powers clearly placed them in a superior position from the start.

On the other hand the titivating theme of sexual licence, the Voracity Syndrome, is, if anything, developed with the emergence of the flesh-and-blood woman. Lust (especially on the part of a widow, the status of so many Warrior Queens, presumably denied that to which she had become agreeably accustomed) remained a popular vice to associate with the name of a female leader, just as it had been a characteristic of a Celtic goddess.

Of course the trailing clouds of the goddess linger. In the case of Semiramis, zest caused the Greek writers to outrun the historical facts and gleefully transform an Assyrian ruler of the ninth century BC into a demi-legendary creature. The historical basis for Semiramis is one Sammu-ramat, the Babylonian widow of the Assyrian King Shamshi-Adad V, and mother of his heir Adad-nirari III. On Shamshi-Adad's death in 811 BC, Queen Sammu-ramat ruled as regent for five years during the minority of her son; beyond the fact that her regency was energetic, which suggests a strong character, little else is known for certain concerning her.[2]

In the hands of the Greeks, Semiramis became a daring character, subject to a series of adventures from birth; being the daughter of the goddess Derceto by an Assyrian, she was exposed in the desert, only to have her life saved by doves, who succoured her for a year. Subsequently she was brought up by a peasant until her beauty secured her two profitable marriages – first to the Governor of Ninevah, and then to Ninus King of Assyria.

Herodotus made Semiramis responsible for some of the remarkable embellishments to the city of Ninevah, which moderated the flooding of the river (although he rated her intelligence lower than that of a succeeding queen, Ninocris); while Propertius wrote that 'with dams Euphrates she controlled, where through her capital it rolled'.[3] But Semiramis' plans for rebuilding Ninevah were less important to her legend than the use she was alleged to have made of her beauty, securing the throne itself from her doting husband Ninus. Having been proclaimed sole Empress of Assyria, Semiramis lost no time in having the foolish Ninus put to death. Unencumbered by male tutelage, she further glorified her capital Babylon, in the time she spared from her military campaigns, by means of which she conquered many of the neighbouring countries of Mesopotamia.

Semiramis, pattern of the Warrior Queen who was nevertheless all woman, was said on one occasion to have been at her toilette when the news was brought to her that Babylon had revolted. Half-dressed, she swore to quell the insurrection before her toilette should be completed. Her voracious sexual appetites were, like the Queen herself, legendary; the most stalwart soldiers under her command were regularly called into a different kind of service; ungratefully if practically, Semiramis was in the habit of putting her lovers to death immediately after a night of love lest the tale of the Empress's desires should be spread abroad. Even more licentious, as well as unnatural, was the passion that Semiramis was supposed to have nourished for her son Ninyas (which in one version of her story caused him to kill her).

At least on her death, Semiramis was supposed to have turned into a dove; or, better still, to have been worshipped as a goddess. It was this identification with mysterious and seductive goddesses of the East, such as Astarte (or Ishtar), who first prowled along the edges of the Classical world and then invaded it, which was probably most important in preserving her story. In this manner it was thrillingly carried away from the small patch of historical ground in which it had originally been rooted.

As for the mother–son relationship, Voltaire employed that in his play *Semiramis*, first performed in 1748 (and used by Rossini as the basis for his opera *Semiramide*). In so doing Voltaire gave the relationship a gloss which made it at once more tragic and more innocent. Once Semiramis had

> led her army and her people captive
> And spite of time, with more than magic art,
> Chained down the minds of men, the universe
> Astonished stood, and trembled at her feet . . .

Now Semiramis is doomed by her love for Arsaces (unknown to her, he is her own son) because love itself, not incest, will rob her of her ability to command her people and her army.

Nevertheless it is difficult to believe that when Voltaire dubbed Catherine the Great his 'Semiramis of the North' he had in mind the possibility of such an agonizing maternal dilemma on her part; surely it was the role of the triumphant female general and even more the out-of-hours employer of strong soldiery, which was the link between Semiramis and Catherine. Voltaire's Semiramis was the lascivious one described by Diodorus Siculus in the first century BC: 'what knight in her eye was the most goodly and personable man, him she would covertly choose out from all her army of people and disport her with him after her appetite...'.[4]

Herodotus had more admiration for the bold Tomyris, Queen of the nomadic Massagetae (living in what is now eastern Iran) than he had for Semiramis. It was to Tomyris, as queen and general of the army, that Herodotus ascribed the death of Cyrus the Great, King of the Medes and Persians, in 529 BC, preferring the account which makes a woman the agent of his fall to all the others. (The point has been made that in half the total mentions of women by Herodotus they are shown as 'actors who themselves determine the outcome of events'.) Tomyris was a widow, left to rule the Massagetae after her husband's death, and Cyrus' first effort to take over her territories was couched in an offer of marriage. Tomyris declined this: 'for the queen was well aware that he was wooing not herself but her dominions'.[5]

What was more, Tomyris then urged Cyrus to leave the Massagetae in peace. As she watched the bridges being built which would enable Cyrus' armies to cross the River Araxes and begin his assault against her people, she sent him a message urging him to desist, containing the not unreasonable plea: 'Rule your own people, and try to bear the sight of me ruling mine.' Unfortunately, as Tomyris herself admitted, peace could scarcely be the aim of the all-powerful Persian King, he who had within twenty years founded an empire based on conquest from the Aegean Sea to the Indus river. So Tomyris' next suggestion was that Cyrus should abandon his bridge-building and a meeting should be set up. Either the Massagetae would retreat three days' march from the river and Cyrus would cross, or Cyrus would retreat and the Massagetae would make the crossing.

According to Herodotus, Cyrus seriously considered this proposal and at a meeting of his chief officers it met with almost universal approval. The exception was Croesus the Lydian whose arguments ended tellingly (invoking the spectre of the Shame Syndrome): 'And apart from what I have already said, it would surely be an intolerable disgrace for Cyrus son of Cambyses to give ground before a woman.' So Croesus advocated crossing the river and getting the better of the Massagetae by a Glencoe-like strategy involving a banquet.

In the event the Persians would have done better to listen to the reasonable Tomyris than to the tricky Croesus. The latter's strategy led successfully in the first instance to the slaughter of a number of Massagetae, sated by the banquet, and the capture of Tomyris' son, Spargapises. This time the message sent back to Cyrus by Tomyris was as follows: 'Glutton as you are for blood, you have no cause to be proud of this day's work, which has no smack of soldierly courage.' She continued grimly: 'Give me back my son and get out of my country with your forces intact, and be content with your triumph over a third part of the Massagetae. If you refuse, I swear by the sun our master to give you more blood than you can drink, for all your gluttony.'

Tomyris saw to it that her vow was horribly fulfilled. The nomadic Queen swept down upon the Persians and after a bloody battle – 'which ... I judge to have been more violent than any other fought between foreign nations', wrote Herodotus – the Massagetae succeeded in slaughtering the Persians, including Cyrus himself. Finding Spargapises had committed suicide in captivity, Tomyris had the dead body of Cyrus brought to her from the field, whereupon she pushed the head of the corpse into a skin which she had filled with human blood, saying, 'Though I have conquered you and live, yet you have ruined me by treacherously taking my son. See now – I fulfil my threat: you have your fill of blood.'

Yet for all Tomyris' courage and a bloodthirstiness in a measure at least justified, it is evident that her reputation survives merely as a footnote to that of Cyrus. Boccaccio, for example, commending her for her courage – she did not look for a place to hide 'like a fearful woman' when faced with the spectacle of Cyrus' army – gave a final verdict with which it is difficult to disagree: 'she was famous in proportion to the power of Cyrus'.[6] The Warrior Queen, whatever her qualities as a general or even as a human being, begins a long career of attachment to some male figure or figures of supreme reputation; she may challenge him successfully (as Tomyris to Cyrus) or she may fail gallantly in the attempt (as Boudica to the Romans) but she begins to be defined, unlike the war-goddess, by the connection: a refinement of the Appendage Syndrome, not in familial but in historical terms.

Fifty years after the death of Cyrus the Great, another brave queen accompanied another Persian king, Xerxes, to war against the Greeks and, although defeated at his side in the battle of Salamis, emerged from the contest with her reputation enhanced. It is true that something of Herodotus' partiality for Artemisia, Queen Regent of Halicarnassus, may be due to the fact that she was the local heroine, Herodotus himself springing from that same rocky promontory on the south Aegean shore (now the site of Bodrum in modern Turkey). Herodotus was born in 484 BC, that is to say he was only four years old at the time of the battle of Salamis; as a boy he listened to the tales of the men who had sailed with the famous Artemisia.[7] As a result Herodotus' anecdotal portrait of the Queen has a vividness and plausibility beyond mere local patriotism.

He began by admitting that it was 'a most strange and interesting thing' that Artemisia – a woman – should have taken part in the campaign against Greece. But he then went on to emphasize that it was not a mere fluke of inheritance that brought Artemisia to command. Of Cretan blood from her mother, Artemisia assumed power on the death of her Halicarnassan father Lygdamis: at first sight this is an example of Warrior Queen as Appendage, following the failure of the male line; but there was in fact a male heir available in the shape of Artemisia's grown-up son. So Artemisia's dashing expedition was due to her own force of character; or, as Herodotus put it, 'her own spirit of adventure and her manly courage were her only incentives'.

Furthermore Artemisia showed herself from the start of Xerxes' fatal naval campaign against the Greeks prudent as well as adventurous. It was Artemisia, alone of Xerxes' commanders, who suggested that the Persian King should learn the lesson of his recent defeat at the hands of the Greeks at Euboea, and not challenge the Greek naval power by putting to sea. Her advice was couched in apparently modest terms: 'The Greeks are as far superior to us in naval matters as men are to women', although she had begun by noting that it was her own courage and achievements at Euboea 'surpassed by none' which gave her the right to speak so boldly. She pointed out that if Xerxes rushed into another naval action, the ruin of his fleet might involve the ruin of his army as well.

Artemisia's intervention was heard with bated breath by the other members of Xerxes' council: her friends feared she had ruined herself, the jealous hoped that her sway over Xerxes would now be diminished. In the event Xerxes disregarded Artemisia's advice – he decided that the failure at Euboea had been due to his own absence, which had enabled his men to shirk their duty. But his high opinion of her perspicacity was at the same time confirmed.

What was more, Artemisia's conduct at Salamis, compared to that of Xerxes' male commanders, called forth the celebrated lament, 'My men have turned into women, my women into men.' It is the cry, an essential part of the Shame Syndrome, which will be heard again and again in the history of the Warrior Queen, down to the twentieth century, when Mrs Gandhi was described as 'the only man in the cabinet of old women' during her first year in office and the Labour politician George Brown called Mrs Thatcher 'the best man in the Tory Party'.[8]

Artemisia's escape from the scene of the naval engagement showed a special bravado. According to Herodotus, 'it was Ameinias who gave chase to Artemisia, and if he had known that Artemisia was on board, he would never have abandoned the chase until he had either taken her or been taken himself; for the Athenians resented the fact that a woman should appear in arms against them, and the ships' captains had received special orders about her, with the offer of a reward of 10,000 drachmae for anyone who captured her alive'.

Artemisia, faced with the problem of eluding Ameinias' trireme, adopted a radical solution. Instead of trying to engage Ameinias, she boldly rammed the ship of one of her own allies. The ruse succeeded. The Greeks assumed Artemisia's ship to be one of their own side and abandoned the chase. At the same time the ramming was noted from afar and brought to the attention of Xerxes himself with the words: 'Do you see, my lord, how well Artemisia is fighting? She has sunk an enemy ship.' For the Persians, like the Greeks, could not conceive of Artemisia ramming one of her own allies.

Artemisia rounded off the campaign, successful at least from the point of view of her own prestige, by giving Xerxes another sage piece of advice. She suggested that the Persian King should now leave his general Mardonius behind in the country to complete the design, since that was Mardonius' wish. 'If his design prospers and success attends his arms, it will be *your* work, master – for your slaves performed it. And even if things go wrong with him, it will be no great matter so long as you yourself are safe.' This time – since Artemisia's advice exactly coincided with his own inclinations – Xerxes followed it. And his admiration for Artemisia was greater than ever.

All in all, it is not difficult to sympathize with the verdict of John Aylmer in the sixteenth century. Put up to defending Queen Elizabeth I against the attacks of Calvin and Knox on female 'regiment' (government), he referred more than once to the story of Artemisia and Xerxes. Artemisia the woman, he pointed out, had shown more talent to rule than Xerxes the man.[9]

The trouble with this perception of the Warrior Queen as one whose behaviour and indeed whose whole career served as an implicit chastisement of the opposite sex was that it existed entirely in the moral sphere of the narrator. As Thomas Heywood observed in his seventeenth-century *Gynaekeion* – although the sentiment was universal from the time of the Greeks onwards – 'I know not better how to express the boldness of women, than by shewing you the fear of men, nor can I more plainly illustrate the valor of one sex than by putting you in mind the cowardice of another.'[10]

Bearing this in mind, the story of Cleopatra's treatment by the Romans in the century before Boudica and above all the story of her treatment as a would-be 'Queen of War' acts as a significant footnote to the history of pre-Boudican female warrior leaders. Where practical politics were concerned, no Warrior Queen could count on the kind of approval meted out by Herodotus to Artemisia in his character study of a woman at once sagacious and brave (beyond the capacity of all the surrounding contemporary males). Like other client rulers, or those designated as such by the Romans, she would be judged entirely by her usefulness to the advancement of the Roman cause (which, put simply, happened to be profitable overlordship of the known world). At the same time sexual licence attributed where possible to a Warrior Queen would be aimed as a barbed political arrow: where Cleopatra was concerned, it was convenient that Artemisia should be forgotten, Semiramis remembered.

Cleopatra VII – as she would become – was born in late 70 or early 69 BC, one of the six children of Ptolemy XII Auletes (the word means the Piper). Of these six, there were two girls older than Cleopatra, Cleopatra VI Tryphaena and Berenice IV; after Cleopatra came a fourth daughter Arsinoe and then two sons by Auletes' second wife, Ptolemy XIII and Ptolemy XIV, born in 61 and 59 BC respectively. There is some doubt about the identity of Cleopatra's mother, but Auletes' first wife Cleopatra V Tryphaena (mother of her two elder sisters) is the most likely choice.[11]

It is of course important to realize that Cleopatra came from a line of Hellenistic queens, something which should not be obscured by the exceptional fame with which literature has endowed her. Equally important is the truth about Cleopatra's blood and upbringing. Shakespeare's 'serpent of the old Nile' was in fact to all intents and purposes a Greek; she had Macedonian, Persian and Syrian blood as well as Greek, but her language was Greek. She had no Egyptian blood, although as an intelligent, well-educated woman she may possibly have spoken Egyptian. Cleopatra's Greek upbringing meant that she had been raised up in the knowledge of the great Hellenistic monarchies which had existed in the past: but she was also aware that these were now mere insubstantial memories, as Egypt had passed under Roman tutelage during the previous century. Cleopatra's father had been established as a kind of puppet monarch during the Roman dictatorship of Sulla; as a child Cleopatra might have known of the typically humiliating incident in which her own father was received by Cato as a course of laxatives were being administered to him.[12]

It is possible that Cleopatra co-ruled with her father for a period of weeks or months before the end of his life; at all events she was pronounced co-ruler with her ten-year-old brother Ptolemy XIII on Auletes' death in 51 BC. Such a union with her brother was a crucial step. Firstly, these repeated Ptolemaic marriages of brother and sister, whatever their genetic consequences, were intended to play upon the Egyptian devotion to their gods Osiris and Isis: the first-born children of the god of the earth and the goddess of the sky who married each other. The Ptolemies, as they enacted the roles of brother–husband and sister–wife, appealed to the patriotism of the Egyptians and at the same time emphasized their own divine origins as lawgivers.

Secondly, from the point of view of Cleopatra, as with her other female relatives, some kind of male ruler was essential, *de jure* if not *de facto* (the notion that these Hellenistic queens were ever considered *de jure* sole rulers cannot be upheld, even if their renown to say nothing of their strength of character far outstripped that of their

fainéant brothers).[13] Cleopatra VII was exceptional in that, as effective ruler in her own right, her head did actually appear alone on
bronze coins inside Egypt. Her female predecessors' heads had only
appeared occasionally on gold and silver coins – and even then in
the guise of Isis.

The picture we do have is of a Cleopatra who was not only
strong-minded but ambitious enough to have her own conception
of empire, involving the restoration of the glorious Ptolemaic
dominion which had once extended as far as Syria and Palestine. As
in the case of another celebrated *femme fatale* of history, Mary Queen
of Scots, a close inspection of Cleopatra's career reveals far more
concentration on power politics and far less self-indulgent dalliance
than wistful popular imagination cares to admit. Whether beautiful
or not (she has a heavy if sultry look to the modern eye), Cleopatra
certainly understood how to make the best use of her fascinating
femininity. After a series of intrigues led to her deposition in 49 BC,
Cleopatra set her sights upon the strong man of Rome, Julius Caesar,
appreciating that he had the power to restore her.

Plutarch tells the celebrated story of her arrival at Caesar's palace
in a sleeping bag rolled up: 'This little trick of Cleopatra's, which
showed her provocative impudence, is said to have been the first
thing about her which captivated Caesar, and, as he grew to know
her better, he was overcome by her charm and arranged that she
and her brother should be reconciled and share the throne of Egypt
together.'[14] (But Ptolemy XIII was in fact subsequently defeated
with Caesar's help, and put to death, leaving Cleopatra to share the
throne officially with her younger brother Ptolemy XIV.)

The birth of a boy known as Caesarion in 47 BC, after Caesar had
left Egypt, further strengthened Cleopatra's hand in view of her
theoretical need for a male co-ruler, and her practical need for a
submissive one. Julius Caesar was generally thought to be the father
of the child, as his name indeed indicates, but later, by officially
ascribing paternity to her brother Ptolemy XIV, Cleopatra brought
the boy within the necessary network of the Ptolemaic royal family.
After Ptolemy XIV had been disposed of, like Ptolemy XIII (and at
another date Cleopatra's sister Arsinoe), Cleopatra was able in time
to establish herself as co-sovereign with her own son as Ptolemy
XV Caesar. This other 'little trick' of Cleopatra's, whatever its
'impudence', has nothing particularly languorous about it.

Meanwhile as Caesar's mistress, Cleopatra journeyed to Rome, a visit either underplayed or excoriated by the Romans in later years. Cicero's description of her sojourn in Rome belonged to the latter category: 'I detest Cleopatra,' he wrote, 'and the insolence of the queen ... when she was in her villa across the river [i.e. the Tiber] I cannot mention without great indignation.'[15] It was a taste of what was to come. At the time Cleopatra was saluted by Caesar with a golden statue of herself in the temple of Venus Genetrix, the publicly proclaimed ancestress of Caesar's own Julian family. She was still living there in 44 BC when Caesar's assassination put an end to her political hopes – from that direction.

The rise of Mark Antony after the defeat of Caesar's assassins at Philippi in 42 BC, presented Cleopatra with another opportunity to exert her wiles in the interest of gratifying her territorial ambitions. She arrived to greet him in Tarsus in Asia Minor by barge up the River Cydnus, a scene originally described by Plutarch that lives forever at the pen of Shakespeare. Outwardly, Cleopatra appeared more as a goddess than as a potential mistress. Plutarch wrote: 'the word spread on every side that Aphrodite had come to revel with Dionysus for the happiness of Asia'.

For Cleopatra herself, although Aphrodite was held in certain circles to be a mother goddess (which was useful), it was Isis who proved throughout her reign the most convenient point of identification. In the East, the cult of Isis stretched back for at least two thousand years: here was the national divinity of Egypt, the Great Mother of all the gods and of nature itself, the equivalent of Dionysus; except that the cult of Isis, which could be followed by both men and women, presupposed the equality of the female sex. Only one Ptolemaic creed connected with the cult has come down to us but it is a remarkable one from the point of view of a putative Warrior Queen: 'I am Isis, the Mistress of every land ... I gave and ordained Laws for men, which no one is able to change ... I am she that rises in the Dogstar, she who is called Goddess by women ... I made man strong ... I am the queen of war. I am the queen of the thunderbolt. I stir up the sea and calm it. I am the rays of the Sun.'[16] At one point, not only did Cleopatra project herself as the New Isis, but she projected her lover Antony as the New Osiris: not an agreeable concept to Antony's political enemies at Rome.

Even more threatening from the point of view of those hostile to the renewal of the Ptolemaic empire were such words as these, taken from the so-called Sibylline books, a corpus of prophetic literature, probably written at the height of Cleopatra's power:

> But when the Tenth Generation goes down to Hades
> There comes a Woman's great power...
> And then the whole wide world under a woman's hand...

Soon Rome, the 'delicate gilded voluptuous maiden', would be at 'a mistress' stern command'.[17]

Cleopatra's territorial fortunes certainly prospered with Antony under her sway. Not only were lands handed over to her far into Asia Minor but her personal wealth was increased with the gift of the Nabatean Arab kingdom, enabling her to exploit its bitumen resources. It has been suggested that new coins issued jointly with Ptolemy XV Caesar (her son) commemorated this fortunate new development.[18] At the same time, the name of Cleopatra's son by Antony, born in 40 BC, Alexander Helios, pointed to the cult of the sun; his twin sister Cleopatra Selene being similarly linked to the moon goddess.

At the Donations of Alexandria of 34 BC, by which little Alexander Helios was to rule Armenia, his two-year-old brother Ptolemy Philadelphus the lands to the west, and his sister Cleopatra Selene Cyrene, all the children were dressed in suitable national garb – Alexander in the traditional high royal cap of the ancient Persian monarchs. When Antony visited Athens, it was the statue of Cleopatra, dressed in the robes of Isis, which the Greeks erected on the Acropolis.

The Roman attitude to the New Isis (and the New Osiris) was very different. As political opposition to Antony on the part of his brother-in-law Octavian hardened, Cleopatra was increasingly depicted as an unpleasant Eastern siren who had seduced the Roman Antony, in order to play out a life of debauchery with him far from his Roman duties (and his wife Octavia). Octavian proclaimed to the Roman people, on the basis of Antony's will, which he seized from the temple of the Vestal Virgins, not only that Antony had given away Roman possessions to Cleopatra, but also that he intended to found a new dynasty with her, based on Alexandria, not Rome. It was thus the destiny of Octavian (the future Caesar

Augustus) to contain her: 'as swiftly as the hawk follows the feeble
dove', wrote Roman Horace with an air of satisfaction not lacking
in vindictiveness for all the trouble Cleopatra had caused. 'So he
sailed forth to bind this fatal prodigy in chains.'[19]

How different, how very different, at least in the popular imagination, was the sensuous and commanding Cleopatra from modest
Octavia at home, Antony's lawful Roman wife! Octavia's admirable
disposition encouraged her to plead for mercy where possible;
ultimately she would bring up the children of Antony and Cleopatra
(the surest test not only of an admirable but of a charitable nature).
As for Fulvia, that vigorous Roman matron, Antony's previous
wife, this was how Plutarch described her: not content to rule a
husband who had no ambition for public life, her desire was 'to
govern those who governed or to command a commander-in-
chief'.[20] But Fulvia's ambitions were also alien to Cleopatra, who
was herself 'the Queen of War'.

The winter of 33/32 BC was spent by Antony and Cleopatra
together at Ephesus. In this period of gathering storm, the perpetual
presence of Cleopatra not only at banquets but at military con-
ferences was criticized by the Roman Ahenobarbus (another character gruffly familiar to us from Shakespeare). While Ahenobarbus
wished in vain for Antony to send Cleopatra away, it was left to
another Roman, Canidius Crassus, to point out another aspect to
the situation. Not only had Cleopatra contributed a great deal from
her own treasury to the expenses of the war (of the five hundred
warships under Antony's command, Cleopatra had provided two
hundred) but she had also ruled a great kingdom without effective
aid for many years – and was by no means inferior in intelligence
to the other kings Antony counted as his allies.

When Octavian formally declared war against Cleopatra (not
Antony) at the end of 32, he also chose to direct his most vicious
attacks against the 'licentious' Egyptian Queen, rather than against
the man who might easily have been regarded as a treacherous
Roman. Antony's subjection to Cleopatra was declared to be incomprehensible (here was the Voracity Syndrome at work, with a
vengeance). The poet Propertius made of Cleopatra 'that courtesan
obscene ... that worst of stigmas branded on the Royal race of
Macedon' who 'dared pit against our Jupiter, Her god Anubis, half
a cur'. In another line, almost risible to modern ears in its disgust,

Cleopatra was accused of longing on 'Tarpeia's rock to set, The effeminate mosquito net'.[21]

This dichotomy between the Cleopatra of independent character and independent wealth described by Canidius Crassus, and the 'courtesan obscene' of Propertius persisted until the very end of the great adventure shared with Antony. It is even possible to argue that the sea battle at Actium in September 31 BC which terminated it, was justifiable, if Cleopatra's view that a land battle would have ensured the loss of her ships be accepted. As for Cleopatra's presence at the scene of the battle (the Romans, like Napoleon later, thought a battle was no place for a woman), that too is explicable if one accepts that she was needed as the figurehead to her own troops; alternatively that her personal safety was guaranteed more easily there than if she had been left on shore.

More starkly, Horace put forward the Roman view that Cleopatra was the 'wild Queen' who had plotted 'ruin to the Empire'. So Cleopatra's reputation was trampled into the mire by the Romans, much as Shakespeare has Cleopatra predict to her waiting-woman Iras at the end of the play that the two of them will be turned into puppets:

> The quick comedians
> Extemporally will stage us, and present
> Our Alexandrian revels. Antony
> Shall be brought drunken forth, and I shall see
> Some squeaking Cleopatra boy my greatness
> I' the posture of a whore.[22]

Like his fellow Romans, Horace ignored the possibility that Cleopatra might legitimately have ambitions of her own – for another kind of empire, under the dominion of a Ptolemaic Warrior Queen. The Roman treatment of Cleopatra in this respect may be profitably contrasted with that meted out to Dynamis of Bosphorus whose name means 'she who must be obeyed' but who is sometimes known as the Bosphoran Cleopatra.[23] Dynamis' husband King Asander had been recognized as ruler of the kingdom of the Cimmerian Bosphorus by both Antony and Octavian, Dynamis herself being the daughter of the late king. In about 17 BC, however, a certain Scribonius, alleged to be Dynamis' lover, instigated a revolt against the now elderly sovereign. Whatever Dynamis' part in the original uprising, she indubitably threw in her lot with Scribonius against her husband, leaving the aged Asander (he was said to be over ninety) to starve himself to death. Dynamis' next step was to assume control of the country herself, her own descent from Mithridates being an important factor in bolstering up her position. The evidence of the coins, showing her head alone, indicated that Scribonius was not invited to share the throne, even if he shared the bed.

Such a revolution in the Bosphoran kingdom could not be regarded with equanimity by the Romans, notably by Marcus Agrippa, Governor of Jerusalem. The kingdom's position both as a bulwark against the wild men surrounding it to the north, east and west, and as a gateway for the empire's supplies, demanded a stable Roman-controlled government.

Polemo, King of neighbouring Pontus, was accordingly sent into the field, having been promised the hand of Queen Dynamis if he managed to subdue the rebel Bosphorans. Reducing the Bosphorans to a state of submission was not difficult in that they had already thoughtfully put Scribonius to death of their own accord. Pontus duly received the kingdom of Bosphorus and he duly married Dynamis.

But Dynamis' story was not to be so tamely concluded. Fleeing from what proved to be an unhappy marriage, she raised a fresh revolt, this time against Polemo, with the help of a Sarmatian tribe. Dynamis now felt herself free to wed a young Sarmatian named Aspurgus. With his help, a series of military campaigns ended with the victory of Dynamis over Polemo, and the death of the latter at the hands of Aspurgus in 8 BC. Still, Dynamis could not rest easy until she had been accepted by Augustus Caesar and his representative Agrippa.

Once this was established, her chequered past, in both moral and political terms, proved no bar to her acceptance by the Romans. So Dynamis became a Roman vassal, receiving the title of 'friend of the Roman people'. Although her head now disappeared from Bosphoran coins, being replaced by those of Augustus and Agrippa, Dynamis unlike Cleopatra lived to a ripe old age, dying in AD 7 or 8.

It was Anchises, father of Aeneas, whom Virgil had prophesy the special destiny of the Romans, when Aeneas encountered him in the underworld: 'You, Roman, must remember that you have to guide the nations by your authority, for this is to be your skill, to graft tradition on to peace, to shew mercy to the conquered, and to wage war until the haughty are brought low.'[24] Of the two striking Warrior Queens whom the Romans encountered in the first century BC, Dynamis' fate illustrated the mercy shown to the conquered regardless of sex or behaviour, when convenient from the point of view of security. But Cleopatra, by placing herself unlike Dynamis in the category of 'the haughty', received a very different kind of treatment. Her fate was that fate of those whose ambitions or pretensions were inconvenient to the mighty Roman Empire.

It was a lesson to be learned again ninety years after Cleopatra's death by another Warrior Queen, Boudica.

CHAPTER FOUR

ICENI:
THIS POWERFUL TRIBE

*We had not defeated this powerful tribe in battle,
since they had voluntarily become our allies.*

Tacitus on the Iceni, AD 47

Boudica, like most Warrior Queens, was royal by birth and ruled over an aristocracy. The later Iron Age society in which she lived might be 'barbarian' by the standards of Rome – the Latin word means literally strange or foreign, not savage as it has come to mean in modern usage – but it was certainly not anarchic. Furthermore, she lived in a period of transition when Roman influences had already been brought to bear upon parts of England as a result of military invasion, commercial dealings and finally military occupation for a generation before her uprising.

This is not to say that the Iceni, the tribe of which she became the leader on her husband's death, were in the forefront of Romanization. There were more sophisticated groups to be found in the middle of the first century AD, using the word sophisticated to denote such matters as literacy and style of living, whose geographical position had brought them into closer contact with the Romans.

Geography indeed plays an important part in the story of the Iceni as it does in that of Boudica herself. The Iceni territories, broadly speaking, encompassed modern Norfolk and north Suffolk, an area which even today can give an impression of rural seclusion, vast tracts of land whose inhabitants are not in immediate daily touch with any metropolis. That natural disposition of the terrain which leaves East Anglia in a sense out on its own large limb was obviously an even more potent factor in preserving Iceni independence in the Iron Age.

Despite this caveat, it would be quite wrong to regard Boudica herself as some kind of violent savage: a woad-stained and shrieking animal. Furthermore, since her behaviour at times can fairly be considered violent, it would be wrong to regard that behaviour also as being merely the mindless outbreak of a female ruffian. Boudica did exist; she did spring from a particular society; her conduct, whether heroic or reprehensible, was the product of that society and its standards.

The first recorded mention of the Iceni tribe occurs, almost certainly, in Caesar's report on his second invasion of Britain, roughly a hundred years before Boudica's rebellion. Julius Caesar's first invasion, in 55 BC, had not taken him across the Thames. The following year however he made the crossing, and following the defeat of a British overlord named Cassivellaunus, received the submission of a number of tribes. Foremost among these were the Trinovantes – Camulodunum (Colchester) was one centre associated with their name – and it was in fact the appeal of the Trinovantes to Caesar for protection against Cassivellaunus' dominion which had provoked the latter's final defeat. The Trinovantes' submission was the obvious corollary to their appeal; the five other tribes who also submitted presumably judged it prudent to do so. Among their names are listed the Cenimagni – 'the great Iceni'. (This is to assume, as is generally done, that the Cenimagni are to be equated with the Iceni: the mention of 'the great Iceni' may of course postulate the existence of another tribe, the lesser Iceni, who did not submit.)[1]

Then Caesar departed for the second time, and this time he did not come again. As the years passed, the British tribes must have hoped or even believed that he had taken away his doughty Roman legionaries forever. The Iceni at least sank back into that kind of historical obscurity to which lack of literary evidence can consign a whole people for a whole century: 'the world forgetting, by the world forgot'.*[3]

* In local British terms, the river name Itchen may be related to the tribal name Iceni, but Ixworth or Ickenham are not thought to be so related.[2]

Even when in AD 43 the Emperor Claudius instigated a fresh invasion – which as it proved developed into four hundred years of occupation – the name of the Iceni did not immediately recur. It is true that there are those eleven mysterious 'kingdoms' – mysterious because unnamed – associated with the Arch erected to Claudius to celebrate his triumph. According to the inscription, the Emperor 'received the surrender of eleven kings of Britain, defeated without any loss', as well as being 'the first to bring barbarian peoples across the Ocean under the sway of the Roman people'. Quite possibly, among these 'kingdoms' (or tribes) whose rulers surrendered are to be found the Iceni.[4]

Nevertheless, the next specific reference to the Iceni occurs in Tacitus' account of their first rebellion. Four years after the Claudian invasion, the Romans, under their governor Aulus Plautius, were pushing north and west. There is some dispute concerning their intentions, fuelled by an obscure text in Tacitus. Did they intend, by reducing 'the whole territory as far as the Trent and Severn', to establish that line of defence now known as the Fosse Way as a kind of frontier? Or did they intend to pursue the possibility of further conquest?[5] Whatever their future plans, the Romans proceeded to deal with those tribes left behind by this advance in a manner which was summary if not sagacious.

For the incoming Governor of Britain, Ostorius Scapula, who arrived in 47, took the radical step of disarming his own allies. He did so in the interests of protecting his rear. Ostorius found himself dealing with escalating guerrilla warfare on the modern Welsh borders, the raiders from beyond the Roman lines being encouraged in their depredations by the charismatic British leader Caratacus. Meanwhile to the north, the attitude of that sprawling federation of tribes, the Brigantes, remained uncertain. Nevertheless the indignation of the British 'allies' to the east thus disarmed was potent: they were after all being deprived of their weapons, in an essentially bellicose world, in anticipation of a rebellion which had yet to take place.

Among the disarmed peoples, there was one whose reaction was especially bitter: the Iceni. 'We had not defeated this powerful tribe in battle,' wrote Tacitus, 'since they had voluntarily become our allies.'[6] It was under the leadership of the Iceni that the neighbouring tribes now rose up against the Romans. The rebellion, generally placed in about AD 49/50, was not successful. The Romans put it down with ease, although Tacitus noted that the British comported themselves bravely to the last, performing 'prodigies of valour' even when there was 'no way out'. The Iceni did however survive as a quasi-independent body: that is to say, they remained as a client-kingdom of Rome, their leader as client-king having specific obligations as well as rights.

It is at about this point that Prasutagus emerges as client-king of the Iceni. No date is known for certain beyond the fact that when he died in 59 or 60 he had been ruling for a long time. Maybe he was already ruling over one branch of the Iceni in 43, and was placed at the head of the other branch – assuming there were two – in 49. Maybe he simply emerged in 49 in the wake of the rebellion as one capable of leading his people in peace. All of this is speculation. What is important from the point of view of this study is the fact of Prasutagus' marriage. At some point equally unclear, but almost certainly before the AD 49 rebellion, Prasutagus had married a woman of royal birth called Boudica.[7]

Already this, the first incontrovertible mention of the Iceni, has painted a picture of a tribe both vigorous and resentful, their voluntary submission humiliatingly disregarded in the wider interests of Roman policy; one, furthermore, capable of showing courage even in despair. In the light of subsequent events, it is a significant image. And another image may perhaps be added to it: that of a young woman – a queen – with her own memories of Roman injustice, revolt and suppression.

What sort of people were they, the Iceni? First of all, it is important to understand their Celtic heritage. That is to say, a thousand years before, their ancestors had formed part of the great Celtic world spread across Northern Europe.[8] It is a heritage which marks the Iceni, despite the fact that by AD 49 their client-kingdoms existed on the very frontiers of the Romanized and apparently settled world. But then it was a powerful heritage, the Classical writers displaying a remarkable unanimity in commenting upon the characteristics of the Celts from the German forests to the sandy stretches of Spain. (They wrote about them either as Galli – 'the Gauls' – or as Keltoi, presumably how such people described themselves.)

We are of course dependent on the views of these outsiders since the Celts themselves, as Caesar noted of the Gauls, considered it 'improper to entrust their studies to writing'. It is true that there is 'presumptive evidence' for the import of writing materials into Britain before the Claudian invasion. In Britain in the years before the Boudican revolt, the unwritten Celtic language was gradually being replaced by the Romans' Latin for purposes of administration and commerce. In the same way, during this period of transition, the native spoken language was being permeated by Latin.[9] Nevertheless the basic culture of the Celts, being an unwritten one, remains destined to be observed from outside, rather than delineated from within.

Above all the Celts were brave: those prodigies of valour noted by Tacitus in 49 were customary, not unique. Like many (but not all) brave people, the Celts also loved the fight itself, dashing joyously and frequently into the fray, laughing and shouting their way either to bloody death or to an equally bloody victory. The traveller and Stoic Strabo, who died in about AD 21, described the Celts in his *Geographica*: the whole race, he wrote, was war-mad, both high-spirited and quick for battle, although otherwise simple and not ill-mannered.[10]

With courage went recklessness. It was, Strabo continued, easy to outwit them, since they were always ready to face danger 'even if they have nothing on their side but their own strength and courage'. The Romans noted their use of single combat upon occasion, the contestants flinging themselves down from their chariots (which would actually be light affairs of bentwood, no knives on the wheels, very different from the chariot supporting Boadicea on the Thames-side sculpture).[11] They also observed that the Celts fought naked, something they were well equipped to do; for this was a robust, well-muscled race who placed much emphasis on physical fitness. Furthermore, the Celts, as perceived by the Classical writers and depicted in Classical sculpture, were not only strong but tall and big-boned, with thick, flowing fair or reddish hair (in contrast to the modern idea of the 'Celtic type' as being small, neat and dark-haired).

Loud noises – trumpets and clappers in the form of animal heads – also attended the conflicts of the Celts. Noise, whether the braying of trumpets, the sounding of clappers or music itself at their frequent feastings, was indeed a universal taste among them. Such hospitable feasts would also be marked by lavish imbibing, either leading to singing or concurrent with it: drink being another universal taste. Wine for the aristocrats and wheaten beer for the rest was the custom, the whole spiced with cumin. Vast loving cups would be handed round, and although the sips taken might be small, Strabo added, 'they do it rather frequently'.

Another passion was for rich personal ornament, something which would now be termed conspicuous consumption perhaps, but was then, in Strabo's opinion at least, part of their general naïve boastfulness. Heavy gleaming gold, twisted and chased, was the best material of all: gold round the neck, gold bracelets on the arms were common to high-born men and women alike. Brooches were enamelled, cloaks were fastened with imposing buckles. Even in war, this passion for ornamentation was not subdued but extended to the helmets of the charioteers and to weapons such as shields. Colour was not ignored: clothing (like Boudica's cloak) was generally stained and dyed in a variety of hues and stripes, making a kind of early tartan.

Starting about five hundred years before the time of Boudica, some of these fighting, singing, drinking, gold-bedecked Celts migrated across the English Channel from what are now the Low Countries to East Anglia. These were the ancestors of the Iceni. The first Celtic settlers who brought the practice of iron smelting were comparatively humble folk. Then in about 150 BC the warlords of the Marne Valley followed, bringing with them their chariots and their ponies (Iron Age horses were only about ten or eleven hands high).[12] Further migrations of so-called Belgic people – the Belgae from North Gaul – are still the subject of dispute, just as the distinction between Celts and Belgic people is itself blurred; but if the southern neighbours of the Iceni – the Trinovantes – were in some manner Belgic, it is the consensus of opinion that the Iceni in their geographic isolation remained 'Celtic', even if some 'Belgic' influences can be discerned as the century wore on.[13]

Whatever these distinctions, certain it is there followed in the first century BC and the years up to the Claudian invasion of AD 43, that flowering of Iron Age civilization and British Celtic art to which recent archaeological finds bear such eloquent witness. Many of the most significant finds have been made in Iceni territory: the Brecklands, for example, an area of forestry and heather and marsh lying between Bury St Edmunds and Norwich, and in northern coastal areas near the Wash. (It is the pattern of archaeological finds, following the cleavage in the terrain, and in its turn providing the pattern of Iceni settlement, which gives some substance to the idea that there may have been two Iceni tribes, the greater and the lesser.)[14]

Many of these finds testify to the fact that this was a society dominated by the horse and, by extension, the chariot: the rich bridle-bits and bronze nave-bands, a charioteer's cap found at Snettisham. The coins of the Iceni are stamped with galloping horses, legs prancing, manes flowing wildly (like the luxuriant locks of their masters enshrined in Classical sculpture). As a result this society, ruled over by the horse-mad, as well as war-mad, chieftains, has been compared to that of other ancient chivalric orders, such as the Samurai of Japan or even the warriors of Homer.[15]

Not only the arts of war – enamelled scabbards and shields – called for the skills of the Celtic craftsmen; a style of living which may even be termed gracious, is revealed by the appearance, both intricate and exquisite, of certain domestic artefacts. Much fine metalwork including dolphin and thistle brooches was discovered in a hoard at Santon in north Norfolk. Moreover if nothing else of late Iron Age society had survived except its decorated bronze mirrors, its sophistication and artistic sense would still have been amply demonstrated. Sir Cyril Fox wrote lyrically of the 'perfection of harmony between hand and eye' which these north Celtic craftsmen displayed in the creation of the mirrors, their 'masterly and apparently effortless technique'[16] – words which are even outstripped by the objects themselves. Once again, Iceni graves have provided richly of these mirrors.

It is however in the massive gold torcs or necklaces (from the Latin *torquis*) that the confident and aristocratic nature of Iceni society is perhaps best understood. Unlike the bronze mirrors, the powerful beauty of these magnificent objects is ill-conveyed even by photographs, let alone in words. Gold – the Celtic favourite – is by far the most popular material, although torcs of bronze and even silver are known. Their precise function will probably never be perfectly understood: Boudica will be described as wearing one round her neck as she harangued her troops on the eve of battle. Yet those who have tried on a torc, even very briefly, speak of the extraordinary weight (those in the Snettisham hoard, to be discussed below, vary between 1,000 and 858 grams).[17] Some are more flexible than others – some are made of gold strands, some tubular with the external diameters between nine and seven and a half inches; but none is flexible and light enough to make long-term wearing anything but a burden. In particular, the possibility of actually fighting in torcs, at any rate those such as have survived in the Norfolk and Suffolk hoards, must be seriously called in question.

Did the torc then have some more ritual function? That is to say, did the Iceni chiefs merely wear them on state occasions when the weight would have to be endured in the interests of majesty, as a British sovereign endures the heavy weight of the Coronation regalia – the crown weighs over 2,000 grams – once in his or her lifetime? A declaration of war on Boudica's part would count as such a state occasion. Perhaps the torc was in fact a votive object which was housed in a sacred place, round the neck of an idol, when not in public use.

Two separate sets of torcs have been exposed by chance since the Second World War either within the main area of late Iron Age Iceni settlement at Snettisham near Hunstanton on the north-west Norfolk coast (1948/50) or contiguous to it, at Ipswich (1968/70).* The Snettisham Treasure, five hoards deposited some time between 25 BC and AD 10, was possibly the stock-in-trade of a metalsmith plying his wares from the south, or possibly Iceni loot after a profitable visit to their neighbours, the Trinovantes. The Ipswich torcs, whose extent suggests a goldsmith's workshop, are so similar in style that it has been suggested they originally came from north-west Norfolk.[18] If the precise significance of a torc is mysterious, the general significance of such a resplendent and indeed ostentatious object is not: a wealthy local dynasty.

In contrast to the torcs, the houses of the Iceni would indeed have a 'barbarous' look to modern eyes. But this is to misunderstand the nature of Celtic society, where domestic comfort, as for example the incoming Romans understood it, was simply not an objective. The houses of the Iceni would have been those circular Iron Age structures with high, sloping roofs which to us now have an African look. (However, a 1973 experiment in reconstruction, the Butser

* A collection of torcs can be seen in the British Museum (from the Snettisham hoard) and in the Ipswich Museum (from the finds made locally).

Ancient Farm Project – the 'Maiden Castle' House – has revealed the durability of these round-houses compared to an African hut: their skilful building methods surviving the storms and rigours of British winters in a way the latter could never do.)[19] An ordinary house would be about fifty feet across, with a central fire. The palace of the Iceni would have consisted of a much larger dwelling – a great hall – constructed along the same lines and smaller outlying round-houses.

But no trace of Prasutagus' palace, and by extension that of Boudica herself, has yet been found. The most likely area for such a discovery is around Thetford. Excavations in the early 1980s at Gallows Hill, near Thetford, raised hopes, before the absence of all domestic detritus inevitable on the site of a palace dashed them again. The Thetford site is now thought to be some form of temple.[20] In the absence of a reliable finding, it is not only the particular situation of Boudica's palace which remains in doubt, but also, more generally, the pre-Roman tribal centre of the Iceni.

When the Roman soldiers were asked to take part in the Claudian invasion of 43, they waxed indignant. This was asking them to carry on a campaign 'outside the limits of the known world'.[21] It was actually true that the world they encountered within Britain both looked and was very different from their own – thatched round-houses in contrast to the Roman houses of brick and tile. The lives of Celtic women were also very different from those of the Roman ladies who increasingly accompanied the occupying troops: while the notion of actual Celtic matriarchy has been dismissed, the women of the Iceni who looked into those exquisitely decorated bronze mirrors led the freer kind of tribal life in which the constraints imposed upon women by Roman law were quite unknown. A Roman female, having no rights at law herself, was from birth to death the property of her male relations.[22]

Roman society has been described as 'essentially a man's world'.[23] This was certainly not true of Celtic society. Not only law but religion, and religious attitudes to the sexes, were important areas of distinction. Women were excluded from the Mithraic religion which was spreading via the Roman armies across the empire. No such exclusion was ever contemplated where the Celts were concerned, a society still haunted by the powerful goddesses discussed in Chapter Two. There is every reason to believe that the priestly caste of the Celts, the Druids, included women as well as men.[24] Boudica's ability to summon up the character of priestess – or even goddess – on the eve of battle was to be an important factor where her war leadership was concerned: a capacity quite outside the experience of a Roman woman, however grand her status.

Caesar describes the entire Celtic people as being 'exceedingly given to religious superstition': that again was written from the Roman point of view. Another way of putting it would be to stress the profoundly religious nature of Celtic society, with every grove and stream and well inhabited by its own deity, and the 'otherworld' ever present in the Celtic mind. In particular the human head in every form, from ornamental depiction to the skull of the enemy, has been described as being as central to the Celtic religion as the sign of the Cross (referring to the central act of the Crucifixion) in Christian contexts.[25]

To the Celts, the head was literally the godhead, the symbol of divinity or the centre of the human soul. The heads of their enemies, decapitated, took on a symbolic importance. Livy wrote of the Gallic horsemen 'with heads hanging at their horses' breasts, or fixed on with their lances, and singing their customary song of triumph'. According to Strabo, the heads of 'enemies of high repute' were then embalmed in cedar-oil and exhibited to strangers; even if 'an equal weight of gold' was offered to ransom them, the Celts would refuse.[26] It is clear from this alone that the Celtic pre-occupation with the head cannot be equated, for example, with the mediaeval display of executed criminals' heads and limbs. It was numinous, not admonitory, in origin.

To the Romans, however, the zest with which Celts exhibited these severed treasures was not so much symbolic as revolting. It aroused the kind of disgust in the Roman breast which so-called superior civilizations have always reserved for the religious practices of those they designate – by right of conquest – to be inferior. Nevertheless, for all the Roman repulsion, this – deified groves, chanting priestesses as well as priests, and decapitated heads – was the religion which animated Boudica, as the Romans would discover to their cost when the conquerors were abruptly transformed into the conquered.

With the Iceni successfully subdued – as it seemed – the Roman action after 49 moved away from East Anglia back to the north and west. Here Caratacus still posed a threat: 'his many undefeated battles – and even many victories', wrote Tacitus, 'had made him pre-eminent among British chieftains'. His were the classical resources of the guerrilla leader, since 'his deficiency in strength was compensated by superior cunning and topographical knowledge'.[27]

The more northerly Brigantes were however soon defeated, as the Iceni had been, and after the deaths of a few 'peace-breakers' the rest were pardoned. Not only did this obviate the danger of a combination between the Brigantes and the 'exceptionally stubborn' Silures of modern Wales, it also presented Rome with a large and friendly client-kingdom across a wide spread of northern territories. Ironically enough, in view of subsequent events among the Iceni, this client-kingdom was ruled not by a client-king but by a queen: Cartimandua. The name Cartimandua, appropriately enough in this horse-haunted world, means 'Sleek Pony' – the kind of pony used to draw a chariot. This particular 'Sleek Pony' may well have been among those unnamed tribal monarchs who submitted to Claudius in 43, since she was clearly an established client-leader by the date of Caratacus' defeat.[28]

Even Caratacus could not hold out forever against the Roman legions. Vanquished at last in 51, he fled north to Cartimandua and the Brigantes (or else was captured by the Queen's trick – there are two different accounts). 'But the defeated have no refuge', wrote Tacitus. He might have added: when that refuge is under Roman protection. Caratacus was duly handed over by Queen Cartimandua, bound hand and foot, in order to appear as the centrepiece of Claudius' triumph at Rome. The client-queen had thus successfully 'furnished what was needed' by the Romans.[29]

Brigantian peace-at-a-price did not last long. Cartimandua's consort Venutius, also of royal blood, headed a revolt against her.[30] At first Cartimandua was able to survive by another of her cunning tricks, for she 'astutely trapped' Venutius' relatives. But then Venutius organized outside support. Tacitus is frank about the reason for this support: Cartimandua's enemies 'infuriated and goaded by fears of feminine rule, invaded her kingdom with a force of picked warriors'. Rome was obliged to come to her support, and it was with Rome's help that Cartimandua was able to remain upon her client-throne.

There is a parallel to be drawn here between Cartimandua and Queen Dynamis of Bosphorus. (But Cartimandua's capacity for survival in troubled times allied, not coincidentally, to a capacity for intrigue entitles her to be considered as the first-century Queen Elizabeth, if Boudica's dramatic end qualifies her perhaps to be its Mary Queen of Scots.) It is evident that whatever the Brigantian nobles may have felt, the Romans had no objection to 'humiliating feminine rule' so long as it suited their particular brand of power politics. The next stage of Cartimandua's story was however closer to that of Cleopatra than Dynamis. Some nine years after Boudica's rebellion, Cartimandua exercised what she clearly thought to be a queen's right to change her mind and acquired a new consort. She swapped the semi-royal Venutius for his armour-bearer Vellocatus. Tacitus, implicitly making the Queen part of the Voracity Syndrome, presents this as being due to lust: '*libido reginae*'. But it has been suggested that Cartimandua may actually have lusted after something very different: political support against Venutius. Once again Cartimandua was rescued by her Roman allies, although this time she did not survive on the throne itself, but was peacefully retired in favour of the *de facto* rule of Venutius.

It had been a long reign. In the extent of her territories and the power she wielded, Cartimandua can be compared to that celebrated southern client-king, Cogidubnus, builder of Fishbourne Palace, near Chichester. It is interesting therefore that Tacitus feels obliged to reflect on Cartimandua's '*libido*' and to treat the episode as a moral issue. (I. A. Richmond pointed out the irony of this in a lecture to Somerville College in 1953 – then as now an all-female institution – 'when the matrimonial experiments of the Julio-Claudian house and senatorial families in general are recalled'.)[31]

Furthermore the subsequent popular reputation of Cartimandua, obeying that rule which links sexuality to the Warrior Queen where possible, has concentrated on her adulterous aspect. Ubaldini, in that history of illustrious women presented to Queen Elizabeth 1, referred to Cartimandua in this fashion: 'she was a warlike woman and her way of acting was an example to the women of her country of how to be licentious, even if they were not born princesses'. Milton, writing a hundred years later in his *History of Britain* (when there was no queen regnant on the throne) was coarser. Cartimandua's military action was described as 'the Rebellion of an adulteress against her husband'. Her subjects were praised for siding with Venutius, since they thus displayed their detestation of 'so foul a fact' (the adultery); at the same time they rid themselves of 'the uncomeliness of their subjection to the Monarchy of a Woman'.[32]

This is to anticipate. The contemporary relevance of Cartimandua's lofty position and long reign with regard to Boudica is of a different nature. Tacitus described female leadership as something known among the Britons as opposed to the Romans, for example, where of course it was not: *neque enim sexum in imperiis discernunt* (they make no distinction of sex in their appointment of commanders).[33] Although no other names of reigning queens are known beyond those of the celebrated duo, Cartimandua and Boudica, these constitute one-third of the total of all the known names of sovereigns/chieftains. When King Prasutagus of the Iceni died in about AD 60, there was an established client-queen presiding over the vast Brigantian territories, a client-queen already supported once by the Romans in difficult circumstances. On grounds of gender alone, Prasutagus had no reason to suppose that his wife Boudica would be unacceptable to the Romans as regent of the kingdom after his death.

With the death of King Prasutagus, the pace of Boudica's story quickens; at the same time the areas where speculation must substitute for certainty by no means diminish. Sir Ronald Syme once wisely observed that conjecture cannot be avoided: 'otherwise history is not writing, for it does not become intelligible'.[34] This is undoubtedly a comforting maxim for the student of Boudica.

Speculation as opposed to certainty gets off to a spanking start in view of the fact that there are only three written sources for the Boudican rebellion which have any claim to be regarded as primary; and one of these survives in an edited form made nine hundred years later. Two of these sources come from the pen of Tacitus, who touched upon the Boudican rebellion both in his *Agricola*, the life of his father-in-law published in about AD 98, and in his *Annals* written fifteen to twenty years later. The third comes from Dio Cassius, who was born in Nicaea, where his father was a senator, in about 163; a monk called Xiphilinus of Trapezus produced 'epitomies' of his work, selections for public reading which included his passage about Boudica, in the second half of the eleventh century.[35]

None of these three accounts is very long. And at first sight each of the three claims to be regarded as a primary source may seem rather tenuous in view of the fact that Dio was born a hundred years after the revolt and even Tacitus a mere five years before it. Fortunately Tacitus, quite apart from his diligent researches in the imperial archives, was able to benefit from the first-hand testimony of his father-in-law. For Agricola as a young man was present in Britain, a member of the Governor's staff, at the time of these stirring events; whatever old men forget, they do not forget the campaigns of their youth. There were other survivors he might have interviewed: the widow of Ostorius Scapula lived on for many years, Tacitus being consul in the same year as his grandson. He has also increased his store of knowledge between writing the *Agricola* and the *Annals*.[36]

Dio's claim is based more modestly on the fact that although there are traces of his having read Tacitus' account, he does not simply reproduce it. On the contrary, so far as can be judged from Xiphilinus' selection, Dio had access to other independent material which has since vanished. It is known that he spent ten years taking notes on the work of other historians.[37]

Mercifully, this paucity of written sources concerning the Boudican episode is counteracted by the burgeoning discoveries of archaeology. Since the Second World War new methods of ploughing and above all the development of aerial reconnaissance in course of such pastoral duties as crop-spraying have led to fresh and exciting finds, even if the increasing demands of the American NATO bases upon East Anglian airspace are beginning to act restrictively.[38] Nevertheless, the fact that the actual date of the rebellion remains the subject of controversy – with dedicated proponents of both AD 60 and 61 – does illustrate the undeniable problems caused by this dearth of evidence.

The argument arises over Tacitus' own placing of the rebellion in 61, a date which does not fit with other information he supplies concerning the governors in Britain and the consulates in Rome. His narrative however makes sense, if the rebellion is put back to 60; the other events such as the change of governors then follow naturally. As against that, Tacitus' care as an historian casts doubt on such a mistake in dating. It is not however a controversy which is of vital interest to the present study of Boudica. Since the preponderance of historians still appear to favour 60, despite some strong contenders in the 61 party, this is the date which without prejudice will here be adopted.[39]

At least the fact of King Prasutagus' death is incontrovertible. What else is certain? He died in 60 – or maybe 59 – having been *longa opulentia clarus* – long renowned for his wealth. He died as a client-king of the Roman Empire, a position which at least from the point of view of the Romans, made his dominions an integral part of that empire – *membra partesque*. He died, we must assume, without male heirs, since the will he made did not mention them, and did mention two daughters. He did not leave the kingdom to his wife, Boudica, but he did entrust her with the regency on behalf of these girls.[40]

The clause in Prasutagus' will which was however to stir up the most trouble at the time, and prove the undoing of his family thereafter, was not to do with the regency. It was to do with that wealth for which he had long been renowned. Prasutagus left his lands and personal possessions partly to the Emperor, and partly to his wife in trust for his daughters (although the exact proportions of the inheritance due to each are not known).[41] He must have hoped that by so doing he had provided for a peaceful hand-over. It was an idle hope.

CHAPTER FIVE

RUIN BY
A WOMAN

Moreover, all this ruin was brought upon the Romans by a woman,
a fact which in itself caused them the greatest shame.
Dio Cassius

Boudica, the widow in whom King Prasutagus of the Iceni had placed such trust, was of royal birth. This much we know from the *Agricola*. But Tacitus, with his eponymous taciturnity, actually leaves open the question of whether she belonged to the royal family of the Iceni or another one. He simply says that Boudica was *generis regii femina*, a phrase that can be (and has been) variously translated as 'a woman of the Royal house' and 'a lady of royal descent'. The Greek of Dio Cassius reads less equivocally: 'A Briton woman of the royal family.'[1]

It is theoretically possible, therefore, that Boudica was actually a princess from a neighbouring tribe. It would be romantically fitting, for example, to derive Boudica from the Brigantes, where that strong female leadership was being exercised from the 40s onwards. Making Boudica the sister, daughter or niece of Cartimandua has, however, no evidence to support it, beyond the vaguely comforting feeling that the only two known Warrior Queens of the period must have been related to each other. (But this is to treat a Warrior Queen as a rarity: as has been pointed out in Chapter Four, this was not necessarily so.) Nor is there any proper evidence for the equally pleasing tradition which has Boudica hailing from Ireland. (The known existence of Irish queens in later centuries and the similarity of the Norfolk torcs to those found in Ireland does not seem quite enough.)[2] In the absence of such evidence, it seems far more likely that, as Tacitus implies and Dio Cassius states, the royal house to which Boudica belonged was that of the Iceni: the tribe she would now successfully stir to action.

Neither Dio nor Tacitus helps us with Boudica's exact age at the time of the rebellion. It is a fair guess that she was somewhere in her thirties. In 60 we know that Boudica had two living daughters who had reached the age of puberty, who were not married and who needed their mother's regency. If these daughters were in their teens, and thus born some time around 45 or 46, a rough calculation brings Boudica's birth to AD 26 or 27, and at latest AD 30. It is this calculation, incidentally, which makes it virtually certain that she was married to Prasutagus at the time of the first rebellion of the Iceni in 49, a mere eleven years previously; otherwise this was a remarkably short period in which to cram marriage and the birth of two children who had reached a nubile age. But if Boudica is not likely to have been under thirty in 60, she could of course have been quite a bit older; supposing these daughters were merely the youngest survivors of a large family, Boudica could have been forty or more. Her precise age, like so much else about her, remains guesswork.

Dio, unlike Tacitus, does give a physical description of the British Queen. She had red hair – a mass of 'the tawniest hair' hanging to her waist – and she was very tall, 'in appearance almost terrifying', with a fierce expression. These attributes were not unusual for her sex and race, at least according to the Classical writers. The proverbial Celtic colouring has been mentioned. The size and indeed strength of Celtic women was also something on which they were prone to comment: Diodorus Siculus went further and complimented them on being the equals of their husbands in courage as well. A celebrated anecdote of Ammianus Marcellinus has a Gaul's wife, even stronger than her husband, battling with swelled out neck and grinding teeth, flaying her arms like a wind-mill, and delivering kicks at the same time 'like missiles from a catapult'.[3]

Boudica also had a notably harsh voice, according to Dio. This is a comment which has an additional interest in a study of the

Warrior Queen at various periods, since again and again the question of the voice will arise. Condemnation of a female leader very often throws in the fact that her voice is harsh or strident. In 1400 Leonardo Bruno instructed Battista Malatesta that 'if a woman throws her arms around whilst speaking, or if she increases the volume of her speech with greater forcefulness, she will appear threateningly insane and requiring restraint. These matters belong to men, as war, or battles...'. As will be seen, allusions to Mrs Thatcher's 'fishwife' voice have been frequent in the 1980s.[4]

At the same time approval for a given Warrior Queen frequently takes the form of endowing her with a persistently dulcet tone, in spite of circumstances when any voice, male or female, might be pardoned for being raised. Thus Matilda of Tuscany, although both tall and strong, retained 'a wonderfully sweet voice', in the account of an admiring monastic chronicler. The Rani of Jhansi, on the other hand, who led the Indian sepoys following the mutiny of 1857, was allowed a remarkably fine figure by the British, but 'what spoilt her was her voice'. The best kind of voice for a female leader, achieved by few, was that allowed to the third-century Queen Zenobia of Palmyra by a contemporary commentator: *vox clara et virilis* – 'clear and like that of a man' (which Gibbon however translated as 'strong and harmonious' – in the eighteenth century, women were not allowed to have manly voices).[5]

Maybe, then, Dio Cassius, who was not after all present to hear Boudica haranguing the Iceni, endowed her with her harsh voice because it was in keeping with what might be expected of a Celtic Warrior Queen; maybe his informants made the same assumption for him. It is even possible that Dio knew nothing of her appearance and merely granted Boudica the likely attributes of such a person. Leaving aside these imponderables, it is sufficient to state that it is from this, Dio's short but vivid account of the strapping, red-haired Warrior Queen, that all other descriptions of her, to say nothing of later impersonations, have flowed.

Dr Johnson once described this world as one in which 'much is to be done and little to be known'. That certainly stands for the narrower world of Boudican research. But the nebulous nature of the information available about Queen Boudica should not cause too much dismay; at least, not in terms of the period in which she lived. It has been pointed out that in a revolt which involved perhaps as many as one hundred thousand people, only ten names are known, all from Tacitus.[6] (Dio added none.) Two are British – Prasutagus and Boudica – and the rest Roman. One more name, that of a Roman woman, Julia Pacata, emerged when the tombstone she commissioned for her husband, Julius Classicianus, was discovered.

It is the contrast between this nebulosity, characteristic of the first century AD and Boudica's – or rather Boadicea's – subsequent transcendent fame, which makes the lack of information so tantalizing. (Although it has to be admitted, from the point of view of myth rather than history, that the fire of popular interest often burns all the more brightly for the lack of dampening facts to pour upon it: Boadicea's lively leaping myth being no doubt a case in point.)

The local Roman administration reacted immediately and unfavourably to the will of King Prasutagus. The latter's intention in dividing his estate and treasure was presumably to placate the Emperor and safeguard his family's inheritance at one and the same time. In the event Prasutagus succeeded in doing neither. But this is not to say that the expedient of sacrificing part of the inheritance in order to ensure the safe bestowal of the rest was a wild or even an original plan. Not only did the Roman nobility of this period often resort to the same device to protect the terms of their wills, but the range and number of royal wills involving Rome has recently been shown to be far greater than is sometimes supposed.[7]

Unfortunately in this case the officials on the spot were either unsympathetic or rapacious – or both. They ignored the will of the King. Representatives of the Procurator Catus Decianus – the chief financial administrator of the British province – seized all the King's estate and the total of his treasure. That was not the end of the depredations. Not only did the Iceni nobles find their own hereditary estates treated as though forfeit to the Romans – for no crime except the death of their king – but members of Prasutagus' own court were humiliated and maltreated. It is obvious that the Iceni nobility, a free-born and independent caste, suffered an extraordinary and unwelcome change in their status. In Tacitus' menacing words: 'Kingdom and household alike were plundered like prizes of war.'[8]

The first step taken by the Procurator's representatives was however in a different class so far as sheer inhumanity and public insult was concerned. Brutally, Boudica, the new Queen of the Iceni, was flogged. Her two daughters, those princesses designated as heiresses by their dead father, were raped.

The names of these young girls, like so many other women's names throughout history, are unknown. Rape, equally, is a fate which has been shared by countless women down the ages, both named and nameless; victims of a male aggression, at once casual and horrifying, simply because, historically speaking, they happened to find themselves in the wrong place at the wrong time. That Roman conquest was not altogether free from this can be seen from the speech made by the Caledonian Calgacus, facing Agricola in battle some twenty years after the Boudican revolt, and reported to Tacitus. He urged on his men by castigating the enemy: 'They rob, kill and rape and this they call Roman rule.' In this case however it is impossible to regard the violation of Boudica's daughters as in any way mindless. This was a deliberate act of policy and as such it was symbolic: this act of rape was what Susan Brownmiller has called 'the vehicle of *his* victorious conquest over *her* being': he in this case being a Roman and she an Iceni royal princess.[9]

Symbolic too was the flogging of the Queen: or scourging, to be exact, for Tacitus' words are *verberis adfecta* – literally, to put to the rods. In principle, the Romans were not merciless or brutal to their captive royal women. One would not expect Cleopatra to have suffered such a fate, nor did she herself anticipate it: for the proud spirit of the 'Queen of War' the prospect of exhibition in a Roman triumph was humiliation enough. The wife and daughter of the British Caratacus were shown clemency once they had performed their own part in Claudius' triumph. On the other hand, the rape of the royal female as a ritual act to signify the suppression of a people is one with obvious psychological connotations.

The young Cesare Borgia held Caterina Sforza, then in her late thirties, incommunicado for a period after he had finally succeeded in storming her stronghold of Ravaldino in 1499; he then committed 'injustices' to her body. This was not lust, nor was she acquiescent (despite Cesare Borgia's coarse joke to his officers afterwards that Caterina had defended her fortress better than her virtue).[10] Cesare Borgia's act of rape was intended to signify the collapse of Caterina Sforza's spirited political and military campaign for independence.

It is generally assumed by historians that some act of defiance on the part of the Iceni must have preceded this brutality of the Romans towards their royal women.[11] Certainly this is perfectly possible, given the natural temperament for resistance the Iceni had displayed in 49 and would shortly display again. But as a matter of fact Tacitus does not say so. On the contrary he lists the cruelties of the Romans (starting with the flogging of Boudica and the rape of her daughters) and then moves to the consequences: 'These outrages and the fear of worse ... moved the Iceni to arms.' So perhaps an unconscious assumption has been made by these historians, in view of the bestiality of the Romans' behaviour, that some gesture or gestures of dissent *must* have taken place to provoke it.

Tacitus, writing shortly after the event, shows proper understanding of the way subject peoples are frequently handled. Given his order of events, the Romans' pitiless treatment of Boudica and her daughters was intended not so much to punish the Iceni for defiance but to emphasize their subordinate status and the uselessness of resistance to Roman rule. The fact that the royal family of the Iceni contained, coincidentally, two young females gave the Romans a nice opportunity for that extra-symbolic violence of rape. As for the scourging administered to the Iceni Queen, the Romans happened to believe that women as a whole were incapable of rule because they were incapable of discipline: 'Woman is a violent and uncontrolled animal, and it is no good giving her the reins and expecting her not to kick over the traces': these were the supposed words of Cato the elder in 195 BC, as reported by Livy two hundred years later on the eve of the Boudican period.[12] To be able to 'control' a woman and figuratively control the Iceni at the same time was another fitting coincidence.

If it was just this symbolic Roman brutality which touched off the Iceni revolt, demonstrating that a Warrior Queen can personify her people to the oppressed as well as the oppressor, that was not its sole cause. For such an intense conflagration as now threatened to destroy the whole basis of the Roman occupation could hardly be set off by that brutality alone, however shocking. It was Boudica who led her people in the general uprising, Tacitus noting at this point that lack of distinction between the sexes in the Britons' appointment of commanders referred to earlier. Furthermore Tacitus had Boudica allude to the outrages performed upon her own body and those of her daughters in the speech he put into her mouth to encourage her warriors on the eve of battle. Nevertheless the rebellion itself had deeper underlying causes. The mere fact that the other tribes to whom Boudica's wrongs would be less personally shocking joined in with the Iceni under Boudica's leadership, shows that this was in fact a widespread as well as dangerous protest against the excesses of Roman rule.

Financial exploitation and land appropriation, two slow-burning fuses liable finally to cause an explosion in any society, were at the centre of the problem. According to Dio, the rebels found 'an excuse for the war' in the fact that certain sums of money granted to leading Britons by the Emperor Claudius and believed to have been gifts were now declared to be mere loans. The Procurator, Catus Decianus, he who was also responsible for the confiscation of that part of Prasutagus' estate willed to his daughters, proceeded to demand the return of these 'loans'. At the same time, Dio accused Seneca, the celebrated Roman philosopher and politician, of first imposing an unwanted financial loan upon the Britons (attracted by the good rate of interest) and then suddenly recalling it in a series of severe measures.[13]

Whatever the truth of these particular exactions – perhaps Dio's cases merely serve to illustrate the general Roman use of short-sighted exploitive methods – the picture which emerges of the Roman administration of its new province is not a pretty one. The Romans were certainly not pursuing that policy of conciliation towards and co-operation with the local magnates most likely to ensure the long-term pacification of 'Roman' Britain. The tribal men of property began by resenting this treatment and ended by rising up against it, since they no longer had anything to gain by backing the Roman cause.[14]

The case of the Roman temple at Camulodunum (Colchester) exemplifies this process of exploitation. The situation in and around Camulodunum was already disturbing for the native Trinovantes in view of the arrogance with which the Roman occupation was carried out. The Roman town of Camulodunum had been founded about twelve years previously. It was designed not as a military stronghold, but as a *colonia*, that is to say, a settlement of Roman army veterans who had received grants of land in the surrounding *territorium* administered by the town, in place of gratuities at the end of their period of service. The term *colonia* also meant that an existing town or city was accorded special municipal status. (Camulodunum was in fact the first town in Britain to receive it.)

The establishment of a *colonia* was always a matter of explicit imperial policy and it was a direct decree from the Emperor Claudius which had brought into being Roman Camulodunum. The intention, obviously, was the 'Romanization' of the new province; civilizing loyal veterans would gradually spread and multiply among the rude British.[15] The native Trinovantes, of course, did not see it quite like that; in particular their reactions were not helped by the manner in which the ex-soldiers possessed themselves of their grants. According to Tacitus, 'the settlers drove the Trinovantes from their homes and land, and called them prisoners and slaves'. Furthermore, excavations at Colchester have revealed the cruel conditions in which the native workers were kept, as they were obliged to carry out the construction works of their conquerors.[16] When the ex-soldiers helped themselves to more land than was legally granted, their comrades still in arms turned a blind eye, hoping for the same licence themselves. With all this in mind, it is not difficult to see how the oppressed Trinovantes, whether the tribal aristocrats or their humbler followers, might brood upon their wrongs.

The temple, erected to the Emperor Claudius at Camulodunum, may have been intended by the Romans to imbue the native Trinovantes with loyalty to their new masters, but that was very far from being the effect it had upon them. On the contrary, the temple appeared, according to Tacitus, as the 'blatant stronghold of alien rule'. The whole concept of civic monument was alien to Celtic society. Moreover the sylvan temples of the Celtic religion had a very different air. This edifice proposing the godhead of a foreign emperor had nothing sublime about it to the indignant eyes of the Trinovantes. What was more, they were expected to pay for it.

It is not clear exactly how much of the temple of Claudius had already been erected by AD 60, since it is no longer thought that construction was begun during the Emperor's lifetime.[17] It would therefore have been building costs, rather than the maintenance of a priesthood to service the temple, which fell upon the Trinovantes. A series of discoveries, beginning in the late seventeenth century when the existing Norman castle (erected in the eleventh century) was demolished, have, however, given some idea of how the hated temple must have looked.

In 1683 the contractor found vaults below the Norman floor; in

1919 Sir Mortimer Wheeler and P. G. Laver revealed that the castle actually enclosed the *podium* or platform of the temple; further excavations have followed in 1950 (the 1,900th anniversary of the foundation of the *colonia*) and 1964. Calculations made from the surviving walls and piers suggest that the temple itself measured some 150 feet by 80 feet, that it was surrounded by a colonnade of columns, thirty-five feet high and over three feet in diameter, and fronted by a sweeping flight of steps where there would have been a series of statues.* [18] Enough of this was already completed to provide a clear and imposing focus for the resentful eye: enough, as it turned out, was already completed to provide a target for destruction.

According to Tacitus, the town of Camulodunum gave out its own desperate but unheeded warning of what lay ahead. The portents were many and various. The statue of Victory fell down with its back turned as though it was fleeing the enemy. Outlandish yells were heard in the senate-house and shrieks in the local theatre (the Romans had indeed gone for those amenities which made their civilization so agreeable to them while ignoring the prime need of maintaining walls round the town). A phantom settlement in ruins was glimpsed at the head of the River Thames. Most troubling of all was the blood-red colour of the sea, and the shapes like human corpses found abandoned at the edge of the shore by the ebb-tide.

Gazing on all these things, the native Britons began to hope – and the Roman settlers began to tremble.

Elsewhere in Britain, there were other frenzied women to be found. These women were not merely chanting, they were delivering their chants as war-cries against the Romans. For as the Iceni rose in revolt, led by the outraged Queen, and the subjugated Trinovantes planned to join them, the Governor of Britain, Suetonius Paulinus, was on the faraway island of Mona (Anglesey). Here, in the celebrated sanctuary of the Druids, numbers of rebels against Roman rule had taken refuge. Suetonius' mission was one of search and destroy. Moreover the destruction was intended to encompass not

---

* A reconstruction at the Castle Museum, Colchester, shows a building of gleaming white, with ostentatious red, blue and golden ornamentation; Roman eagles and a triumphant statue of the Emperor Claudius at the front steps make it easy to understand Tacitus' reference to a blatant stronghold.

66

only the rebels, but also the host of Druids as well.

The scene at Mona is vividly described by Tacitus. The dense armed mass of the enemy confronting the Roman army included 'black-robed women with dishevelled hair like Furies, brandishing torches'. Close by stood the Druids, 'raising their hands to heaven and screaming dreadful curses'. For an instant the Roman host stood as if paralysed by the weird spectacle. But then they urged each other, and were indeed urged by Suetonius himself, not to be afraid of a pack of fanatical women.

In that businesslike way which had made their soldiers the disciplined wonder of the world, the Romans bore irresistibly down on the varied multitudes of their opponents. Curses and women's cries were no match for them. The torches of these Celtic Furies were actually turned against their brandishers. After the assault, in an equally businesslike fashion, Suetonius had the sacred groves of Mona cut down, so that, as Tacitus put it, Mona's 'barbarous superstitions' could no longer be practised; in these Tacitus included the drenching of the altars in the blood of prisoners, and the consulting of the gods by human entrails. From Suetonius' point of view it had been a highly satisfactory operation. In that military rivalry with Corbulo to which Tacitus attests, he had now surely scored a victory to rank with Corbulo's conquest of Armenia.

It was at that very moment that the news of the horrifying disaster which had overcome the Roman settlers of the eastern *colonia* reached him.

Suetonius was by now a man of about sixty. As a veteran commander, he knew how to handle the kind of mountain warfare with which the Welsh terrain confronted him: he had campaigned in the High Atlas mountains.[19] He had been Governor of Mauretania, and in a distinguished career had shown himself not only a brilliant general but also an accomplished politician. The question remains as to why, at this combustible moment in the history of the province he had been ruling for the last two years, he found himself at the very limits of his territory: as far from the turbulences in the east as it was possible to be.

Was it a coincidence? Was Suetonius merely led on by his own military ambitions at what proved to be an exceptionally ill-timed moment? Or is there some more sinister – and more exciting – interpretation to be placed upon the fact that Suetonius was besieging the Druid sanctuary at the exact moment that the eastern tribes chose to rebel?

As the priest-class of Celtic society, the Druids were drawn from among the tribal aristocracy.[20] The Druids of Gaul, in the time of Caesar at least, were believed to constitute an important nationalist focus for their people. Caesar was also convinced – a hundred years before the Boudican revolt – that Druidism was an import from Britain to Gaul, with Druids returning to Britain again in order to refresh their knowledge. Even if the Druids were not as politically influential as was supposed by the Romans, it was this belief which was the important point. At any rate, the Druids were suppressed, either for their 'barbarous practices' (the official reason given) or for their political activities.[21]

What were these barbarous practices? The normal priestly concerns of the Druids were all those of ritual magic, including of course intercession to the gods via animal sacrifice. Gibbon acquitted the Druids of actual *human* sacrifice, supposing the charge to be a mere excuse for suppressing them on other (political) grounds, and wrote feelingly of the Celtic religion: 'the deities of a thousand groves and a thousand streams possessed in peace their local and respective influence'.[22] But it is generally believed nowadays that the references are too numerous to be ignored; at some point in the past the Druids must have practised it, though it may well have died out by the first century BC.[23]

Human sacrifice was something from which the Romans shrank in fastidious horror (although the unarmed Christians, matched in the arena against wild beasts for the delectation of the emperor and the Roman crowd, might have found such disgust ironical). The notion of human sacrifice, like the notion of nationalist political influence, combined conveniently to present the image of a body both hateful and threatening and thus ripe for suppression. This is not to dismiss Gibbon's equally evocative image of tranquil sylvan deities, which may represent another part of the truth.

In the early nineteenth century Gérard de Nerval wrote of the history of the death of religions as being even more terrifying than the history of the fall of great empires: 'all of us must sometimes tremble to find so many dark gates opening out to nothingness'.[24] Certainly to contemplate the Druids themselves in the absence of any literature (non-existent because they were non-literate) is to gaze through a very dark gate indeed. The Classical writers, who must under the circumstances remain our only guides, are not necessarily equipped for the task. To discern actual policy in the disparate actions of a body, whose motives and practices are completely alien, is difficult if not impossible.

Returning to the British Druids of Mona, a hundred years after the time of Caesar, they were, according to Tacitus, harbouring rebels at their sanctuary, thus transforming it into a form of political refuge. Does that mean that Druids of first-century Britain were also busily fomenting anti-Roman feelings elsewhere?[25] In short, were the British Druids actually responsible for the coincidence – the planned coincidence – of the East Anglian uprising and Suetonius' absence in remotest Wales? Tempting as such a theory might be, there is no hard evidence for such a collusion. That might not be relevant if, as was suggested by Sir Cyril Fox, the Druidic hierarchy were busy organizing the gold trade of the Iceni via the sea ports of the Wash.[26] Certainly the coastal access of the Iceni, which made their peaceful attitudes interesting to the Romans, is not to be ignored.

In the absence of any proof, however, one is thrown back on the palpable injustices which the Iceni had unquestionably endured, as had the Trinovantes to the south. There was quite enough here to whip up a revolt. It therefore seems more plausible to regard the uprising now led by Boudica as a spontaneous explosion for which there were deep-rooted causes, financial and economic, with a particular incitement of the Iceni arising from the treatment of their queen, rather than something planned or fomented by the Druids of Mona.

If there was a religious dimension to the Boudican revolt – and it seems from Dio's account of the British behaviour that there was – then it sprang from two sources. One was that natural equation of a popular religion and political resistance which occurs when the religion of the conqueror is markedly different from that of the conquered. (Irish history since 1650, the Catholicism of the people versus the Protestantism of the Ascendancy, is the classic example of this.) Such an equation needed no encouragement from afar. The second source would be Boudica's own self-identification as a religious figure, whether as priestess, prophetess or even quasi-goddess.

Boudica, according to Dio, addressed her tribe at enormous length on the eve of the rout which would lead them towards Camulodunum. The enunciation of such elaborate orations, if not the common practice of barbarian Warrior Queens (we cannot know), was certainly the common practice of Classical historians, who were accustomed to put these setpieces into the mouths of their characters on appropriately dire, solemn or patriotic occasions. Tacitus gives Boudica his version of a speech both queenly and bellicose at a later point: on the eve of the final battle.

Dio begins his account with that physical description of Boudica quoted earlier, gives her a spear to rattle in her fist ('to shew herself the more dreadful', as Holinshed would later have it) and describes her clothing: 'a tunic of diverse colours over which a thick mantle was fastened with a brooch'. This, he tells us, was her invariable attire. He then elevates her high on a tribunal, the kind of raised platform used by Roman magistrates and generals. The speech which follows has not fared well at the hands of later historians. Milton, in fine misogynist form, sneered at it in his *History of Britain*. He ran it together with Tacitus' version and put Boudica, somewhat opprobriously, 'on a high heap of Turves in a loose-bodied gown [so much for her Celtic dress] declaiming ... fondly', that is, foolishly. 'A deal of other fondness they [Dio and Tacitus] put into her mouth, not worth recital; how she was lash'd, how her Daughters were hand'd, things worthier silence, retirement, and a Veil, than for a Woman to repeat as done to her own person, or to hear repeated before an host of men.' Sir Ronald Syme, who otherwise found Dio's account 'verbose and miserable', regarded the speech as 'a monstrosity'; more recently it has been described as 'long, not to say exhaustive'.[27]

Clearly Boudica did not address her tribe in the terms given to us by a second-century Greek, epitomized by an eleventh-century monk and here translated into early-twentieth-century English. But the sentiments she is made to express do at least serve to remind one quite vividly of the recent treatment of the Britons at the hands of the Romans. Boudica talks about the difference between freedom and slavery which they have learned from experience (Tacitus at this point merely has the Britons in general, without mention of Boudica, arguing for freedom over slavery) and touches on their ancestral mode of life, boasting of their hardiness. She points out how the Britons have suffered since the Romans appeared in Britain. 'Have we not been robbed entirely of most of our possessions, and those the greatest, while for those that remain we pay taxes?' Although the Britons should rightly have repelled the Romans when they first invaded, it is not too late for them to act now, if only for the sake of their children, lest they too be raised up in bondage.

It is however what Boudica does, rather than what she says, which gives its importance to Dio's account. For having spoken, the Queen suddenly released a hare from the folds of her dress 'as a species of divination'. As the hare fled, it was seen by the multitude to run 'in the auspicious direction'. There were general shouts of delight at what was clearly a favourable omen for the uprising (as it was clearly intended to be, for one imagines that Boudica, astute enough to install the hare, was also astute enough to ensure that it ran in the right direction). The choice of a hare was also deliberate. This is an animal which features mysteriously and excitingly in the mythology of many countries, from the Far East to the pre-conquest inhabitants of North America, and it had been mentioned already by Caesar as among those animals sacred to the Britons. Various traces of hares in outline and other depictions of them as hunted beasts have been preserved; these may well have religious significance.[28]

Boudica then prayed to a goddess named Andraste (or Andaste in one manuscript). 'I thank thee, Andraste, and call upon thee as woman speaking to woman.' Although this is the only specific mention of the name Andraste/Andaste, it may well relate, given the process of translation and epitomization, to that of the goddess of the Vocontii in south-east Gaul, Andarta, and a general British goddess of Victory, mentioned by Dio later, Andate. It could also be some compound derived from Anu, one of the names of the Celtic super-goddess, the mother of all the mothers, as it were. The name is however less important than the type: for while the local Celtic deities have hundreds of names, the types remain consistent. Andraste was presumably the war-goddess of the Iceni. (One goddess portrayed on an Iceni coin 'with an individuality and a vigour atypical of classical art' may be intended to depict Andraste.)[29]

This is not the unique reference to a woman enacting a prophetic role in this period. Tacitus commented that the German tribe 'traditionally regard many of the female sex as prophetic, and indeed, by excess of superstition, as divine'. About ten years after the Boudican uprising, 'an unmarried woman' designated as Veleda (the word in Celtic implies the functions of a prophetess) was described by him as enjoying wide influence over some Rhinelanders called the Bructeri.[30] A captured legionary legate, Munius Lupercus, was despatched to her as a gift, although put to death before she could bend him to her purposes, whatever they might have been. Veleda's prestige was further enhanced when she foretold the massacre of the Roman army at Vetera. Later Veleda was used as an intermediary by the citizens of Cologne. Personal approaches to Veleda, of any sort, were not permitted; her relatives, with the idea of increasing the aura of veneration about her, kept her immured in a high tower, one of their number transmitting questions and answers, 'as if he were mediating between a god and his worshippers'. Nor did the Romans attempt to dispute her sacred credentials: it seems that when they finally captured Veleda, she was installed in the service of a temple at Ardea.[31]

Similarly Boudica – whose eventual fate was to be very different – in releasing her hare and issuing her supplication not only associated herself with the goddess, but assumed a composite role of priestess, prophetess and war leader – Holy (Armed) Figurehead – in accordance with Celtic tradition and myth.

So Boudica, Queen and leader of the Iceni, swept down upon hapless Camulodunum in her chariot. She had assembled an initial host of 120,000 according to Dio. It was the apparent suddenness of the attack upon a defenceless city which made it so horrifying in its consequences. But of course the fact of a British assault should not have come upon the Roman inhabitants so suddenly, just as Camulodunum itself should not have been so defenceless. The suddenness was not so much in the British attack itself, as in the minds of the Romans who faced it.

The Roman veterans, happily enjoying their generous grants of land, including those tracts to which they had helped themselves, must have ignored other signs, which should have been more telling to them than the blood-red sea and the outlandish cries in the theatre. Tacitus mentions the fifth column within the city who made sure that it was not defended properly; but this fifth column (*occulti rebellionis conscii*, literally 'secret conspirators in the rebellion') must have consisted of native Trinovantes, whose loyalties, given that they were first dispossessed, then ill-treated, should never have been taken for granted.

To explain the Roman negligence, Donald R. Dudley and Graham Webster, authors of the authoritative study *The Rebellion of Boudicca*, called attention to 'that overconfidence that often besets colonial powers'. Writing in 1962, they pointed out that the British had shown an equally negligent attitude towards the Mau Mau tribal insurrection in its first stages, for which oversight an official report had recently criticized the government of Kenya.[32] The comparison is certainly a valid one, not only for the tribal–nationalist character of both uprisings. The Roman settlers of Camulodunum, confronted by a series of atrocities apparently totally unheralded, must have experienced something like the same appalled bewilderment as the British settlers of Kenya some nineteen hundred years later.

The plain fact was that the Romans simply could not conceive that the Britons could do this to them: rise up, sack a city and massacre its inhabitants. History after all provides plenty of examples of this kind of tragic error. It is a common mistake on the part of the conquering power to consider a rebellion of the conquered to be impossible, because they find it unbelievable. The Romans of Camulodunum merely joined in this error and suffered for it.

Nor was disbelief confined to Camulodunum itself. Once the situation was accepted within the *colonia* for what it was – serious but not yet desperate – there was still time for the veteran settlers to send for reinforcements from London to the few men still under arms at Camulodunum. Here, however, the Procurator Catus Decianus, showing himself to be complacent as well as rapacious, thought it sufficient to despatch a mere two hundred men (who would perish with their former comrades). Around the wall-less town itself not even a rampart or a palisade was erected, for which there must have been time if reinforcements could still be summoned from afar.[33] Most tragic of all, the women, the children and the old people were not sent away.

The town was overrun without difficulty. Archaeological evidence not only confirms that there were no walls – as Tacitus stated – but that the original defences erected by the legionaries had actually been levelled down. Over them were built a series of houses made of wattle-and-stake, and filled in and covered with daub. These houses were separated by narrow gravelled alleys. All of this would be easy to destroy by fire – and it was. So fierce was the fire that whole buildings became baked into a kind of clay: a section of one such house (discovered in 1972 in the Lion Walk near the site of the temple) can still be seen preserved in the Colchester Castle Museum. The carbonized remains of twill mattresses were found, and other domestic objects such as Samian ware, burned black, as well as food: the charred remains of imported fruits, including dates, plums and figs.[34]

Even today, in modern Colchester, traces can be seen of a way of life which came to a halt abruptly nearly two thousand years ago. (Modern Colchester has incidentally considerable archaeological value as a site since it had to be totally rebuilt by the Romans following the holocaust of AD 60, allowing precise dating for certain discoveries.) The excavated site of a centurion's camp gives the visitor a strange Pompeian feeling of the past arrested. This camp, founded about twelve years before, would have been part of the sketchy defences of the town. A Roman grid cooking-iron has been discovered (such grids, by being pressed flat into the earth, have a good chance of survival). One may reflect that the last meal cooked on that iron was cooked in AD 60.[35]

Moreover there have been plenty of new opportunities for excavation, due to the levelling of one lot of buildings and the erection of another as the town has been rebuilt by stages during the twentieth century. In that brief interval allowed by the grace of the developer can be seen once again the blackened Samian ware and the scorched earth – literally – of the Boudican sack: an extraordinary orange–red hue.* However, curiously enough, of actual skeletons there are very few traces. It is to be assumed that sometime later the Romans came back and cremated the remains of their slaughtered comrades.

Three surviving artefacts, two of them of stone and one of bronze, also bear witness to the savagery of the British attack – as also to the motives which inspired it. At some point the British tribes swooped down upon the Roman cemetery to the west of the town where the old soldiers had been interred, as it was hoped, for an eternal rest after their long and honourable labours. The tombstone

---

* As for example at a site in Culver Street, Colchester, destined eventually to be a car park, visited by the author in the summer of 1985 when it was worked by the Colchester Archaeological Unit.

of one Marcus Favonius Facilis of the xxth Legion shows him standing confidently in full military panoply, including his *vituus* or vinestick (the modern swagger stick) in his right hand and his sword in his left. But the tombstone (discovered in 1868) has been broken into two pieces; more significantly still, the face has been hacked away.

In 1928 another tombstone was discovered, that of a man who died at the age of forty belonging to the first *Ala* (auxiliary cavalry unit) of the Thracians. Named as Longinus Sdapezematygus, his adoption of a Roman name in addition to his Thracian one was a characteristic practice. Unfortunately for his survival, Longinus was depicted as mounted upon an enormous rampant horse while below him crouched some troglodyte figure of a man, who probably symbolized death, but could well have had to the British attackers a more unpleasant symbolism of subjugation. At all events the tombstone of Longinus Sdapezematygus has been set about with a will, the face of Longinus himself and the nose of his horse violently obliterated.

Lastly, a bronze head of the Emperor Claudius was fished out of the River Alde, near Saxmundham in Suffolk, in 1907 by an astonished boy who had gone swimming. This head too has been subjected to violent treatment, as can be seen from the jagged edges at the neck where it has been hacked away from the body. Once thought to be the head of the great equestrian statue of the Emperor which would have fronted the temple erected to his memory, its comparatively moderate size and provincial technique are now considered to rule out that possibility. It must have belonged to some lesser statue erected in the body of the town. From the point of view of the sack of Camulodunum, it is of course more evocative to regard this head as one which might have been once carried on a pole through the burning streets of the *colonia* – if not the live head of the Emperor, at least the symbolic head of the enemy.* Since the Alde findspot is in Iceni territory, one imagines that the head, a peculiarly incriminating piece of evidence, was finally flung away there, after the defeat of the tribe.[36]

The temple itself held out for two more days following the sack of the town. The old soldiers congregated there as in a redoubt

* It is now in the British Museum. Both the military tombstones can be seen in the Castle Museum, Colchester.

for one last desperate effort to survive until reinforcements came. Weapons and armour, rusty with disuse, have been discovered, which the veterans must have hastily routed out and donned.[37] The picture of these old warhorses, once the masters of Europe, now destined to die, antiquated weapons to hand, at the hands of the despised barbarians outside the limits of the known world (as they had once complained to Claudius) has its own poignancy. For unlike Lucknow and Mafeking, there was to be no relief for this particular garrison. The gaudy temple was battered down and fired, the veterans, like their families, put to the sword.

The Britons under Boudica surveyed the smoking town and turned their faces towards London. For the Romans, when news of the holocaust reached them, there was an additional humiliation to be faced. 'Moreover,' wrote Dio Cassius, 'all this ruin was brought upon [them] by a woman, a fact which in itself caused them the greatest shame.'

CHAPTER SIX

THE RED
LAYER

Far below the modern streets of the City of London the events of AD 60
are indelibly scorched on the soil as a red layer of burnt debris...

Peter Marsden, *Roman London*

One should be in no doubt about the dangerous nature of the
situation then facing the Romans in Britain. And there was worse
to come.

The Boudican revolt has been described as 'the most serious
rebellion against Roman rule in any province during the early
Principate' next to the great Batavian (Rhinelander) revolt under
Julius Civilis ten years later;[1] Julius Civilis being another charismatic
native leader of royal descent ill-treated by the Romans – he was
sent in irons to Rome – before he rebelled. The Romans were
experiencing for themselves the ugly truth, as expressed by Tacitus,
that they had broken the Britons into obedience, 'but not as yet to
slavery'.[2] Now that the habit of obedience had been boldly flung
off, the Britons were facing their oppressors with all the banked
energies of the unfairly subjugated, not the lethargy which long
generations of serfdom can breed. It was clear to the Romans
themselves that such a British onslaught, in equal measure surprising
and horrifying, must be checked and as soon as possible, lest the
entire occupation of the island be imperilled.

With the Roman commander at distant Anglesey, the nearest
available Roman force had to be flung into the fray, in order to stop

the British triumph at source, following the sack of Camulodunum. That honour fell to the ixth Legion Hispana – one of the legions which had taken part in the Claudian invasion, taking its name from the Spanish province where it had served with distinction.[3] The commander of the ixth Legion, Petilius Cerialis, set off for Camulodunum with the intention of rescuing his compatriots, or at least of inflicting a smashing defeat upon the rebels. He probably came from a camp at Longthorpe, near Peterborough, some eighty miles from Colchester, and despite Tacitus' assertion, was not accompanied by a full legion, which would have comprised approximately five thousand men, but something under three thousand.[4]

If however the exact quantity of cohorts at Petilius' command is in doubt, their fate at the Britons' hands is not. Somewhere to the north of Camulodunum a British contingent was lying in wait: this would presumably have been a separate striking force from the army which had sacked the city and was probably detailed to cover just such a Roman advance. (We do not know precisely which tribes joined under Boudica, other than her own Iceni and the Trinovantes; some of the Coritani and the Cornovii from the Midlands were probably also there and maybe some disaffected Brigantes from further north; Dio's figure of 230,000 for Boudica's army at the final battle is obviously wildly exaggerated, but does at least convey the massive nature of the rising which Tacitus described as universal.)[5] The ambush was as bloodily successful as the sack of the city had been. Petilius' infantry was cut to pieces. He himself, according to Tacitus, escaped with his cavalry and took refuge back at the legionary camp.

Perhaps he had contributed to this defeat by acting rashly. Petilius' later career, which brought him into contact with that other native rebel, the Batavian Julius Civilis, showed him to be a general of daring rather than cautious instincts;[6] but at this point, while the Roman mentality still grappled bemusedly with the notion of British insurrection, caution would have been more desirable in a commander than daring. At least Petilius had survived to fight another day: and after his campaigns against Civilis he would end up as Governor of Britain. But for the present the Romans had now lost a further estimated 2,500 men, and were no nearer to stemming the British advance.

At this point, the Procurator Catus Decianus, he 'whose rapacity
had driven the province to war' as Tacitus pointed out, exercised
the traditional prerogative of the rat and fled the rapidly sinking
ship. He took with him not only all his papers, but all his officers:
Roman Britain was now without an administrative structure of any
sort, and still the Governor Suetonius, hastening from Mona, had
yet to arrive to save the situation – or so it was hoped.

Tacitus tells us that Suetonius was 'undismayed'. That was just
as well. He certainly made excellent speed in his 250-mile dash
towards Londinium since he managed to reach it in advance of the
British hordes from Camulodunum (a mere sixty-three miles away).[7]
Or perhaps the natural if damaging British concentration on plunder
following the sack of the veterans' wealthy city was already weak-
ening their original determination to extirpate the Roman rule. It
was the element of surprise which had enabled the British tribal
forces to slaughter Petilius' well-equipped and well-trained men of
the ixth Legion. Since the Governor of Britain could hardly be
expected to linger in western Mona once the startling news of the
fall of Camulodunum reached him, it might have been as well for
the Britons to employ the element of surprise once again, either
by ambushing Suetonius on the route to Londinium as they had
ambushed Petilius, or by occupying Londinium itself. But this was
not to be.

So Suetonius reached Londinium unscathed, and reached it some
short time ahead of the Britons; but it was an interval at least long
enough for him to appraise the situation with his accustomed quick
intelligence. Tacitus tells us that Suetonius had pressed on towards
Londinium with the original intention of using it as a military
stronghold. But it is important to realize, as Suetonius soon discovered, that Londinium at this point was not actually a fortified
city. Nor for that matter was it the capital city of Roman Britain, a
fact which may be difficult for twentieth-century Britons to appreciate, trained by long historical usage to think of London as the centre
of their world at least, and perhaps of other worlds as well.

If not a military stronghold, what was the nature of the city to
which Suetonius had hastened, and at which the marauding and
triumphant Britons would soon arrive? Despite all the recent archaeological activity in this area, the exact origin of Londinium has not

yet been established beyond all possibility of doubt.[8] Caesar does not mention Londinium at all in his account of the second (54 BC) campaign in the course of which he crossed the Thames; while it was the twelfth-century chronicler Geoffrey of Monmouth who was responsible for spreading the enduring legend of a pre-Roman city, something for which there is no support from archaeology. Since the name Londinium itself does derive from something pre-Roman, it was perhaps some obscure farm on a bend of the river which gave its name forever to the future mighty conurbation.[9]

Be that as it may, the archaeological evidence indicates that Londinium as known in the first century owed its foundation to the Romans. There are two main theories: the first suggests that Londinium was founded as a military base at the time of the Claudian invasion of 43. The second envisages it as 'a carefully planned civil trading settlement of Roman merchants'. It is the lack of military equipment among the discoveries unearthed which argues against the theory of the military base: unlike Colchester, for example, which is known to have been established in the first place as a fortification before being transformed into a *colonia*, and where a plethora of military remains have been turned up. The military argument cannot however be conclusively demolished. For one thing, the new settlement undeniably occupied a situation of strategic importance: it would make sense if its earliest Roman use was in fact as a place of river crossing, and that would suppose some form of military presence.[10]

The dating of the coins however suggests a town which began to flourish from about AD 50 onwards. Recent archaeological work has indeed tended to reinforce the notion of a town planned from the first and rapidly expanding. Traces of a major north-east–south-west Roman road have been revealed in Southwark, crossing the Thames just below the modern London Bridge (and above the mediaeval one). This is in addition to the long-known major east–west road, nine metres wide, which has been replaced by the modern Cheapside, but parts of which have been integrated into Lombard Street and Fenchurch Street. Traces of this north–south road, on the north bank of the Thames, were found in the winter of 1984/5 in King Street, between the Guildhall and St Paul's; already in the AD 50s it was attended by thriving shops.

There are also traces of a central square, probably a market square, under Gracechurch Street, as well as these broad roads, and although the Boudican destruction followed by Roman reconstruction makes it impossible to be certain, there may well have been an early temple; if so, it would notionally lie beneath the site of that temple, recently rediscovered, which is dated about AD 70. We know that there was at least one large building, a Roman version of a modern shopping mall; this had a deep verandah or portico running along in front of it, obviously intended for a series of different shops, which indicates that the Roman version of the developers were also present.

'Boudican' Londinium spread over thirty acres at least and may have had as many as thirty thousand inhabitants.[11] The limits of the city are indicated by various factors including of course those fire deposits which provide brutal evidence of how soon all this development was to be suddenly and violently shattered. The siting of the Roman cemeteries of this period is also important, since they had by law to lie outside the bounds of the city. Londinium in these early days would have centred round modern Lombard Street where it is bisected by Gracechurch Street, and continues into Fenchurch Street, with the findspots of shards and so forth heavily grouped near Leadenhall Market. A stream, later named the Walbrook, flowed through it (its course lying beneath the modern Bank of England and Mansion House). The eastern limits of Londinium would have been not much further than Mincing Lane; the Fleet from which modern Fleet Street takes its name, then a navigable river, must have acted as a virtual boundary in the west.

Unlike hapless Camulodunum, the first British *colonia*, and the *municipium* of Verulamium to which Boudica's army would shortly turn its attentions, Londinium had as yet no official status. This is the description given to us by Tacitus: Londinium 'did not rank as a Roman settlement, but was an important centre for businessmen and merchandise'. The word which Tacitus uses for businessmen, *negotiatores* – bankers or those engaged in financial transactions as opposed to *mercatores*, merchants – suggests incidentally that Londinium in its occupational use in AD 60 was not so far from that of the City of London, which now occupies more or less the same area.[12]

Although lacking a charter, the city may have enjoyed some kind of self-government under military control.[13] For whatever the origins of the site, it is clear that by AD 60 a teeming energetic cosmopolitan city, connected with Europe and beyond, full of confidence in its commercial future, occupied it. Londinium at this point should not be regarded as a 'British' city. It may have been temporarily swollen with British refugees, given the impending arrival of the Boudican army, already laying waste the countryside of the Thames between Camulodunum and their new target. But the city was not a natural focus for any particular British tribe, as the fact that it had taken a Roman foundation to conjure it into existence bears witness.[14]

The cosmopolitan nature of this busy community is on the contrary well illustrated by the kind of belongings and household objects it left behind, many of them luxuries which had to be imported from some far-flung town or country. Objects have been found as geographically diverse as red-pottery tableware from southern Italy, still showing traces of Vesuvian ash, amphorae, probably containing olive oil, from the Seville region of southern Spain, smaller amphorae for wine from Rhodes, and glassware from Syria. Here were wealthy merchants, already beginning to live in the kind of comfortable lifestyle they had enjoyed at home, not necessarily Roman, but from the easeful Mediterranean. As with Camulodunum, a growing body of expatriates had come to profit from the opportunities presented by the new Roman province, serenely confident that the graph of their prosperity must inevitably soar with the passage of time.

Then Suetonius arrived from Mona, took one look at Londinium and decided to abandon it to the enemy. The town, he believed, could not be defended and the horrifying recent experience of Petilius left him disinclined to emulate that commander's rashness; he was well aware of the inferior numbers of his own men compared to those of the Britons. It was better to live to fight another day. As Tacitus coolly and succinctly expressed it: 'He decided to save the whole situation by the sacrifice of a single city.' It was a radical and unsentimental solution.

In vain those about to be sacrificed – civilians all – prayed and wept not to be left to their fate. Suetonius gave the signal for departure. The brave Roman cavalry clattered away. The legionaries, those that there were, marched off. The able-bodied must have tried, many of them, to leave with him. At any rate, 'those who could keep up with him' were given a place. Others would have escaped up the waterway of the Thames to the safer territories of the Atrebates, with their capital at Silchester and their king Cogidubnus, like Cartimandua of the Brigantes, friendly to the Roman interests.[15] But there remained behind in Londinium, according to Tacitus, all those who could not travel, either because of their sex, or because they were too old (or, as he might have added, too young). And there was a third category, equally poignant from the point of view of the historian, of those who remained behind voluntarily because they were 'attached to the place'. Already it seems the city had its inveterate inhabitants, who if not native Britons, were in another sense already Londoners: these too stayed behind as centuries later Londoners would refuse to leave their homes during the Great Plague, the Great Fire and the Blitz.

'Never before or since has Britain ever been in a more disturbed and perilous state': thus Tacitus, later, on the state of the Roman province at this time, and it is worth recalling that Tacitus had a first-hand witness to the events and emotions of that terrible period in his father-in-law, then a young man and a member of Suetonius' staff. With the veterans and their families massacred, a *colonia* burned to the ground, at least part of a Roman legion wiped out – a minimum of two thousand men – and now a populous merchant city abandoned, it is difficult to see that Tacitus was exaggerating.

Indeed, if the Boudican revolt was the second most serious provincial rising in this century, for a parallel to the Roman situation on the abandonment of Londinium it is suggested that one should go back a hundred years to Gaul.[16] Here the young champion of the Arverni, Vercingetorix, defeated Caesar at Gergovia in 52 BC, and at the head of a general army of the Gauls very nearly succeeded in throwing the Roman yoke off altogether.

The lamentations of the helpless inhabitants of Londinium had not been misplaced. Their city was to be destroyed and they themselves were to be sacrificed, in certain cases quite literally so. From the very first, serious excavations of the city of London – beginning in 1915 but with a rapid increase after the First World War – have indeed provided startling evidence of the violent demolition of an earlier foundation in the middle of the first century AD.[17]

The process of discovery, in connection with the building and rebuilding in this area, has continued in various phases ever since, with the depredations of the Blitz during the Second World War providing of course ripe opportunities. If not all of these were taken in the past – where archaeological discovery is concerned one might well adapt the words of Thomas Hood concerning a noted sportsman: 'What he hit is history; what he missed is mystery' – fortunately the present climate is increasingly favourable to co-operative ventures between archaeologist and developer.*

In this way fragments of burned roofing tiles, wood ash conveniently accompanied by burned coins of the reign of Claudius – seventeen such bronze coins were discovered at a depth of seventeen feet when Lloyds Bank was built – burned grain from a merchant's stock he could not carry away, burned Samian ware, all these have provided mute testimony of the great fire which finally completed the holocaust of London. The civilized homes of the wealthy businessmen, made of timber and some clay, with their white plaster work, some of it decorated with colours, with their thatched roofs and their wooden floorboards, burned merrily. The elegant pots, the amphorae for the Greek wine and the Spanish oil, the decorated pottery lamps imported from the Mediterranean, all these witnesses to the sophisticated tastes of the first Londoners were first smashed by desecrating hands then baked in a furnace of destruction. The fact that some of these houses even had running water by this date would have been of little significance in view of the fiery furnace which now engulfed the centre of the city: it has been estimated from tests on burned Samian ware that the heat must have been in excess of 1,000°C (to be compared with the similarly estimated heat in the firestorms in Hamburg during the 1943 bombings, with all the additional aid of high explosives).[18]

Above all, more vivid to the eye than in the diagram and most vivid of all perhaps to the eye of the imagination, there is the red layer. Lying about thirteen feet below the surface and approximately sixteen inches deep, the red layer is the substratum of burned debris which serves as a perpetual reminder to the archaeologist of the severity of the Boudican attack. 'Far below the modern streets of

---

* Excavations of a site off Leadenhall Street during 1985–6 took place during a pause granted by the developer Legal & General before the erection of Leadenhall Court, a new centre of shops and offices; they were jointly supported by the Museum of London, English Heritage and the developer, who together formed the Roman Civic Centre Project.

the City of London', writes Peter Marsden, 'the events of AD 60 are indelibly scorched on the soil . . .'.[19]

The massacred inhabitants have left no equivalent red layer. As with Camulodunum, where, as has been seen, similar conditions of fire and slaughter prevailed, we can presume that the Romans returned to the smoking ruins – or perhaps long after they had grown cold, for the time scale of all these events remains mysterious – and gave the wretched victims a mass cremation. There are no skeletons, skulls or mere bones which can be ascribed to the first-century sacking with the same conviction as can for example the Samian ware baked black or the hoard of burned bronze coins in the foundations of Lloyds Bank.

If there can be no certainty, there are nevertheless some grisly relics which have been interpreted as coming from the Boudican era, since their actual form – skulls of heads which had been hacked off the body – fits plausibly into the known pattern of Celtic tribal practice.[20] Some of these decapitated skulls may have been discovered in the Walbrook stream as early as mediaeval times: Geoffrey of Monmouth's story of the mass beheading of a legion on its banks at the orders of Allectus, who led a revolt at the end of the third century, was perhaps an imaginative response to their persistent appearance as wells were being dug. In recent years at least 140 skulls have been turned up on four sites around the crucial Walbrook area, with references to a possible further large number on a fifth site. In no case have skeletons or other bones been found adjacent to these skulls.

There are various possible explanations for such large-scale finds. Since the earliest cemeteries – those just outside the city limits – are not far from the Walbrook area, these vagabond skulls might in theory have somehow been swept by the stream from their original sites, although it has been pointed out that the Walbrook even in its prime was never particularly fast-flowing. Furthermore it seems a strange coincidence that only the skulls were displaced. The skulls certainly belong to the early Roman period, first or second centuries, with at least one of them embedded in a wall erected in 200. It is surely legitimate therefore to connect them, however tentatively, with the one large-scale massacre known to have taken place within Londinium at this time, one moreover conducted by tribes with an historically known taste for the ritual use of water, wells, groves

and streams in worship, and the ritual involvement of the head —
both in life and death.[21]

Despite the absence of physical relics, Tacitus leaves us in no
doubt that an immense number of people died at the hands of the
Boudican armies. It is true that his estimated figure of seventy
thousand Roman and provincial dead, counting the sack of Verulamium yet to come, is once again likely to be an exaggeration. But
actual figures in these matters, even if verifiable, have a way of
being secondary to the impact of the event itself. (For instance,
the Cromwellian massacre at Drogheda killed three thousand Irish
according to the official verdict, four thousand at most: it is hardly
necessary to emphasize the resonance of *that* event down the ages.)[22]
It is the overall picture of an 'indescribable slaughter' taking place, as
perceived by the Romans, remembered by the surviving witnesses,
which is both appalling and convincing.

Nor do Tacitus and Dio combined spare us concerning the
atrocious manner in which many of these victims died. In the
Agricola, Tacitus merely makes a general statement that 'there was
no form of savage cruelty that the angry victors refrained from'; in
the *Annals* however he explains further that the Britons never
thought it worthwhile to take prisoners in order to sell them (as
was sometimes done at the time) or to exchange them for their own
men. On the contrary: 'They could not wait to cut throats, hang,
burn, and crucify...'. Dio's account is even more specific and as a
result even more dreadful.[23]

'Those who were taken captive by the Britons were subjected to
every known outrage', he wrote. 'The worst and most bestial atrocity committed by their captors was the following. They hung up
naked the noblest and most distinguished women and then cut off
their breasts and sewed them to their mouths, in order to make the
victims appear to be eating them; afterwards they impaled the
women on sharp skewers run lengthwise through the entire body.'
On one level, the symbolism of these skewers with which the
formerly oppressed tortured and killed the womenfolk of the former
oppressors is sufficiently obvious, if horribly so. But Dio makes
the point that these obscene cruelties were also accompanied by
'sacrifices, banquets' and what he calls 'wanton behaviour' which
took place in the Britons' sacred places, and in particular in the
grove of Andate, their goddess of Victory whom they regarded with

'most exceptional reverence'. Taking Boudica's earlier invocation to the Iceni goddess Andraste (or Andaste) 'as woman speaking to woman' and putting it together with this mention of Andate and her sacred groves, it would seem that the general slaughter practised by the Britons had some distinctly religious or ritual element attached to it; as did the Iceni rising, with a Holy (Armed) Figurehead at its head.

The presence of a ritual element does not of course palliate the fact of the slaughter – or the atrocities which accompanied it; on the other hand it should not make them seem worse. It is natural of course for a later age, sharing neither the religious obsessions nor the oppression which had provoked the rebellion, to shrink back in horror from details such as Dio's. Tacitus' explanation for these cruelties is however a significant one: the Britons must have had a premonition of what was going to happen to them: they acted 'as though avenging, in advance, the retribution that was on its way'. As will be seen, he relates the Romans' own final full-scale slaughter of the Britons, including their women and their very baggage animals – 'transfixed with weapons' – without emotion; no need is felt here to explain let alone justify such ferocity. The Romans were the winners, and the implacable destruction of the losers was their right and even, it might be argued, their duty.

For Roman civilization itself was far from lacking the concept of revenge. The most celebrated temple in all Rome was that dedicated at the turn of the last century BC to the god of vengeance, Mars Ultor. (While in Mars' wife Bellona the Romans had their own ferocious chariot-driving spear-waving goddess of war, to whom future Warrior Queens would sometimes be compared, or compare themselves.)[24] This temple was dedicated by Augustus after the battle of Philippi when he considered that he had avenged the murder of Caesar: here magpies and vultures and larger victims, horses and wolves, were sacrificed on the bloodstained altars. If it is argued – inverting Tacitus as it were – that the Romans in Britain after Boudica's defeat were merely avenging what had gone before, then it must be pointed out that Roman history was certainly not deficient in instances when hapless civilians had been massacred. Returning once again to the comparison with Vercingetorix, Caesar, for example, put all the innocent inhabitants of Avaricum (Bourges) to the sword during the period of his wars against the Gallic leader.

It has been remarked more than once that at the hands of the Romans the weak had no rights.[25] Momentarily under Boudica, the Britons – like the Indians at the time of the Mutiny in 1857, to which we will return – had ceased to be the weak. Zestfully, they did not hesitate to take full advantage of their new strength. Where historical massacres are concerned, twinkling as they do like innumerable black stars in the moral galaxy of history, it seems fairest to divide them into two categories: those where the oppressed rise up and strike down their oppressors, exacting vengeance in the process, and those where the rulers or invaders exact their own vengeance on a particular section of the population, for their own reasons. The Boudican vengeance fell into the former category, which has at least the merit of being the more comprehensible of the two.

Curiously enough, Boudica's own reputation as the leader who headed this avenging force has remained remarkably free of the taint of atrocity. Boadicea, as she must now become in reference to her later reputation, is frequently seen as a partisan queen of considerable nobility. Her lethal scythe-wheeled chariot also features more often than not – the chariot that never was – but somehow Boadicea herself never seems to leap down from it to take part in the bloodstained termination of a Roman civilian life. This may well be accurate, and again it may not. The highly limited sources available neither implicate Boudica personally in the bloodshed nor defend her from it. History – legend – has however by implication defended her from the charge of atrocity by glossing over it where she herself is concerned.

Beneath this lies the incontrovertible fact of Boadicea's feminine gender. It is as though a woman leader can mount a ritual chariot, wave a metaphorical banner in the air, invoke the spirits of revenge in return for intolerable wrongs done to her, but she must not actually be involved in the killing itself. After all, if there is no direct evidence that she was so involved, there is also no evidence against it. Boudica at all points cheered on the Britons and urged them to defeat the Romans. So the well-attested massacres – as well attested as any other part of the story of Boudica, since both Tacitus and Dio report them – vanish in favour of the patriotic female leader on high in her chariot: high that is, morally as well as physically, above the inevitable consequences of her oratory.

There is an appropriateness about this, which does not necessarily relate to historical truth. Boudica's sex and that of her children made them peculiarly vulnerable targets to the Romans, intent on making a series of symbolically brutal gestures to indicate the uselessness of British resistance. So Boadicea's sex has subsequently saved her legend from the tarnish of Dio's revelations, for which in fact as the effective leader of the Britons she must have been morally if not physically responsible.

Meanwhile the red layer beneath the City of London serves as a different kind of *memento mori* of the Boudican sacking and perhaps a more pertinent one. Its existence is a perpetual reminder that even the most thriving commercial city can be laid low, and that by a people generally despised as slaves, and that all in an instant of time: the destruction of everything made of clay, timber, thatch – or even other, far more durable modern materials – is guaranteed.

For afterwards, after Boudica and her troops had streamed on to enjoy one further fevered hour of triumph before turning towards oblivion – as it seemed – Londinium too fell into a state of decay and became a kind of ghost town. (Even the great new roads north of the river were abandoned: those newly excavated in the King Street site show a period of about twenty years' disuse.)[26] In the nineteenth century Macaulay imagined a situation in which some kind of 'malady' would be engendered within 'the bosom of civilization itself' to bring about the collapse of the then flourishing city of London: 'is it possible that, in two or three hundred years, a few lean and half-naked fishermen may divide the ruins ... with owls and foxes, may wash their nets amid the relics of her gigantic docks, and build their huts out of the capitals of her stately cathedrals?'[27]

But in the middle of the first century AD it had already happened.

CHAPTER SEVEN

EIGHTY THOUSAND DEAD

It was a glorious victory, comparable with bygone triumphs. According to one report, almost eighty thousand Britons fell.

Tacitus, *Annals*

After the fall of Londinium, there was still a third city to be sacrificed. Not yet gorged with slaughter or, more to the point, plunder, the Britons under Boudica swept on to Verulamium (St Albans). The city was not defended. Suetonius, the Roman commander who had coolly appraised the necessity of deserting an entire expatriate community, was not likely to hesitate over the fate of Verulamium. This was primarily because Suetonius' attention remained focused on those measures likely to stave off Roman defeat in the first place, and then turn the whole pulsating British advance to the Roman advantage: it was after all for the long-term victory, or at least the saving of the province, that he had taken the decision to abandon Londinium.

At the same time Verulamium as a city was quite different in kind from both Camulodunum and Londinium. It was populated neither by Roman veterans and their families nor by Mediterranean businessmen but by Britons – albeit Britons friendly to the cause of Rome. Tacitus tells us categorically that Verulamium by this date had been granted *municipium* status, which ranked it below a veterans' settlement (a *colonia*) but above an ordinary native tribal town (a *civitas*).

This privileged status must have had its roots in the events of the Claudian invasion in 43 when the Catuvellauni, in whose territory lay the town of Verulamium, had acted helpfully towards the Roman cause. Certainly Tacitus' testimony is born out by archaeology. A Belgic stronghold called Verlamio had antedated Verulamium on the same site, but excavations (by Sir Mortimer Wheeler and later Sheppard Frere) have revealed that a carefully planned new British city was laid out from about AD 49 onwards. Furthermore, traces of a country house, a villa made of timber at Gorhambury, reveal that the loyal – to the Romans – Britons at Verulamium were beginning to live as did their new masters and allies.[1]

As Verulamium's privileged status harked back to the events of 43, so the rivalries and hatreds of its inhabitants' fellow Britons must also have played their part in the destruction which followed. A favourite notoriously has no friends. There was little sympathy and much jealousy to inspire the horde which now swooped down on its third municipal victim (Dio suggests that only two cities were laid waste but, since he does not name them, Tacitus' testimony of three, bearing in mind his connection to the eyewitness, Agricola, is to be preferred). The fine Gorhambury villa was jealously destroyed by fire, as was much of the rest of the town.[2]

Once again excavations have provided evidence of a red layer of burned daub and ash far below modern St Albans: three shops disinterred from 1955 onwards give the same impression of normal busy life rudely interrupted, a first-century time warp, as has already been noted at Colchester and London. The modern focus of historical attention is however the later Christian town: the Roman city which was resurrected after the Boudican sack is now the site of a car park and an ornamental lake; the relics of the Roman theatre which can be inspected nearby are witness more to this placid prosperous centre than to the British *municipium* which the Queen of the Iceni and others in her army set on fire. Early British Verulamium has left little trace compared to these glamorous later developments.

But if there is evidence of fire, the same proportion of charred personal belongings has not survived. The fate of the residents of Camulodunum and Londinium served as an awful warning to the Britons of Verulamium; they had no wish to share it. These more fortunate citizens were able to make their getaway well in advance, taking their portable valuables with them. At least their furious fellow Britons were able to revenge themselves on the buildings of the favoured *municipium*, and that must have been satisfactory. The other principal aim of the Boudican army was to amass yet more booty.

Once again Tacitus is clear on this point: 'The natives enjoyed plundering and thought of nothing else. Bypassing forts and garrisons, they made for where the loot was richest and protection weakest.' Even if one allows for Tacitus' natural tendency to emphasize the superiority of the Romans, it must be admitted that Boudica – or whoever actually decided the direction of the British army under her titular command – had made a strategic mistake in ignoring for the second time the need to strike at Suetonius while he was at his most vulnerable.

For all Suetonius' rapid and ruthless retreat from Londinium, he remained at risk until he had secured reinforcements for his own small force. This urgent need for reinforcements provides indeed the strongest argument for the theory that Suetonius must now have turned back to the Midlands and away from the London area. (The sources give us neither a specific geographical setting nor a time scale for the crucial events following the sack of Verulamium and leading up to the so-called 'last battle' between Romans and Britons.) The principal asset of the Boudican army was its size, enormous if now unquantifiable, but doubtless swollen with each successful foray, as the local tribes increasingly came to see the British side as the winning one. Then there was that famous Celtic courage, rashness if you like, which was particularly effective in surprise attacks and ambushes. Both these assets were liable to diminish as Suetonius caught up with his desired reinforcements, seasoned troops, and the British numerical superiority declined. And an element of surprise in the British attack could obviously not be long preserved, certainly not long enough for the Britons to gorge themselves in a further feast of municipal plunder along the way.

As it was, Suetonius had to face yet another reverse, this time one dealt out to him by his own side. Suetonius' plans for bolstering up his own numbers from among the various legions scattered about the province included summoning the IInd Legion Augusta – so called because it had been raised by the Emperor – whose base was in the south-west at Exeter. The designated meeting place would have been modern Wroxeter (then known as Viroconium) or somewhere thereabouts in the West Midlands. Unfortunately Poenius Postumus, the Roman commander in charge of the IInd Legion – his actual title was *praefectus castrorum*, that is, camp commandant – failed to bring his men to the appointed rendezvous.

Poenius Postumus' reasons for ignoring the summons are unknown: he may even have been pinned down by another tribe and had no choice in the matter. But his failure to arrive certainly increased Suetonius' problems. Lacking the men of the IInd Augusta, the latter was left to pull together the XIVth Legion and a detachment of the XXth (these had been with him on the Mona expedition) and the nearest auxiliaries available; out of all these Suetonius welded together a force of men variously estimated at between ten and fifteen thousand. Even if Dio's estimated figure of 230,000 for the Boudican army is reduced to a hundred thousand or less, Suetonius' troops must still have been heavily outnumbered. On the other hand these were hardened fighting men.[3]

Under the circumstances, Suetonius decided to attack the Britons without further delay. The bold decision that Boudica – or her deputies – should perhaps have taken themselves was in fact taken by the Roman Governor. This at any rate is Tacitus' version of events, and it fits with what we already know of Suetonius' character and his approach to strategy. He needed every advantage he could get against the numerically unequal odds; to choose the site of the battle himself and thus by implication its timing was to award himself two vital ones – as indeed it proved. It is true that Dio suggests to the contrary that the battle was imposed upon Suetonius against his better judgement as his legionaries grew short of food and the barbarians pressed him. But once again, Tacitus' access to Agricola means that in a contradiction of this sort, especially over matters of military detail, his version takes priority. Furthermore Tacitus is convincingly explicit about the terrain chosen by Suetonius – without unfortunately naming it: 'a position in a defile with a wood behind him'. This meant, as Suetonius realized, that he would only have to face an enemy at his front and here there was 'open country without cover for ambushes'. These details smack of actual decisions taken and recollected in tranquillity long after.

· · ·

Much ink has been spilt over the site of Boudica's last battle, figuratively as well as actually, since it continues to be spilt in what might be described as the post-ink age. With Dio passing over the subject altogether – he tells us nothing at all about the actual site of the battle, not even the nature of its terrain – and Tacitus confining himself to the physical characteristics quoted above, an atmosphere had prevailed in which supposition, proposition and opposition have all been able to flourish happily. (In the 1980s two scholarly disputants concerning the location of the site did agree about one thing, that 'the search for the pattern of the Boudica campaign is great fun'.)[4] The key question must remain the view taken of Suetonius' movements after his departure from Londinium, and during and after the sack of Verulamium.

If it is accepted that Suetonius went in search of reinforcements in those areas – basically to the west – where the scattered legionary fortresses and garrison could most easily succour his limited force, and then chose the position for the engagement for which he was now himself prepared, then a convincing argument can and has been put forward for a West Midlands site.[5]

In centuries gone by, however, a romantic attachment was felt to the notion of a last battle in London itself with special heed given to the area around King's Cross station, built in 1852 and for which the name Boadicea's Cross was at one point even proposed. The name Battle Bridge for an old crossing of the Fleet river near King's Cross was held optimistically to offer encouragement. Thomas Nelson, author of *The History of Islington*, printed in 1811, was among antiquaries who were attracted by the idea of locating thereabouts 'the operations of the Roman General in his arduous contest with that injured and unfortunate Princess'. In his long but spirited biography of 1937, *Boadicea*, Lewis Spence took much trouble, by the use of ancient contour maps, to point out the existence of some kind of defile around York Road and the Caledonian Road, between the 'acclivity' of Pentonville and the high ground near Gray's Inn Land.[6]

Nor has London and its environs been allowed to dominate the field entirely: other suggested localities have included Wheat-hampstead, while Ambersbury Banks, a large earthwork in Epping Forest, is among local sites where the tradition of the last battle is cherished. Moreover in 1983 a revisionist argument for the Staines area was put forward by Nicholas Fuentes in the *London Archaeologist*; concentrating on the age-old valley between the well-wooded Shrubs Hill and the River Thames, and placing the 'defile' approximately where Virginia Water station is today. This argument however demands a radical reassessment of Suetonius' campaign following Mona, including the theory that he actually brought his entire task force to Londinium, not merely his cavalry; it also proposes that Cogidubnus and the Atrebates of the Silchester area were somehow involved in the last battle; in the absence of firm new archaeological evidence, all this seems a revision too far.[7]

So for the time being at least the West Midlands region remains the most plausible locality, one supported by the known deployment of the Roman military forces around AD 60, the forces upon which Suetonius now drew, as Tacitus quite clearly tells us. Attention has been focused in particular on the Warwickshire area north-west of Nuneaton, near Atherstone; here, at Mancetter (Roman Manduessum), a steep escarpment can be seen rising from the plain. The discovery and exploration of a Roman camp here, which was the site of the XIVth Legion until it moved up to Wroxeter in about AD 55, has underlined its claims as a possible site of the last battle. Although the XIVth Legion would have departed by the time of the Boudican rebellion, auxiliary units – trained non-Roman troops – would presumably have still used the camp, and that would have made Manduessum, coupled with its terrain (still today conforming quite markedly to Tacitus' description) an ideal focus for Suetonius' strategic plan.* It would of course take the discovery of 'some quite remarkable finds ... such as a mass burial with closely identifiable weapons in association' for the status of Mancetter/Manduessum to be finally verifiable.[8] In the meantime no more plausible alternative has been put forward.

If the site of the last battle is finally unknown and perhaps unknowable, the course of the battle presents a different problem. One travels back in time from the suppositions of the twentieth-century archaeologists – agreeing only on the lack of certainty possible and the 'fun' involved in the discussion – to the ancient historians, who express their respective certainties by once again

---

* Nowadays the London–Manchester InterCity railway line passes through the site of the battle; the historically minded traveller may salute the memory of the Queen of the Iceni from the windows of the train.

contradicting each other, as they do over Suetonius' role in its inception. Once again, and for the same reason, Tacitus' is the preferred account.

There was one matter on which the two ancient historians did agree – that the battle itself was preceded by a series of set speeches. But as with Dio's earlier Boudican speech, recounted in Chapter Five, this was more a question of contemporary protocol than historical accuracy. In this case Tacitus and Dio give us a total of three speeches: one apiece for Boudica and Suetonius from Tacitus; Dio, having already given the Queen her say, contents himself with awarding Suetonius a tripartite speech, delivered in turn to his three divisions. It is Tacitus' portrait of the Queen on this occasion, driving round and round the assembled tribes in her chariot, with her daughters in front of her, which has made an indelible impression. It has become joined to that physical description given by Dio on the earlier occasion of the tall, splendid and ferocious red-haired Celt in her war panoply; together they form the popular image of Boadicea.

'We British are used to women commanders in war' the Queen cries, before adding, with that neat lack of logic many other Warrior Queens will be found to echo: 'I am descended from mighty *men*!' Otherwise Tacitus' Boudica emphasizes her ghastly treatment at the hands of the Romans – 'I am fighting as an ordinary person for my lost freedom, my bruised body and my outraged daughters' – and dwells further on other Roman atrocities, as well as denigrating the Roman courage. She ends with this clarion call to invoke – like so many Warrior Queens – a sense of masculine shame: 'consider how many of you are fighting – and why. Then you will win this battle, or perish. That is what I, a woman, plan to do! Let the men live in slavery if they will.'

Suetonius, according to Tacitus, also stressed the feminine presence in the British ranks, but in this case he did so only in order to hold it to scorn: 'In their ranks there are more women than fighting men.' Dio's Suetonius equally took the opportunity to sneer at the natives: 'Fear not, then, their numbers or their spirit of rebellion; for their boldness rests on nothing more than headlong rashness unaided by arms or training!' The Britons' achievement in capturing the two cities of Camulodunum and Londinium is dismissed as being due to betrayal in one case and abandonment in the other. With the confidence of a member of the master race, Dio's Suetonius

The bronze statue of Boadicea and her daughters, in a scythe-wheeled chariot, sculptured by Thomas Thornycroft between 1856 and 1885, and finally erected by the London County Council in 1902. The lines of William Cowper are inscribed upon the plinth: 'Regions Caesar never knew / Thy Posterity shall sway.'

Images of Boadicea. Above: Illustration to Thomas Heywood's *Exemplary Lives* of 1640 showing her in the Caroline court dress of the period, with plumed headdress and one breast exposed, the torc having become a pearl necklace with a cross, and the spear a baton. Right: Engraving of the 'Thrice Happy Princess' by W. Fairthorne; an illustration to Aylett Sammes' *Britannia Antiqua Illustrata* of 1676.

'Boadicea haranguing the Britons' by H. C. Selous (*c.* 1840); the Queen's ill-treated daughters can be seen in a fainting condition at her feet.

Illustration by A. S. Forrest to *Our Island Story, A Child's History of England* by Henrietta Elizabeth Marshall; first published in 1905 – and written in Melbourne, Australia, for the author's children – this work provided formative images of history for many British children in the first half of the twentieth century, including the author.

The Boudican firing of Londinium in AD 60, illustrated by Richard Sorrell, from the Museum of London; a red layer, about 13 feet below the streets of the modern City of London, still attests to the fierceness of the holocaust.

Two impressions of the Britons' last battle against the Romans. Opposite below: An illustration to Holinshed's *Chronicles* of 1577, showing Boadicea and her ladies in Tudor dress faced by Romans in helmets and doublets, armed with guns. Above: A realistic recreation by Alan Sorrell, from the Museum of London.

A *crater* of 460 BC showing Sthenelus, a companion of Heracles, in his war against the Amazon women; encounters with Amazons were often used in Greek art to symbolize the Greeks' victories over their male enemies.

Left: The voluptuous European conception of Cleopatra; an engraving by J. Chapman of 1804. Right: Ptolemaic votive plaque believed to depict Cleopatra as a goddess.

Judith beheads Holofernes in a nineteenth-century engraving by Schnorr von Carolsfeld.

The romantic European image of Zenobia; an eighteenth-century engraving by William Sharp from a drawing by Michelangelo.

Semiramis, the legendary Queen of the Assyrians (based on Sammuramat, Babylonian widow of a ninth-century BC Assyrian king), seen in an engraving c. 1800.

The sisters Trung Trac and Trung Nhi, Vietnamese heroines who led the first rising in their country against the Chinese in AD 39; from a popular Vietnamese print. The characters on the flag give the family name 'Trung' and above the sisters (right) their own names; at lower left is Su Ding, the Chinese governor, and top left the legend 'Queen Trung drives out the Han'.

Vietnamese print of Trieu Au, who raised a thousand troops to liberate her country from the Chinese in AD 248; like the Trung sisters, Trieu Au is regarded as a patriotic heroine in modern Vietnam.

declares: 'let them learn by actual experience the difference between us, whom they have wronged, and themselves'.

The rightness of the Roman cause is indeed one of the major themes of Dio's Suetonius: 'the gods are our allies', he goes on to say to his third division, 'for they almost always side with those who have been wronged'. His other theme is the natural superiority of their heritage: 'we are Romans and have triumphed over all mankind by our valour'. Lastly Dio's Suetonius does at least envisage the possibility of defeat, if only to allow the author to dwell once again on those British atrocities which he had already described so vividly apropos the women sacrificed to Andate. If the Romans did not triumph and were captured, they could expect to be impaled, to look upon their own entrails cut from their bodies, to be spitted on red-hot skewers, to be melted in boiling water ... In a word, 'to suffer as though ... thrown to lawless and impious beasts'.

In the event Suetonius' confidence was justified: except that the courage was found equally on both sides, the skill and experience solely on that of the Romans. Even before battle was joined, the two armies drawn up for battle would have presented an extraordinary contrast in their equipment and the manner of their array, a contrast which only became more intense as the conflict proceeded.

Here were the Britons, a vast concourse of them it is true, but in no sense a standing army: the fact that they were farmers, that they had literally come off the land, would be cruelly emphasized in the aftermath to the battle. The Celtic sword was the traditional weapon of such people, a sword with a long history, a sword such as the sword with which 'the wild deer', Cúchulainn, had been able to despatch all fourteen soldiers sent after him by the wicked Queen Medb. They wore no body armour of any sort, except perhaps a pair of loose trousers (if we judge by the Gauls depicted on the Roman sculptural reliefs). The fine helmets and decorated shields which this civilization has left behind were for the aristocrat–warriors among them: these too would have been mounted on the light wickerwork chariots, like to their queen's, from which they habitually dismounted to fight. (The chariot was however already slightly old-fashioned and had vanished altogether from the British/Celtic host by the second century AD.)[9]

We may believe that this concourse had the noisy, shambling quality of the Celtic array, with its music and its shouting and some hoarse amalgamation of the two. Perhaps the most significant difference of all between the British army and the one which faced it within the defile was that the Britons had brought along their families to see the fun. There they were, women and children, in a series of wagons stationed at the edge of the battlefield – which meant, given the lie of the land, at the back of it. One imagines a certain boastfulness in the mounted warriors of the Britons, and in their foot followers too, as beneath the eyes of their dependants they 'seethed over a wide area in unprecedented numbers'. The presence of these innocent camp followers, in a position which might well and in fact did prove extraordinarily dangerous, illustrates perfectly how war for the Britons, with its joy of fighting, its hope of plunder, was a serious but also a tribal business.

For the Romans on the opposite side, war was not only a serious business but the only business. It was for this that the legionaries had been trained, trained in many cases over long years and in the hard school of continental warfare; above all it was for this business of fighting that they were equipped, and equipped in a manner which was developed further each decade with the sole aim of making every legion a superb fighting machine. Against their naked or near naked opponents, they wore helmets including neck protection, light body armour to the waist, broad leather belts with metal-tipped leather thongs falling below it, and studded open boots like hobnailed sandals.[10]

When it came to weaponry, the Roman cavalry had their lances, while the infantry, as well as curved wooden shields with bosses, had a pair of javelins per man. These javelins were seven feet long with a three-foot iron point, difficult to remove once embedded: but their long wooden shafts made them easy to throw. With the aid of his javelin, the legionary could render his opponent's shield useless, or even pin the two of them together. Furthermore a legionary also had a shorter two-foot sword (his *gladius*, hence *gladiator*) and a dagger. It was the long hero's sword of Cúchulainn against a battery of professional weapons. But the legionaries of Rome were not to be equated with the soldiers of Queen Medb. Alas, this was not a contest which the epic hero – or heroine – was destined to win.

At the first charge of the Britons towards the defile which contained their enemy, the Roman legionaries deliberately held their ground without counterattacking, as they had been trained to do. But when the order finally came to burst forward with their lethal javelins, they did so in wedge formation and to murderous effect, accompanied by the infantry of the auxiliaries. Finally it was the cavalry's turn to demolish all resistance. We do not know how long the battle raged – all day? less than that? The duration was of less significance than the final result.

The Britons, by dreadful irony, found themselves pinned in against this fierce counterattack by their own wagons, those wagons brought along so blithely for their families to see the show. It was in this way, in this death-trap, that the Romans were able to put to death the British women, as well as the British baggage animals (which were transfixed) at the same time as they despatched their menfolk. 'According to one report', says Tacitus carefully, eighty thousand of the Britons died, compared to four hundred Romans killed, and others wounded.

Was Queen Boudica herself to be numbered among the eighty thousand British dead? The indications are that she did not actually die on the battlefield, but shortly afterwards and by her own hand: Tacitus tells us that she took poison. (Dio's story that Boudica fell sick and then died is not incompatible with this, since poison would obviously have brought about sickness, however short-lived, and it may have been this aspect of the story which Dio picked up.) As for the Queen's daughters, their fate, like their names, remains unknown to history since it is not mentioned by Tacitus, while their very existence is ignored by Dio.

For once, however, the many fictional accounts of Boadicea's life, be they plays or novels, which have her administering poison to her daughters as well as to herself, are not straining credulity too far. In Beaumont and Fletcher's play, for example, the heroine's younger daughter momentarily shrinks back from the mystery of death – 'O but if I knew but whither . . . ' – as her mother offers her the fatal draught. The Queen comforts her and issues her last rallying cry:

> Keep your minds humble, your devotions high
> So shall ye learn the noblest part, to die.[11]

For if the Iceni princesses did survive the wanton slaughter at the end of the battle, it is surely not likely that their mother, having decided to poison herself, would have risked them falling into the hands of the Romans – a second time.

As it is, myth surrounds Queen Boudica's burial place as with everything else about her. Dio tells us simply that the British gave her a costly burial, Tacitus nothing. The seventeenth-century story that Boadicea (as she now becomes) was given this 'costly burial' at Stonehenge has a great deal to commend it of neatness and romance – if nothing of historical truth – since two mighty legends are disposed of together, the immemorial stones and the woman. The celebrated if equally unhistorical connection of the Druids with Stonehenge only dates in fact from the later years of the seventeenth century: in 1624 for example, the antiquary Edmund Bolton, believing Stonehenge to be the work of Britons ('the rudeness itself persuades'), concluded that here was to be found the tomb of Boadicea. This theory was rebutted in 1655 in a posthumous publication from notes by Inigo Jones. He pointed out that 'a mighty Prince may be buried with great Solemnity, yet no material Monument be dedicated to his memory'; adding that it was unlikely the Romans would have permitted 'an everlasting Remembrance of Boadicea'.[12] (Although the Romans had in fact a tradition of allowing their enemies to carry away their dead for burial – to avoid evil spirits – so that the erection of 'an everlasting Remembrance' was not out of the question in Iceni country.)

To many other neighbourhoods and many other monuments, however man-made or otherwise, clings obstinately the tradition that 'Here lies Boadicea'. Counted among them are a mound on Hampstead Heath known as Boadicea's Tomb (in reality more likely to be a Roman burial place); various sites around Parliament Hill, following the legend of the London King's Cross battle; Warlies Park, Waltham Abbey, in Essex; the Bartlow Hills in the same county; and a tumulus known locally as The Bubberies in the grounds of a parsonage at Quidenham in Norfolk – the name being hopefully regarded as a corruption of Boadicea or Boudica. The legend of the King's Cross battle is also responsible for periodic bursts of enthusiasm (most recently in 1988), suggesting that the British Queen must lie buried under Platform 8 of the station itself, a story which may at least divert the weary traveller, causing him or her to ruminate on the possible advantages of the chariot over the train as a means of conveyance.[13] The discovery of a mid-first-century British burial place, containing the bones of a woman of royal rank, would be exciting enough in its own right; it would also, for better or for worse, put an end to such innocent local fantasies.

Whatever the truth of the costly burial and its precise situation – and as with the royal palace of the Iceni, one must not give up all hope of finding it within the tribal area – it is reasonable to assume that Queen Boudica took her own life. Let us suppose that the Emperor Nero did choose to exercise clemency towards this barbarian princess, once she had served her purpose in the triumphal procession (as Claudius had exercised clemency towards Caratacus). Let us suppose that the offer was made, and the Iceni Queen believed that the promise would be kept. She would not have wished to live out her days a slave. Shakespeare's description of Cleopatra not wishing to see 'some squeaking Cleopatra . . . boy her greatness' on the Roman stage would surely have been paralleled by Boudica's own profound wish not to experience further humiliation.

There were royal 'slaves' who settled down in Rome – Queen Zenobia of Palmyra will provide an interesting example of such in the following chapter; there were also the barbarian captives described by Gibbon: 'taken in thousands by the chance of war, purchased at a vile price, accustomed to a life of independence, and impatient to break and revenge their fetters'.[14] Everything we know about Boudica, one certainly accustomed to a life of independence, suggests that she would have fallen proudly into the latter category. As for slavery, there is of course also no guarantee that she would have been offered that option. It is true that the womenfolk of Caratacus had been well treated following his ritual exhibition in a Roman triumph. But Caesar earlier had executed Vercingetorix after a similar display. Caratacus' womenfolk were also women who had acted within the Roman meaning of the word: they had not challenged the might of Rome successfully. Boudica, who had already experienced Roman brutality before ever she rebelled, had no reason to suppose that the penalties which followed it would be any less severe. As the Queen herself was made to exclaim by Tacitus: for her as a woman it was a case of winning this battle or perishing. She had not won; we must therefore believe that she kept her word and perished.

The vengeance of Suetonius against the Britons was every bit as frightful as that of the rebel Britons had been towards Rome. (A further convincing argument for the death of Boudica shortly after the end of the battle lies in the fact that she would otherwise surely have featured in it.) The British must have suffered shockingly, and not all of the victims had taken part in the rising. For not only those who were judged hostile but those who were deemed to be 'wavering' were 'ravaged with fire and sword': the latter category, being in the eye of the Roman beholder, could encompass almost everybody and justify many a retributive cruelty. Even more terrible were the Britons' sufferings from famine, for the Iceni in particular had neglected to sow their own fields before departing on their victorious rampage, taking everyone with them: the cheerful intention had been to seize the Roman supplies.

Some of the Britons went on fighting. Confusion has arisen about their desperate continuance of the struggle which was manifestly lost, and there is a suggestion that it was bound up with the implacability of Suetonius towards those who had recently humiliated him by ravaging the province under his command.[15] This is Tacitus' story in the earlier of his two accounts, the *Agricola*: 'Excellent officer though he [Suetonius] was, it was feared that he would abuse their surrender and punish every offence with undue severity, as if it were a personal injury.' So some of them fought on, feeling that at this point they had nothing to lose.

In the later *Annals* however Tacitus linked this ultimate British stand to the mischievous influence of the new Procurator, Julius Classicianus, he who came to replace the fugitive Catus Decianus. Julius Classicianus disloyally hinted that it was in the Britons' own interest to prolong their activities until a new or less personally involved – and thus milder – governor should be sent out from Rome. Whether Tacitus' slur on Julius Classicianus' loyalty is justified, or whether he was merely seeking to defend the reputation of his father-in-law's old commander, it is true that a 'milder' governor was finally sent out from Rome: Publius Petronius Turpilianus, who had just finished being Consul. This followed a report by the Emperor Nero's emissary, the former slave Polyclitus, who tried to reconcile Governor and Procurator, and ended by criticizing Suetonius for not terminating the war. Peace was finally restored. With peace however came repression.

If the execution of the Roman vengeance lacked those picturesque atrocities depicted by Dio (so far as we know) it partook of the equally grim nature of long-drawn-out persecution including whatever brutal measures were thought necessary under the circumstances. Fresh troops were brought from Germany to fill out the ranks of that legion brought low by the first British onslaught; auxiliaries, both infantry and cavalry, were also imported. The Iceni paid dearly for their crowded hour of glorious life, and were condemned to live out instead that traditional alternative to it, a dismal age without a name. Excavations of the post-Boudican age reveal that a detailed policy of repression was enacted towards the guilty tribe, including slavery and transportation. Temporary Roman forts were put up at strategic sites for the control of the population, such as Great Chesterford north of Saffron Walden, Coddenham near Ipswich and Pakenham near Ixworth on the borders of Suffolk and Norfolk.* [16]

Farms were burned, sanctuaries such as that of Arminghall desecrated; some of the buried hoards of torcs, coins and other precious golden objects referred to in Chapter Four, such as that at Santon, may owe their origins to this terrible time. The draining of hitherto unoccupied territories in the Iceni area and the conversion of them into fertile land was probably carried out by deported Iceni slave labour (using Roman drainage systems). So the Iceni, proud and independent of yore, were made subject, and this time they did not revolt again. The evidence is that in punishment for their rebellion the Iceni lands remained wasted into the next century. To the Caledonian leader Calgacus, via the pen of Tacitus, went the last word, when he was raising his own rebellion (put down by Agricola) in the 80s. Of the Romans, he said 'they create a desolation and call it peace'.[17]

So Britain as a whole settled down to be a Roman province: or as the unknown but free-spirited Briton inspecting from an observation point some excavations of the Roman period at Leadenhall Court in the City of London observed to the present writer

---

* From time to time traces of these forts, symbolic of the repression of the Iceni, emerge as a result of drought and aerial photography: in this way the Roman camp at Pakenham was shown up in 1976, and excavated in 1985 before being engulfed by a bypass.

in 1986, 'That's the Romans for you – four hundred years of occupying *our* country.'

Were these four hundred years of occupation inevitable (leaving aside the question of whether they were desirable)? How far did Queen Boudica of the Iceni really progress in the direction of eliminating that occupation? The Romans in Britain trembled and with good reason, but what about the imperial power itself? Did Rome tremble? Should it have done so? The answers to these questions, fascinating if finally imponderable, are linked in part to Tacitus' own estimate of Suetonius' achievement.

Tacitus quoted the last battle as being 'a glorious victory' for the Roman side, 'comparable with bygone triumphs'. Poenius Postumus, that senior officer who had failed to answer Suetonius' summons to a rendezvous, subsequently fell on his sword because he had robbed his own legion of the possibility of sharing in all this glory. If Suetonius really triumphed with great difficulty over Boudica – against overwhelming odds as well as overwhelming numbers – then the Iceni, and the other tribes who joined with them, must have nearly succeeded in their objective, the overturning of odious Roman rule.

Against this picture of Boudica having suffered a last-minute reverse due to the military cunning of Suetonius and the experienced, courageous brilliance of his Roman legionaries – so that it was indeed in Roman terms 'a glorious victory' – has to be put a more cynical picture. It has been pointed out with truth that the southern tribes, notably the ever friendly, ever powerful King Cogidubnus and his Atrebates of Silchester, showed no signs of joining in the fun with their more northerly fellow tribesmen and women.[18] If some disaffected Brigantes probably rallied to Boudica's side, her fellow Queen Cartimandua certainly did not: hence the grateful support the latter would receive from Rome at the time of her own tribulations around AD 70.

On the military level, it is perfectly true, as Suetonius was made to point out by Dio in his speech, that the Britons never had to besiege a city which was actually defended properly by the Romans, since Camulodunum's defences were pitiful, and Londinium's non-existent. Their defeat of Petilius was due to the success of the ambush: when the experienced Roman legionaries lured the wild

Britons into their trap, they were able to cut them down without much difficulty.

And yet this is only a part of the story ... the force of a patriotic flash flood (as Boudica's rebellion is most plausibly seen) should never be underestimated. If positive hindsight, the explaining of why what did happen absolutely had to happen, is one enjoyable historical occupation, then the negative rather more dream-like dwelling on the what-might-have-been is another. Personalities come into play. The Procurator Catus Decianus fled from Londinium at the news of the fall of Camulodunum; Petilius' recklessness led to his vanquishing; it would also have been perfectly possible for Suetonius to flee from Glevum (Gloucester) and reach the continent if things had turned out differently or if he had been of a different nature. As to Queen Boudica's tactics and the potency of surprise, it was Mao Tse-tung in his brilliant and demonstrably effective essay on guerrilla warfare who advocated seizing the initiative whenever possible so that a small band of poorly equipped guerrillas could cause havoc and defeat a well-equipped army.[19]

The more victories the Britons clocked up, the more allies among their fellow tribesmen they would have gained. It was the winning side which was seductive to those with an eye to a profitable future. The Roman rule in Britain in AD 60, seventeen years after the invasion, was clearly neither so extensive nor so settled as it was afterwards to become; the memory of the people concerned is an important element where any occupation is being considered, an element not always sufficiently regarded. Many of the Britons in AD 60 – certainly Queen Boudica herself – could remember a time before the Romans came, and before the Romans ruled, and being blissfully unaware of the 'historical inevitability' of the four hundred years of Roman occupation, may have genuinely believed that they could enjoy freedom in the future.

What kind of freedom was envisaged? The answer to that question surely lies in the Roman maladministration which provoked the Iceni in the long term, as the Roman maltreatment of the Queen and her daughters provoked them in the short. The indignation of the native inhabitants of Camulodunum, compelled to labour and pay for an imperial cult, an imperial temple, alien to their religion and to their way of life, falls into the same category. It was as a patriot – of the Iceni cause – and a partisan that Queen Boudica rose. It is as a challenge to the Roman might by tribes generally termed inferior – 'nothing to fear from the Britons who are too weak to cross the sea and assault us', Strabo had written in an age before the invasion – that her uprising is best seen.

Had Queen Boudica continued her rout, challenged the army of Suetonius at a place of her own choosing – with her numbers and her desperate courage – she might have presented the picture of the winning side to the other tribal leaders. The 'glorious victory' might just conceivably have gone the other way. But this is to make her a prudent calculating Roman leader as Suetonius was. She remained and remains a Celt, bold, inspiring, but not so far as we know calculating.

And in this manner her story ends. Or so it must have seemed to those who knew her, with the enforced 'pacification' of the Iceni by just that fire and sword which Boudica herself had temporarily and bloodily employed. But Boudica's story did not end there. The death of this obscure British queen, buried in an unknown grave, was in fact only the beginning of the story. The phoenix Boadicea would rise from the ashes of Boudica. What happened to this phoenix later, why Boudica/Boadicea did not rest forever forgotten, is one theme of the rest of this book. The other interwoven theme is the multiple fascination exercised by the Warrior Queen, illustrated in so many different civilizations, including those where the Roman writ never ran and where the name of Boadicea was never known, each story contributing to the mosaic.

The first story – that of Zenobia – is however given as a dramatic coda to that of Boudica, because she too in her time challenged the might of Rome.

CHAPTER EIGHT

O ZENOBIA!

How, O Zenobia, hast thou dared to insult Roman emperors?
Aurelian to Zenobia, Queen of Palmyra

The story of Zenobia, third-century Queen of Palmyra, another adversary of Rome, provides not only a dramatic coda to the story of Boudica, first-century Queen of the Iceni but also, at first sight, a peculiarly appropriate one. There are so many interesting parallels to be discovered between their respective experiences quite apart from the simple fact that Zenobia, like Boudica, led her people to war. Both women were widows when they assumed power, both women ruled in theory as regents for their offspring, both women had been married to client-rulers of Rome, both women led revolts (that is, from the Roman point of view) destined to upset an existing relationship with Rome which had apparently been comfortably established under their late husbands' sway.

Of course the status of widowhood is far from being peculiar to Boudica and Zenobia in the consideration of historic Warrior Queens. The frequent recurrence of what has been termed earlier the Appendage Syndrome – the Warrior Queen seen as an extension or prolongation of the rule of a particular great man – has produced widows as well as daughters. The nineteenth-century Rani of Jhansi is another prominent example of widowhood, as Queen Tamara of Georgia, Queen Elizabeth I of England and Indira Gandhi represent daughterhood. In her own way, the Rani of Jhansi comes close to fulfilling those conditions observed above concerning Boudica and Zenobia; not only was she a widow and a would-be regent, but she duly challenged an imperial power, except that the power in question was British not Roman.

For all these overall similarities linking the Warrior Queens of many different ages, at first inspection the Roman connection does seem to constitute a special link between Boudica and Zenobia. Once again some two hundred years after the death of Boudica, a Roman general found himself 'waging a war with a woman'. This was the accusation made against Aurelian by his fellow Romans, leaving him to expostulate in reply: 'As if Zenobia alone and with her own forces only were fighting against me ... as a matter of fact, there is a great force of the enemy ...'. Here is another familiar syndrome at work, that of Shame, the one which caused the Romans to bow their heads in dismay after the destruction of Camulodunum, for, in the words of Dio Cassius quoted earlier, 'all this ruin was brought upon [them] ... by a woman'.[1]

It is only the cooler light of second inspection which uncovers important differences between the two queens, both as they behaved and as they were treated. These differences serve as a salutary reminder, just before the 'real' Boudica is abandoned for the legendary Boadicea, that a host of very diverse women throughout history have fought beneath the generalized banner of 'Warrior Queen'. The similarities are often imposed from outside by the existence of the stereotype. Where the stories are undoubtedly superficially alike, as with Boudica and Zenobia, one should be careful not to ignore the dissimilarities, to enable the individual female character to struggle out from beneath the web of legend – in the case of Zenobia a rare character indeed.

Zenobia was an Arab. That is to say, inscriptions give her the full names of Septimia Zenobia in Latin or Bat Zabbai in Aramaic. Her father may have been called Zabbai (although 'Bat Zabbai' can also mean 'daughter of a merchant' in Aramaic). At all events this father was probably a native of Palmyra or Tadmor, to give the city its historic name (the exact etymology of these two names, respectively Greek and Aramaic, remains obscure). He would have been part of the proud, cultured and wealthy Arab merchant-aristocracy who inhabited this splendid city, half religious monument, half commercial centre, situated at a vital confluence of caravan routes in the Syrian desert.[2]

If Zenobia's descent was predominantly Palmyrene Arab, she may well have had dashes of many other bloods including Aramaean. She flourished after all in that interesting Middle Eastern area, the world's ancient crucible, where the three languages Greek, Latin and Aramaic, in which Palmyrene inscriptions are expressed, stand for a confluence of cultures and races as well as trade routes. Some Jewish blood has been suggested on the ground that she treated the Jews of Alexandria sympathetically; but this was in fact a comprehensible political move, the Jews always forming a potential anti-Roman force since Titus' destruction of all Jerusalem in AD 70. (Individuals who treat a given Jewish community with sympathy are often supposed to be of Jewish descent: a commentary on the long history of the Jews as a persecuted people.) But it is significant that Zenobia, who made much of historic bonds, never claimed one with Solomon, which in view of his mythic connection to the fortress of Tadmor would seem to dispose of a real Jewish link.[3]

The great Cleopatra (herself predominantly Greek but acting out the Egyptian with verve) was as it were the role model to which Zenobia aspired. Moreover the Palmyrene Queen claimed very firmly to be descended from her; there was a certain history of Alexandria, dedicated 'to Cleopatra', of which Zenobia must have been the actual dedicatee. The claim is generally thought to be false, although Zenobia's knowledge of the Egyptian language and her predisposition towards Egyptian culture may conceivably indicate that her mother was Egyptian.[4] The real significance of the claim is as a proof of Zenobia's intelligence: she quickly appreciated the self-aggrandizement to be derived from a glamorous historic connection. As Cleopatra used the image of the goddess Isis, the Queen of War, to lend exciting credence to her own dreams of empire, so Zenobia drew Cleopatra's own image to her. She also incidentally associated herself with Semiramis, and loved to dress up 'in the robes of Dido':[5] one has the impression that no queen, however unfortunate her history, was left unturned in Zenobia's relentless (but practical) evocation of female majesty.

Zenobia's fantasies about Egypt should not be allowed to obscure the strong tradition to which she actually belongs. Zenobia is in fact part of a discernible pattern of pre-Islamic Arabian queens with military connections, many of them coming from her own Syrian homeland or areas adjacent. The researches of Nabia Abbott have revealed at least two dozen of these formidable ladies over six centuries, following the visit of the Queen of Sheba to Solomon in the tenth century BC. Various origins have been ascribed to this fabulous Queen including south Arabian and Abyssinian: more importantly she exemplifies 'the exercise of the right of independent queenship among the ancient Arabs'.[6]

The Assyrian records give glimpses of troublesome Arab queens such as Zabibi, finally subjugated and forced to pay tribute in 738 BC, and Samsi, who may have been her successor and, after military defeat, underwent the same fate. It was from the royal house of Emesa, annexed to Syria, that the Emperor Septimius Severus in about AD 185 chose as his wife Martha, the daughter of the priest–king – she who became the powerful Julia Domna and introduced the Semitic goddess Tanit (as Caelestis Dea) to the Roman world. Mamaea, the redoubtable daughter of Julia Domna's sister, Julia Maesa, ruled for her son the Emperor Alexander, even accompanying him on the German campaign in 234; a generation older than Zenobia, but hailing from the same 'Syrian' cradle, she was described by Gibbon as having 'manly ambition'.[7]

Nor did this tradition end with Zenobia herself: from about AD 373 to 380, a hundred years after Zenobia's disappearance from the scene of history, we encounter another Syrian Arab queen named Mawia, probably a Ghassanid. Mawia too rode in person at the head of her army, made excursions into Phoenicia and Palestine, ravaged the land to the frontiers of Egypt, and defeated the Roman armies; later she sent her fleet of Arab cavalry to the aid of the Romans when they in their turn were hard-pressed by the Goths. The last 'queen' of pre-Islamic Western Arabia was the famous – or infamous – Hind Al-Hunūd about whom many traditions have congregated, some bloodthirsty, but all pointing to her independence. And it is worth recalling too that as late as 656 Aishah, 'the beloved of Muhammad' (the Prophet's last wife), was present at the Battle of the Camels at the heart of the fighting. More than that, Aishah's role in the internecine strife of which this battle was the culmination showed that at this date men would still follow a woman to war.[8]

Zenobia may have looked to Cleopatra for inspiration, but Zenobia's Arab tradition in which, as with the Celts, queens could ride to battle (and to victory) was an important element in her story. And the Holy Figurehead element in a woman's presence at the scene of battle as an inspiration, even a quasi-goddess, was also common to the Arabs, as to the Celts, in the pre-Islamic tradition of the Lady of Victory. By this tradition, some woman of quality would be placed within the portable *qubbah* or sacred pavilion of the tribal deity and, with her attendants, form a sacred group within sight of the warriors, singing songs of encouragement to them. The Lady of Victory, her hair flowing and her body partly exposed, embodied an appeal to valour and passion. (As late as the nineteenth century, William Palgrave described one particular 'huge girl' who encouraged the Amjan Bedouins against the heir to the throne of Nejed in this manner; when she was slain, they were defeated.)[9]

Another crucial element in Zenobia's career was the geographical situation of Palmyra itself, halfway between the two mighty and contending empires, one of which was Roman. It would be equally unsuitable to regard Zenobia as some kind of Hollywood 'Desert Queen', riding out of a dust storm, with a tent for her court and a palm frond for her sceptre, as it would be to regard Boudica as a woad-stained shrieking Celtic savage. Both women – both leaders – came from complex civilizations; in the case of Zenobia, the civilization from which she sprang had been affected deeply by that of Rome.

Around AD 114, Palmyra had theoretically become part of the Roman Empire, while the Emperor Hadrian judiciously allowed the city considerable liberty in order to benefit from its celebrated archers as defenders of what was now his own frontier against the Parthians. Moreover the Palmyrenes were allowed to be responsible for their own municipal taxes: another wise move. Palmyra flourished under this loose mutually beneficial tutelage. At the beginning of the third century the Emperor Septimius Severus made Palmyra into a colony and allowed a properly elected senate to manage its affairs; distinguished Palmyrenes began to add Roman names to their Semitic ones.

As Zenobia was not an unsophisticated Bedouin queen, so Palmyra itself was not a remote and ruined city lost in the midst of sands, as some ancient geographers suggested. On the contrary, vital caravan routes linked it to the seaboard cities of Phoenicia, to Emesa, to Damascus and to Egypt itself, Palmyra providing the link between these and Seleucia, and the more distant eastern regions. Foreign armies might not easily penetrate the intervening deserts, but the camel caravans of the merchants had no such problems. So the substantial animals toiled endlessly to and fro – camels in prime condition could carry loads of up to 200 kilos – and thus the Palmyrene merchants emulated Macaulay's Lars Porsena, who 'bade his messengers ride forth, East and west and south and north, To summon his array'; except that the camels of the Palmyrenes bore back with them an array of goods, not soldiers: from perfumes and aromatic oils to skins and salt. A tariff of commercial dues dated AD 137 reveals how far afield the tentacles of Palmyrene trade actually spread: silks and jade from the Chinese frontiers are listed, and from India muslins, spice, ebony, ivory and pearls.[10]

The merchant–aristocrats lived well: in their day two emperors visited Palmyra. The merchants made great profits and patronized the arts with their money (it is always agreeable to find these two activities considered compatible). A hundred years before Zenobia, a special tax was imposed on imported bronze statues and busts; the wealthy citizens had a special penchant for erecting columns and colonnades and adorning them with self-congratulatory inscriptions. Jewellery loaded down the women – how Zenobia would one day come to feel the weight of those splendid jewels! If the colonnaded edifices showed the influence of Rome, the shadow of Palmyra's other great neighbour also fell across her culture: local deities might be given Roman names but wear Parthian dress. Later Persian costume, rugs and jewels mingled with the Roman styles.

Central to Palmyra was the great Temple of the Sun.[11] Yet by the third century the official sun worship of the Palmyrene state was being supplemented by an alternative religion: a vague yet spiritual kind of monotheism – the worship of the unknown god, to whom those inferior categories of women and servants also made offerings. Here, where the unknown god and the celestial pantheon of other gods were content to receive harmless sacrifices of incense and wine, a generally liberal atmosphere prevailed, in which, according to inscriptions, the Jews also found their place (and adapted to Palmyrene customs).

The collapse of the Parthian Empire and the arrival of the Sassanids to the newly imperial throne of Persia in AD 227 put an end to a status quo which had been prosperous and far from disagreeable for Palmyra. At the same time the worldwide vigour of imperial Rome was declining – or to be more specific the emperors were obsessed by the Gothic threat on their northern frontiers. Obviously new perils threatened what was, to outsiders, essentially the buffer state of Palmyra. It was against this background of transitional turmoil that Odainat (otherwise Septimius Odenaethus), husband of Zenobia and self-styled King of Palmyra, decided like Shakespeare's Henry v to pluck the flower of opportunity.

Zosimus, a fifth-century Greek whose history of the Roman Empire up till 410 casts an interesting light on Zenobia, refers to Odainat as a 'person whose ancestors had always been highly respected by the emperors'. Certainly Odainat came of an illustrious family. His grandfather – or possibly great-grandfather, at any rate another Odainat – had become a Roman senator in about AD 230, eighteen years after all free men within the Empire were made Roman citizens. The son or grandson of this first Odainat, Hairan (Herodianus) was the first to bear the equivocal title of chief of Palmyra – or in Aramaic Ras Tadmor.[12]

Odainat, son of Hairan and husband of Zenobia, was made a Roman consul in AD 258. Two years later the Roman Emperor Valerian was defeated by Sapor I of Persia, held captive in disgusting conditions and finally killed. It was under these circumstances that Odainat took to the field with the archers and spearmen of Palmyra on the one hand, the cavalry of the desert Arabs on the other; remnants of the tattered Roman legions may also have assisted him. Palmyra might have preferred to lean towards Persia rather than towards Rome, in view of the latter's debilitated state. It was the Persian Emperor who declined to lean towards Palmyra. Under the circumstances Odainat had little choice but to sally forth against him.

As it was, Odainat's forces swept all before them, and according to one chronicler they finally captured the magnificent treasure of the Persian Emperor. In 261 Odainat secured another victory at Emesa (now Homs) in western Syria, where a Roman general had taken advantage of the fluid times to set himself up as a usurper. Very likely, Odainat had been given some general title of command by Rome before he sallied forth. But in 262 the incoming Roman Emperor Gallienus – himself incapable of avenging the murdered

Valerian – made Odainat, the man who could actually do so, officially *dux romanorum* and later *imperator*.

There is some understandable confusion over what these titles actually meant. For one thing, they must have meant different things to the Romans, who were particular about the niceties of such things but absent, and to the Palmyrenes themselves, not so particular but on the spot. There is no evidence that Odainat was granted the distinctive title of Augustus by Gallienus or, more to the point, claimed it. He did have himself inscribed as 'King of kings' at Palmyra – but then Palmyra was a long way from Rome.[13] Odainat was a realist: he showed himself content with the substance of his power, the fact that he had saved the fortunes of the Roman Empire in the east and shored up those of Palmyra.

It was however not Odainat himself but Zenobia who mesmerized ancient historians. The so-called *Scriptores Historiae Augustae* – a collection of biographies, probably written in the fourth century, dealing with the Roman emperors from AD 117 to 284 – are full of her praises. Of the six authors to whom the *Scriptores* are attributed, 'Trebellius Pollio' and 'Flavius Vopiscus' are responsible for the period in which Zenobia flourished.[14] 'The noblest of all the women of the East', wrote Trebellius Pollio, dilating also on her personal charms: she was also *speciosissima* – 'the most beautiful' – and elsewhere *venustatis incredibilis* – 'of an incredible attraction'. His description of Zenobia – eyes black and powerful beyond the usual wont, teeth so white that many believed she wore pearls in her mouth, complexion wonderfully dark – suggests that we may look for her type among the surviving portraiture of Palmyrene art, where the impressive women with their strong noses and enormous almond-shaped eyes look out with baleful dignity; a type indeed not far from that of Zenobia's proclaimed ancestress Cleopatra.[15]

At the same time these historians, writing of course with hindsight and a full knowledge of Zenobia's remarkable career, were quick to praise her more 'masculine' qualities: her hardihood for example. Odainat himself was celebrated for his hunting; he would live in the forests and endure heat, rain and other hardships in pursuit of lions, panthers and bears: in this way he was naturally equipped for the rigours of his Persian campaigns. But Zenobia too went on these hunting trips, and so she was fit enough to accompany him on his military sorties.

Not only was she fit enough – disdaining the comfort of a woman's coach and even a man's chariot, in favour of a horse – but she was also sufficiently daring. Zosimus considered flatteringly enough that Zenobia had 'the courage of a man; and with the assistance of her husband's friends, acted in every respect as well as he had done'. But Trebellius Pollio went much further. When he wrote that Zenobia 'in the opinion of many was held to be *more* brave than her husband', he was expressing an opinion, often linked to the Shame Syndrome, but also a syndrome in its own right, which makes the woman 'the better man of the two'. There is no real reason to suppose that Zenobia was more courageous than Odainat, who sounds to have been both a vigorous general and a brave soldier; she was undeniably more reckless. It was Zenobia's gender which gave her the advantage. Because of that, even to parallel the achievements of her husband inexorably made Zenobia the Better-Man.

In other ways the idealized portrait of Zenobia as a Warrior Queen neatly encompasses the most useful qualities of both sexes. Her voice, as has been mentioned apropos that of Boudica, was not harsh (unfeminine) but clear and manly (useful for rallying the troops). Leaping off her horse, she could walk with her footsoldiers three or four miles. Indeed, Zenobia had little taste for having other women about her, eunuchs being preferred to maidservants. She could also drink-with-the-boys (like the voice, the question of drinking-with-the-boys being another perennial if unstressed problem for female rulers). But her chroniclers emphasized that Zenobia never drank without an ulterior motive: either she drank diplomatically with foreigners such as the Persians in order to get them drunk; or she drank graciously with her own generals. Either way, this rare creature was, it seems, never by any chance intoxicated.

Then there is the bizarre matter of Zenobia's famous 'chastity'. The exact number, order of birth and indeed names of Zenobia's various sons are not clear. What is quite certain is that she gave birth to at least three and possibly more. Marital relations with Odainat therefore could hardly be denied. But by a brilliant piece of propaganda, Zenobia's undoubted periodic admission of Odainat to the marriage bed was transformed into actual evidence of her chastity: 'she would not know even her own husband, except for the purpose of conception', wrote Trebellius Pollio. 'For when once she had lain with him, she would refrain until the time of the month to see if she was pregnant; if not, she would again grant an opportunity of begetting children.'

Zenobia's semi-Lysistratan policy was to gain her the awed respect of subsequent (male) historians, as it impressed the fourth-century Trebellius Pollio. Gibbon allowed Zenobia to surpass Cleopatra in both '*chastity* and valour' and one cannot help thinking that her reputation for the former subtly helped on her reputation for the latter. 'How praiseworthy was this decision in a woman!' wrote Boccaccio, describing Zenobia as 'so virtuous ... that she must precede all other foreign women in fame'. He then indulged in a wonderful fantasy concerning her tomboy girlhood. Boccaccio has Zenobia scorning womanly exercises and wandering the forests instead to kill goats and stags with her arrows. She also wrestles with young men, carefully preserving her virginity at all points, in the passage – strongly reminiscent of Virgil on the subject of Camilla of the Volscians – cited earlier. As a grown woman, Boccaccio's Zenobia hides her beauty under armour, and never speaks to her soldiers except behind the protection of her helmet, a detail captured by Ben Jonson in his *Masque of Queenes* of 1610, whose illustration shows Zenobia 'the chaste' in her 'cask' or helmet but with long curling hair flowing beneath it, to say nothing of one exposed breast, liable, one would think, to inflame the least wanton soldier.[16]

Naturally the truth of the legend concerning Zenobia's 'chastity' can hardly be established at this point. A sceptic might be forgiven for requiring further evidence that this alluring wife of an Eastern potentate actually carried out her stringent method of sex control. But that is less important in the context than the excitement which the legend of the husband-denying Zenobia produces. The Chaste Syndrome accords well with a satisfyingly puritanical picture of the warrior–woman, the pure figurehead, her holy virginity equated with the holiness of her cause. By throwing in the theory of sex control, even married women like Zenobia can belong to it.

Around AD 266 or 267 the problem of marital attentions, if it existed, ceased to trouble Zenobia altogether. Under circumstances which have never been fully unravelled, her husband Odainat met his death. The ostensible assassin was his nephew Maeonius, whom Odainat had punished for insubordination. In the same attack also died Odainat's presumed heir, Hairan; this was the son of his first marriage, the typically unsatisfactory offspring of a successful general, being given to 'Grecian luxury'. That left Zenobia, the second wife, to assume the regency of Palmyra on behalf of her own son Vaballathus Athenodorus.

Any stepmother who sees an elder son preferred by right of birth to her own, and then lives to witness her own offspring benefiting from this son's premature death, stands to be suspected of complicity in the crime.[17] If Zenobia did help Hairan on his way, she was certainly not the first stepmother to do so. The hard evidence against Zenobia does not seem to go further than this *post hoc, propter hoc* kind of argument, nor does the ambitious temperament she subsequently revealed necessarily make her a murderess even if matters had indubitably turned out conveniently for her. Zenobia however is far from being the only person who had something to gain from the death of Odainat. There is also the question of Rome.

Although the Romans appeared to acquiesce in Odainat's tacit assumption of viceregal powers, they had plenty of historical experience of self-styled emperors-in-the-East, none of it satisfactory. The perennial problem was how to secure their frontiers and yet keep down their various mushrooming lieutenants. It may be that the removal of Odainat, that hardy and effective general, was not displeasing to them; it may even be that they conspired to secure it. A youngish woman as regent for a boy would present much less of a threat. Or so the Romans thought.

As it was, Zenobia's immediate reaction to her new position was more that of the swift voracious hawk than that of the placid domestic dove. Swiftly she struck against Egypt, taking advantage of the fact that the Roman Empire itself was being hard-pressed on its other frontiers, notably in northern Italy, by those unwelcome strangers at the European feast, the Goths. (Their first attacks had occurred about thirty years earlier.) By 269 her general Zabdas had secured most of the country; at the same time Zenobia had simply annexed most of Syria to the Palmyrene kingdom. Some local difficulties with Egypt – where many distinctly preferred the distant Roman overlordship to that of neighbouring Palmyra – meant a second campaign by Zabdas. But in neither case – Egypt or Syria – was the beleaguered Roman Emperor Gallienus in any position to protest.

It was then the turn of Asia Minor: by 270 Zenobia had conquered as far as Bithynia, which commanded the Bosphorus. Only at Chalcedon were the gates closed against the Palmyrenes, who, far from their base, could not take the city. Nevertheless in the few years since her husband's death, Zenobia, in a great swathe of conquest, had sickled out a vast new empire for the tiny Palmyrene state from Egypt in the south right up to the Bosphorus in the north. And to crown it all Zenobia now took a step which Odainat had never taken: she declared herself formally independent of Rome.

By this time, Zenobia was controlling not only much of the commerce so vital to Rome – which depended for example on Egypt entirely for corn supplies – but also the trade routes with Abyssinia, Arabia and India. In addition, her northern swathe brought her in touch with the Bosphoran route to Thrace. Yet despite the menace of this eastern situation, the Roman Emperor still preferred – however grudgingly – to allow some form of concordat with Zenobia, while the still greater Gothic threat remained to be eliminated. In the words of the *Scriptores Historiae Augustae* on the fortunes of Rome at this point: 'Now all shame is exhausted, for in the weakened state of the commonwealth ... even women ruled most excellently.'[18]

Whether Zenobia ruled excellently or not, depending on one's view of extended conquest, she certainly ruled, and with a deliberate pomp which pointed most magisterially back towards that of Cleopatra; even the gold vessels used at her banquets were said to have been those bequeathed by the great Queen. Furthermore Zenobia established a court known however briefly for its intellectual brilliance as well as the more material coruscation of its jewellery. Prominent among the scholars and men of letters who surrounded her at her invitation was Cassius Longinus, the eminent writer on Greek rhetoric and philosophy, himself probably Syrian. Then there was Callinicus Sutorius, originally from Petra, a sophist and historian who had taught at Athens. It was Callinicus who actually wrote that history of Alexandria – significantly, capital of the Ptolemies – which was sometimes ascribed to Zenobia herself. But then the desire, however wistful, to be known as a published scholar is not in itself an ignoble ambition for a prince – or a princess. Moreover Zenobia's was an empire founded on tolerance rather than exclusivity. Her benevolence towards the Jews of Alexandria has been mentioned. According to tradition, she also established relations with Paul of Samosata, the Christian Bishop of Antioch, condemned for certain doctrinal errors at the Synod of Antioch held in 268.[19]

What was the mainspring of all this imperial – and imperious – activity on the part of the Palmyrene Queen? The recreation of vanished Ptolemaic glories was a thrilling pursuit indeed, yet it was a chimera, one which had never haunted the more hardheaded and practical Odainat. With Zenobia, acting on behalf of her son Vaballathus, on the other hand, one can trace the mounting tenor of her claims through various inscriptions in Egypt, Syria and Palmyra, as the break with Rome gets nearer. Vaballathus was not only *dux romanorum* like his father, but *rex* and *basileus* (Greek for king) and despot – ruler. Zenobia herself was *regina* and *basilissa* – queen – and, most magnificently, the two of them were Augustus and Augusta. Finally, at some date after 11 March 271 and before August, Zenobia on behalf of Vaballathus struck money in both their names.[20] This was a declaration of war against the Empire.

The French authority on the history and customs of Palmyra, J. G. Février, knew the answer to Zenobia's driving force. For the impartial historian, he wrote, one trait dominates her character: '*une ambition féroce, insatiable*'.[21] One may be far more partial towards Zenobia, sympathetic to the problems which she overcame and to the near-miraculous achievements which for however short a span were hers, and still find the answer to be the right one. How else could she have urged her troops on that extraordinary sweep of conquest, how else set up her Cleopatrine court, if she had not been animated by ferocious and certainly insatiable ambition? This is where Zenobia, as a type of Warrior Queen, parts company significantly with Boudica, and with many others of the Boadicean ilk, who for one reason and another were driven into a military solution.

Unlike Boudica, Zenobia had not been wronged: she had not been scourged, her daughters had not been raped, the Romans had not taken over her people's land nor imposed lethal taxes upon Palmyra. Following the pattern of Odainat, there was an opportunity here for renewed Palmyrene aggrandizement while the Empire remained weak, even if the Palmyrene archers, no longer supplemented by Roman legionaries, would have to look out for the Persian enemy on their other frontier. But Zenobia – in this indeed like Cleopatra – preferred a bolder course.

It is not clear whether Zenobia ever claimed formal joint rule with her own son[22] and since she enjoyed effective power during Vaballathus' youth one can only imagine how she would have dealt with the problem of his majority had the Palmyrene Empire survived so long. As it was, her style of majesty, like the Palmyrene culture to which she belonged, took profitably from the worlds which she straddled. Symbolically, the vast oriental jewel which hung from her helmet was not the kind of brooch generally worn by women, but that of Eastern kings, for Zenobia copied the regal pomp of the Persians in her banquets and the obeisance she received; on the other hand she stepped forth to public assemblies like the Roman emperors. Zenobia was the type of striking and intelligent woman whose original Appendage status is soon forgotten. When the enveloping masculine carapace was broken, she stepped out from the fragments of the shell with zest.

Zenobia was not to be allowed to pursue her daring course with impunity forever. It is generally and plausibly believed that the new Roman Emperor Aurelian took the initiative in what followed. The time was at last propitious. Aurelian, a general who probably originally came from Lower Moesia, had done well in northern Italy against the invading Alemanni and Juthungi. The Dalmatian invasions were for the time being held off, and at home a revolt in the Senate had been quashed. Nor could Palmyra look towards Persia for any assistance against the traditional Roman enemy: it was now the turn of that empire to be paralysed by inner troubles following the death of Sapor I. Even if Zenobia provoked the actual outbreak of hostilities by cutting off the vital supply of Egyptian corn to Italy, she could not have expected her joyous suzerainty over such a vast area – all of it contiguous to the Roman overlordship – to remain unchallenged for long once Rome itself had the energy to spare.

Aurelian's first task was to secure the reconquest of Egypt, under the generalship of Probus. This was not a task which presented too many difficulties since the Palmyrene presence was still the cause of much Egyptian resentment. At a conference at Palmyra itself, on the other hand, in August 271, a bare year since Zenobia's bold essay of independence, pledges of loyalty were given to the family of Odainat, in effect to the Queen.

Two oracles were now consulted by the Palmyrenes concerning the fate of their eastern empire: the Apollo Sarpedonius at Seleucia and the Venus Aphacitis (of Aphaca in Syria). On a grander scale, it was a situation reminiscent of Boudica's rally when she first invoked the goddess Andraste and then released the hare from the folds of her skirt 'as a species of divination'. But the hare – doubtless by careful stage management – had run off in an auspicious direction. The Apollo Sarpedonius returned an answer which indicated that he found the mere enquiry odious:

> Accursed race! avoid my sacred fane
> Whose treach'rous deeds the angry gods disdain.[23]

As for the Venus Aphacitis, she declined to instigate that phenomenon of a rounded airy figure, appearing from a lamp of fire, which sometimes greeted the fortunate; and the Palmyrene offerings at her cistern floated unhappily on the surface, a sign that the goddess had rejected them.

As things turned out, Boudica's auspiciously lolloping hare proved to be a false prophet, whereas the Apollo Sarpedonius and the Venus Aphacitis could have claimed the satisfaction, in some pantheon where they had gloomy colloquy with each other, of getting things absolutely right. But then what omen, favourable or otherwise, has ever altered the course of history? The fact was that with a strong Roman presence back on the Eastern scene, the luck of Zenobia – and Palmyra – was fast running out.

Aurelian's first campaign took him as far as Ankara. The city duly opened its gates since the Palmyrenes had not left behind a garrison, either because Ankara was judged too far from their centre of operations, or because they had insufficient troops to do so. The first resistance encountered by Aurelian was in the defiles of Taurus, commanded by the city of Tyana, which the Palmyrenes held. Possibly aided by treachery, Aurelian was able to prevail. But he did not permit his troops to sate themselves on pillage in the customary manner – yet. After all, as he pointed out, resplendent and wealthy Palmyra lay ahead.

The Palmyrenes fell back on the line of the Orontes river, which flows north-west from Emesa to Antioch. Here just outside Antioch the two armies faced each other: but it was far from being such a disparate confrontation as that of Romans and Britons at Boudica's 'last battle'. It is true the Roman legions were once again veterans of a life of war, such as those Suetonius had had at his command; Aurelian also had some light cavalry. But he had no archers or heavy cavalry. The Palmyrenes on the other hand had both: and the prowess of their archers was renowned throughout the East. Zenobia's line of battle consisted of a line of archers on foot, with an imposing mass of both cavalry and infantry behind; unfortunately her cavalry, famous too for its zest and power, had a tendency to lose touch with the infantry due to the unchecked depth of its charge.

In the battle which followed, with Zenobia seen galloping alongside her troops although transmitting orders through her general Zabdas, this lack in restraint on the part of the Palmyrene cavalry proved crucial. Zosimus tells us that the Romans pretended to flee, luring the Palmyrenes on until both men and horses were 'thoroughly tired, through the excessive heat and weight of their armour'.[24] As a result the Palmyrene cavalry was cut off and subjected to the most frightful slaughter.

Following this reverse, it even took a trick on the part of Zabdas to secure his re-entry to Antioch (he pretended to be leading in the captive Aurelian) since the waning fortunes of the Palmyrenes were evident to their subjugated neighbours. Zenobia, pursued by Aurelian, now fell back on Emesa, and it was here, on the banks of the Orontes, some five or six miles north of modern Homs, that her 'last battle' took place. According to Zosimus, Zenobia at this point still had, out of those Syrians loyal to her, seventy thousand men. But Aurelian's own troops, augmented by reinforcement, may by this stage have been almost as numerous.

The battle was long and fierce: but in the end the fiery Palmyrenes, for all their archers and their cavalry, were no more match for the seasoned Roman legionaries than the warriors of the Iceni had been, with their decorated shields, chariots and long swords. The Roman staying-power could not be gainsaid. Once again the Palmyrene cavalry failed to re-form after its initial charge, and the Emperor was able to throw in his footsoldiers against them. 'The slaughter was promiscuous,' wrote Zosimus, 'some falling by the sword and others by their own and their enemies' horses.'[25] The field was covered with dead men and animals. So fell the flower of the Palmyrene aristocracy.

But Zenobia did not fall. After a grim council of war, the decision was taken to abandon Emesa for the base stronghold of Palmyra, where at least the Palmyrenes would not have to contend with growing Syrian hostility. Zenobia's withdrawal across the desert to Palmyra – a distance of perhaps one hundred miles – was something to which custom had habituated both her and her Arab troops. Aurelian's pursuit, given the terrain and the ability of the nomads who inhabited it to harry him, was more of an ordeal and thus more of an achievement. And, once he had arrived to set up his blockade, Palmyra's isolated position, with the caravans no longer active, told against her rather than her enemies. In the subsequent siege, it was famine as much as anything else which ravaged the inhabitants.

Zenobia however had not lost her spirit. It was at this point that her chronicler has her engaging in a correspondence with Aurelian on the subject of surrender.[26] Aurelian was already publicly bemoaning his fate in being matched against a woman in that passage quoted earlier: 'as if Zenobia was contending against me with her own strength alone . . .'. To the Queen herself he wrote in contemptuous terms: 'And you, O Zenobia, may pass your life in some spot where I shall place you in pursuance of the distinguished sentence of the Senate; your gems, your silver, gold, silk, horses, camels, being given up to the Roman treasury.'

'Thou askest me to surrender', replied the Palmyrene Queen proudly, 'as if thou wert ignorant that Queen Cleopatra chose rather to perish than to survive her dignity.' In answer to Aurelian's indignant question: 'How, O Zenobia, hast thou dared to insult Roman emperors?' she answered: 'Thee I acknowledge to be Emperor, since thou hast conquered', but the rest of them, including Gallienus, she did not consider worthy of the name of chief – *princeps*. She added: 'Believing Vitruvia* to be a woman like me, I desired to become a partner in the royal power, should the supply of lands permit.'

At the same time as firing off this defiant letter – about the authorship of which there would later be some significant dispute –

---

* Victoria or Vitruvia, the influential mother of the rebel Gallic Emperor Victorinus (who succeeded Postumus in 268/9); she also helped the next Gallic Emperor, Tetricus, to power.[27]

Zenobia sought assistance from the Persians. It is kindest and by no means unreasonable to regard Zenobia's subsequent secret flight from Palmyra as part of her plan for securing this Persian help, since Aurelian blocked off not only supplies but also any overt Persian relief force. Taking a female camel – 'which is the swiftest of that kind of animal, and much more swift than horses' – she managed to slip out of the beleaguered city. Riding furiously, Zenobia got as far as the Euphrates. Here she was captured as she was boarding a boat, either recognized or betrayed. Taken to Emesa, Zenobia found herself once more facing the Emperor Aurelian, but this time unaided by Palmyrene archers or cavalry.

Palmyra itself was captured and sacked. But in the persons of Aurelian and Zenobia an interesting battle of the sexes was joined, one from which the Palmyrene Queen undoubtedly emerged victorious. Aurelian for his part remained uneasy at his triumph over a mere woman, and reflected that in ages to come it might not redound entirely to his credit to have done so. He therefore continued to stress at length the amazing qualities of the Palmyrene Queen: a woman perhaps, but what a woman! So brave, bold, daring, prudent in council, firm in purpose, etc., etc. Moreover Odainat's victories in Persia were due entirely to her, 'such was the dread entertained of this woman, among the natives of the East and of Egypt, that she kept in check the Arabians, the Saracens and the Armenians'.[28] Frantically Aurelian attempted to elude the taint of the Shame Syndrome, generally supplied to those who were actually defeated by 'mere women' like Boudica, but still capable of adhering to those who defeated them.

Zenobia on the other hand displayed an impudence which should make her the admiration of any strong-minded woman finding herself in a tight corner in a masculine-oriented society. She simply turned round and claimed immunity on the grounds of her sex. In short, she 'produced many persons, who had seduced her as a simple woman'. Even her bold letter of defiance to Aurelian was now ascribed to the scholar Longinus, although another scholar Nicomachus asserted to the contrary that Zenobia had dictated the letter to him personally, in order that he should translate it into Greek.[29] As a result, Longinus was executed. Zenobia however survived, as presumably had been her intention: for nothing more was heard after this of her bold desire to 'perish rather than lose her dignity'.

All the evidence points to the fact that Zenobia was now taken captive to Rome. Zosimus is the only dissenting voice, but then in suggesting that Zenobia died on her way to Europe by her own hand he was manifestly trying to emphasize the identity of Zenobia with Cleopatra. Other versions agree with a wealth of circumstantial detail that Zenobia reached Italy in safety where she was obliged to walk in the Emperor's triumph.[30]

One would like to have witnessed this apotheosis of the Emperor Aurelian, although preferably not in chains. First came a parade of the most curious wild beasts, including not only elephants but tigers, giraffes and elks: subsequently the prudent Aurelian gave this menagerie to various Roman citizens so that the privy purse would not be burdened with their upkeep. Then came the gladiators and then the ambassadors of such diverse empires as Ethiopia, Persia, India and China. The human menagerie which followed was of no less interest to the inquisitive spectators: captives from, as it seemed, every corner of the globe attesting to the range of Aurelian's victories, and all neatly labelled with placards round their necks to din in the geography lesson (as diplomats today are labelled at a United Nations session). In this manner there trailed past not only the recent victims of the East, but also Hibernians, Vandals, Franks and Swabians. Among these last were a group of Gothic women who had been discovered fighting in men's clothes: helpfully the placards round their necks read 'Amazon'.

Four chariots in all formed part of the procession. One of these, which had once belonged to the King of the Goths, was drawn by stags: at the Capitol the stags would be slain and vowed to the altar of Jupiter. The others were of Eastern provenance: the chariot of Odainat, adorned with silver and gold, the chariot given to Aurelian by the Emperor of Persia, and the chariot of Zenobia (that chariot in which she had often disdained to ride, preferring with her 'masculine energy' the hardihood of horseback).

It was indeed Zenobia herself, walking in front of her chariot, who was the focus of every eye. She bore no placard round her neck, nor was she labelled 'Amazon' or for that matter 'Penthesilea' or 'Hippolyta'. Nevertheless the half-fainting Palmyrene Queen (for once she might have been glad of that chariot), shackled by golden fetters and weighed down by the very mass of those jewels she had once displayed so proudly, stood by her very presence for Aurelian's victory in the East, much as the Greek heroes' legendary victories over the Amazons had symbolized the victory of Greeks over the barbarians.

Zenobia, the great survivor, survived the ordeal of the Triumph. She did more than that: she built a new life.[31] At some later point, she seems to have married a Roman senator. At any rate she was able to retire in affluence to a villa, granted to her by the Roman state, at Tibur (Tivoli), near that of Hadrian. A hundred years later her descendants, either by this second husband or by Odainat – Vaballathus disappears from view, but two other sons walked with her in the Triumph – were known in senatorial circles; the fifth-century Bishop of Florence, Zenobius, may have owed his unusual name to a still remembered ancestress.

Zenobia's instinct for survival, unlike her forcible marital chastity, has received a bad press from historians, although one can detect a certain gloomy satisfaction at finding a woman, however bold on the field, choosing to behave really badly in a genuine crisis. Theodor Mommsen thundered: 'Zenobia, after she had for years born rule with masculine energy, did not now disdain to invoke a woman's privileges and to throw the responsibility on her advisers.' Gibbon was more philosophical: 'as female fortitude is commonly artificial, so it is seldom steady or consistent'.[32] For tradition has it that Zenobia, unruffled by such considerations, had the bad taste to enjoy her life as a Roman matron. She held a fashionable salon in her villa, where only her outlandish Roman accent (but then she did speak Greek, Aramaic and Egyptian) betrayed her exotic origins. As Zenobia dispensed hospitality and perhaps told stories of her tribulations walking in the Triumph or even tales of desert rides – did she ever dream of that female camel, the swiftest in the business? – Aurelian was obliged to return to Palmyra. There he quelled another insurrection. Finally both Palmyra and Alexandria were plundered to excess and the Palmyrene civilization passed away.

So finally the story of Zenobia and the Romans, as a coda to that of Boudica, reminds one that there could be advantages in being a Warrior Queen – as opposed to a Warrior King – as well as disadvantages; or at least so far as the queen herself was concerned. Boudica was scourged (and her daughters raped), which it has been suggested was a deliberate outrage on the part of the Romans, connected to Boudica's sex; Zenobia on the other hand betrayed

Longinus with impunity, if one leaves out of account her short bejewelled travail on foot. The Only-a-Weak-Woman Syndrome – 'I am as good as (or even better than) a man when I ride to victory but I'm Only-a-Weak-Woman when I'm defeated' – is also part of the history of the Warrior Queen.

None of this should detract from the achievements of Zenobia in her prime. There is a figure of Arab legend called variously Zebbâ, al-Zabbà or az-Zabbà: a beautiful warrior who leads her troops to victory in a series of confrontations, as well as indulging in some wily tricks, based on her own charms.[33] Zebbâ has two fortresses on the left and right banks of the Euphrates – in some stories her sister called Zainab (the Arab version of Zenobia) occupies one of them – and in one legend at least remains chaste; moreover Zebbâ, like Zenobia, is captured in an incident at a river. Although an exact connection between Zenobia and Zebbâ cannot be made – just as a historical figure like Boudica can never be exactly connected with the legendary Boadicea – nevertheless there are too many coincidences between them to dismiss it altogether.

It therefore seems fitting, as we go forward on the long march of Boudica's mythical history, to remember that Zenobia also has her own lively myths in her own Arab culture (Zainab is a popular name in Syria today). A modern play by Assi and Mansour Al-Rahbani ends with Zenobia poisoning herself just before the Roman soldiers bind her in chains. She dies with the words 'O Liberty!' on her lips, and her mourning people promise themselves never to forget her (or the idea of liberty).[34]

It is good to bear this Arab heroine in mind; for we shall find the 'chaste' Zenobia appearing from time to time in a somewhat pallid disguise in Europe:

> That lovely form enshrines the gentlest virtues
> Softest compassion, unaffected wisdom,
> To outward beauty lending higher charms[35]

as an eighteenth-century play had it. It is difficult to imagine this 'beauteous mourner' raising her 'suppliant voice' for 'mild humanity' carving out an empire from Egypt to Asia Minor in defiance of Rome itself. 'O Zenobia, hast thou dared to insult Roman emperors?' wrote Aurelian to the real-life Queen: she had and she did. It is

Zenobia's courage which links her to Boudica; her ambition (and her instinct for survival) sets her apart.

PART TWO

CHAPTER NINE

MATILDA, DAUGHTER OF PETER

The daughter of Peter and the faithful hand-maid of Christ
Pope Gregory VII to Matilda Countess of Tuscany

'To you, my most beloved and loving daughter, I do not hesitate to disclose any of these thoughts, for even you yourself can hardly imagine how greatly I may count upon your zeal and discretion.' The writer of this letter in late 1074 was Pope Gregory VII. The 'most beloved and loving' daughter in question was Matilda Countess of Tuscany, a woman now in her late thirties, who had inherited vast dominions in northern Italy from her father some twenty years back. As she moved towards independence from the various tutelages of mother and stepfather, increasingly she was acting as the 'faithful hand-maid' of St Peter – a hand-maid with a sharp sword in her hand and an army at her back.[1]

The combination of Countess Matilda's prolonged military endeavours with her own sense of a holy mission is what made her egregious among her contemporaries: 'For St Peter and Matilda!' her men shouted as they stormed the fortresses of the Apennines while she termed herself 'Matilda by the Grace of God'. It also inspired their admiration – if they were on the same side.

The approval which Matilda received from her allies and subordinates, based on her gender, not despite it, clearly related to the apparently 'holy' nature of her chosen role. The pious Christian Matilda would not have relished a comparison to pagan Boadicea, with her invocation to Andraste on the eve of battle a thousand years earlier. As a matter of interest, she would not even have recognized the allusion. Penthesilea was not forgotten and Matilda would receive the usual ration of such comparisons to the Amazonian Queen. However, not only had Boadicea vanished into her unknown grave but her very name had been forgotten, awaiting the rediscovery of Tacitus' manuscripts in a monastery library in the fourteenth century.[2] Yet Matilda's role represents an important aspect of the subject of the Warrior Queen, that of Holy (Armed) Figurehead. Just as Boadicea must have gained strength from the image of the Celtic goddess in her people's minds, so Matilda received practical support from the notion of the halo round her head – and the sword in her hand.

Not surprisingly, it was just this shining white garment of virtue which Matilda's (political) enemies sought to defile. Calumnies included the suggestion of a carnal relationship with the Pope, and the suggestion that the 'chaste' Matilda actually had one of her husbands killed, and possibly her children as well. This was a deliberate attempt to counteract the undoubted propaganda value – to the papal side – of the image of Countess Matilda, both pure and powerful, encouraging her troops to the rescue of the Holy Father. The scandals as well as the paeans of praise bear witness to the successful possibilities inherent in the idea of the Armed (Female) Saint.

The Pope, assisted by his loving daughter, was involved for most of the years of his reign in an incessant power struggle with the German Emperor Henry IV. From the point of view of Countess Matilda, it was an armed struggle which over thirty years would have enabled her to have claimed, with Schiller's Wallenstein, 'our life was but a battle and a march'. So in a sense the Countess Matilda did lay down her life for the papal cause – the cause of Christ, as she firmly believed.

The life she dedicated to the cause was that of a wealthy, high-minded and extremely religious aristocratic woman, who might otherwise have ruled her dominions and endowed her pious foundations with the suitable expectation of peace in this life and further peace to come 'in the heavenly country'. This was the life she finally led as a very old lady, when these papal–imperial troubles were in any case subsiding, helmet and mail finally, as it were, put away.

Yet as the devout and filial language of the 'hand-maid' Matilda towards the Pope indicates, fully reciprocating his own intimacy, the sacrifice, if sacrifice it was, was one that she herself felt called by God to make. At one point she borrowed the words of the Apostle to say that neither tribulations nor anguish, nor hunger, nor peril, nor persecution, nor swords, nor death, nor life, nor angels, nor principalities, nor virtues, nor the present could ever separate her from the love of Peter.[3]

Matilda of Tuscany – Matilda of Canossa as she is sometimes known – was born in about 1046 somewhere in northern Italy.[4] Her father was the Margrave Boniface II, head of a family based on the mighty Apennine fortress of Canossa, and invested with the office of Margrave by the Roman Emperor-cum-German King, Conrad II, in 1027. Boniface's lands stretched roughly speaking from the Apennines to the Alps, sweeping across the wide plain of Lombardy; but he held many of them in feudal tenure to Conrad II since in a revival of the idea of the 'Roman Empire' of Charlemagne, the elected German King was in his capacity of 'Roman Emperor' currently exercising lordship over northern Italy.

Charlemagne's 'Roman Empire' had been conferred on him in 800 by the Pope and brought back for the German kings in the middle of the tenth century. Officially, therefore, Conrad, like other German kings of this period, owed his position in Germany to election by the German princes; while he had to be crowned by the Pope as Roman Emperor. That at any rate was the theory of the thing.

Matilda's mother was Boniface's second wife Beatrice, daughter of the Duke of Upper Lorraine. Hereditarily speaking, Matilda must have owed at least as much to her clever, capable mother as to her rough warlord of a father; while in terms of environment Beatrice's influence must certainly have been paramount since the Margrave Boniface was killed when Matilda was six.

It was to be a turbulent childhood, a presage of Matilda's adult life. The death of her father and the deaths of her brothers – their precise number is in question but the relevant point to Matilda's story is that they did not survive – left Matilda theoretical heiress of Boniface's extensive lands. But the rules of inheritance, given the vital imperial exercise of Italian overlordship, were not at this date quite so simple. The Emperor Henry III, for example, who had succeeded Conrad II in 1039, claimed the right to invest a male child with those of Boniface's Tuscan territories which he had held in feudal tenure, although this still left Matilda as heiress to the Canossa family heartlands. Moreover Henry III was in an increasingly strong position to enforce his wishes since the fortunes of the German-ruled 'Roman Empire' were waxing. Burgundy had fallen to Conrad II by inheritance; Henry III himself had extended his sway over Bohemia, Bavaria and Hungary, as well as over the Normans in the south of Italy.

In any case the question of female inheritance in this age dominated by force turned more on practicalities than on theories. Where an heiress was concerned, her husband would tend to exercise her military obligations because he was judged physically capable of doing so, although she herself might literally inherit (and later transmit possession of her lands to her children). Similarly, where kingdoms, duchies and counties were at stake, a female's ability to inherit in fact rather than theory often depended on what masculine support she could muster. This is illustrated by the story of the fight for the English crown between Stephen and his cousin Matilda (or the Empress Maud) to be considered in the next chapter: by modern rules of descent, Maud, the King's daughter, had a better claim than her first cousin, Stephen, son of the King's sister. But, as will be seen, such a claim was not necessarily upheld if it could not be enforced. The need for strength or at least protection, and marriage for the sake of protection – these were the elements which dominated the lives of women (and little girls) in high positions, as the need for strength and powerful allies dominated the lives of their menfolk.

Under these circumstances, the swift remarriage of Matilda's mother Beatrice to her cousin Duke Godfrey of Upper Lorraine a year after Boniface's death is easily understood; although by choosing a husband who was at the time in open revolt against the German Emperor, she was hardly likely to achieve a reconciliation in that direction. At one point Beatrice and Matilda were taken hostage. It was not until after the death of Henry III in 1056 that some kind of political calm was temporarily established. The new Emperor Henry IV was another child (at six years old, he was four years younger than Matilda) and the regency was left in the hands of his mother, the Empress Agnes. The conditions of Matilda's own life became less perilous: Duke Godfrey, no longer considered a rebel vassal, was allowed together with her mother Beatrice to govern Matilda's estates during her minority.

Where the chroniclers of her education are concerned, naturally the Tomboy Syndrome is found to be at work.[5] Matilda, like Zenobia, was said to have been eager to learn martial accomplishments to the detriment of traditionally female arts like embroidery: 'Disdaining with a virile spirit the art of Arachne she seized the spear of Pallas', wrote Vedriani in 1666; Arduino della Paluda, later a general, was said to have taught her to ride like a lancer, spear in hand, to bear a pike like a footsoldier and to wield both battleaxe and sword. Fortunately for these activities, Matilda grew up under this treatment tall and strong, if slender. According to later tradition, she was certainly accustomed to the weight of armour: in his lifetime Vedriani declared that he knew of a suit of her armour sold for a song in the Reggio market in 1622.

Whether or not Matilda actually wore armour, which is doubtful, she did, as a matter of fact, embroider: she embroidered well and she sent presents of her work (an embroidered standard) to male contemporaries such as William the Conqueror.[6] The stereotype of the tomboy has to disdain 'the art of Arachne' (spinning) if she dares to pick up the spear, but the real woman had no intention of sacrificing a possible advantage by disdaining those pursuits common to her sex and rank which signalled femininity and gentleness.

Furthermore, Matilda's education left her accomplished in four languages – the four languages concerned, German, French, Italian and Latin, expressing the polyglot nature of her future responsibilities – and, in an age when most Northern rulers usually signed documents with a mere cross, this female would in adulthood be able to write letters herself unaided by a clerk. One should not ignore the effect of this excellent education in giving her confidence to rule her estates. (Queen Elizabeth I had the same kind of education and exhibited the same kind of intellectual confidence towards her male contemporaries.)

At some point during her youth Matilda was married. Like her mother's second marriage, this was another inevitable and practical step, although myth, wishful thinking and the fact that it had taken place beyond the Alps combined to allow a lot of nonsense to be written on the subject later on. The chosen bridegroom was the son of Duke Godfrey by an earlier marriage, a boy known – all too accurately, alas, since he was severely deformed – as Godfrey the Hunchback. Three facts can be extracted for certain out of the various fantasies surrounding this, the first of Matilda's two marriages: that she did marry, that the marriage was consummated because at least one child, who died in infancy, was born of the union, and that the marriage itself was a failure.

The various elaborate legends on the subject divide into those intended to bolster up Matilda's 'holy' image (that the marriage if indeed it took place was never consummated, or, if consummated, only reluctantly in the line of duty) and those intended to denigrate her by making of her some kind of insatiable witch-like creature. It is significant that exactly the same kind of legends – the Chaste Syndrome versus the Voracity Syndrome – attached themselves to Matilda's second marriage at the age of forty-three to Welf of Bavaria. According to the scurrilous accounts, both Godfrey and Welf were supposed to have been impotent in face of Matilda's treatment – in the case of Welf, Matilda was alleged to have boxed his ears with disappointment and sent him home; Godfrey was supposed to have been killed, as were Matilda's two children by Godfrey, both hunchbacks.[7]

On the other hand, a pious story has Matilda cropping her hair deliberately short on her wedding night, adopting a hair shirt and then starkly inviting her husband to a joyless but dutiful coupling for the sake of the dynasty: 'Come, let us to our union.'[8] It is possible of course that the two versions, lubricious and pious, actually bear some relation to each other: one cannot help observing that Matilda's wedding-night tactics required a delicate balance to be struck between performance (desirable) and pleasure (undesirable) in which there may have been an unfortunate degree of miscalculation on her part.

On the subject of Matilda's chastity, two important sources for her life unite in following a more moderate course. The *Vita Mathildis* is a long biographical poem in Latin by the Countess's chaplain Donizo which he intended to present to her personally; her death intervened and the poem was published later. For all its flourishes, it preserves details which would otherwise be lost, and the fact that it was designed for Matilda's own perusal suggests that wild inaccuracies would not have been permitted. Donizo stresses

Matilda's personal holiness, while not actually claiming her celibacy. Rangerius, biographer of Anselm of Lucca, Matilda's spiritual adviser, takes the same line: Matilda, he wrote, was not keen on the carnal aspects of matrimony, nevertheless 'her mother's exhortations prevented her from committing herself to the deep religious desire for a chastity which was, in her case, no longer permissible in view of the obligations she had assumed'.[9]

Donizo and Rangerius between them put forward a plausible picture; it is certainly more plausible if less exciting than that of an eighteenth-century Italian work, for example, with the full wind of myth in its sails: 'Matilda, embellished with all the virtues, had the rare destiny of causing lilies to bloom among her martial laurels, and these she bore ever unharmed to her tomb; wife and widow to be sure, but always a virgin too.'[10] Matilda's marriage, for which she had not felt much enthusiasm in the first place given the unprepossessing nature of her husband, petered out with her return to Tuscany from beyond the Alps and her enthusiastic adoption of the papal cause. It ended technically with Godfrey the Hunchback's death in 1076 but before that politics, far more than physical disinclination, had driven the couple apart.

The politics which transformed Matilda from a dissatisfied but dutiful wife into the right-hand woman warrior of Pope Gregory VII were painted in theory on a broad canvas of noble aspect. The eleventh century witnessed that great battle between Pope and Emperor to exercise jurisdiction over each other – and each other's subjects – which had at its heart the relative importance of Church and state in directing men's lives.

Two and a half centuries later, Dante would suggest in *De Monarchia* that the divine plan for the government of the world consisted of a universal emperor acting in harmony with a universal pope; man had 'a twofold end', both spiritual and temporal, and thus needed 'a twofold directive power' to achieve it: 'to wit, the supreme pontiff to lead the human race, in accordance with things revealed, to eternal life; and the Emperor to direct the human race to temporal felicity, in accordance with the teachings of philosophy . . .'.[11] Nothing like this ideal was however established in the lifetime of Matilda. And there were some murky details in the corners of the broad canvas of Church and state. As emperors deposed popes to set up rival popes in holy Rome and popes interfered with German affairs by declaring emperors excommunicated (which might result in their own deposition) their motives might be construed as spiritual (the preservation and purification of the Church of Christ) or they might be seen as the less sympathetic ones of power-seeking and power-broking.

It is probable that Matilda's first appearance on the public scene was at just such an ambivalent occasion. In 1059, when she would have been about thirteen, she was present with her mother and stepfather Godfrey of Lorraine at the Council held at Sutri, in the mountains between Rome and Viterbo. The death of Pope Stephen IX, Godfrey's brother, in March 1058 had been a blow to the family interests when the Roman nobles took the opportunity to elect their own candidate. He was however deposed at Sutri in favour of the Bishop of Florence, backed by Godfrey's faction, who took the title of Nicholas II. The death of Nicholas II in 1061 produced yet another crisis. While Anselm of Lucca – a worthy incumbent of the office – was duly elected as Pope Alexander II, a sense of the imperial interests in Italy, somewhat dormant during the childhood of Henry IV, began reviving in Germany. Thus an anti-pope was put forward in the shape of Caladus of Parma, a prelate of notoriously evil character (according to his enemies) who took the title of Honorius II; what was more the lax bishops of Lombardy preferred his cause to that of Alexander II, fearing the upheavals in the name of Church discipline which the latter had promised.

The circumstances surrounding the Council of Sutri of 1059, the election of Alexander II and the years of fighting which followed it give an indication of the background, turbulent, complicated, ever-changing and contentious, against which Matilda grew up. If it were true to say that 'mere anarchy' was 'loosed upon the world' in which she lived, her devotion to the papal cause in the shape of the Pope she principally served, Gregory VII, was the natural reaction of a singularly unanarchic character to such a situation. It was however to be over a decade before the Papacy was so vigorously incarnated. In the meantime Matilda was learning the arts of battle.

So far as one can piece together her story, she made her first foray on the battlefield at the side of her mother, defending the interests of Alexander II against those of the schismatics in 1061 shortly after his election. The seventeenth-century account is eloquent: 'Now

there appeared in Lombardy at the head of her numerous squadrons
the young maid Matilda, armed like a warrior, and with such
bravery, that she made known to the world that courage and valour
in mankind is not indeed a matter of sex, but of heart and spirit.'[12]
Matilda was also probably present in 1066 when her stepfather
finally put an end to the Roman and Norman support for the anti-
Pope Honorius II: at the battle of Aquino, at which Godfrey of
Lorraine defeated the Normans, she is even said to have shared
the command of four hundred archers with the General Arduino,
although this is surely an exaggeration.

According to Vedriani, Matilda was by now generally seen as 'the
new Bellona among the armed companies'.[13] But although there are
later reports to establish Matilda's presence at various military
engagements in the 1060s in the cause of Alexander II, it seems
unlikely that she had carried out any kind of real military command
before the death of Duke Godfrey in 1069.* This was the effective
moment in Matilda's life when, aided by her mother, she began to
exercise proper authority in Italy – in the absence of any male figure
able to stop her. Her husband, Godfrey the Hunchback, battled on
in Lorraine (physical disability did not prevent him being a doughty
fighter) but increasingly failed to support Matilda in Italy with
reinforcements.[14] The fact was that Lorraine was beginning to turn
away from the Papacy back towards the imperial cause, just as
Matilda's own commitment became yet further strengthened by the
election of a new pope.

In the summer of 1073 the great reformer and former monk
Hildebrand was consecrated as Pope Gregory VII. A strong character, believing in the centralization of the Church as a means to this
reform, Hildebrand had already acted as the power behind the
throne during the pontificate of Alexander II. In particular he was
dedicated to rooting out that practice of lay investiture, by which
the symbols of their office were granted to ecclesiastics by laymen.
The new Pope Gregory was convinced that the Church would never
be purified so long as laymen had in effect an opportunity to buy
and sell Church offices, although he would initially have preferred
to work through rather than against the Emperor. (In the previous

---

* The metaphors of strife and battle used by commentators on both sides at the time
make it difficult (except in the case of Sorbara) to be certain when Matilda actually led
her men, as opposed to commanded them.

reign, Henry III had been a noted supporter of Church reform.)

In 1075 Pope Gregory prohibited lay investiture under pain of excommunication, and later that year carried out that sentence against various offenders: these included favourites of Henry IV who had been appointed to the vacant sees of Milan, Fermo and Spoleto. At Mass in Rome on Christmas Eve 1075, however, as part of the rough internal politics of the city, the Pope was first violently assaulted and then abducted. The intention was to take him as prisoner to Germany. Only the furious uprising of the Roman people (to whom he had endeared himself) rescued him.

The incident, shocking in its brutality, may well have put the finishing touches to the unofficial break-up of Matilda's marriage. Although there is some evidence that Godfrey the Hunchback suggested a reconciliation about this point, Matilda did not take up the offer: the fact that Godfrey's sympathies were increasingly towards the imperial cause was hardly likely to endear him to her, in view of the Holy Father's beleaguered state. For was not Matilda, wife of Godfrey, by now happily transformed into Pope Gregory's hand-maid, and one 'distinguished by her excellence' (*egregia indolis puella*) in his own words?[15]

The Pope's excellent hand-maid was recommended to throw herself at the feet of the Blessed Virgin whom she would find more attentive than any human mother; frequent Holy Communion was suggested in order that Christ himself might nourish her. Matilda for her part declared herself as devoted to Gregory as Paul had been to Christ. While nothing in Gregory and Matilda's language – or indeed their respective characters – gives any credence whatsoever to the calumnies of their opponents concerning their carnal relationship, the intensity of the mission which they shared cannot be doubted. Matilda, a deeply religious woman, victim of an unhappy marriage, had found a far more satisfying role as the Pope's 'daughter Matilda'. Unlike anything more sinister, the paternal role which Pope Gregory played in Matilda's life – he was twenty-six years older than the Countess – does emerge very strongly through their correspondence.[16]

It was Matilda's good fortune that the love which she undoubtedly bore for Gregory, a love compounded of veneration and affection, was an emotion actually sanctified by the Church since it was the prescribed attitude of any pious Christian 'daughter' towards the

'Holy Father'. Writing of a period many many centuries before the emergence of psychoanalysis, it is fruitless and anachronistic to probe further into the sexual elements which may have lurked into this 'daughter's' passionate devotion to her 'father', since if they existed Matilda herself would have been quite unconscious of them. To make a more pagan allusion, however, Matilda's reporting of her military victories to Pope Gregory sometimes reminds one of Wagner's Brünnhilde reporting her triumphs to her godly father Wotan.

It was Anselm of Lucca, her spiritual adviser, who commented that Matilda combined the will and energy of a soldier with the mystic and solitary spirit of a hermit.[17] Fighting for the head of the Church gave an opportunity to fulfil both sides to her nature; marriage to Godfrey the Hunchback, on the contrary, not even solid in his support of the Papacy, gave her an opportunity to fulfil neither.

At all events 1076 was to be a dramatic year in Matilda's life, as well as in the fortunes of the Papacy. Matilda found a new independence: Godfrey was killed in Antwerp in February and her mother Beatrice died in April. Ironically enough the fact that Matilda's child (or children) by Godfrey had died in infancy added to this independence since Matilda had no male heir to challenge her position. At the same time the Emperor Henry moved against the Pontiff: at the Council of Worms in January 1076 he had renounced obedience to 'Hildebrand, now not Pope but false monk' and declared him deposed. Lastly, and most dramatically of all, Gregory employed the most powerful weapon at his own command in retaliation, a mighty one indeed, that of excommunication.

The terms worked out at Canossa were as follows: an excommunicated monarch – even an emperor – had twelve months in which to make penance; otherwise his subjects were absolved from all obedience to him and he himself forfeited all civil rights and stood to be deposed from every civil and political office (which meant that the Pope was in effect interfering with the political affairs of Germany, much as the Emperor's practice of lay investiture was now seen as interfering in Church affairs). Of course the practical consequences of such a ban depended very much upon the behaviour of those in a position to benefit from the possibilities of independence it offered: that is to say, the Emperor's vassals. When

Henry's Saxon subjects used the excuse to rise up in revolt again – for they had rebelled earlier – they made it unpleasantly clear what the consequences were likely to be, including the most hideous possibility of all, the election of another king of Germany. So, as Henry's other vassals began to fall away from him, the stage was set for that celebrated scene of political (and politic) repentance: at Canossa, Matilda's Apennine fortress, in January 1077.

The Pope was already on his way to Germany, for a consultation with the German princes, including bishops, at Augsburg, when the dramatic news of the Emperor's dash towards Italy across the Alps reached him. Such a journey from Rome to Germany – as the brutal events at Christmas 1075 will have made clear – could not have been made by the Pontiff without suitable armed escort, since Piedmont and Lombardy supported the Emperor. This escort was already provided by the troops of Matilda. The Emperor's action demanded a new schedule. The Countess probably came to join the Pope at Florence on about 28 December in order to ride with him personally to Canossa. The choice of this virtually impregnable fortress, lying in the heartland of Matilda's territory, was doubly significant. It symbolized not only security, essential in view of the still unknown intention of the Emperor, but also the powerful protection which Matilda herself was exerting, had exerted and would continue to exert towards the Holy Father.

Canossa stood – and its ruins still stand* – on a spur of the Apennines about twenty-five kilometres south-west of Reggio. On a clear day there you could see if not forever at least the rising cities of the Italian plain: Modena, Parma and even Mantua, as well as Reggio. Only one side of the fortress was remotely accessible and that was guarded by three walls; the rest was guarded by the terrain itself. The chaplain Donizo romantically referred to Canossa as a 'new Rome'; if an excess of praise, the description did at least convey that a proper little town existed within the fortress itself: domestics, animals, shopkeepers and men-at-arms jostling with the influx of mighty visitors.

'Lo, I possess at once the Pope, the King [Henry], Matilda, princes of Italy, of France and of those beyond the mountains. Those also of Rome, prelates, sages, venerables...'. In his bio-

---

* But only the foundations of Countess Matilda's fortress remain; the ruins above ground date at earliest from the thirteenth century.

graphical poem, Donizo had the fortress of Canossa itself chant this proud refrain.[18] Among the prelates present, to be listed also among the notables, was Hugh, the celebrated Abbot of Cluny, that Benedictine monastery in Burgundy which was one of the sources of the movement for the spiritual reform of the Church; he was accompanied by his secretary Odo, later as Pope Urban II to be Matilda's second guiding 'Holy Father'. Then there were the unhappy German clergy who by participating in the Council of Worms had risked anathema themselves; the Emperor's relations came also to ask for mercy.

Henry IV probably made his first stop at Matilda's outlying sentinel fortress of Bianello; there the Countess visited him, accompanied by Abbot Hugh. From his point of view, a quick absolution was essential if he was to shore up his political situation in Germany. The Emperor besought the intervention of both (Abbot Hugh had been made his godfather by Henry III) in order that he might be relieved at once of his excommunication. According to Donizo, the Emperor believed, and Abbot Hugh confirmed his belief, that Matilda's intercession was the best hope of melting the hard papal heart: 'Plead for me, cousin,* plead for my forgiveness with the Holy Father ... Go therefore to him, Oh! most valiant cousin and make him bless me again. Go! I beseech you!' (One notes that Matilda was not thought to have sacrificed the traditional intercessionary powers of a woman.)

There is some evidence that Matilda did intercede and also a suggestion that the Pope became irritated at her persistent efforts. No doubt, he preferred her practical exertions as the Pope's armed hand-maid to her enactment of the more traditional female role of mediator. An illustration to Donizo's *Vita Mathildis* shows an enormous Abbot Hugh (in a monk's robe and carrying a crozier) with a tiny Henry kneeling beneath him. The Emperor's supplication is clearly addressed to Matilda, shown medium-sized, and extending her own hand pleadingly on his behalf. Gregory did not in any case grant the Emperor the speedy relief he desired, sending messages instead regarding the forthcoming Council of Augsburg. So the Emperor's situation was not shored up, or not for the time being.

Instead, in the freezing weather – the winter of 1076/7 was

* Matilda was second cousin to Henry IV through her mother Beatrice of Lorraine.

exceptionally severe – the Emperor was obliged to stand barefoot in a coarse woollen penitential garb outside the gates of Canossa itself. Fasting for three days, from 25 to 27 January, there he stood during the hours of daylight, a visible symbol of imperial penitence. From time to time he knocked on the doors of the fortress and still he was not admitted. Inside Canossa the Pope, silent and as it seemed remorseless, remained in the imagination of the world as the invincible symbol of papal determination. To some he stood for more than that. The whole matter of the excommunication with its concomitant of interference in German affairs was to many minds dubious in canon law. 'This was not apostolic severity but rather the cruelty of a tyrant!' Gregory himself admitted in his subsequent account of the episode to the princes and bishops of Germany: 'he did not cease to implore with many tears the apostolic clemency' so that all present were found 'marvelling at our unusual hardness of heart'.[19] But outside Canossa, while still under ban, Henry for the time being had no choice but to persevere.

Finally on the fourth day, the shivering Emperor was allowed to throw himself at the Pope's feet and receive mercy. Even so, his absolution was in theory granted to him only as a man, not as a king: that would still have to wait for a conference at Augsburg. (Although the conference never took place, and Gregory did refer to Henry as king after Canossa.) It was undoubtedly at first sight a sensational victory for Gregory. For all that Henry did not keep his word regarding the notorious investitures – strife between Pope and Emperor persisted well into the next century – he had at least been obliged to bow his neck to the Pope's authority on this single most celebrated occasion. The Emperor had in short 'come to Canossa' and so that famous phrase signifying the recantation of a previous proudly held position, for humbling oneself on a grand scale, was born.

Furthermore, Canossa, where it all happened, was the stronghold not of a prince or bishop, but of a woman. (No wonder that Canossa with its infinite possibilities of defence was the favourite residence of Matilda.) This extra bit of symbolism concerning Canossa's female ownership is however generally missing from the catchphrase which has come down to us.

The practical triumph of Pope Gregory was short-lived. The last years of his life were spent in an unenviable series of confrontations with the Emperor, ending with Gregory's death in exile at Salerno while an anti-pope, Clement III, Henry's nominee, occupied St Peter's. Civil war in Germany – where the princes persisted in electing a new king in Rudolf of Swabia despite the lifting of the ban on Henry – occupied the Emperor until 1080. After that Rudolf's death in battle freed him to return across the Alps to Italy and, after ravaging the north, besiege Rome itself. Here, with William I of England and Philip of France carefully neutral, Matilda was, as Donizo put it, the only soldier of St Peter left.[20]

Nor had her own affairs prospered since Canossa. The rising Tuscan cities, in particular Lucca, were beginning to desert her cause – since the townsmen, wanting independence, regarded the hereditary ruler of Tuscany as their natural foe. On his return Henry marched on Lucca, had Matilda judged guilty of high treason for refusing feudal allegiance to him, and placed her under the ban of empire which meant that all her goods were confiscated. On the papal side there was nothing but praise for the sturdiness with which Matilda met the fate which her loyalties to the Holy Father had brought about. Anselm of Lucca, the Pope's Vicar in Lombardy, praised the heroic Countess for amassing 'eternal treasure in heaven' by her efforts, confident that she would 'fight with her blood' until God delivered over his enemy (Henry) 'into the hands of a woman'. But the fact was that Matilda's earthly treasure was fast diminishing as a result of her ceaseless campaigns, a fact recognized by Pope Gregory when he pleaded for assistance for 'our daughter Matilda ... otherwise she will be forced to make peace with Henry or lose all her possessions'. By the spring of 1082, Matilda's finances were in ruins, and much of the gold and silver in the treasury at Canossa had to be melted down to remedy them. Yet still, according to Rangerius, Matilda feared neither dark nor cold and nothing separated her from her soldiers. Nor did she retreat into neutrality.[21]

Matilda's military triumph at Sorbara in July 1084 was a bright spark in the increasing gloom of the papal fortunes. At Easter the anti-Pope Clement III had crowned Henry at Rome, with Pope Gregory held in the Holy City. Subsequently the Norman leader Robert Guiscard liberated Gregory and took him back with him to Salerno where he died the next year; Robert Guiscard also sacked the Holy City, causing the Emperor to flee. North of Rome however

Henry's allies continued to harry Matilda's possessions: her castle of Sorbara, on the plain about fifteen kilometres north-east of Modena, seemed an ideal target to invest because of its accessibility compared to, for example, Canossa. Matilda retaliated with a surprise attack late at night when the enemy soldiers were asleep; the celebrated war-cry 'For St Peter and Matilda!' rang out as Matilda personally led her small force to victory. According to tradition, she carried the 'terrible sword of Boniface' (i.e. her father's sword) as she massacred the enemy, standing in her stirrups before her troops.[22] Militarily, one Sorbara did not make a summer, however satisfying to Matilda. The Emperor Henry continued to ravage her possessions.

It is indeed the stoical resistance of Matilda to the idea of making peace with Henry, because it necessitated recognizing the anti-Pope Clement III, which compels admiration over the next fifteen years of her life. As the champion of St Peter, she tried in vain to persuade Gregory's short-lived successor Pope Victor to take up residence in Rome; then the succession of Odo, the former prior of Cluny, as Urban II in 1088 brought about the second great partnership of Holy Father and armed daughter.

It was Pope Urban who, in the need for allies, recognized that Matilda's theoretical marriageability must be employed once more in the cause of Christ. In 1089 the forty-three-year-old Matilda was married to the seventeen-year-old Welf v of Bavaria, thus introducing Bavaria into the papal alliance. The fury with which Henry IV greeted the match demonstrates the success of the move on the political level. In the case of the participants, Matilda's personal reluctance was probably equalled by that of the youthful Welf: some six years later he separated from his masterful bride, his senior by a whole generation, tired of her dominance in the cause of papal politics. As for Matilda, various suitors had been mentioned for her hand over the years since Godfrey the Hunchback's death, without conclusion; it was significant that her second marriage was not only arranged by the Pope, but arranged for the benefit of his cause. To that kind of marriage, Matilda could agree.

There was a moment after Henry had taken Mantua in 1091, followed by Ferrara and other important Italian cities, when peace was once more proposed with Tuscany's *gran Contessa*: if only she would acknowledge Guibert of Ravenna as Pope Clement III. There were by now many who begged her to accede. 'You have struggled long enough, oh! most valiant lady, you and your serene consort, to uphold the dignity of the Pontificate.' Matilda's reaction can however be most closely gauged by an outburst at the same council of war, held in the Apennines, by one Hermit John: 'Are you not that Matilda who glories in the title of daughter of Peter? ... What sort of peace can be made with the impious?'[23] No peace was made.

It took a series of deaths, marking the passing of a whole generation who had lived most of their lives entrenched in conflict, to pave the way for Matilda's comparatively serene old age. Pope Urban II died in 1099 and the anti-Pope Clement III in 1100. Lastly the death of Matilda's old enemy Henry IV in 1106 ushered in a new era. The Concordat of Worms of 1122 – a compromise by which a clear distinction was made between a prelate's position as a landed vassal of the crown and his spiritual office – was hammered out towards the end of the reign of his son and successor Henry V.

A new age was dawning in more senses than one. Matilda continued to regard the struggles of the Italian cities for independence as part of her own struggle to establish a free Papacy. She had been born too soon or had spent too much of her life in conflict to understand that as the commercial importance of Pisa and Lucca developed, this was a phenomenon in its own right.[24] And yet as a governor she was far from being naturally despotic: she patronized jurists such as Ubaldo da Carpineti and Irnerius. One has the sad impression that Matilda's long fights with the Empire, while granting her her reputation in the pantheon of Warrior Queens, actually robbed Tuscany of the possibility of strong, intelligent and benevolent female rule over thirty years.

The new Emperor Henry treated Matilda, towards the end of her life, courteously. He called upon her at Bianello, the sentinel fortress of Canossa, where once his father had set off to shiver in the snow, 'swearing in the whole earth there could not be found a Princess her equal'. But Matilda, as her health failed, spent more and more time at Polirone, a Benedictine monastery near Mantua founded by her grandfather. (Although when there was an uprising in the city of Mantua in 1114, this gallant old lady still threatened to command an army against the unruly townsfolk.) Polirone had been the first northern Italian monastery to accept the reformed Cluniac rule: both Anselm of Lucca and Matilda's second spiritual adviser Bernard of

Vallombrosa had been monks at Polirone. The illuminated so-called Matildine Gospels presented by the Countess to Polirone (now in New York, in the Pierpont Morgan Library) commemorate not only her generosity towards the monastery, but also, in the nature of their illustrations, those spiritual sympathies which Pope Gregory and Pope Urban had inculcated.[25]

It was at Polirone that Matilda died on 15 July 1115, in her seventieth year, leaving Donizo (his biographical poem unpresented) to repine, 'Now that thou art dead, oh great Matilda, the honour and dignity of Italy will decline.' It is however a curious postscript to the life of Matilda that her testamentary dispositions brought about considerable trouble – for the Emperor Henry v and also for the Pope. The Countess, childless if not virgin, left no direct heir since with her own death her family died out. Thus in two separate wills of 1077 and 1102 Matilda had transferred all her allodial property – that is, the Canossa inheritance, not within the feudal structure of the Empire – to the chair of St Peter. After peace was made with Henry v, Matilda willed her feudally held possessions back to him, although Henry seized the opportunity to claim the whole of her territories. This left the Pope, at the next moment of strength, to claim Matilda's allodial property in his turn. Ironically enough, even in death Matilda, the Warrior Queen in the course of peace, had not brought about that tranquillity between Emperor and Pope which she so ardently desired for the sake of the Holy Father.

Countess Matilda was originally buried at the monastery but in the seventeenth century her body was transported to St Peter's, surely the appropriate resting-place for her who had been the Pope's 'hand-maid'. Certainly the 'daughter of Peter' would have been a more comforting title in death to the Countess herself than that allusion to Penthesilea inscribed on her original tomb. The first of the three Latin inscriptions contained this passage: 'This warrior–woman disposed her troops as the Amazonian Penthesilea is accustomed to do. Thanks to her – through so many contests of horrid war – man was never able to conquer the rights of God.'[26] And yet, whatever the pious Matilda's reactions, there remained the need to compare one Warrior Queen to another, for verification as it were, however far-fetched the comparison.

Anselm of Lucca himself, in her lifetime, compared Matilda to the Amazonian Queen; he also compared her to the Queen of Sheba.[27] Where Matilda was concerned, however, Anselm was careful to add that 'the garb of a Penthesilea' hid 'the messenger of mercy'. That is, on the judgement seat, God would see in Matilda not the stern avenger of crime but rather the compassionate mother of the feeble and oppressed. For another perceived need was to prevent Matilda losing her proper femininity due to her military command. Matilda's latter-day reputation includes a possible tribute from Dante in the *Purgatorio*: the 'Lady Beautiful' encountered beside the waters of Lethe, who draws him through its drenching waves to the blessed shore, is named Matilda (although there are other more likely claimants for the poet's inspiration). A more valiant and thus more verisimilitudinous picture emerges from Tasso in *Jerusalem Delivered*:

> With manlike vigour shone her noble look,
> And more than manlike wrath her face o'erspread...
> Henry the Fourth she beat, and from him took
> His standard, and in Church it offered
> Which done, the Pope back to the Vatican
> She brought, and placed in Peter's chair again.[28]

In general, however, the many tributes to Matilda both in her lifetime and afterwards, down to the twentieth-century biographies of the Countess, are careful to stress the compassionate side of her nature. Like Boadicea, she is excused the final responsibilities for her actions and their consequences by her sex. At Sorbara, for example, the warrior maid with the 'terrible sword of Boniface' raised above her head was also depicted as begging a halt to the slaughter once the fortress was surprised: slaughter, it could be plausibly argued, that she herself had initiated. 'Her heart did not grow hard – she cared for the sick, nursed the wounded, made bandages and dressings, prepared and distributed food, and nourished and clothed the destitute, dispossessed by the German scourge.' So runs a hagiographical modern life of Matilda, published in Italy in 1937.[29]

The judgement delivered by Leone Tondelli in his classic modern biography of Matilda, which has run through many revised editions since its first publication in 1915, is on firmer ground; for throughout it stresses the religious inspiration which not only supported Matilda in her 'so many contests of horrid war', but also justified her participation in them to her contemporaries.[30] The Countess Matilda, wrote Tondelli, was 'a heroine of Christian Italy'. Her whole life constituted 'luminous proof' that if a Christian upbringing tends, with 'modest self-effacement, self-reflection and a mystical union with God, to elevate and refine the spirit', it nevertheless does not take away vigour in action. Most significantly of all, it is to Matilda's 'Christian upbringing' that Tondelli ascribes that martial ability so uncharacteristic of her sex. In moments of need, Tondelli continues, such an upbringing can suggest 'even to a woman's heart the heroism of chivalry and it can mould the female soul – usually rich in generosity but little resistant to long-lasting tests' – shades here of Gibbon and Mommsen on the subject of Zenobia – 'into an indomitable constancy'. One feels that that is a judgement with which the *gran Contessa* herself – 'Matilda by the Grace of God or she is nothing' – would have agreed.

CHAPTER TEN

ENGLAND'S
DOMINA

On bier lay King Henry
On bier beyond the sea,
And no man might rightly know
Who his heir should be.

Piers of Langtoft on the death of Henry I (1135)

In 1114, the year before the death of the *gran Contessa* Matilda of
Tuscany, there took place the May-and-December marriage of an
English princess to the German Emperor Henry v. The girl herself,
who was variously known as Matilda or Maud (but owing to the
plethora of Matildas in this period, will be here generally described
as Maud), was a mere twelve years old, having been betrothed and
sent to Germany four years before.[1] Her bridegroom, nearly twenty
years older, was a veteran of many a military campaign and military
struggle. He had taken part in the prolonged investiture arguments
with the Pope, and had actually enforced the abdication of his father
Henry iv, scourge of the Countess Matilda, before his death in 1106.

At the time it hardly seemed likely that the young Empress Maud,
or Matilda Augusta, daughter of King Henry i of England, would
be called upon to take to the field of battle; but perhaps the unlikely
nature of their destiny is one of the few things that all the Warrior
Queens outside the antique days have in common. Her married life
with the Emperor Henry v was as it turned out comparatively brief
in a long and eventful life: he died in 1125. Nevertheless Maud's
youth at the moment of her transference from the royal English

court of her powerful Norman father to the imperial court of Germany ensured that these were formative years. The Emperor sent away her English attendants – there were to be no Scottish Maries, as would escort the infant Mary Queen of Scots to France – and he had Maud carefully instructed in the German language and customs.

Some of the apparent haughtiness of which, as we shall see, the Empress Maud was to be later accused must have sprung from these early experiences, working upon a naturally strong character. (It is noteworthy indeed how many of the female descendants of William the Conqueror show a vigour and even guts worthy of their great progenitor, starting with his strong-minded and intelligent daughter Adela of Blois.) Here was a girl who was crowned in Germany before she was in her teens and whose official title was 'Queen of the Romans'. Yet at the time, Maud, having a natural outlet for her energies by contemporary standards for females, in her position as consort to the Emperor, secured nothing but golden opinions. To her German subjects, she was 'the good Matilda'; a description which would have had an ironic ring to many of those English upon whom she attempted to lay her rule, in the course of her prolonged martial dispute for the crown with her cousin Stephen during that English period known as the Anarchy.

It was the death of Maud's brother William in 1120, drowned in the tragedy of the White Ship, which brought about the first stage in her transformation. The Empress Maud was now the only surviving legitimate child of Henry I since Henry's second marriage to Adeliza of Louvain was to be childless (although he was to have more than twenty bastards). The death of Maud's husband, the Emperor Henry, leaving her also childless and thus without stake in Germany, brought about the second stage. The Empress now returned to the court of her father, and Henry now set about making Maud his heiress with all the considerable energies still at the forceful old King's command.

Maud had been well fitted to her imperial role, not only by her dignity and her benevolence but also by her beauty, to which all contemporary chroniclers, English and French as well as German, bear witness.[2] But as to her new role as heiress to the throne, no one knew what the qualities were which might fit her for that, since there had been no queen regnant in England within historical memory – or at least not indisputably so.

What precedents were there for a female ruler? There were some but Boadicea was not among them. It has been mentioned in the previous chapter that the name of Boadicea had vanished from the written records in England and would not reappear for several hundred years (we cannot of course know about folklore). It is true that Gildas, the sixth-century monk who defended Roman Britain, in order to excoriate against the degraded rulers of his own day offered his own version of the events of the British revolt five hundred years earlier.[3] It was not a flattering one. He did not name the war leader of the Iceni, but termed her 'that deceitful lioness, who put to death the rulers they [the Romans] had left in Britain, to unfold more fully and to complete the enterprise of the Romans'. Nor did Gildas allow those 'crafty foxes', the Britons, any credit for the courage of their attack, or for their bravery against the Roman counterattack; on the contrary he described them as having 'offered their necks to the sword and stretched out their hands, like women, to be bound'. This double insult both to the Britons and to the sex which had produced Boadicea was, as we have seen, also historically quite inaccurate. Bede and Nennius both referred briefly to the revolt without mentioning Boadicea or indeed any ruler of either sex.[4]

Negative evidence for the disappearance of Boadicea is indeed provided by the fact that Geoffrey of Monmouth, who discusses the claims of Maud to her father's throne at length, does not mention the British Queen; while he does produce numerous historical instances of reigning women. For although knowledge of Boadicea might have disappeared on a literary level, history pointed to the fact that the instinct for bellicosity in the female sex had not: where there was a need or, as some might say, an opportunity for 'severe womanhood' to exercise its powers.

The phrase is that of Ruskin, gazing in excited awe at Botticelli's portrait of the biblical Judith in the nineteenth century, and calling her 'not merely the Jewish Dalilah to the Assyrian Samson, but the mightiest, purest, brightest type of high passion' into the bargain, displaying 'the purity ... and severity of a guardian angel'.[5] A thousand years earlier, the militant character of contemporary Judiths had caused no revulsion. The best-known example of a female exercising power before the time of Maud was King Alfred's eldest daughter Aethelflaed (or Ethelfleda), whose marriage to Aethelred, earlderman of the Mercians, led to the completion of the union of Wessex and Mercia under the West Saxon kings.

Aethelflaed, born about 870 and dying in 918, was generally known as the Lady of the Mercians rather than Queen (although the *Annales Cambriae* referred to her as *Regina* at her death). Whatever her title Aethelflaed seems to have held joint authority with her husband during his lifetime, profiting from his illness and subsequent death to assume sole control; her numerous campaigns against the Danes and the Norse included leading her troops personally to victory at Derby. In an interesting variant of the Chaste Syndrome – carrying the alleged policy of Zenobia one stage further – Aethelflaed was said by William of Malmesbury to have abandoned marital relations altogether after the birth of her only child, a girl. The risk of childbirth was too great, and, she declared, 'it was unbecoming the daughter of a king to give way to a delight, which after a time produced such painful consequences'.[6] It is this Lady of the Mercians who probably inspired the tenth-century Old English poem *Judith*.[7]

In this poem, Judith's 'severe womanhood' is treated with a respect worthy of Ruskin: Judith herself is 'white and shining', 'noble and courageous'. The poem also quite ignores the fact that the biblical Judith was actually a widow (of Manasses) in order to concentrate throughout on her virginity: 'wise Judith' is 'the noble Maid', 'the holy virgin' who has been led to the pavilion of Holofernes. Here, where Holofernes 'thought to stain the radiant woman with pollution and foulness', Judith was in principle saved by her belief and her trust in God. In practice 'the creator's handmaiden with curling tresses', the 'valorous virgin' was equipped with a gleaming sword with which she struck off the head of the hostile foe: 'Judith ascribed the glory of all that to the Lord of Hosts'.[8]

As with the life of the Countess Matilda of Tuscany in the following century, there is a perceived connection between the 'purity' of Judith and her severity: the former makes the latter admirable. But it is finally religion, Christianity in the case of Countess Matilda (or some other cause holy to its advocates, that of the goddess Andraste for example), which exercises a benediction over what might otherwise be deemed unsuitable female activity. This becomes relevant in the case of the Empress Maud, who in her claim to the English throne was the recipient of no such healing benediction. No 'holy' war-cry as, for example, 'For St Peter and Matilda!' was appropriate to the lips of her followers: Maud's cause was that of a royal person, who happened to be a woman, asserting a superior right to the throne by force. Being part of the Appendage Syndrome did not save her at a time when she needed in fact to pose as a Holy (Armed) Figurehead. The result was a charge of overweening arrogance on the part of the daughter of Henry I, which the Pope's 'daughter Matilda' never had to sustain.

The ten years between the death of Maud's husband and that of her father were stamped by the energy with which Henry I, now in his late fifties, prosecuted her cause as his heiress. This vigorous campaign was necessary, not only in view of the questionable status – at best – of a female ruler, but also because of the threat posed by an alternative male heir. At this point one must bear in mind the ramifications of the Norman dynasty founded by the Conqueror. Countess Matilda of Tuscany had inherited the lands of the Margrave Boniface as a girl after the deaths of her siblings with the aid of a powerful stepfather to uphold her rights; it was also important that there were no immediate rivals in her family circle (as we have seen, the line came to an end with her own childless death). Maud's situation was very different.

A number of elements went into the making of a king at this period and it could be argued that the most important of all was the king's demonstrable ability to occupy the throne:[9] forcible seizure of it being one good way of demonstrating this ability. Certainly male primogeniture itself – the right of the heir male to succeed in all circumstances – did not apply. Henry I himself was the third son of William the Conqueror and had succeeded the Conqueror's second son, William Rufus, as King of England; he then wrested the other part of the inheritance, Normandy, from the Conqueror's eldest son Robert Curthose. The heir male to the Conqueror's line was undoubtedly Robert Curthose's son William Clito; but Henry I did not acknowledge his claims any more than he had respected those of his father.

If male primogeniture, strictly speaking, did not apply, blood itself was not to be ignored, otherwise Maud – 'Matilda the Empress, daughter of King Henry' as she liked to term herself, a neat exposition of the Appendage Syndrome – would not have entered the picture in the first place. Henry's own marriage to the daughter of Malcolm Canmore, King of Scotland, had been an acknowledgement of the power of blood. For his wife's mother, St Margaret, a great-niece of Edward the Confessor, had been herself a member of the English (Wessex) royal house, 'the true royal family of England' in the words of the *Anglo-Saxon Chronicle*.[10]

There was however a veil – almost literally so – around this 'true royal' marriage since as a girl the Scottish Princess had been brought up in a convent. A seventeenth-century biography of St Margaret phrased it most romantically: the saint's daughter came 'out of the Monastery' to marry Henry 'as a fair star, dispelling by her rays the cloud that had obscured, and hid her for some time from the eyes of man'.[11] But if the Scottish Princess had actually taken vows as a nun, then these vows, less romantically, would have rendered her subsequent marriage vows void. It does not seem that this was so; nevertheless it was an argument which the enemies of her daughter Maud would use against the latter's legitimacy.[12]

Meanwhile there was another strong candidate for the English throne: Stephen of Blois, son of Henry's sister Adela, who had been brought up at his uncle's English court. (But again, like his royal uncle, he was not the eldest son of the family.) In the five years between the deaths of Henry's son and Maud's husband, it may have occurred to Henry to make Stephen his heir; at all events he arranged a significant marriage for him to the heiress Matilda of Boulogne. This Matilda could also claim descent from 'the true royal family of England', her mother being Mary of Scotland, another daughter to St Margaret and Malcolm Canmore.*

Now the widowhood of the Empress Maud meant that, in one of those swift dynastic transformations, Henry's only daughter became instantly marriageable; the joyful possibility of the continuance of his own line loomed before him. The King's first step was to impose an oath of fealty on his *Curia Regis* – his council of nobles and ecclesiastics. On Christmas Day 1125 they swore to acknowledge Maud – Matilda Augusta – as 'lady of England and Normandy'. The oath emphasized the double nature of her claim;

---

* Thus Matilda of Boulogne and her husband Stephen were both first cousins to the Empress Maud (but not to each other); Matilda through Maud's mother and Stephen through Maud's father.

both Norman and English. To her alone 'the legitimate succession belonged from her grandfather, uncle and father who were kings as well as from her maternal descent for many ages back'. The question of Maud's next match was clearly crucial. In his turn, according to William of Malmesbury, the King promised not to give her away outside England, except by the counsel of the magnates.[13] In the event neither promise was kept, King Henry being the first to break his word. A second oath of fealty was sworn at Northampton in 1127. But then to her own great reluctance, and to the disgust of the young gentleman concerned, Maud was despatched to Anjou to wed the Count's teenage son, Geoffrey.

Part of the importance of Anjou to Henry was geographical: it lay next door to Normandy and the King feared its counts; so coolly Henry bought off Angevin pressure with his daughter's hand. At the same time, the King may also have had his eyes on his son-in-law as his successor, an effective co-ruler with Maud. But from her point of view, to be Countess of Anjou was hardly a distinguished position for one who had been Empress of Germany, and was born a Princess of England. Nor was the ten-year gap between the ages of the bride and bridegroom a good omen for this marriage of state. Maud, having been married to a veteran statesman as a child, was now linked to a boy. Understandably she resented her altered status, life in this petty countdom; there was an initial separation. The couple were however reunited, and reunited most successfully in dynastic terms; for Maud produced two sons before her father's death in 1135 (and one more in 1136). Whatever Henry's intentions towards Geoffrey, the ultimate prospect of a male succession obviously bolstered Maud's position as heiress: the eldest of these sons – the future Henry II, known then as 'Henry FitzEmpress' – was included in the third oath of fealty sworn to Maud. But Maud was not present at her father's deathbed in Normandy; although he had in fact renewed his disposition of his crown to his daughter, her absence gave her enemies the opportunity to pretend afterwards that he had disinherited her.[14]

The immediate situation on Henry I's death was summed up by a rhyme of Piers of Langtoft:

> On bier lay King Henry
> On bier beyond the sea,

And no man might rightly know
Who his heir should be.[15]

Then a *coup d'état* by Stephen, resulting in his coronation in Westminster Abbey at the end of 1135, made it clear who that heir might rightly be – at least for the time being. As for the Archbishop of Canterbury, who crowned him, he absolved the nobles from their oaths of fealty to Maud on grounds of duress.

In the contest for the succession which followed, personalities as well as rights became of importance, particularly in view of the nebulous aura surrounding those of the female. The husband was very likely to exercise those rights, as Stephen ruled Boulogne in right of his heiress wife Matilda. Henry I had not allowed Geoffrey of Anjou and Maud to build up what has been described as 'some kind of power base' in either England or Normandy, despite his wish for his daughter's succession.[16] One possible solution to the English succession was to make the infant Henry FitzEmpress king; but this had the disadvantage, from the point of view of the English and Norman baronage, of making Geoffrey as well as Maud regent.

Stephen of Blois on the other hand, five years older than his cousin Maud, was not only reputedly the handsomest man in Europe, but also 'unassuming, generous and courteous' in the words of the *Gesta Stephani*, 'a thing acknowledged to be very uncommon among the rich of the present day'. Maud's supporter William of Malmesbury gave the same picture: 'by his good nature and the way that he sat and ate in the company of even the humblest', he wrote, Stephen 'earned an affection that can hardly be imagined'. Events would show a lack of iron in this agreeable soul: Stephen was 'kind as far as promise went, but sure to disappoint in its truth and execution'.[17] At the date of his *coup d'état*, however, Stephen could well be regarded, in contrast to unsuitable female Maud, as the ideal of the (male) monarch.

As time went on, a further comparison would be made between Stephen's wife, Queen Matilda, and her first cousin, the Empress Maud. Queen Matilda was another of those public women, intelligent and capable, with whom this early mediaeval period abounds. (Queen Matilda, like her cousin Maud, was also beautiful.) In Norman England, female capability was not infrequently tested when ladies had to hold castles against siege in their husbands' absence, as the Countess of Norfolk had held Norwich in 1075. During the long battling years of the Anarchy, other women would come forward and perform a similar service, as the situation demanded it. Matilda of Ramsbury for example, mistress of Bishop Roger of Salisbury and mother of his children, commanded the Bishop's castle of Devizes.[18]

Like the Empress Maud, Queen Matilda conducted sieges and defended castles. She first appeared in the field in 1136 and received the surrender of Derby. But there was one obvious difference between the respective images which the two women presented to the world. Queen Matilda was acting on behalf of her husband and her young son Eustace, Stephen's heir; the Empress Maud – 'Matilda daughter of Henry' – was basing her right on her father, but claiming it for herself. Just as Countess Matilda of Tuscany had a perfectly valid excuse to ride to battle, so did Queen Matilda of England; she could conduct herself as a Warrior Queen, unlike the Empress, without losing her notional femininity or being exposed to accusations of arrogance.

The comparison between Maud and Matilda reached its apogee in the nineteenth century in the reign of Queen Victoria with Agnes Strickland's well-researched *Lives of the Queens of England*, which built on the presence of another queen upon the throne. The author dedicated this massive work by permission to Queen Victoria, quoting those words of Tacitus concerning Boadicea's leadership, 'they do not discriminate against women in matters of military command', and adding a phrase from Boadicea's own speech: 'We British are used to women commanders in war.' Agnes Strickland hereby explained that Queen Victoria ruled 'not only by rightful inheritance and the consent of the people, but also in full accordance with the ancient British custom'. But a few chapters further on, Agnes Strickland is praising 'the good Queen Matilda whose feminine virtues, endearing qualities and conjugal devotion ... created the most powerful interest in her favour' compared to 'reports of the pride and hardness of heart of her stern relative and namesake' (Maud). Above all, with a sublime unawareness of any possible irony involved, Agnes Strickland commended Queen Matilda for avoiding 'all Amazonian display by acting under the name of her son'.[19] (It was not an example that Queen Victoria inclined to follow with the future Edward VII.)

. . .

In his *Historia Regum Britanniae* Geoffrey of Monmouth was (as has been noted) concerned to dredge forth numerous examples of female sovereignty in Britain's remote past. In his version of the story of King Lear, for example, the King's youngest daughter Cordelia reigned in Britain after the death of her father and husband: 'And Cordelia, now mistress of the helm of State in Britain ... governed the kingdom in peace...'. That is, until her sisters' sons rose up and 'took it in high dudgeon that Britain should be subject to the rule of a woman'. (He may have based the story on the adventures of an actual queen of Central Gaul.)[20] But as a matter of fact a queen regnant was not literally unknown in Europe at this period.

Queen Urraca of Aragon, who belonged to the generation older than Maud (she was born about 1080 and died in 1126), managed to maintain her sway successfully over an enormous tract of territory in Spain (as did her half-sister Teresa later in Portugal). Urraca was a twenty-seven-year-old widow, with two infant sons, when the death of her father resulted in her succession to his kingdom of León-Castile. Thirteen of her seventeen years as queen were in fact to be spent campaigning against her boorish second husband, a king of Aragon with the discouraging name (to an estranged wife) of Alfonso the Battler.

Among Urraca's qualities however was an ability to manage the system in which she found herself. It used to be thought that Urraca's policy decisions were the result of the advice of her supporter Bernard Archbishop of Toledo or of her lover the Count of Lara (Urraca's reputation as a Warrior Queen formed part of the Voracity Syndrome: she too was no Holy Figurehead). A recent study has however suggested that it was the Queen herself, on the available evidence, who was very much in control.[21] In particular she showed herself adept at managing the question of her son's – and heir's – rights, calling him to her aid by having him crowned with her at exactly the right psychological moment.

With Geoffrey of Anjou as a husband, this was not a solution which could immediately present itself to the Empress Maud. Significantly, it was in King Stephen's acknowledgement of Henry FitzEmpress as his heir (following the fortuitous death of his own son Eustace in 1153) that the whole grisly matter of the Anarchy and the English succession was to be finally settled. That, however, in September 1139 when the Empress Maud landed on the south coast of England in pursuit of her claim, was more than a decade and many a battle away.

Joining forces with her stepmother, Henry I's widowed Queen Adeliza, Maud first held Arundel Castle against Stephen's besieging forces. At this point, in one of those odd twists in the lives of Warrior Queens, as when Zenobia managed to avoid execution on grounds of feminine irresponsibility, Maud's sex told in her favour. For Stephen, reluctant to be seen besieging two high-born and presumably gentle ladies, allowed Maud to depart in order to join her loyal ally and half-brother (one of her father's numerous bastards) Robert of Gloucester in the west. The Empress herself on the other hand displayed no such 'female' clemency when shortly afterwards the tide turned in her favour with the aid of the western barons. In February 1141 Stephen was captured. Maud, unmoved by the pleas of Queen Matilda and her son, sent him in chains to Bristol Castle.

The Empress now made a triumphant entry into Winchester, having assured its bishop Henry of Blois (one of Stephen's brothers) that if he would join her she would make him chief among her counsellors, otherwise she would 'lead all the host of England against him at once'. Bishop Henry accepted this offer that he could hardly refuse. At Winchester, Maud was duly acknowledged 'Lady of the English' (*Domina Anglorum*). The new Domina was not at this point additionally claiming the title of queen: or not generally so. *Domina Anglorum* was her style on the charters and of the two charters extant in which she is termed *Regina Anglorum*, one is described as 'probably spurious'.[22]

It was not customary to employ the style of queen before coronation: it may be however that Maud did anticipate the style in an occasional charter out of impatience and a need to underline her authority. If so, this merely emphasized the fact that Maud's coronation was of particular consequence both to her and to her supporters since her rival Stephen had of course already been crowned more than five years before. He thus enjoyed the sacramental benefit of an anointed king. At midsummer 1141 Maud, Domina as well as Empress, moved on to London, took up residence at Westminster and prepared to be crowned at its Abbey in her turn.

Unfortunately for Maud's cause, Domina never was to be

transformed officially into Regina. For the rest of the years of her conflict with Stephen, Maud had to endure the fact that, unlike herself, Stephen had received his crown at the hands of the Archbishop of Canterbury. This was no small advantage in this period when an ill-defined notion of kingship jostled with respect for the Church, a respect that the Church for one was keen to see maintained. (Repeated appeals to the Pope to ratify their claims were to be made by both contestants for the throne.) As it was, an uprising by the Londoners, incensed by Maud's new financial exactions, caused her to flee precipitately to Oxford. Significantly in the context of the Warrior Queen, criticisms were uttered of the very voice in which these exactions were set out: 'she sent for the richest men and demanded from them a huge sum of money, not with unassuming gentleness, but with a voice of authority'. And at the richest men's refusal 'her forehead wrinkled with a frown, every trace of a woman's gentleness removed'. With hindsight, one may wonder whether the most dulcet and submissive tone would actually have persuaded the citizens to part with their wealth – and whether Maud's lack of 'a woman's gentleness' did not merely provide an excellent additional excuse for not doing so. Nevertheless the check to her fortunes was severe. Maud now ran from the very banquet – 'a well-cooked feast' – arranged on the eve of her coronation, as the enraged Londoners poured forth 'like thronging swarms from beehives'.[23]

At the same time Maud no less than Stephen was showing herself incapable of handling the restlessly self-seeking baronage of England, who took advantage of the prevalent Anarchy to demand grants of land and other favours from each side in turn. It is to this period that the many accusations of Maud's arrogance and intractable temper belong: 'arbitrary and headstrong in all she did ... mightily puffed up and exalted in spirit' are some of the phrases used. Certainly it was foolish – to say the least of it – for Maud to cancel the grants made by Stephen; by confiscations on an even greater scale than his, including the lands of the Church (which had hoped for better things), Maud hardly endeared herself.

It is notable that if Maud the woman was accused of being too harsh, Stephen the man was accused of being too soft. Both reproaches may well have been justified, but of course both reproaches were also in truth politically useful to batter away at the central royal authority, whoever was deemed to hold it. As for Maud, it could be argued that she was in an impossible position. On the one hand the fighting blood of the Conqueror and of the Saxon kings was said to flow in her veins, justifying her original claim to the throne despite her sex. On the other hand, if she tried to display herself as the strong monarch the situation demanded – for which this fighting blood certainly had equipped her – she was immediately accused of being proud and domineering. Any signs of royal strong-mindedness in Maud had a propaganda value for her enemies, just because she was a woman.

As it was one may doubt that either Maud or Stephen or indeed any other monarch alive in this period threatened by a disputed succession, possessed the requisite qualities to bring peace to a land now so beset by horrifying violence of all sorts. In the words of the *Anglo-Saxon Chronicle*, it 'was said openly that Christ and his saints were asleep'.[24]

Thereafter the cause of the imprisoned Stephen began to wax again in the hands of his wife, the 'good' Queen Matilda. In September Maud found herself blockaded within Winchester, once the scene of her triumph, by 'the King's Queen', as Stephen's Matilda was known in a contemporary attempt at clarity, 'with all her strength'.[25] Maud broke out with her vanguard, but after heavy losses, had to flee as far as Devizes with only one follower. Here Maud resorted to an even more desperate expedient to escape. Still in terror of pursuit and rightly recognizing the all-importance of her personal safety to her own side (remembering the blow which Stephen's imprisonment had dealt to his) Maud embarked on a macabre masquerade. It was dressed as a corpse, in 'grave clothes' and roped to a bier, that Maud, once Empress of Germany, was finally carried into the secure town of Gloucester.

Despite Maud's daring escape, the deathblow to her hopes in England had probably been dealt on this same occasion of the break-out from Winchester. This was because her ever-loyal half-brother Robert of Gloucester, while covering for her escape, fell captive to the Queen. A bargain was now possible to secure Stephen's liberty. One prominent prisoner being exchanged for the other, King Stephen was finally set free on 1 November. Naturally his re-emergence gave a new impetus to his supporters. An appeal by Maud to Geoffrey of Anjou for help had to be made in person by

Robert of Gloucester — at Geoffrey's insistence. And then, busy with his Norman invasion, the Count of Anjou merely sent his eldest son Henry as a pledge of support. Maud herself was once more blockaded and besieged, this time by Stephen, and within her own headquarters of Oxford.

As the autumn of 1142 passed, Maud and her supporters were brought to the brink of starvation; high hopes were raised of the Empress's capture. But just before Christmas, in another daring coup, Maud once more eluded her would-be captors. Thick snow blanketed the city and its environs; the surrounding river was frozen. Dressed all in white, with similarly white-clad attendants, Maud stole out of a small postern gate of Oxford Castle on to the surface of the icebound Thames. Noiselessly and in their white garments virtually invisible, Maud's party were able to pass through Stephen's pickets, which were 'everywhere ... breaking the silence of the night with the blaring of trumpets or the cries of men shouting loudly', like so many ghosts. No sentinel challenged them. The royal party then made its way on foot across the snowy wastes to Abingdon, some six miles away, before riding onwards — Maud 'in the male fashion', that is astride. By daybreak, Maud and her attendants had reached Wallingford and safety.

Agnes Strickland ascribes this escape with an air of covert disapproval to 'female ingenuity'. Whosoever the ingenuity was (quite possibly Maud's) it was certainly a remarkable feat and has been rightly celebrated both in myth (where Maud is supposed to have let herself down by a rope from a tower) and in more accurate annal. William of Malmesbury on the one hand called it 'one of God's manifest miracles' and on the other hand praised Maud herself: 'necessity sometimes ... discovers means and ministers courage'.[26] Maud's reward was to be reunited with her nine-year-old son Henry and her half-brother Robert. For all that courage Maud's cause was still lost, if Stephen's was not exactly won.

Maud lingered in England for several years, mainly in the west, before returning to the safety of Normandy. In any case pressure was now upon the next generation to solve the state of anarchy by arms or treaty. With the agreement of Geoffrey, Maud increasingly allowed her eldest son to exercise her own rights of succession. The death of Stephen, followed by the undisputed accession of this son as Henry II in 1154, left Maud free to complete her life in peace.

As for the whole question of a queen regnant in England, nothing had been proved either way. The fact that Henry II was manifestly ruling in the lifetime of his own mother, and yet his blood claim must have come through her, meant that the matter was left in abeyance. There it remained for the next four hundred years until the death of Edward VI, only son of Henry VIII, leaving only two Tudor sisters Mary and Elizabeth to succeed him, brought it sharply into question again.

Now Queen Dowager, Maud found herself again in a role both highly respected and properly conventional, as she had been in her youth. Maud became to the Normans, as she had been to the Germans twenty years before, 'the good Matilda'. Once more she displayed all those qualities of piety and grace which had made her so beloved; age had brought with it an appropriate wisdom as well. The Dowager Queen and Empress now occupied herself chiefly making a series of pious foundations; but she also dispensed some excellent advice along the lines of moderation and practicality to her son on the throne of England. She persuaded Henry for example not to invade Ireland in 1155. And it was Maud who urged the King not to appoint Thomas à Becket as Archbishop of Canterbury (an unparalleled piece of good advice as it turned out, but, like most really good pieces of advice, it was ignored by its recipient). Subsequently Maud acted as mediatrix between King and Archbishop, as well as endeavouring to bring about peace with the Pope after Becket's death.

The golden opinions won by the Empress Maud in the first and third stages of her life are in such marked contrast to the accusations of pride, temper and intractability which surrounded her in her middle years that it has been suggested that these faults might have had a physical cause. The Earl of Onslow, one of Maud's male biographers, suggested (in 1939) that her change of attitude was due literally to a change of life: 'Maud was now in her thirty-ninth year (on arrival in England) ... she may have attained that time of life when physical conditions are apt to react on the nervous system'. This suggestion was however firmly refuted by her (female) biographer Nesta Pain in 1978; leaving aside the fact that thirty-eight was early for the menopause even in the twelfth century, she pointed out sensibly enough that 'Not many women are seized with sheer folly at such times.'[27]

It is surely closer to the truth to suppose that Maud, first the child-wife to an older man, then the reluctant wife of a boy (for all the formidable character that Geoffrey of Anjou would later develop), saw, on arrival in England, an opportunity to exert that independence for which as 'Matilda the Empress, daughter of King Henry' she may have long secretly yearned. The other side to this independence was a tenacity and sheer steadfastness which must compel admiration – think of her two remarkable escapes – from the disinterested observer. But of course none of the observers of twelfth-century England was disinterested. Her character and indeed her whole intervention earned her universal abuse from those for whom it was politically awkward. It is true that Bishop Arnulf of Lisieux, her supporter, referred admiringly to Maud's 'intrepid spirit' which had 'nothing of the woman in it'. Far more characteristic was the reaction of a contemporary chronicler (and opponent): at the moment of her greatest triumph at Winchester he referred to her 'scornful and arrogant air' instead of 'the modest and gentle demeanour proper to her sex'.[28]

Maud died in Normandy in 1167. Her epitaph referred to the three men sharing the same name who had dominated the passage of her life, two English kings and a German emperor. 'Here lies Henry's daughter, wife and mother; great by birth – greater by marriage – but greatest by motherhood.'[29] (It was of course an epitaph composed in the lifetime of Maud's son.) Unlike the monument to Countess Matilda of Tuscany which recorded her martial achievements, there was no mention in Maud's epitaph of that period when she had battled her way across England in her own right as a Warrior Queen, or been acclaimed as Domina – 'the Lady of the English'.

CHAPTER ELEVEN

LION OF
THE CAUCASUS

A lion's cubs are lions all, male and female alike
Rustaveli, *The Knight in Panther's Skin*, c.1200

To pass from the Anarchy of mid-twelfth-century England to late-twelfth-century Georgia is to pass from mire to mountain. Under its great Queen Tamara (or Thamar), a character both wise and splendid, powerful and beloved, the Caucasian kingdom of Georgia flourished as never before – and indeed never since. Memories of its golden age dominate both Georgian history and myth, and these memories are intricately connected to the story of Tamara. Alone of all the Warrior Queens considered in this book, Queen Tamara succeeded lawfully to her father to the acclaim of her people, added to both the prestige and the dominions of her country, and died leaving a legally begotten male heir to succeed peacefully in his turn. In actual fact, her gender, so far from detracting from all this glory, seems to have added to it.

Yet, even here, there has to be some canker on the rose. To the leading Georgian historian of today, Tamara is 'the symbol of Georgia's political might and cultural progress'; but in Georgian folklore and myth her reputation, in addition to this fame and as though provoked by it, is that of a woman of voracious sexual appetite. This Tamara was crystallized in Lermontov's famous ballad *The Demon*, 'with scant regard for history', in the words of his biographer Laurence Kelly, as having the face of an angel but with a heart 'like sprites from hell'.[1]

She dwells in a tower on a gloomy crag, the sight of whose golden firelight 'promising warmth and rest' lures the unwary traveller out of his way. Within the tower, Tamara's strange magnetic voice 'brimming with passion o'er', urges her suitors to enter. Then:

> Warm arms with arms wound eagerly,
> And lips to hot lips flew,
> And sounds of strange wild revelry
> Echoed the long night through . . .

But in the morning, Tamara's wild passion slaked, each suitor would be hurled to death over the precipice.

> Lo! A lifeless corpse is carried,
> Sounds of moaning voices swell,
> From the tower a white gleam shimmers,
> Comes a distant cry, 'Farewell'.[2]

Today in Georgia, part of the Soviet Union, legends concerning Tamara abound. (And since the name was a common one in the Georgian royal family, the existence of other less famous and less austere Tamaras, such as the Queen's granddaughter, contributes to the myth.) There are also the familiar modern developments of a legend: there are statues to her, to say nothing of Tamara cigarettes, restaurants and comic-strips. The Lermontov tale of the man-destroying Princess loses nothing in the telling. Since the real Tamara was very different, a woman subsequently canonized by the Georgian Church, certainly more of a matriarch than an erotic heroine, her story provides peculiar evidence of the almost wilful connection of a Warrior Queen with sexuality in the (male) imagination.[3] The two syndromes are ready to claim her: if holy chastity happens not to be the desired image, then extreme voracity replaces it. These are two sides after all of the same coin: as though the one thing that a Warrior Queen cannot be is a 'normal' woman; an oddity in political terms, she is also assumed to go to one sexual extreme or the other.

The Georgian kingdom to which Tamara formally succeeded in 1184 has been compared to the Norman kingdom of Sicily in its cultural importance, as the royal house of Bagrationi, to which she belonged, has been compared to that of the Angevins; her great-grandfather David the Restorer in particular resembling in his vigour and intelligence a Norman king.[4] Certainly both Bagrationis and Angevins had to deal with a troublesome warrior nobility. But there were obvious differences between the Norman world and that of the Caucasus. One of these differences is indeed indicated by the very different fate of Queen Tamara to that of the Empress Maud as heiress to her father: both being only surviving children at their royal father's death and succeeding – or attempting to succeed – according to similar claims.

'A lion's cubs are lions all, male and female alike': so ran a significant line in Rustaveli's epic poem *The Knight in Panther's Skin*, thought to allude to the accession of Tamara; with her father King Giorgi III as the lion.[5] It was a sentiment to which Henry I of England, unlike his baronage, might well have acceded. This notion of the inherited might of the female via her father was not, however, such a bizarre one to the twelfth-century Georgian as it might be to the English or Norman baron.

Queen Tamara's royal position fitted into certain primitive conceptions supported by embedded memories, as it has been argued that Boadicea's own regality derived from the richness of Celtic legend. But in England much of Celtic culture, including gods, goddesses and religious traditions, had been transmogrified into that of the Romans; Boadicea herself was preserved in Tacitus' (Roman) narrative. When Rome itself fell and Roman history vanished, Boadicea vanished with it; England – and Europe – awoke to a Christian culture where a Warrior Queen must incarnate the 'severe womanhood' of Judith in the Bible.

For all the tales of Geoffrey of Monmouth, with his optimistic interpretation of Lear's story – the happy personal rule of Queen Cordelia – the English point of view in the twelfth century was better expressed by the Archbishop of Canterbury releasing the nobles from their oaths of fealty to Maud as having been taken under duress. Queen Tamara on the other hand was nourished in the popular imagination by lurking memories of those goddesses of ancient Georgia – Itrujani, Ainina and Danana – whose cult looked back to the Great Mother; and given Georgia's geographical situation there were later influences of Eastern goddesses. Even with the Christianization of Georgia in the fourth century, these folk memories of the mother goddess did not entirely die away, as reverence continued to be given to mother saints (as opposed to virgin ones) while Lermontov himself may derive his pejorative if exciting picture of Tamara from the kind of orgiastic rites which celebrated the cult of the Eastern goddess Astarte.[6]

The position of women in Georgian tradition and myth was then an honoured one: and as a matter of fact the coming of Christianity supplied yet another legend, honouring the female sex. Where England was proselytized by a man – St Augustine – the Georgian kingdom of Kartli, according to a variety of sources, owed its conversion to St Nino, a slave-woman from Cappadocia possessed of miraculous powers who healed its Queen Nana.

In other ways than that of matriarchal folk memory, geography, both internal and external, is crucial to an understanding of the mediaeval kingdom of Georgia. The fertile trough in which the country lay was bounded by the Black Sea in the west, reaching towards the Caspian in the east; beyond the Caspian but accessible from its shores were Persia, India and Central Asia. To the north the great mountain range of the Caucasus acted as a barricade against southern Russia; to the south the mountainous plateau of Armenia exercised another kind of barricade against the empire of the Seljuk Turks.

On the one hand therefore Georgia occupied a strategic position on the borders of Christianity and Islam from which, under favourable circumstances – if the kingdom itself was strong – it could aspire towards conquest and overlordship of many different empires. On the other hand the fact that the country was diagonally split by its own mountain range meant that the inhabitants of West Georgia (ancient Colchis, Lazica or Egrisi) were historically inclined to be in conflict with those of East Georgia, including part of Daghestan and Caucasian Albani (modern Azerbaijan). If the kingdom was weak, Georgia obviously lay in an exceptionally vulnerable position, accessible in its turn to numerous conquerors.

The people who inhabited this debatable land shared many of the striking qualities of the Celts to which attention has been drawn in Chapter Four; although possessed since ancient times of their own written and spoken language, they did not share that aspect of Celtic civilization – its lack of written record – which makes it so elusive. Unlike that of the Celts, the Georgian love of the arts could be attested, other than orally and visually. But in other ways the feasting, the splendour of personal adornment and above all the fighting recall those singing, drinking, gold-bedecked Celts, ancestors of the Iceni, who migrated across the English Channel to East Anglia. When the Patriarch of Jerusalem wanted to describe the Georgians in 1225, he called them 'very warlike and valiant in battle ... much dreaded by the Saracens with their long hair, beards and hats': words which recall those of Strabo concerning the Celts, a whole race high-spirited and war-mad. Here too were chieftains and aristocrats, and by the twelfth century a society which could be described as feudal in Norman terms, that is with a strong tradition of kingship balanced by a strong tradition of warrior independence. (It has been said that in Georgia every peasant is a prince, or behaves like one.)[7] Above all the Georgians enjoyed their roistering if feudacious lives – as, given the slightest opportunity, they have continued to do ever since.

The ancient history of Georgia stretches back to that fabulous time when the Argonauts, some fifteen centuries before Christ, set out for Colchis to recover the golden fleece.[8] (Medea, tragic prototype of the woman scorned, was the daughter of the Colchian King.) But the whole legend may reflect the actual journeys of the Greek adventurers from Miletus to benefit from the mineral wealth of the Caucasus. The kingdom of Colchis was certainly flourishing about the sixth century BC and the powerful kingdom of Kartli at the beginning of the Christian era, itself falling under the sway of the miracle-making St Nino in about AD 330. The partial Arab conquest of the seventh century brought Georgia into the oriental world: at the same time it was subject to the territorial ambitions of other aggressive neighbours, the Byzantine Empire to the west and the Armenian monarchy to the south. It was not until the late tenth century that the unification of East and West Georgia into an independent feudal monarchy was made possible by the collapse of Muslim power in the Caucasus, and the waning imperialism of both Byzantium and Armenia.

The ruling family of Bagrationi were the beneficiaries. Originally hailing from the marchlands of Georgia and Armenia, the Bagrationis had travelled northwards and, by a mixture of dynastic luck and political energy, garnered to themselves a number of princely patrimonies including Kartli. Bagrat Bagrationi was crowned in AD 975. It was a taste of things to come – as well as underlining the honour paid to women – that a woman regent in the shape of the intelligent Queen Dowager Mariam Artsruni should rule most successfully in the early part of the eleventh century. It was however the Bagrationi King David II, known for his achievements in raising his country from its state of collapse as the Restorer (or Builder), who was responsible for the most memorable epoch of Georgian history before the age of Tamara.

David the Restorer was crowned at the age of sixteen in 1089, that is, some twenty years before Henry I ascended the throne of England, and died ten years before the English King, in 1125. In his celebrated will, David the Restorer bequeathed to his royal heir a state 'from Nikopsia [on the Black Sea] to Derbend [on the Caspian] and from Ossetia to Arragat'.[9] It was not an idle boast. As his ancestors had benefited from the collapse of Muslim power and the decline of the Byzantine empire, David the Restorer in his turn benefited from the effects of the First Crusade of 1096, and the Norman–French campaigns against the Seljuk Turks. The Turkish victory of Manzikert in 1071 had brought their menacing presence close to the very borders of Georgia; in the 1080s hordes of Turkish nomads began to roam the Georgian heartlands of Kartli. After years of campaigning, it was the achievement of David the Restorer to push them back successfully: after the victory of Didgori in 1121, in which some Crusaders participated, Georgia was increasingly seen as a Christian bulwark.

Finally, in the climax of his reign, David the Restorer recovered Tiflis (Tbilisi) the ancient Georgian capital, which from the Georgian point of view had languished as an Islamic city for nearly four hundred years. The fortress of Rustavi built to the south of Tiflis signified a new security. And in his last years David the Restorer, as a Christian, was even able to exert overlordship over Muslim Shirvan. It was a hegemony made easier to endure by the essentially constructive nature of David's sovereignty (as his sobriquet indicates): his newly acquired Muslim subjects within Tiflis, for example, were granted an amnesty. 'He soothed their hearts', wrote a Muslim contemporary of this act of grace, 'and left them alone in all goodness.'[10]

With such a progenitor (who also patronized scholarship and

building) it might seem that the reign of Tamara, great-grand-daughter to David the Restorer, was assured of glory: not so. In the intervening years – nearly sixty of them* – before Tamara's assumption of sole rulership, Georgia, that bold ship surrounded by so many troubled and troubling seas, ran into rough weather once more.

The twenty-five-year reign of David's successor, Dimitri, has probably been treated too cursorily by the annalists writing in the reign of his younger son (and Tamara's father) Giorgi III.[11] This was because Giorgi II succeeded (somewhat as did Richard III of England) in place of his own great-nephew Demna, heir to Dimitri's elder son, David III, who reigned a mere six months. Propagandists wisely did not care to emphasize the virtues of the father at the expense of those of the son. Nevertheless it is indubitable that King Dimitri failed to hold on to the signal conquests of David the Restorer, as the Muslims began to recover strength and the Crusader kingdoms of Syria and Palestine in turn began to fail.

If one overlooks the coarseness and cruelty of Giorgi III, it has to be admitted that he kept the thrusting nobles in check: on the other hand he indulged freely in favourites. Nor is the cruelty easy to overlook. When Demna attempted to regain his rightful throne in 1174, with much support from the princely houses of the kingdom, he was defeated in battle at Hereti. After that, cornered at Lori, in a scene which once again needs Shakespeare's pen, Demna, the rightful heir, was first blinded and then castrated.

Thus it was that Tamara, last of the direct line of the Bagrationis, thanks to the careful atrocities of her father, came to inherit.

The accession of Queen Tamara had not been without careful preparation on the part of the previous monarch. Where King Henry I of England attempted to bond his nobles to his heiress with oaths of fealty (but did not associate her with his rule) King Giorgi had his daughter actually crowned as co-ruler in 1178, six years before his own death. Declaring Tamara to be the 'bright light of his eyes', he hailed her as queen with the assent of the patriarchs,

---

* It gives some indication of the time scale involved to point out that Queen Tamara stood in the same relationship to David the Restorer as Queen Elizabeth II of Great Britain to King Edward VII; although Elizabeth II acceded only forty-two years after her great-grandfather's death, as opposed to fifty-nine in the case of Tamara.

bishops, nobles, viziers and generals. The new Queen sat on her father's right dressed in purple ornamented with gold and silver fringes. Giorgi gave her the official title of 'Mountain of God' and placed on her head a crown richly encrusted with rubies and diamonds.[12]

At the death of Giorgi in 1184, Tamara became sole ruler, and was consecrated queen once more by the Archbishop of Kutaisi. She was also proclaimed 'King of Kartli', by that interesting expedient by which the royal title magically transforms the sex of its bearer rather than the other way round. (The Georgian word was *Mepe*, there being at this date no word for queen in the language.)

Queen Tamara was in her late twenties at the time of her accession.[13] Even so, she was put under the official guardianship of her father's sister Rusudani. It is suggested that she felt some impatience at the 'domination of women', but as an unmarried queen regnant there was of course another domination to which she must sooner or later subject herself – that of a husband who would, if nothing else, generate those heirs of which the house of Bagrationi stood in urgent need. The first husband chosen on the insistence of her aunt was George Bogolyubski, son of the Grand Prince Andrew of Suzdal from the adjacent south Russian kingdom of Kiev, who had been exiled as a child. They were married in 1187.

It proved to be an ill-fated union, not least because it was the union of an ill-matched pair. Tamara's natural austerity of temperament, even puritanism, has already been mentioned. No such restraints troubled Prince George Bogolyubski. A series of military expeditions against the Muslims in the south brought him some popularity among a fighting people; the man of war did not easily adapt to the manners of Tamara's court. The couple's rare moments of happiness together were experienced out hunting: Tamara, like many another Warrior Queen, enjoyed the mimic battle charge of the chase. Otherwise it was a disaster. The Queen might have dealt with his overbearing and truculent demeanour or even his drunkenness, as indeed for two years she endured the excesses of his debauchery with numerous slaves and concubines. But the fact that Tamara remained childless – something for which her husband reproached her personally in public, a notable affront – meant that there was no practical motive for shoring up the marriage. She had no real need to overlook his gross sexual misconduct further.

The Queen however refused to have her husband punished, a sentence which in that age and in that country might have been harshly carried out (witness Giorgi III's handling of his great-nephew). She allowed him simply to go into exile; furthermore she sweetened his dismissal with opulent gifts. There is no evidence that Tamara regretted her leniency, despite the subsequent attempts of her first husband to raise the standard of revolt against her in her own country: the ghost of her father might have pointed out that dead (or imprisoned and blinded) husbands were in no position to foment rebellion.

All this lay ahead. In the meantime Tamara was married – with renewed celebrations to signify renewed hope – to David Sosland. This Ossetian prince came from an especially suitable background in that he was descended from the half-brother of a former Bagrationi monarch: he was also an excellent horseman, something to appeal to the Georgians (as it would have appealed to the horse-mad Iceni). In other ways he proved suitable: a son Giorgi was born in 1194 and a daughter Rusudani the following year. The succession was secure. This second marriage freed Tamara to pursue those policies of military expansion which, if they did nothing else, would engage her nobles in their favourite pursuit of war, thus taking them away from their other favourite pursuit, jockeying for power and position.

Certainly from the start Queen Tamara, with the assistance of her aunt Rusudani, showed in dealing with the various factions in her nobility a delicate appreciation of the need for tact which the Empress Maud, for example, signally lacked. The possible unrest at the prospect of female rule was assuaged by giving a noted general command of the province of Lori; other commands were given to sons of prominent nobles to bind them to her side. The promotion of upstart favourites of her father's reign had aroused indignation then and was liable to arouse something more than mere indignation now that Giorgi was no longer there to support them. But Tamara, by honouring former supporters of her wretched royal cousin Demna on the one hand and drawing in Sargis Mkhargrdzeli, one of Giorgi's Kurdish minions, on the other, managed to tread the tightrope. A move to limit the powers of the sovereign by setting up what has been described as 'a kind of House of Lords' – to be compared with the trial of strength between the baronage and King John in England at roughly the same date – did not succeed.[14] There was to be no Georgian Magna Carta.

Instead there were to be Georgian military triumphs. But before Tamara could seek to bring these about wholesale, she had to deal with the problem of the dispossessed – in every sense – George Bogolyubski. In 1191 with the probable assistance of the Seljuk Sultan of Erzerum, the Russian Prince attempted to seize the kingdom, aiming at the support of those disaffected nobles still resentful of the power of the central monarchy at the expense of their own. Although the rebellion failed – following two pitched battles won by the Queen – such a failure was by no means a foregone conclusion since originally only the eastern sector of Georgia remained solidly loyal to the Queen.

The errant Prince was finally captured and brought before the Queen. Once more she treated him with a clemency which it might seem appropriate at this point (since it was done twice) to describe as characteristic: George Bogolyubski was permitted to withdraw to Byzantium.

This was not the last internal revolt which faced Tamara, nor the last attempt by George Bogolyubski to recover by force that position which his own violence had sacrificed in the first place. The mountain lords of Samtzkhe rebelled against the Queen a few years later and in 1200 George Bogolyubski, at the head of Turkish troops, had to be driven off once more. Indeed, the fact that for twenty years after the first revolt of 1191 Tamara pursued policies of extreme military aggression – virtually until her death in 1212 – must in part be seen as an eloquent commentary on the internal problems which faced her.

War, for Queen Tamara, was what compulsory court attendance was to Louis XIV: a method of keeping control over those not naturally prone to be controlled by their sovereign. As a matter of fact, when campaigning was in abeyance Queen Tamara employed Louis XIV's plan of insisting on personal court attendance as well. Sport – the hunting which enabled her too to 'ride to battle' – was another method of ensuring that Satan did not find conspiratorial work for these idle hands.[15]

Of course the actual conduct of a campaign always presented problems for a Warrior Queen unless she literally took part in it all the grim way: control in time of war (as Queen Elizabeth I was to be gloomily aware) tending to pass from the woman on the throne to the man on the spot. Each successful Warrior Queen had to find her own solution to this dilemma. There were two possible approaches. One was to inspire from on high as if in the guise of a goddess – or as a Holy (Armed) Figurehead. The other artifice – rather more physically testing – was to provide from time to time, as Zenobia had done, the spectacle of a fragile female sharing the military rigours: such a display of courage in the notoriously timorous sex being equally calculated to inspire.

Queen Tamara practised both arts, presenting herself now as the presiding goddess or figurehead, now as the Queen–general by the side of her men. At home she made plans and plotted battles, displaying a flair for military strategy. On the field she made speeches: before the battle of Cambetch in 1196 she spurred on her men with a rousing address, ending 'God be with you'. 'To our *king* Tamara!' her men shouted in reply.[16]

At the famous battle of Basiani in 1205 in which Tamara's troops routed the Turkish army under the Seljuk Sultan of Rum, the Queen began in one incarnation and ended as the other. On the eve of the conflict Tamara (who was now in her forties) marched with the vanguard of her army to the encampment – traditionally, the Queen went barefoot. She then harangued her men, receiving once again the loud huzza: 'To our king!'

The following day it was the Queen – or should one say the King? – who gave the command to mount. But at this point the Queen, the goddess and the ikon, became too precious to trust to the clash of battle: Tamara the referee took up a presiding position from which she could watch the event. In no way, however, should the hardihood which Tamara showed in following her men, if not actually fighting, be underestimated: as her chronicler commented on the course of her last illness (when she was in her late fifties), a woman's constitution was bound to suffer from the hardships of continual campaigning.[17]

The conquests for which this exhaustion was the price were extensive indeed: on the map the breadth and depth of the early-thirteenth-century Georgian territory astound, as does the dimension of Zenobia's enormous if short-lived empire a thousand years before. After the capture of Byzantium in 1204 by the promulgators of the so-called Fourth Crusade, Tamara sent troops to Trebizond and Kerasund, as a result of which her relative Alexios Comnenos was established as emperor. But this new empire was in effect a Georgian Christian protectorate. There were to be other Muslim semi-protectorates, over which Tamara exerted a loose sway; while beyond the great range of the Caucasus to the north, some of the south Russian peoples paid her tribute.

Where a protectoral relationship did not follow, there could still be substantial rewards for military raids. The Emir of Ardabil, crossing the Arak mountains, indulged in a colossal slaughter of the Georgians in 1209 – twelve thousand killed and others taken into slavery. The next year Queen Tamara ordered Ardabil to be taken by surprise: in revenge an equivalent number of its inhabitants were killed including the Emir himself; and this time the Christians captured the slaves. Daring raids on Marand in Azerbaijan, Tabriz and Kazvin took the Georgian troops deep into north Persia; on their return they brought a good proportion of its treasure back with them. The victory of Basiani had resulted in the surrender of Kars by the Sultan, to which Tamara's son Giorgi was eventually appointed governor.

With Tiflis, the capital, a city of some hundred thousand people, with Georgia trading not only with its neighbours but far afield, with Russians, Armenians, Persians and Turks among others bowing to her command, Queen Tamara had by the time of her death fulfilled the wildest dreams of her great-grandfather David the Restorer. 'One knows a lion by its claws and Tamara by her actions': so ran a contemporary saying.[18]

Queen Tamara's mercy towards her first husband has been mentioned; it is further to the credit of this Warrior Queen that her administration was generally marked by benevolence. The appalling punishments inflicted by her father found no place in her scheme of government.[19] This in itself contradicts the suggestion that Shakespeare in *Titus Andronicus* legitimately founded the character of the Queen of the Goths – 'that heinous tiger Tamora' whose life was 'beast-like and devoid of pity' – upon that of the Georgian Queen. According to this theory, the Byzantine Emperor Andronicus I, who reigned from 1184 to 1185, would have supplied some of the inspiration. One may remark in passing that the dreadful vengeance on Titus Andronicus' daughter Lavinia for which Gothic Tamora is remembered with a shudder was set off, rather like Boadicea's bloody rampage, by the cold-blooded murder of her own two sons 'for valiant doings in their country's cause'. But in any case it is generally thought that the sources of the play lie quite elsewhere and Georgian Tamara is acquitted.[20]

She has her own literary monument. For it is finally in the great Georgian renaissance of letters and arts that Tamara's glory lies, as much as in her conquests, and above all in the inspiration given by her – and her court and culture – to Georgia's national poet Shota Rustaveli. (Georgian brides still regard his poetry as an essential part of their trousseau, so as to teach it to their children.)[21]

Rustaveli's exact date of birth is unknown although his birthplace is presumed to be, from his name, the town of Rustavi, south of Tiflis, founded by David the Restorer.[22] Tradition declares that he was educated in Athens and travelled in Asia – hence the Eastern influences in his work; most importantly tradition declares that he loved Queen Tamara. As a result, he was said to have retreated to the Monastery of the Cross at Jerusalem where he became a monk (there is no suggestion that the love was requited). Whatever the truth of this romantic legend, Rustaveli's passion for the Queen would not have been that of a languishing poet for some unseen *princesse lointaine*. He was a court official, possibly the Royal Treasurer and even perhaps the Queen's chronicler who thus described her 'sevenfold brilliance': God 'who in six days brought forth out of nothingness all that is, rested the seventh day in the sweet and gentle spirit of Tamara'.[23]

The Knight in Panther's Skin, Rustaveli's great epic poem (of about sixteen hundred quatrains) concerns the long and various adventures of Avtandil and his brother-in-arms Tariel (he of the panther's skin), in the style of an Eastern romance. It has been described as 'a hymn to friendship, loyalty and high endeavour' as well as giving an allegorical portrait of Georgia's golden age.[24] If Rustaveli's poem is also 'the Odyssey of Georgia', it is unfortunate that because of the closed nature of the Georgian language to most foreigners (unlike classical Greek taught for so long in English-speaking schools) *The Knight in Panther's Skin* has never enjoyed the same lyrical appreciation outside its country of origin. An eloquent tribute paid to it by Sir Maurice Bowra in *Inspiration and Poetry* (1955) gives however some indication of the riches in store even in translation: 'It is notoriously dangerous to write about the poetry of a language which one does not know ... Yet sometimes [i.e. in the case of Rustaveli] the temptation is too strong.'[25]

The poem* is dedicated to Queen Tamara, 'the jet-haired and ruby-cheeked', and it is believed that the description of the Princess Tinatin, beloved of the knight Avtandil, stands as Rustaveli's tribute to his queen. As in a fairy story, Tinatin is 'radiant as the rising sun, born to illuminate the world around her, so fair that the very sight of her would make a man lose his wits. It would need ten thousand leagues and the wisdom of the sages to utter the praise of the king's daughter.'

Beautiful as Tinatin may be, the story has to begin with the decision whether she – the only child of the King, but female – may reign after him. The verdict of the viziers, leading to Tinatin's coronation, is a deliberate echo of the circumstances of Tamara's own accession: 'Woman though she is, God had created her to be a sovereign. We may say without flattery that she knows how to rule, as indeed we have often remarked among ourselves.' In short: 'A lion's cubs are lions all, male and female alike.'

In spite of this, one notes that Tinatin's father is still sad at his lack of a son, which means that he has no knight who is his equal. Yet Avtandil, sent out into the world by Tinatin, describes her to strangers in formidable terms: she is 'the sovereign of Arabia whom her hosts of strong-armed vassals regard as king'. Nor is Tinatin the only powerful female character in the story. Quite apart from Avtandil's own valorous travels, *The Knight in Panther's Skin* gives a fascinating picture of a world where men and women mix as equals. There is no hint here, in what the author himself described as 'a Persian tale' found in Georgia, of the restrictions of the Islamic world; women receive men freely in their chambers, for example, clearly knowing nothing of the harem or purdah.

Dularkukht is another princess who succeeds to the rule of a kingdom, in this case on the death of her brother: moreover she is described as a Warrior Queen: 'though she is a woman, [she] is hard as rock – even her fighting men cannot excel her in feats of arms'. Another princess, Asmat, is made ruler of a seventh part of India, and instructed to 'take the man of your choice for consort'. It is

---

* Here quoted from Katharine Vivian's prose translation for the Folio Society 1977. A 'poetic recreation' in English by Venera Urushadze was also published in Georgia, 1979.

indeed with marriage that the poem ends: Avtandil marries Tinatin and ascends the throne as 'lord and sovereign of Arabia'.

Queen Tamara died on 18 January 1212, having reigned for twenty-four years, and was buried at Gelati, the tomb of her ancestors. Her son Giorgi, then eighteen, succeeded her. But with her death the golden age of Georgia was fast fading away, even as the adventures of the knight Avtandil had drawn to a close. Giorgi gave himself over to base favourites and died leaving only an illegitimate child. His sister Rusudani was then proclaimed 'King of Kartli'; her lusts too were in stark contrast to the pious austerity of her mother. On the horizon the drumming hordes of Genghis Khan promised a threat to Georgia in the future far greater than these unfortunate dissipations on the part of her royal family.

In 1236, little more than fifty years after Queen Tamara's accession, her daughter Rusudani fled Tiflis from the Mongolian invasion, leaving her lands, once the great empire of Tamara, to be ravished. The golden age of Georgia had become a memory. In the words of the Epilogue to *The Knight in Panther's Skin*:[26] 'Their tale is ended like a dream of the night. They are passed away, gone beyond the world. Behold the treachery of time; to him who thinks it long, even for him it is a moment...'.

CHAPTER TWELVE

ISABELLA
WITH HER PRAYERS

She with her prayers
He with many armed men
Juan del Encina on Ferdinand and Isabella of Spain

It was in April 1492, at Santa Fe, an encampment outside the recently conquered Moorish town of Granada, that Christopher Columbus received the final agreement to explore the new world. He set off a few months later. Columbus was granted the vital backing by a woman as well as by a man: by Isabella of Castile as well as Ferdinand of Aragon. For the two were independent monarchs and had been so since the inception of their reigns. Their extraordinary partnership had lasted twenty-odd years so far. Instead of confirming Isabella as a typically devout and secluded Spanish princess, leaving the sphere of action to her dominant warrior husband, the passage of time had actually transformed her. To the Pope himself, Ferdinand and Isabella were jointly the 'Catholic kings' and in a phrase euphonious to modern ears, 'the athletes of Christ'.[1]

In the forging of this partnership, both destiny and the laws of inheritance played their role; and so did the necessity for armed conflict which preoccupied the royal pair from the earliest moment of their joint reign in Castile. A contemporary, Juan del Encina, described the relative contribution of Ferdinand and Isabella to their conquests in these conventional terms: they fought, 'She with her prayers, He with many armed men'.[2] But while in no way deriding the efficacy of Isabella's prayers (a subject about which no positive information can be garnered) one must also note that she made a public contribution to their victories which puts her in a unique category in this book: the Warrior Queen as partner. Moreover the Queen's military fervour in the cause of right both nurtured her marriage to Ferdinand and was in turn nurtured by it. Her crusades, jointly carried out with her husband, took on some of the sacramental nature of marriage itself in the eyes of a deeply religious woman. As for her contemporary reputation, the decorous wifeliness with which she conducted herself within this partnership earned general approval. At the end of the chapter this approval will be contrasted with the disapproval shown to Caterina Sforza – a would-be Warrior Queen who was neither decorous nor wifely.

Queen Isabella was a woman of forty-one – with twelve more years to live – when Columbus was authorized to return to the Indies 'and supervise the preserving and peopling of them, because thereby our Lord God is served, His Holy Faith extended and our own realms increased'.[3] She was in fact born in the same year as Columbus himself (King Ferdinand was a year younger). With hindsight, this patronage of Columbus resulting in the European discovery of America can be seen as the Spanish 'Kings'' most resonant achievement; but the endless sound waves which would flow from this decision were hardly foreseen at the time. Ferdinand and Isabella had already presided over one dazzlingly successful crusade: to restore the Moorish kingdom to Catholic Spain after eight centuries. At the instance of their religious advisers, they would promulgate a further internal crusade, less dazzling because less practically beneficial: to expel the Jews along with the Muslims.

The relative importance – and approval – which history would give to these respective crusades would have been incomprehensible to Queen Isabella, the denizens of one age rarely comprehending the apparently weird standards of another. To modern appraisers, the protective attitude of Ferdinand and Isabella towards their new Indian subjects – 'What does he [Columbus] think he is doing with my vassals?' Isabella is supposed to have asked – contrasts most favourably with their chilling attitude to the Jews who had been citizens of Spain for centuries.

After 1492 the latter, if they failed to convert, were cast out. According to the priest–chronicler Bernáldez:

They [the Jews] went out from the land of their birth boys and adults, old men and children, on foot, and riding on donkeys and other beasts and in wagons ... They went by the roads and fields with much labour and ill-fortune, some collapsing, others getting up, some dying, others giving birth, others falling ill, so that there was no Christian who was not sorry for them ... the rabbis were encouraging them and making the women and boys sing and beat drums and tambourines, to enliven the people. And so they went out of Castile.[4]

Similarly, the Moors who were originally granted generous terms after the fall of Granada in the same year, including their own laws, their own religion and their own dress, ended by being expelled in their turn if they did not accept conversion. In 1487 during the series of campaigns known as the Reconquista Queen Isabella had given money for the Moors to be reclothed in the Castilian fashion as a propaganda exercise; in 1508, four years after her death, Moorish dress, in a final insult suggesting the total suppression of a culture, was prohibited altogether.

To Isabella herself, however, the need for religious unity in Spain put these expulsions on quite a different level from the protection a sovereign must accord to distant subjects.* Furthermore the expulsions were recommended by her rigorous confessors, including the formidably bigoted Cardinal known as Ximenes (or Francisco de Cisneros). This was a woman who stepped out of the role expected of her sex in one direction – she had become a public crusader expressing such (male) sentiments as 'Glory is not to be won without danger'. One can understand how she might compensate for this in another direction by extreme spiritual humility in private, and devotion to the will of her (male) religious advisers.

In the earlier years of her reign, such complications were not evident. Other perils had to be faced. And Isabella's personal crusading impulse, the product of faith and determination, was not only approved by her contemporaries, but also seen as a holy destiny which might be implicit in the union of the crowns of Aragon and Castile. 'With this conjuncture of two royal sceptres,' wrote

---

* 'Religious unity cannot easily be criticized as an objective by those who live in a world of mutually repellent secular orthodoxies, quite as compelling and all-inclusive in their claims', wrote J. N. Hillgarth in 1978.[5] It is an apt comment. Nevertheless many manage to do so.

Bernáldez, 'Our Lord Jesus Christ took vengeance on his enemies and destroyed him who slays and curses.'[6] First, before that destiny could be accomplished, Ferdinand and Isabella had to destroy those who threatened to slay them – or at least rebelled vigorously against Isabella's succession to the throne of Castile.

It was the death of Isabella's half-brother, Henry IV, son of John II of Castile by his first marriage, in 1474 which provoked this crisis. Although he had acknowledged Isabella as his heir, Henry IV did have a daughter of his own. This girl however was reputedly illegitimate (either the King was impotent or his wife was wanton or both), her nickname Juana la Beltraneja making scornful reference to her supposed conception by Don Beltrán de la Cueva. Whatever the truth of Juana's legitimacy,[7] there were plenty of potentates to seize the opportunity of backing her in their own interests; particularly since she was unmarried, her hand bringing with it the possibility of the Spanish throne.

Isabella's own husband, Ferdinand, whom she had married five years earlier, also had a claim to the throne, since he too had his place in the Castilian succession (Isabella and Ferdinand were second cousins). It is true that the royal house of Aragon was only a minor branch of that of Castile; but then he was a man. This was more relevant in Aragon where the Salic Law operated – that law originating in France in the early fourteenth century which precluded females from the royal succession – than in neighbouring Castile where it did not. Nor had Ferdinand, in his marriage treaty of 1469, pressed his public claims unduly; at that date securing marriage to the heiress Isabella, from his own lesser position, had been the prime consideration.[8]

As it happened, Isabella was in Segovia when her brother died, while Ferdinand was away campaigning for his father, the King of Aragon. It was in order to cope with the threat of Juana's pretensions – she being temporarily captive to a Castilian noble – that Isabella immediately had herself proclaimed *Reina Proprietaria* (Queen Proprietress). She also had herself crowned, still in Ferdinand's absence; and she had the unsheathed sword of justice carried before her at the ceremony, a revival of an ancient practice it is true, but one that had never been performed for a female monarch before. Ferdinand, when he heard the news, is said to have cried out publicly: 'Tell me, you who have read so many histories, did you ever hear of carrying the symbol of life and death before queens? I have known it only of kings."[9]

All this was however directed by Isabella rather against Juana and her supporters than against Ferdinand her husband. In addition, the proud Castilian nobility would not welcome subjection to an Aragonese. Isabella's personal 'proprietorship' of the crown, regardless of her sex, also carried an important point of principle with it for the future, as she pointed out to Ferdinand. Supposing their own surviving child or children were also female? (This was the actual case during the early years of Isabella's reign and would also incidentally be the case at her death.) If Isabella's personal hereditary right in Castile was not acknowledged, then the 'Princess our daughter's' right would be similarly endangered at her mother's death.

In effect, Ferdinand did always act as co-ruler with Isabella. Proclamations in Castile were probably from the very first in their joint names; both their effigies were displayed on Castilian coins; whereas when Ferdinand succeeded to his father's throne of Aragon in 1479 (where the Salic Law ran) Isabella was merely in title his Queen Consort. Gradually as the years passed and the marriage – the partnership of state – flourished, rights and titles in both countries were ignored in favour of the delights of joint rule. The deliberate impression was given of Ferdinand and Isabella 'sharing a single mind'. The fact that the Castilian castles and the Castilian crown revenues were reserved in theory to Isabella personally – 'at the Queen's will alone' – faded in importance compared to Ferdinand's free exercise of power in Castile; similarly Isabella, despite her technical position as a consort, was allowed to administer justice in Aragon.[10] The monarchs came to resemble two great oaks whose roots were inextricably entwined somewhere below the surface.

In 1474, however, the determination which this young woman of twenty-three displayed, far from her husband's side, was crucial in holding on to that throne of which she judged herself to be Queen Proprietress. She showed herself from the first a remarkable character as well as a redoubtable one. It was not as if Isabella had been educated in any way to handle matters of state; she had been raised in virtual seclusion by her mother, after her father's death when she was three years old, having another elder (full) brother who before his premature death was regarded as heir presumptive to Henry IV. The rigorous intellectual training granted to the young Elizabeth Tudor for example – whatever the constraints of her situation – was quite absent from the upbringing of the Castilian Princess. As a result, Queen Isabella set herself much later to learn Latin, the language of diplomacy and statecraft, in order to talk to foreign dignitaries – a decision which will earn the sympathy of all those deprived of necessary languages in resilient youth, and condemned to learn them in far less elastic middle age. (In urging on the production of a Castilian–Latin dictionary, she would observe that it was necessary because women too often learned their Latin from men.)[11] Her own daughters – including Catherine of Aragon – were notably well instructed by the great Spanish educationalist Vives; the obsessive education of daughters is often the sign of a mother who has regretted her own deprivation in that sphere.

Nor was there any sign of the Tomboy Syndrome here in childhood, no tales of a childish Isabella riding freely in the forests, no comparisons to Camilla of the Volsci. Once again it was in later years that Isabella had herself instructed in those martial arts and exercises that she would have learned in childhood had she been born a prince rather than a princess. Yet in another way Isabella's enclosed upbringing, coupled with the subsequent scandals centred round the name of Henry IV's queen, and the disputed birth of Juana la Beltraneja, had left a deep mark upon her.

The pious austerity for which she was renowned must surely be ascribed not only to a natural inclination in that direction but also to an awareness of the dangers brought to a queen, expected to be the bearer of a royal family, by incontinent sexuality. Isabella's nineteenth-century biographer W. H. Prescott (whose great work can never be entirely superseded, if only for the incomparable style in which it is written) suggested that like The Lady in Milton's *Comus*, Isabella enjoyed divine protection at the court, thanks to her own virtue:

> So dear to heaven is saintly chastity . . .
> A thousand liveried angels lackey her
> Driving far off each thing of sin and guilt.[12]

In the forging of this virtue, however, childhood influences must also have played their part.

Austerity in private even extended to her own personal adornment. Isabella understood perfectly well the need for public ceremonial, the jewels, the gorgeous brocades and richly embroidered velvets which must be draped heavily around the woman who wore the crown for Castile. Off-duty as it were, her tastes were very different: she once related to her confessor as a matter for self-congratulation how she had worn 'only a simple dress of silk with three gold hem-bands'.[13] (That was not a boast which would have dropped easily from the lips of Queen Elizabeth I.)

It was appropriate, given her religious temperament, that Isabella should remain devoted to her wedded husband from the moment when, according to tradition, she instinctively picked him out from among a group of other young men crying: 'That is he! That is he!'[14] With less virtue and more human feeling she also remained jealous of Ferdinand's numerous *amours*. Adopting the obviously feminine role beloved of some Warrior Queens – like Matilda of Tuscany – she occupied herself in embroidering Ferdinand's shirts, as though the flashing needle might weave him closer to her side. It was not to be. Unfortunately for Isabella, Ferdinand's own natural inclinations were very far from lying in the same chaste direction.

Isabella's portraits show her with a long nose and a down-turned mouth, characteristics not likely to inspire fidelity in one predisposed to philander. (Portraits of Isabella's daughter Catherine of Aragon, in a time of youth and hope, show a certain similarity although the expression is much softer and the mouth turns upwards; Catherine's unhappy daughter Queen Mary Tudor, on the other hand, displays quite a marked resemblance to her grandmother, including the same glum expression.) According to the evidence of their respective suits of armour, Isabella was also taller than Ferdinand by as much as an inch: a superiority not always welcome even in a royal wife.

Yet in real life, whatever her physical imperfections, Isabella must have been endowed with charm as well as authority; for goodness does radiate its own kind of charm. Her famous virtue, the key to the generally pure tone of her court (never mind the Aragonese King's very different attitudes) was much praised. The chronicler Bernáldez called her 'a fine example of a good wife'. Isabella, like another virtuous sovereign, Tamara of Georgia, also had her bards protesting their respectful passion. The famous chastity did not preclude such ardent literary offerings as this, probably by Alvaro

Bazán, which made of the Queen the object of a cavalier's unrequited adoration:[15]

> When we part
> Departs my heart
> Glory hides
> Sorrow abides.
> Victory vanishes
> Memory languishes
> And grievous smart.

Even more significant were the comparisons literary and otherwise which made of Queen Isabella some kind of mystical figure, akin to the luminous pictures of the Blessed Virgin by Isabella's favourite Flemish artists. The poet Montoro for example went as far as to declare the Queen worthy to have given birth to the son of God. He was not alone in the comparison. After the restoration of southern Spain to Christianity by her agency, Isabella was frequently pictured as a second Virgin Mary, repairing the 'sin of Eve', in the words of Fray Inigo de Mendoza. Following her death, there would be moves to canonize Isabella, moves not limited to distant times, but recurring in the twentieth century.[16]

This latter-day history illustrates how close the halo always hovers above the head of the Warrior Queen, who has presided over a war of avowedly religious purpose: the Holy (Armed) Figurehead. At the time, it was more relevant that with her authority threatened, her pretensions questioned, these comparisons undoubtedly stood Isabella herself in good practical stead.

Civil war between Isabella's supporters and those of Juana la Beltraneja followed shortly after the death of the King of Castile. Juana, not lost for suitors under the circumstances, became affianced to King Alfonso v of Portugal; the conflict which ensued was thus in a sense as much a tug-of-war as a civil war, since the outcome would decide whether Castile in the future leaned west to Portugal or east towards Aragon.

It was Ferdinand, naturally, who was in charge of the prolonged military campaigning. As an Aragonese, he brought knowledge of new military techniques, as well as the possibility of northern alliances.[17] But Isabella, as the official co-ruler – and the Castilian – also had to play a figurehead's visible role as the inspiration of her party. She did more than that. She participated personally and effectively. It may be impossible to assess the precise military achievement of Queen Isabella, due to the general rule obtaining that any female presence or initiative upon the battlefield is greeted with a special enthusiasm born out of surprise at the successful upsetting of the natural order: as when the Venetian minister, Viaggio, wrote that 'Queen Isabel by her singular genius, masculine strength of mind and other virtues, most unusual in our own sex as well as hers, was not merely of great assistance in but the chief cause of the conquest of Granada'.[18] Nevertheless there is sufficient contemporary evidence to support the picture of a genuine contribution beyond those 'prayers' which the poet juxtaposed with Ferdinand's 'many armed men'. For one thing, it was in these first five years of that civil war that Isabella discovered in herself a vital capability for the organization of supplies which complemented the gifts of her husband.

It is true that Isabella deferred to her husband publicly, almost ostentatiously, on all military matters in her official guise of Only-a-Weak-Woman: 'May your lordship pardon me for speaking of things which I do not understand', she began one intervention. At the same time, she was not above employing the useful Shame Syndrome when necessary to secure her own way. During the reconquest of Granada, some younger nobles were trying to persuade Ferdinand to retreat, against Isabella's advice. Isabella succeeded in gaining the day: 'The grandees, mortified at being suspended in zeal for the holy war by a woman, eagerly collected their forces.'[19]

Over the organization of supplies, and above all in the founding of the first military hospital in Europe, the Queen had less need of these tricks and ploys, since supply, possibly, and nursing, certainly, were of course traditional female concerns. Isabella has been described as 'a great general but an even greater quartermaster-general'.[20] Pioneers in thousands were recruited by the Queen (as Bernáldez attests) to build roads for the passage of the guns, while it was the King who concentrated on their disposal once they arrived. It was Isabella at the beginning of the Reconquista who engaged Don Francisco Ramírez, known as El Artillero; he saw to it that the Castilian army was equipped with expert smiths and gunners. She approved the sending for seasoned troops in the shape of Swiss mercenaries, a very practical step. As for nursing, the equipment of 'The Queen's Hospital', six vast tents trundling from siege to siege equipped with beds and medicines and bandages, anticipated Napoleon's ambulances by more than two hundred years.

Not that the soul was ignored in all this concern to heal the body. One notes that chaplains were an essential part of Isabella's hospital force, just as Mass was always celebrated in the centre of the camp with prayers for victory, the altar plate being provided by the Chapel Royal. Even where the mercenary Swiss were concerned, Isabella convinced herself that they were good people who only 'took part in wars that they believe just'.[21]

From the first in the Civil War, the Queen did not spare herself. She rode hundreds of miles, often across the bleak Castilian mountain lands, pleading for support, invoking loyalty. Her early history of miscarriages must be attributed to these ordeals; this was especially unfortunate since the birth of a son would as ever in the case of a queen regnant have bolstered up her cause (as the birth of the future Henry II had improved the chances of the Empress Maud). In any case a daughter could not succeed in Aragon. It was not until 1476 that Isabella's only son, Prince John, was born.

One of these miscarriages occurred in the summer of 1475 after the Queen herself had taken command at Toledo, riding among her men dressed in full armour, Ferdinand being absent. Her presence – whether or not because she was careful to end each exhortation with a prayer invoking 'the aid of Thine arm' – was said to inspire exceptional confidence. But the welcome respite which the Queen's illness gave to her enemy Alfonso of Portugal illustrates all too neatly the unenviable fate of the Warrior Queen as would-be mother (a complication to which the story of Louise of Prussia will also bear testimony).

The encouraging victory by which the Castilian troops recaptured the northern castle of Burgos in January 1476 was celebrated in the presence of the Queen. The Castilians now needed to repossess Toro and Zamora, two fortresses on the River Douro which controlled the route into their country from Portugal. Ferdinand however failed to take Zamora and the Portuguese retreated to Toro, an apparently unassailable stronghold. Since Isabella's new baby was to be born in June, she must once more have been pregnant. Nevertheless it is said that Isabella herself gave the courageous advice to pursue them, into what might well have proved a Portuguese trap. When Toro was taken, boldness paid results: Zamora itself fell shortly afterwards. Then the baby was born and it was a boy.

The child, symbol of hope, was displayed to his people in the presence of his mother, who abandoned her preferred simplicity for such an important public occasion: 'The Queen went capering on a white palfrey in a very richly gilt saddle and a very rich harness of gold and silver and she for her dress [wore] ... brocade with many pearls of different kinds.'[22] Nor was the hope disappointed. The birth of the boy, named John after both his grandfathers, kings of Aragon and Castile respectively, did indeed signal the decline of the Portuguese cause; Juana, the loser, ended by being locked up in a nunnery, abandoned by the rapacious King Alfonso. When Ferdinand succeeded in his turn to the throne of Aragon in 1479, the stage was set for that momentous crusade, the reconquest of the last Moorish kingdom of Spain.

Ferdinand and Isabella gave their own version of the motives behind the Reconquista: it was not undertaken in order to 'lay up treasure', for they could have stayed at home 'with far less peril, travail and expense'. But 'the desire which we have to serve God and our zeal for the holy Catholic faith has induced us to set aside our own interests and ignore the continual hardships and dangers to which this cause commits us'.[23]

It is true that at one level this explanation (given incidentally to the Pope) is evidently too simple. In the words of J. H. Elliott, 'The Reconquista was not one but many things. It was at once a crusade against the infidel, a succession of military expeditions in search of plunder, and a popular migration.' This southwards migration suited the Queen of Castile, whereas the King of Aragon for obvious geographical reasons remained preoccupied with his northern French neighbour. Then there was the question of the restless Castilian nobles: as Queen Tamara had discovered in Georgia, repeated conflicts against foreign neighbours constituted one good way of occupying them and maintaining perforce their loyalty to the crown.[24]

But given the millenarian atmosphere of fifteenth-century Europe following the capture of Constantinople in 1453, and given the devout character of Isabella herself (Prescott called her 'the soul of this war'), the statement of the 'Catholic Kings' should never be dismissed by a later age as in itself insincere. 'It is very true that your war is a just one,' wrote Isabella to Ferdinand of his French involvements, 'but my war is not only a just one but a holy one.'[25] She made much of the distinction.

In 1482 the Christians captured Alhama, south-west of Granada, and from that date onwards there was a series of campaigns, as the Moors were stalked through their once proud kingdom by the predatory Spanish tigers. These were stirring days for Christians, particularly those who had long been held as prisoners of the Moors. When Ronda was recaptured, the filthy and emaciated prisoners who emerged from its dungeons were comforted by the Queen herself. The royal entry into recaptured Moclín was marked by a solemn Te Deum sung in the royal chapel; as the words were being intoned, those present heard faint underground echoes and it was gradually realized that the dungeons lay somewhere beneath the chapel. In a scene reminiscent of the prisoners' emergence in *Fidelio*, the Christian captives, long incarcerated in darkness, were led forth.

It was helpful however that the Moors were disunited by this date. A feud within the family of the aged Nasrid King Mulay Hassan meant that the realm itself was split. When Mulay Hassan's son Boabdil was captured in April 1483, he thought it worth his while to bow as a secret vassal in order to combat his father, just as Ferdinand, in those negotiations at which he was expert, thought it worth his while to accept the notion of a two-year truce. Boabdil was a faltering ally at best – at the final siege of Granada in late 1491 it was once again Boabdil who would defy the Spaniards after various changes of side in between. But his vacillations, besides giving strength to his enemies, enraged his family. His father's brother, the champion known as El Zagal ('the Valiant') preferred in his turn to surrender to the Christians after the fall of Baza in 1480, rather than to Boabdil.

This is not however to denigrate the staunchness of the Spaniards. They were obliged to mountaineer as much as fight in stark and inhospitable country, at least in the early stages of the campaign. And if Boabdil was no great general, El Zagal on the contrary justified his name by inflicting a crushing defeat on the Christians in 1483.

Isabella's own efforts divided, like those of Queen Tamara, into her private strategic contributions and her public 'Figurehead' appearances. The latter included the ceremonial occasions, such as that at Seville, when the militia were reviewed in full battle array, with successive battalions lowering their standards as the Queen passed. Isabella was seated in a saddle-chair embossed in gold and silver, borne by a chestnut mule whose bridle was of crimson satin covered in gold embroidery. At this review Isabella formally raised her hat to her husband (which meant that her head was still covered by her coif) and the 'kings' bowed to each other thrice.

But there are also numerous glimpses of her, splendidly serene and courageous before sieges: it was lucky for her, perhaps, in terms of public display of her person, that the Reconquista was predominantly a war of sieges. The latter created their own mythology by which the arrival of the Queen was said to spur on the Castilian troops, to the extent that victory, previously in doubt, became certain. Her visit to Málaga for example, in the summer of 1487, came as it turned out at the end of three months' arduous siege: for on 18 August Málaga finally surrendered, a turning-point in the Reconquista, after which it was doubtful that the Moors could long preserve their kingdom. The arrival of the Spanish mascot – or rather Holy Figurehead – came to spell doom to the Moors. It was the arrival of Isabella before the walls of Baza late in 1488 which broke the gloomy news to the inhabitants (led by El Zagal) that the siege was to be prosecuted with renewed vigour.

We hear of the Moors craning their necks over the walls of the city in order to catch a glimpse of the legendary Queen. They must have felt shock as well as curiosity. Certainly Isabella in her mail ('No bad personification of chivalry' in this attire, Prescott called her) constituted a very different feminine image to that of the bewitching Sultana Soraya, Boabdil's mother. Although originally a Christian captive, Soraya had accepted the rich opportunities for intrigue and influence – but not for overt warfare – presented by the world of the royal harem. 'Weep for it like a woman, since you have failed to defend it like a man', Boabdil was told by the Sultana when he finally left Granada and turned back for one last melancholy look towards the lost Paradise.[26] But the woman at whom the Moors gaped from the walls of Baza did not weep; on the contrary, she passed her whole army in review mounted on a spirited Andalusian horse with a flowing mane. The cry which sprang from the lips of her soldiers will come as no surprise to those who have followed the fortunes of Tamara, King of Kartli: 'Castile, Castile, for our King Isabella!'[27]

And so the Christian campaign moved forward inexorably to the final siege of the city of Granada late in 1491. For this siege that celebrated camp – as it was then – of Santa Fe, to which Columbus would repair, was specifically created. To the last Isabella maintained the traditionally double role of a Warrior Queen: on the one hand she continued to plot the final strategy to secure Granada with Ferdinand, and has sometimes been credited with the idea of encirclement which proved so successful. On the other hand she maintained her figurehead's role: the chivalrous 'Queen's Skirmish' took place when Isabella was spied aloft with her children, out to view the exotic palace of the Alhambra (curiosity was not all on the Moorish side). A javelin with an insulting message 'for the Queen of Castile' affixed to it had been hurled in the direction of her quarters; single combat between the Moorish champion Yarfe and the Christian Garcilaso de la Vega, which the Christian won, was held to settle the matter.

Boabdil formally surrendered on 2 January 1492. Four days later, on the feast of the Epiphany, Ferdinand and Isabella entered the city of Granada in triumph. By this time – in a gesture which was both symbolic and practical – the principal mosque had been reconsecrated as a church; here Mass could be celebrated and thanks for the great victory could be given. After that the two 'kings' processed to the Alhambra and in the *Mexuar* or presence chamber in another symbolic gesture possessed themselves of the seats of the Moorish rulers of Granada. Soon the flag of St James, Christian patron of the crusade, would fly above the town; and the traditional cry of 'Santiago! Santiago!' would join the universal acclamation: 'Granada, Granada, for the illustrious kings of Castile!' An eye-witness termed it 'the most distinguished and blessed day there has ever been in Spain'.[28]

. . .

The imperialist energies of the 'Catholic kings' (the Pope gave them the title following the Reconquista) were naturally released by the end of the military engagements which had preoccupied them for the last eighteen years. On the one hand Columbus was sponsored in his western venture. On the other hand Ferdinand began to look elsewhere in Europe; not only towards neighbouring Navarre, but to the south of Italy. Here he desired to establish the kingdom of Naples as an appurtenance to that of Aragon, much as Isabella had added Granada to Castile. In so doing, he introduced the influence of Spain into that mess of duchies, despotisms, cardinals and *condottieri* which constituted late-fifteenth-century Italy. One of the duchies was the Sforza duchy of Milan. When Ludovico Sforza invoked the aid of the French King to bolster up his doubtful claim to rule it, he did more than merely add to that general central Italian turmoil. For France – the House of Anjou – as well as Spain, had its pretensions towards the debatable kingdom of Naples.

The story of Ludovico's niece, Caterina Sforza, bold and tragic, both virago and victim, provides a melancholy footnote to these Spanish endeavours, which were ultimately successful and went towards establishing the vast Habsburg Empire, including Spain, Spanish America and Naples, which was ruled over by Isabella's grandson Charles v.* In a sense the fortunes of Isabella the Catholic and Caterina Sforza are as much a counterpoint to each other as were those of Matilda of Tuscany and the Empress Maud. Unlike the latter pair, Isabella and Caterina were in effect contemporaries. But Caterina, subject throughout her life to convenient scorn on the ground of her sex by her political enemies, ended by being violated at the hands of her conqueror. Isabella, as has been noted, was not only a possible early candidate for canonization soon after her death but remained one.

As with Matilda and the Empress Maud, it was religious purpose which was the apparent difference. To Isabella in August 1492 the Borgia Pope Alexander vi could write: 'Your serenity, as greatly befits a monarch, from whom others must copy the example of virtuous living, desires to protect and defend the Catholic faith . . .'.[30] This was not the language which the Pope felt inclined

---

* Although if, as has been suggested, Caterina Sforza was the 'cultural model' for the queen in the game of chess, which attained its present power as a piece in the late fifteenth century, then she has achieved another kind of immortality.[29]

to use towards Caterina Sforza, who ruled Forlì and Imola, part of the territory stretching from Ravenna through the Romagna over which the Pope claimed overlordship. Caterina was on the contrary in one papal bull 'the daughter of iniquity' and in another communication 'the daughter of perdition'. But it was not in fact the relative morality of the two ladies (far apart as that might be) which was at issue. The truth was more cynical, or perhaps one should say more political.

Alexander vi (by birth from Valencia and thus a subject of Ferdinand) passionately needed the support of the 'Catholic kings' in his papal campaigns and intrigues: Spain was finally part of the Holy League including the Pope and the Emperor which would drive the French out of Naples and establish Ferdinand's claim to southern Italy. On the other hand Alexander's son, Cesare Borgia, needed those lands ruled over by Caterina on behalf of her young son in order to form a powerful central Italian bloc. The sexual freedom of choice which Caterina Sforza determinedly exercised gave useful ammunition to those opposed to her for quite different reasons; here was a Warrior Queen whose lustfulness could be denounced to good effect. For Isabella there was the Warrior Queen's other potential reward of the halo.

Caterina Sforza was born in 1462, the illegitimate daughter of Galeazza Maria Sforza, later Duke of Milan, and his mistress.[31] She was brought up by her grandmother Bianca Visconti-Sforza. Her father was assassinated by the Viscontis in 1474, the year in which Isabella ascended the throne of Castile. Three years later, Caterina was married off by proxy to Girolamo Riario, nephew of the then Pope Sixtus IV.

Caterina was well educated according to the humanist tradition, and even in youth was said to have been fascinated by the deeds of famous men and women. The Tomboy Syndrome is here seen at work. Unlike Isabella, Caterina is said to have excelled at boisterous athletic sports: she was obsessed by hunting and dogs – big dogs such as bloodhounds, setters and greyhounds. (And unlike Isabella, Caterina was beautiful.) Her earliest soldiering was in 1483 when she defended her husband's territory of Forlì from the Venetian threat. From the first Caterina relished such martial activity as she had once relished hunting; she maintained an iron discipline, not always without the aid of cruel punishments. The death of the Pope, her husband's uncle (and the fear of the decline in the Riario cause) found Caterina, riding at the gallop with a cry of 'Duca, duca, Girolamo! Girolamo!', to hold the fortress of Sant' Angelo until it could be handed over to the legal successor of Sixtus. Significantly, Caterina, once inside the fortress, invoked the name of Galeazza Maria Sforza – the nearest strong male figure – to illustrate her defiance. She had as much brains as her father, she shouted to those who wished her to admit a plenipotentiary to negotiate.

Caterina was seven months pregnant at the time and in her gold satin gown with a vast train, a huge velvet hat with long plumes, a contemporary wrote that 'only her belt with the curved sword and bag of gold ducats hanging down from it was masculine'. He might have added: that and the free cursing towards the soldiers in which Caterina on that occasion and many others indulged.

The illness of Girolamo Riario meant that Caterina effectively ruled Forlì; his death in 1488, slaughtered by the Orsi, meant that she ruled it entirely, if nominally for their son. For the next twelve years, she led a life of extreme turbulence as she attempted to maintain her independence in the light of neighbourly oppression, papal claims and finally the arrival of the French forces. Her refusal to surrender the fortress of Ravaldino stands in general for her attitude towards her own rights – theoretically those of her family, but in fact one detects in her a more personal stubborn refusal to be consigned to the female world of submission. (Not that she was above invoking the image of Only-a-Weak-Woman like many other Warrior Queens when it was to her advantage: 'nobody believes me ... being just a lady and timid too', she wrote to her uncle Ludovico Sforza concerning the Venetian threat to Marradi which she had persistently predicted.)

When Caterina's large family of children were held hostages for the surrender, she is supposed to have shouted – in a famous story related in a series of versions of increasing coarseness: 'Do you think, you fools, that I haven't the stuff to make others?' And so saying, she scornfully lifted up her skirt. (In the version which Caterina Sforza's biographer, Ernst Breisach, thinks the most likely, Caterina pointed out that she was already pregnant with another child when her existing children were threatened, adding that even if she wasn't she could always remarry and have another family.)[32]

As for her bloodthirstiness, Caterina's treatment of the Orsi family who were the assassins of her husband recalls the vengeance of Boadicea against the wreckers of her daughters: in both cases the details justify that primitive fear concerning the virago unloosed as being deadlier than the male. There were public executions and secret stranglings, followed by the frightful death of the eighty-year-old Andrea Orsi. Dressed in a vest, shirt and one sock, with his hands tied, the patriarch was first of all condemned to watch his house being pillaged and demolished. Then he was dragged round a square tied to a board at a horse's tail; finally his heart was cut out and his aged body dismembered, the pieces thrown to the crowd.

'Oh glorious Madonna, be merciful with a miserable sinner', pleaded Simone Fionni, another potential victim. But Caterina replied: 'Let vengeance rule, not pity. I shall let the dogs tear you to pieces.' (In the event he was spared and managed to escape.)

Then there were the lovers, increasingly young, continuously virile: placing Caterina within the Voracity Syndrome may have been politically expedient for her enemies, but it was not exactly unjust. The vengeance which Caterina would take in 1495 upon another family responsible for the death of her beloved castellan Giacomo Feo (he who transported her into 'the heaven of Venus and Mars') would rival that exacted upon the Orsi. The assassin was killed, his wife and sons flung down a well and left to die. But on the other hand Giacomo himself, probably with the connivance of Caterina's legitimate sons, had been speared and then horribly mutilated before he was killed.

The sufferings of the Jews, Muslims and suspect Christians at the hands of the Inquisition in distant Spain were inflicted on the orders of Isabella's religious confessors, not her own; Isabella herself disliked the shedding of blood (including, incidentally, bullfighting). Once again it was easier to be the pious Isabella at her prayers than Caterina, who on certain occasions could hear the sound of the tortures she had ordered in her own chamber. Yet the Orsi and the murderers of Giacomo had personally bereaved and insulted Caterina; the victims of Isabella the Catholic died for a principle – a principle of religious unity. But in the judgement of history where a Warrior Queen is concerned, it seems to be better to be associated with religious principle than with personal vengeance.

First of the lovers was Mario Ordelaffi, with whom Caterina was probably in love, in an idyll which lasted through the summer of

1489. Then the Pope took the opportunity to announce that because of 'Caterina's disorderly life' he intended to award Forlì to his own son, Francescolotto Gibo, whose life was quite as dissolute. The trap lying in wait for a Warrior Queen (who could not be compared to 'the new Eve', like Isabella the Catholic) becomes apparent.

Caterina's recipe book shows herself obsessed by the preservation of her beauty, in the most traditionally feminine manner: Queen Elizabeth I could not have done more, and in fact where teeth were concerned did less. Lotions of nettle-seed, cinnabar, ivy leaves, saffron and sulphur were applied to maintain the fairness of her celebrated blonde locks. Other lotions removed unwanted hair from her wonderfully white skin. Pearly teeth were guaranteed by daily applications of charcoaled rosemary stems, pulverized marble and coral cuttlebone. There was rose-water to bathe famously blue eyes, and cream for her white breasts. These appurtenances and practices of a Renaissance beauty were all very well; but when Caterina fought a long battle – masculine by the standards of the time – to hang on to her beloved territories of Forlì against the Pope's desire to grant them elsewhere, she found that her very femininity was gleefully turned against her.

In 1497, for example, Venice expressed itself shocked by her 'boundless sensual appetite', when the real problem was that of Florentine aggression, which it was believed that Forlì might encourage. It hardly needs saying that a 'boundless sensual appetite' was if anything the mark of a Renaissance prince. But Caterina was not born a 'prince' – nor had she established herself as such in the minds of her people, once again unlike Queen Isabella.

The accession of Louis XII to the throne of France in 1498 brought with it new turmoil for central Italy. Cesare Borgia went secretly to France, where a deal was struck that Louis would help Cesare to drive the ruling families out of the Romagna in his own interests, while Louis' own claims to Milan and the southern Italian kingdoms of Naples (also claimed by Ferdinand) would be respected. The Treaty of Blois of February 1499 was an especial blow to Caterina by which Venice, her traditional predatory enemy, allied with France. Finally on 9 March Alexander VI promulgated that papal bull which designated Caterina as the 'daughter of iniquity' – and formally invested Cesare Borgia with Imola and Forlì.

By the autumn of 1499 Milan had fallen to the French and

Ludovico Sforza had fled. Beset in Forlì, Caterina wrote to Ludovico: 'should I have to perish, I want to perish like a man'. That bold wish was not however to be granted to her.

Imola proved finally impossible to defend against Cesare Borgia. Caterina however clung on to Ravaldino fortress and refused to flee. Some of her plans for defiance were perhaps over-optimistic, such as sending the Borgia Pope Alexander VI letters which had been impregnated with poison or left in a plague chest (it needs a long spoon to poison a Borgia and the plan was bungled). On 12 December she said that she would 'show the Borgia that a woman too can handle artillery'. The town itself capitulated by the end of 1499. Still Caterina maintained her defiance within the stronghold even after the inhabitants of the town had been given short shrift – rape as well as pillage described by Caterina robustly as 'just punishment for a city which had surrendered like a whore'. Caterina continued to refuse such inducements as a safe conduct and a pension (showing herself in this respect more of a Boadicea than a Zenobia).

The final assault took place in January 1500. Cesare asked for '*la bellicosa signora di Imola e Forlì*' dead or alive, and on receiving her alive – despite the fact that she had been captured by a French officer and was thus officially the captive of the French King – held her incommunicado for forty-eight hours while he treated her as his soldiers had treated the women of Forlì. Bernardi wrote of the 'injustices committed to our unfortunate Madonna Caterina Sforza who had such a beautiful body'. But Cesare quipped to his officers that Caterina had defended her fortress better than she had defended her virtue.

Still Caterina would not sign away her rights to Imola and Forlì. She was not released until June 1501 by which time her beauty, that carefully tended asset, had vanished. She still tried to negotiate the return of some of her rights, but in vain. Her last years were happier, however; she began to train up her young son by Giovanni de' Medici, Giovanni della Banda Nera, born in 1498, to be a soldier, a worthy member of the house of Sforza. She died in May 1509.

It could be argued that at least as a mother Caterina died with more hope than had Isabella the Catholic five years earlier. The Castilian Queen's only son, Prince John, whose birth had been attended by such rejoicings, had died in 1497. Of her three surviving daughters, Juana was mad: but she inherited the crown officially since her husband Philip the Fair of Flanders refused to allow Ferdinand more than the regency after his wife's death. (Isabella's defence of female inheritance had born fruit.) Another daughter Maria, who had been married to the King of Portugal, was already dead, as was her son Miguel, who might have united in his person the crowns of Portugal and Spain, as once his grandparents had united those of Aragon and Castile. Isabella's third daughter Catherine of Aragon was already a widow following the death of her first husband Prince Arthur of England; she lingered in that country with a view to marrying – perhaps – his younger brother Henry.

Ferdinand expressed his own reaction to his wife's death: 'there is therefore hope that Our Lord has her in His Glory, which for her is a better and more lasting realm than those she ruled here'. Peter Martyr of Anghiera, on the other hand, the humanist historian, did not forget her martial achievements: the world – not only Spain – had lost its noblest ornament, he wrote, since Isabella had been the mirror of every virtue, the shield of the innocent 'and an avenging sword to the wicked'.[33]

Isabella's own will, however, expressed the matters which had preoccupied her on earth, including the unity of Spain for which she had fought, and just rule for the Indians in the New World.[34] But her instinct for simplicity prevailed at the last: she requested that there should not be an extravagant funeral; instead money should be spent on providing dowries for poor girls (otherwise unable to get married) and ransoms for the Christian captives in the hands of the Moors in Africa. And Isabella, still with her prayers fighting the fight for the Faith, prayed that Ferdinand should continue to expand Spain into Muslim Africa, as he had once expanded Castile into Granada with Isabella at his side: she with her prayers (but in full armour), he with many armed men.

CHAPTER THIRTEEN

ELIZABETHA TRIUMPHANS

They couch their pikes and bow their ensigns down
When as their sacred royal Queen passed by
In token of their loyal bearèd hearts
To her alone, and none but only she –

Elizabetha Triumphans (1588)

The reign in which the character of chariot-driving Boadicea was destined to be restored to British mythology (or history) did not begin under auspicious circumstances for a woman ruler. The concept was on the contrary generally attacked. 'Murmur ye at mine anointed because she is a woman? Who made man and woman, you, or I? If I made her to live, may I not make her to reign?' These affronted questions were put into the mouth of Almighty God in a pamphlet of 1559: *An Harborowe for Faithfull and Trewe Subjectes against the late blown Blast*. The anointed woman in question was Elizabeth Tudor, who had succeeded to the throne of England in the previous year at the age of twenty-five. The author was John Aylmer, newly restored Protestant Archdeacon of Stow.[1]

Aylmer's intention in quoting God, as it were, was to defend the new Queen from a far noisier piece of propaganda: John Knox's *The First Blast of the Trumpet against the monstrous regiment of Women*. The virulence of Knox's language in attacking the whole concept of female sovereignty can scarcely be exaggerated. Neither the passage of time nor the standards of another age have paled the rich colours of his abuse.* [3] 'How abominable before God, is the Empire or Rule of a wicked woman, yea of a traiteresse and bastard...' he writes. Again: 'For promote a woman to bear rule, superiority, dominion or empire above any realm, nation or city, is repugnant to nature, continuously to God, a thing most contrarious to his revealed will and approved ordinance, and finally it is the subversion of good order, of all equity and justice.' As for women in general: 'their sight in civil regiment is but blindness; their strength, weakness; their counsel foolishness and judgment frenzy, if it be rightly considered'.

The fathers of the Church are quoted, including St Paul, Tertullian (the whole sex is 'the port and gate of the devil') and St Augustine ('woman ought to be repressed and bridled betimes, if she aspire to any dominion'). Then nature is brought into play: 'no man ever saw the lion make obedience, and stoop before the lioness...'. Finally history is invoked: 'For when the males of the kingly stock failed, as oft chanced in Israel and sometimes in Juda, it never entered into the hearts of the people to choose and promote any of the king's daughters...'. In short: 'where a woman reigneth and papists bear authority... there must needs Satan be president of the council'.

The reference to papists is significant. The 'Regiment' or rulership (its contemporary meaning) of females to which Knox so furiously objected was that of three Catholic queens – Mary of Guise, regent of Scotland in the absence of her daughter Mary Queen of Scots (crowning her was 'to put a saddle upon the back of an unruly cow'),[4] Catherine de' Medici in France, and Mary Tudor in England. It was a classic piece of historical bad timing that no sooner had Knox denounced the female regiment than a Protestant monarch – but one who unfortunately for Knox happened to be a woman – replaced Catholic Mary on the throne of England. Nor was Knox alone in his denunciation. The great Calvin too had joined in deploring such an unnatural development.

Speedy and embarrassed revisionism was the order of the day lest Elizabeth, the hope of the reformers, be fatally offended. It was particularly awkward that both Calvin and Knox, in an extension of that idea attributed to Muhammad that 'a people who place a

---

* But the nineteenth-century editor of Knox's works – male – observed that if John Knox had foreseen Queen Victoria ruling over a vast Christian empire, he would have died happy, like Simeon singing the Nunc Dimittis in the temple![2]

woman over their affairs do not prosper', had stated that civil wars generally tore apart those kingdoms ruled over by women.[5] Insecure at the beginning of her reign, Elizabeth would hardly welcome the notion that God himself might foment a rebellion in her own realm, just because she was a woman.

Calvin wrote a mortified letter to Elizabeth's Secretary of State, William Cecil. He admitted that Knox had asked him in a private conversation what he thought of female sovereignty. 'I candidly replied, that as it was a deviation from the original and proper order of nature,' among the punishments Man had to endure since the Fall 'it was to be ranked no less than slavery.' On the other hand, individual women *were* occasionally well endowed to govern, evidently raised up by God's authority, either to condemn the inactivity of the opposite sex or simply to set forth His own glory (as a creator). Calvin instanced the biblical Deborah and Huldah and quoted the prophet Isaiah: 'Queens should be nursing mothers of the church.' (Knox had dismissed both Deborah and Huldah in *The First Blast*.)[6]

Even Knox himself was compelled to backtrack. In July 1559 he wrote with the best air of apology he could muster to the English Queen. 'Nothing in my book conceived is, or can be prejudicial to your grace's just regiment,' he declared, adding characteristically, 'providing that ye be not found ingrate [ungrateful] unto God.' The official line to cope with Elizabeth's presence on the throne was that indicated by Calvin to Cecil: female rule was still unnatural but every now and then God would provide for it for His own good reasons. Knox however added the rider that this put a special burden upon a female (as opposed to a male) sovereign to prove herself worthy of the task. In general the Protestants now fell back on the distinction between Good Queens and Bad Queens: useful in an age which would be marked by the ostensible public rivalry of a Catholic Mary Queen of Scots and Protestant Elizabeth.[7]

Aylmer's defence in *An Harborowe for Faithfull and Trewe Subjectes* leaned heavily on historical precedent.[8] The stage army of Warrior Queens was dutifully paraded across his pages, including those who had enjoyed an 'antique glory' such as Artemisia, famous for vanquishing Xerxes. Revisionism was not entirely on the side of the Calvinists: Aylmer pointed out that it had been an obvious error to prefer Stephen to Matilda (the Empress Maud), since England had been punished with prolonged civil war for ignoring the claims of the rightful heir to the kingdom – or in this case heiress. This stood the previous Calvinist argument on its head. But perhaps the most remarkable piece of revisionism was that which introduced the name of Anne Boleyn among celebrated women of the past such as Margaret of Flanders:* for had it not been Anne Boleyn who had brought about the wonders of the Protestant Reformation?

Historical precedent apart, Aylmer's point of view was not really so far from that of Calvin, as revised, or even that of Knox. It was God who had appointed Queen Elizabeth to reign, as part of His divine plan: even, as in the selection of a female governor, working through weakness. When Aylmer wrote that if God made her to live, might He not also 'make her to reign?', he was expressly defending the divine selection of Elizabeth Tudor; in no way did Aylmer, Elizabeth's other defenders, Elizabeth's other critics and above all the Queen herself attempt to defend the right of women in general to rule equally with men.

As it is impossible to exaggerate the virulence of Knox's language in *The First Blast* it is also impossible to exaggerate the general distaste and anxiety felt towards the notion of a female ruler. When Elizabeth's half-sister Mary Tudor ascended the throne in 1553, many questioned whether it was even legal for a woman to inherit: there had been no queen regnant since that doubtful, because unsubstantiated, claim of the Empress Maud four centuries before. The rights of the female in the table of royal succession had generally been subsumed into those of her husband, who would often have a lesser claim of his own. Thus in 1485 Elizabeth of York had in fact an infinitely better dynastic claim to the throne than her future husband, Henry VII, *de facto* monarch after the battle of Bosworth. Then their marriage added her right to Henry's might and he was of course the one out of the pair who ruled (Elizabeth being merely Queen Consort). The will of Edward VI had concentrated on the *male* heirs to females within the English royal succession such as his Grey cousins, although it was finally disregarded in favour of the

---

* It was another awkward situation that Henry VIII's Act of Succession of 1536 declaring Elizabeth to be a bastard had never been repealed. Nor was it repealed now.[9] Since Elizabeth was able to succeed under the terms of her father's will, it was thought more tactful to let that sleeping and by now rather embarrassing old dog of King Henry's matrimonial entanglements lie.

superior dynastic claim of his elder half-sister Mary Tudor.[10]

Where might and right did not coalesce, the choice of a husband was always likely to be the problem in the case of a queen regnant. It was not at all clear that the husband of such a queen might not have the actual right to be regarded as the king: when the youthful Mary Tudor was betrothed to her cousin the Emperor, Henry VIII was worried whether he might not thus secure a title to her throne. One Chief Justice advised that although the husband could not call himself king by right, because the crown lay outside the bounds of feudal law (the husband of a feudal heiress automatically assumed her titles, rights and possessions), the Queen Regnant could grant him the title if she chose.[11] In the event Mary Tudor's actual husband, Philip II of Spain, was considered to be King of England as well (a worrying precedent). Mary Queen of Scots' disastrous second husband, Darnley, whom she married in 1565, was always referred to as King Henry.

Under the circumstances it was understandable that Cardinal Reginald Pole should have tried to persuade Queen Mary Tudor to take that course actually adopted by Queen Elizabeth: no marriage, but a single-minded devotion to that role granted her by heaven, and for which through many dangers she had been signally spared.[12] (Where marriage and position were concerned, as the relative fortunes of the unmarried Elizabeth and much-married Mary Queen of Scots demonstrate, queens regnant in the sixteenth century resembled career women in the late twentieth century, in that they experienced regrettable difficulty in 'having it all'.)

The objections to female regiment were not entirely theoretical. As Sir John Neale pointed out in his biography of Elizabeth I, government itself was 'a masculine business, with its world a court constructed for a king'. The idea of protecting a queen from the rigours and difficulties of government was of course implicit in the concentration on the topic of her marriage; Elizabeth's widowed brother-in-law Philip II (and putative suitor at the beginning of her reign) advised her to marry soon, if only that her husband could then relieve her 'of those labours which are only fit for men'.[13]

In vain the coronation tableaux leaned heavily on such stories as that of Deborah, ruling for forty years of peace. The popular mood was better expressed by the fears of the Spanish Ambassador de Feria following Elizabeth's accession: 'what can be expected from a country governed by a Queen, and she a young lass, who though sharp is without prudence?' This was not mere chauvinism – in both senses of the word. There was trouble in the House of Lords over Elizabeth's title as 'Supreme Head of the Church' in view of her inconvenient sex, and Nicholas Heath, Archbishop of York, made what were described as some 'ripe remarks' on the subject. In the end the Queen became the 'Supreme Governor'.[14]

This, then, was to be the triumph of Queen Elizabeth I. She ascended the English throne at a time of outright popular hostility towards female sovereigns, and by a mixture of artfulness, intelligence and instinct survived to rule for forty-five years, her personal prestige – both as a woman and as a monarch – growing with every year.

Such a triumph did not happen overnight. Two years after Elizabeth's accession – in 1560 – when the question of her own successor was being raised, the claim of Henry Hastings, Earl of Huntingdon, the last of the Plantagenets, was advanced over those of a host of females of royal Tudor descent (including Mary Queen of Scots): 'the cry is that they do not want any women rulers'. How sublimely different was the mood of Leicester's will of August 1587 in which he hoped Queen Elizabeth, now in her fifties, would prove to be 'the eldest [i.e. the longest-living] prince that ever God gave over England'! If Leicester, the favourite, is held to be a prejudiced source, then one might cite the tribute of the Pope Sixtus V, around the same time, against whom the same charge of prejudice can scarcely be laid. The Queen of England might be only a woman, he wrote, and only mistress of half an island, yet she had made herself feared by Spain, by France, by the Empire and 'by all'.[15]

The triumph also remained personal to Elizabeth. Forty years on, when this question of the old Queen's successor had become acute, it was Mary's son, Scottish James, who was the front runner (even though excluded, as an alien, by the will of Henry VIII), not only because he was of commensurate rank, but also because he was a man. The ever-confident French Ambassador – ultimately however no great prophet – wrote that it was 'certain' that the English would never again submit to the rule of a woman.[16] The early years of James's reign were also marked by a warmth on the part of the English towards the new ruler – just because he was a man, and a vigorous one in his prime – which is often overlooked in view of their subsequent disillusionment.

The general estimate of the female sex, never high, not only declined in the seventeenth century, but declined amid perceptible relief, now that humble lip-service did not have to be paid to She-who-was-on-the-Throne. In a poem printed in 1650 in memory of 'our dread Virago', Elizabeth, Anne Bradstreet called attention to this decline following the Queen's death: 'Now say, have women worth? Or have they none? Or had they some, but with our Queen is't gone?'[17]

The fact was that the 'dread Virago' herself had never made any effort to improve the general appraisal of woman's worth; for cogent reasons, that was the very last of her intentions. An interesting article in *Feminist Review* of 1980 by Allison Heisch considers Queen Elizabeth I at length in terms of those women who are 'honorary males', and thus have no particular impact 'unless indirect and negative' on the status of women of their time.[18] (The same 'negative' argument is often applied by feminists to the presence of Mrs Thatcher as Prime Minister of Great Britain since, as will be seen, Mrs Thatcher has explicitly denied any debt to Women's Liberation.) Queen Elizabeth would hardly have approved of the source of these sentiments – a feminist review. Had she been granted a glimpse into the future to witness the rise of feminism, she would, one must believe, have greeted the spectacle with a royal shudder; just as Queen Victoria, another Queen Regnant, looked on Women's Rights with abhorrence.[19] On the other hand, Queen Elizabeth I would have heartily approved of the verdict of 'honorary male'.

It was customary for her to deride her own sex along stereotyped lines, out of policy. For example, women were popularly supposed to be chatterboxes: when the Queen was congratulated on knowing six languages, she remarked wryly that it was 'no marvel to teach a woman to talk; it were harder to teach her to hold her tongue'.[20] She also believed what she said. For she was different. That was the constantly reiterated message.

The differentness of the Queen from all other female subjects was the cornerstone of her self-presentation, worked out or perhaps simply instinctively felt, by a genius at the art. Her weapons in this self-presentation were two. Firstly, she worked upon her female nature to provide a delicate, exquisite image of the lady who needed to be protected – and the goddess who had to be adored. Secondly, she presented herself as a 'prince': like many successful pieces of composite propaganda, the second part was in direct contradiction of the first.

In all this, there was one real danger and another possible one. The possible danger was of a husband, bringing with him perpetual masculine control. But by maintaining herself as a virgin goddess to the end of her life, despite a farrago of courtships, the Queen avoided that particular peril. Sir James Melville, visiting the English court on behalf of Mary Queen of Scots, observed to Elizabeth when she had been on the throne five years without committing herself to a bridegroom: 'Madam ... you think if you were married, you would be but Queen of England, and now you are King and Queen both; you may not endure a commander.'[21] He went to the heart of the matter although neither he nor the Queen herself – whose most profound decisions were taken by the highly round-about method of endless procrastination – can have envisaged that Elizabeth would end her life, still King and Queen, still without suffering a commander.

The real danger to Elizabeth, both as goddess and as 'prince', was war. For in the late sixteenth century Europe was a sphere where control passed inevitably to a man. In his *History of Scotland* George Buchanan, tutor to the young King James of Scotland, digressed in his turn on the unnaturalness of female government, especially in war: ''Tis no less unbecoming [in] a Woman to pro-nounce Judgment, to levy Forces, to conduct an Army, to give a Signal to the Battle, than it is for a Man to tease Wool, to handle the Distaff, to Spin or Card, and to perform the other Services of the Weaker Sex.' For that which was reckoned 'Fortitude and Severity' in a man turned to 'Madness and Cruelty' in a woman.[22] This was one challenge to her authority that Elizabeth could not avoid. When and if war broke out, the Queen not only had to suffer a commander, but she also had to go further and appoint one.

Under the circumstances, it is hardly surprising that Queen Eliza-beth showed from the beginning of her reign to the end a dislike and fear of war verging on the pathological. Her very jewels – always the emblematic messengers of her true feelings – spoke in favour of peace; as the years passed, she took to wearing jewels in the shape of spring flowers, in order to symbolize the peace which she was proud to have brought to the kingdom.[23] As to her commanders, she was of course extremely careful that they should be seen at all times as the royal representatives. The first need for a military initiative on the government's part came in 1569 when the northern earls revolted. (Eleven peaceful years had passed since Elizabeth's accession: in a poem written to celebrate the suppression of this rebellion, the Queen was to refer – without regret – to 'our rusty sword'.) The revolt was put down by Lord Hunsdon. But when the Queen thanked him officially, it was for being 'by God appointed to be the instrument of *my* glory'.[24]

Then the Queen used every conceivable card in her hand – including that potential ace of trumps (which would never in fact be played), her marriage, in order to avoid military involvement in the Netherlands, where Protestant rebels were locked in conflict with the overlordship of Catholic Spain. When Elizabeth could hold back no longer, and command had gone to Leicester, she enjoined him firmly 'not in any sort to hazard a battle without great advantage'. (There were to be no false heroics about the sheer glory of the contest here.) That zest for conquest which possessed Zenobia and Tamara was quite lacking in Queen Elizabeth I, who made of this deficiency – as some might have rated it – a virtue: 'In my ambition of glory I have never sought to advance the territories of my land ... I have used my forces to keep the enemy from you.' She added pointedly, 'I have thereby thought your safety the greater and your danger the less.'[25]

War of course brought another kind of bondage, and this bondage applied to monarchs male and female alike: for war was liable to bring the monarch under the control of those who financed it, notably Parliament voting for the necessary taxation. Elizabeth practised an ostentatious parsimony in this respect, regarding war as a 'cancer' which ate up private men and their patrimony, princes and their estates. As Simon Adams has written recently, not only did Elizabeth have 'no martial ambitions' but she had on the contrary 'a healthy suspicion of expensive military adventurism'.[26] This sensible attitude (to those indifferent to the rival claims, so costly in men and money, of national glory) was especially prudent in view of her sex. If she were to exercise any control in the sphere of war, such a control might be considered unsuitable coming from a woman: in or out of her control, a war might bankrupt her.

It was Mary Queen of Scots, not Elizabeth, who referred to herself in the sad declining years of her captivity as one who would rather pray with Esther than take the sword with Judith; but the English Queen too was no Judith at heart. As a result of avoiding Judith's severe and sword-wielding womanhood, Elizabeth had by 1574 freed herself from debt for the first time. This has been significantly contrasted with the situation in the last years of her reign, when she was no longer able to emulate peace-loving Esther or peacefully ruling Deborah: war now cost her the horrifying sum (then) of three and a half million pounds.[27]

Part of the trouble with the ambitious young Essex in the 1590s was that his hotheaded love of war was inimical to his royal mistress, dote as she might upon his stylish rashness when it was displayed, for example, in a court tournament in her own honour. When Francis Bacon was advising his patron Essex how to secure a reconciliation with the Queen, he suggested that he should not be so warlike in his talk 'for her majesty loveth peace'.[28]

As the young Indian braves in Western films used to be routinely portrayed as eager for war, where their elders were content to smoke the pipe of peace, so Elizabeth and Essex were ranged against each other by their generations, he as a war-loving young man, she as a peace-loving old woman. It proved a recipe for disaster, but thanks to Elizabeth's long practice of what she called the 'wit of the fox', it turned out in the end to be Essex's disaster, not her own. The reference is to the Queen's interview with the historian William Lambarde. In 1601 Lambarde presented her with his *Pandecta*, the various records of the Tower of London during the Middle Ages. A discussion concerning the meaning of certain mediaeval legal terms followed in which the Queen was pleased to demonstrate her own considerable learning. Were *rediseisnes*, for instance, as she supposed, unlawful and forcible throwing of men out of their lawful possessions? Lambarde confirmed that they were. 'In those days', the Queen observed with satisfaction, 'force and arms did prevail: but now the wit of the fox is everywhere...'.[29]

Integral to Queen Elizabeth's creation of herself as a 'prince' were sedulous references to her descent from King Henry VIII – 'Great Harry' – in a rich working of the Appendage Syndrome. Knox had advised the Queen in his somewhat limited apology not to 'brag of your birth' but brag she did, in full measure, and over and over again. ('Well did she show, great Harry was her sire, Whom Europe did for valour most admire', wrote Lady Diana Primrose after the Queen's death.) Elizabeth was also artful in associating herself with contemporary male leaders, in order to underline her possession of 'masculine' courage. It was her recurrent theme (not only in that reverberating speech at Tilbury to which we will return) that she had 'the heart of a man', not of a woman. 'And I am not afraid of anything', she added on one occasion, having made the familiar boast to the Spanish Ambassador, declaring herself in the process to be quite as brave as the kings of Spain, France, Scotland and the whole house of Guise.[30]

The greatest art of all was deployed paradoxically in persistently reminding her audience that she was Only-a-Weak-Woman, in order to evoke the desired reaction of wonder and disbelief: for surely here was the equal of any prince of the past! In 1586 for instance, Queen Elizabeth described her reaction to her accession: 'bethinking myself on those things that fitted a King'. And she listed 'justice, temper, magnanimity, judgement' among them, adding modestly: 'As for the two latter, I will not boast; my sex doth not permit it.' The implication was clear. The Queen kept up these quasi-modest allusions to the end of her life. In almost her last public speech she reminded her audience of her 'sexly weakness', before going on to boast once again that God had given her a heart 'which never yet feared foreign or home enemy'.[31]

Then there were the numerous otherworldly references to Diana, Juno, Astraea, Gloriana, Sweet Cynthia, the Fairy Queen and so forth and so on, as a goddess untouched by the depredations of time. (An ode celebrating her funeral referred to 'this sweet slumbering *maid*' with the air of one on her way to Parliament, not to her burial.) The extensive researches of Roy Strong in art and history have exposed the workings of this subtle and brilliant campaign – like some huge campaign for re-election lasting forty-five years, except the votes were cast in loyalty, not at the polling booth – by which Queen Elizabeth I secured first the affection, then the adoration of her people.[32] In the apogee of this campaign, the 'Accession' picture of 1600 showing the triumph of Astraea, the Queen had finally been transformed into the first Virgin of Virgil's Fourth

Eclogue: Virgo and Venus (at the age of sixty-seven) ever young and ever beautiful.[33]

Nor, happily, did this self-presentation as a virgin goddess prevent the Queen from appearing also in the guise of the mother of her people, as the years passed. When Leicester expressed that hope in his will that Elizabeth would be the longest-reigning 'prince that ever He [God] gave over England' he went on to wish, in a splendid transfer of genders, 'that she may indeed be a blessed mother and nurse to this people and church of England'. Sir John Harrington referred to her as the 'natural mother' of her subjects; Thomas Dekker, in his epitaph, described her as 'having brought up (even under her wing) a nation that was almost begotten and born under her'.[34]

For gradually her femininity, which called for a chivalry and protection denied to a king, became an asset, not a weakness. At the beginning of her reign at a tournament given in honour of the Duc de Montmorency, Queen Elizabeth watched with her ladies at the tiltyard while the earls of Rutland and Essex charged at each other at a signal given by her. But it had to be admitted that for all the prettiness of the torchlit spectacle – the two earls in blue and silver, the young Queen gilded and radiant – it was not thus that Great Harry had conducted himself at the beginning of his reign, he who had tired out eight to ten horses hunting, and then played tennis, and finally jousted himself. Twenty years later when the Queen, still more gilded, yet more radiant, watched a tourney of armed 'Amazons' versus knights, she had become the centre of an astonishing cult, in which even the warlike 'Amazons' had to be played by men, since such games were far too rough for the delicate sex of which she was the most delicate of all.[35]

There is a special piquancy in this respect about Queen Elizabeth's legendary meeting with Grace O'Malley, the Irish pirate captain, who is supposed to have appeared before her at Greenwich in 1593, barefoot, dressed in wild and ragged Irish costume. (One should say that this meeting is legendary only in the sense that it has given rise to many legends: the meeting did take place, as a result of Grace O'Malley's petition to the Queen regarding her family and properties, although unfortunately no other details concerning it are known.) For Grace O'Malley, a woman of about the Queen's own age – that is, sixty – had led exactly the kind of buccaneering life which went to make up an old-style Warrior Queen. 'This was a notorious woman in all the coasts of Ireland', wrote Sir Henry Sidney in 1577 of her numerous piratical ventures. Even if Grace O'Malley was not actually in rags, as the legend has it, the weather-beaten appearance of this real-life Warrior Queen must have provided a sharp contrast to that of the bedizened and bejewelled English sovereign, pampered by a lifetime at a chivalric court.[36]

Of course the process of incarnating the goddess Diana meant that hunting, that standby occupation of the Warrior Queen, could be vigorously pursued. The Queen, who had had arrows headed with silver and flighted with peacock's feathers when she was a mere princess at Enfield, hunted with enthusiasm till the end of her life. On the other hand her renowned progresses around the country – that art form of self-display which she did not invent but energetically developed – showed her more statically: her purpose was to look, as a contemporary wrote, 'like a goddess such as painters are wont to depict'.[37]

And all the time, the tributes, the sonnets, the literary sighs and the long lyrical eulogistic poems poured forth. It was indeed a measure of the Queen's success that in the last decade of her reign Shakespeare could create in *Henry vi* the savage character of Margaret of Anjou, and be confident that lines such as these following would not be regarded as treason.[38] Here York, smeared by Queen Margaret with his own child's blood, crowned by her in mockery with a paper crown, knows that he is about to die:

> How ill-beseeming is it in thy sex
> To Triumph like an Amazonian trull
> Upon their woes whom fortune captivates! . . .
> O tiger's heart wrapped in a woman's hide!

When Shakespeare had York tell Margaret of Anjou (who was of course French):

> Women are soft, mild, pitiful and flexible
> Thou stern, obdurate, flinty, rough, remorseless

he could not possibly be thought to be addressing Gloriana, Sweet Cynthia, Venus, Virgo, Astraea – or his sovereign. A man's heart was evidently easier to accommodate within 'a woman's hide' than a tiger's.

History, as well as art, was summoned to the aid of Queen Elizabeth. The return of British Boadicea, driving her 'cart' as it was unromantically known in the sixteenth century, contributed most helpfully to the picture of a patriotic female leader. But there was also a fruitful cross-fertilization. For in turn the presence of a queen regnant on the throne ensured that when Boadicea did quite coincidentally re-emerge from the historical mists into which she had vanished, she was accorded respectful treatment. The first English translation of Tacitus was that of Sir Henry Savile in 1591: it was dedicated in flattering terms to Queen Elizabeth herself. Perhaps his own humble efforts might encourage the Queen to share with the world her own 'rare and excellent translations of Histories', wrote Sir Henry, 'if I may call them translations which have so infinitely exceeded the originals'. The printer however issued a different message to the reader, according to that custom of the time by which some pertinent moral lesson was expected to be drawn from a historical work.[39]

This was the moral of Tacitus: 'If thou mislike their wars be thankful for thine own peace; if thou dost abhor their tyrannies, love and reverence thine own wise just and excellent Prince. If thou doest detest their Anarchy, acknowledge our own happy government, and thank God for her, under whom England enjoys as many benefits, as ever Reign did suffer miseries under the greatest Tyrant.' And so we come back, but now in English, to the fortunes of the Britons' previous queen 'Voadica [sic], a lady of the blood of kings: for in the matter of governing in chief, they make no distinction of sex.'

The story of Boadicea had already been introduced to readers in Latin through the works of Polydore Vergil, an Italian humanist, who came to England at the beginning of the sixteenth century and became a member of the circle of Sir Thomas More. Polydore Vergil's *Anglica Historica*, written about 1512, with its first printed edition in Basle in 1534, drew on both Tacitus in the original and those epitomes of Dio Cassius, which were the only form in which his works survived.[40] It was Polydore Vergil who divided the protean Warrior Queen into two: in his case named Voadicia and

Bonduica, using Tacitus for one and Dio for the other, an error which along with his confused geography was later copied by the Scottish chronicler Hector Boëce.

Boëce, a native of Dundee also writing in Latin, followed Polydore Vergil by placing all the fatal events of Boadicea's rebellion in the north: his Queen Voada, as he calls her, is the widow of Arviragus (Prasutagus), and when she is daily lashed with 'insufferable stakes' while her daughters are deflowered, she appeals to her brother Corbrede, King of Scots, to avenge her. The King does send a message of protest to the Romans, only to receive an 'outrageous answer' loftily dismissing the protests of a mere 'barbarian people', with a reference to the 'majesty' of Rome itself.[41]

It was Boëce's *History of Scotland* which Ralph Holinshed quarried for his own chronicles, first issued in 1577; just as Shakespeare in his turn would work over Holinshed's material.[42] It must indeed remain one of the minor but titillating What-might-have-beens of literature to speculate what would have happened if Shakespeare's fancy had lighted on the story of Boadicea instead of, say, that of Macbeth, also taken via Holinshed from Boëce. Holinshed's Queen Voada – a woman 'not unworthy to be numbered among doughty chieftains' – strongly resembles that of Boëce except that she has been brought slightly further south. The characters of her two daughters, unnamed by Tacitus or Dio, are also for the first time developed, as they were to be in subsequent seventeenth- and eighteenth-century dramas.

The elder daughter, also named Voada, subsequently marries that 'noble Roman' called Marius 'who had deflowered her before her time'. (This sexual theme of the raped daughter either marrying a Roman or falling in love with him will be developed in the Boadicean plays of the seventeenth and eighteenth centuries.) The younger daughter, Voadicia, having gathered together a crew of soldiers on the Isle of Man, attacks the Romans as her mother had done, and is captured in Galloway by the Roman Petilius: 'Upon her stout answers made unto him as he questioned with her about her bold enterprises, she was presently slain by the soldiers.'

The false distinction created by Polydore Vergil between Voadicia and Bonduica was one which Petruccio Ubaldini, an enterprising Florentine desiring royal patronage, kept alive. After a series of travels, including a visit to Scotland, Ubaldini, born in about 1542, settled down in England under the patronage of the twelfth Earl of Arundel. But he was after bigger game. In 1576 he presented to Queen Elizabeth the manuscript of *Le vite delle Donne illustri del regno d'Inghilterra, e del regno di Scotia,* which was printed still in Italian in 1591 (Italian was of course among the many languages in which the Queen was proficient).[43] There is a long dedicatory epistle 'to the most serene and very wise Elizabeth, most powerful Queen of England...' in which Ubaldini manages to blow his own trumpet as a scholar with almost as much vigour as he proclaims the Queen's manifold virtues, which include, incidentally, her 'valour' in defending her peoples from the enemy, as well as her 'clemency'. Among the illustrious ladies considered are Cartimandua, 'a warlike woman', and Matilda Augusta (Maud), praised for playing a manly role (*intervenedo virilmente*), which demonstrates that 'women can be wise, prudent and capable...' so long as they eschew all 'softness'.

The next year Ubaldini gave Queen Elizabeth a further volume in manuscript, 'Le Vite e i Fatti di sei Donne Illustri', which was never printed, perhaps because it did not involve British queens. The six ladies included Zenobia who was described as *virile*: 'in that while her husband lived she was his equal in virtue and valour, and after his death she became famous far and wide for her great achievements in peace and in war'. Thanks, presumably, to this historical barrage, the relationship flourished: not only in 1577 but in 1588 the Queen and Ubaldini exchanged New Year gifts. [44]

Both Spenser in the reign of Queen Elizabeth and Ben Jonson in that of James I (for his *Masque of Queenes*) drew upon the *Britannia* of William Camden for their allusions to Boadicea. Camden's is an upbeat picture: 'the Britains under the conduct of Boadicea had unanimously resolved to recover their old liberty'. It is also scholarly: based, as ever with Camden, on a proper study of the available sources, including not only Tacitus but the monk Gildas.[45] And although he hesitates over the name of the Warrior Queen as many have done before and since – Boadicea? Bunduica? *Boodicia?* – he places the Iceni in roughly their correct geographical position; it is true that Boadicea is described as capturing Maldon in Essex instead of Colchester, but the East Anglian Queen is no longer driving her chariot through the mountain passes of the north.

Spenser's Warrior Queen, 'stout Bunduca', is one of the several 'women valorous' who are celebrated as the ancestresses to his 'fair martial maid', Britomart. It is a sympathetic portrait, with 'stout Bunduca' seen as a patriot, who 'up arose and taking arms the Britons to her drew'; there is no hint of any atrocities being committed. Even her defeat is blamed upon the treachery of her captain, here named as Paulinus, and as for her suicide, that too is seen as glorious:

> And yet, though overcome in happless fight,
> She triumphed on death, in enemies despite.[46]

Britomart herself, who dresses in man's clothes for convenience, has had the classical Tomboy upbringing: as her father's only daughter and his heir, she is taught to upset the most warlike rider with her spear and shield. (She naturally loathes such ladies' pastimes as 'to finger the fine needle and nice thread'.) Britomart's whole delight is in 'feats of arms': the feat to which she is set by Spenser is that of rescuing the knight Artegall from the clutches of the evil Radegunde, Queen of the Amazons.

Nothing illustrates more forcibly the distinction successfully made by the 1590s between one valorous female warrior and the general notion of female rulership than Spenser's treatment of Radegunde and Britomart respectively. Like the other captured knights in the Amazonian stronghold of Radegunde, Artegall is set to spin and sew: nor is there a choice in the matter for this captive househusband, for Artegall has to spin before he is allowed to eat. This behaviour on the part of the Amazons represents an odiously unnatural order to Spenser, as it did to the ancient Greeks. The Amazons are cruel (like Queen Margaret of Anjou) just because 'they have shaken off the shamefast band, With which wise Nature did them strongly bind', which is to obey the orders and laws of men. In short:

> Virtuous women wisely understand
> That they were born to base humility
> Unless the heavens them lift to lawful sovereignty.

Britomart herself, her task of rescue performed, and the 'Tyranesse' Radegunde defeated, removes the helmet which made her look like the war goddess Bellona, and drops her shield. She now becomes 'a gentle courteous Dame'. For a while she remains with the chastened Amazons, to be adored as a goddess; taking the opportunity however to repeal that 'liberty of women ... which they had long usurped; and them restoring to men's subjection ...'. Her story ends with her happy union with the knight Artegall, the warrior maid symbolizing Chastity – one of the many allegorical figures representing Queen Elizabeth in the poem – united to the knight who symbolizes Justice.

Throughout *The Faerie Queene* there are plenty of other women lifted (like Queen Elizabeth) to 'lawful sovereignty', who exist to be contrasted with those evil or licentious creatures such as Radegunde, Semiramis and Cleopatra.[47] The last named, a figure of lust, is now to be found in the unpleasant House of Pride: in contrast the lawful queens are virgins or at least chaste. There is Belphoebe (one of Elizabeth's favourite allegorical incarnations), the huntress who puts Braggadochio to flight; Mercilla, 'a Maiden Queen of high renown', who wins her duel with the malevolent Duessa, representing Mary Queen of Scots. Most powerfully described of all is Spenser's Gloriana, 'the flower of grace and chastity'. Having been chosen – like Queen Elizabeth herself – to rule by God, Gloriana inspires a 'sacred reverence' in all her subjects, as being 'Th' Idol of her makers [God's] great magnificence'. It was this sacred reverence which Queen Elizabeth I, no Radegunde at the head of an unnatural order of cruel women, had worked so hard to inspire.

Queen Elizabeth's incandescent appearance at Tilbury in August 1588, at a moment of national peril, affirmed in practical terms her theoretical triumph. It was just on thirty years since Elizabeth's tricky accession to the throne of England, when the cry was 'they do not want women rulers'. Now her country was facing, as it was thought, the assault of the Spanish Armada. Here was one challenge from which this reluctant Britomart could not gracefully extricate herself. Instead, how brilliantly she made of the challenge the apogee of her glory both as a monarch and as a Warrior Queen!

Leicester described how her appearance 'inflamed the hearts of her poor subjects'. Bishop Goodman spoke for many who would now freely 'adventure our lives to her service'. Camden, as her first historian, summed it up: 'Her presence and words fortified the courage of the captains and soldiers beyond all belief.'[48] Emulating chaste Diana might be her preferred course in public, but in 1588 Bellona too proved to be within Elizabeth's range: at least, her own special version of Bellona.

This was her version and this was her performance. A woman in her mid-fifties, raddled and rather overdressed, mounted on a carefully selected docile horse, reviewed loyal troops on top of a small hill in Essex. Yet that feat on the part of the Queen – if feat it can be called – quickly passed into the romantic annals of our history as a deed of daring to be ranked with the first charges of Boadicea's scythe-wheeled chariot fifteen hundred years before. Boadicea and her daughters were said to have lived again at Tilbury 'through this our Queen, England's happie Queene', in the words of a contemporary poet (James Aske); their bravery no greater 'in those actual deeds ... than did our sacred Queene, Here signs display of courage wonderful'.[49]

The Earl of Leicester officially invited his sovereign to visit Tilbury on 27 July 1588. He did so in his capacity of the 'Queen's lieutenant' or the 'Lord General' as he was sometimes otherwise known. Tilbury Camp – actually at West Tilbury where a church recently turned to a private dwelling now stands – contained the flower of the Queen's troops and was consequently known as the Camp Royal. Tilbury Fort itself, on the River Thames, some twenty-six miles below London Bridge, had been constructed by Henry VIII in 1539. Some two miles from the river, the site of the camp had been chosen with a view to blocking the Spanish invader from reaching London either by road or river, part of a network of defensive fortifications. Since it lay on a kind of plateau on top of its hill – its sides about one hundred and fifty feet high – the camp provided 'as goodly a prospect as may be seen or found'.[50]

It was on 20 July that the Spanish Armada had been sighted approaching the English Channel; whereupon the English fleet engaged it. Such was the good fortune of the English fireships that by the end of the month the Spanish fleet was compelled to flee northwards, 'driven like a flock of sheep' in the immortal phrase of Sir Francis Drake. At this point however the stately Spanish galleon–sheep vanished from view. It is important to realize that just because they did vanish, the extent of their dispersal and damage was not appreciated for some time. (Some messages concerning the damage were received while the Queen was actually at Tilbury.) Elizabeth's appearance, *dea ex machina*, at Tilbury, should not therefore be understood in terms of an empty exercise. It was an exercise, it is true, but one intended to perform a vital function in rallying the national morale in time of war. 'Ye shall comfort not only these thousands', wrote Leicester of the camp's inhabitants, 'but many more that shall hear of it.'

The Queen set forth for Tilbury by water on 8 August. Silver trumpets blew to mark her progress, or as one of the contemporary eyewitness accounts had it, with a characteristic allusion to her illustrious parentage:

> And to barge upon the water
> Being King Henry's royal daughter
> She did go with trumpet's sounding...

But when she landed at about midday (at the present blockhouse of the fort) there was music of a more martial kind: drums, fifes were heard and finally the guns thundered. And so like Boadicea – in the words of the Essex historian Morant like the war goddess Bellona, or like 'a king' in other contemporary accounts – Queen Elizabeth was brought ceremonially into the centre of the Camp Royal.

The method of transport used was a coach: but this bejewelled and spangled affair was indeed different from Boadicea's mythical chariot, and different again from the light wooden structure of the Celts which that forgotten figure Boudica would actually have used. This chariot – never intended to see a battlefield – was chequered with precious stones in patterns of emeralds, diamonds and rubies. According to the poet James Aske (who was present among the soldiers) it reminded observers of nothing so much as 'the heavenly car' of the sun god Phoebus, drawn by his 'foaming steeds'.

One side-effect of Elizabeth's thirty-year propaganda campaign was the frantic desire to protect and cosset the Queen's own person, a desire which of its very nature could never have been applied to the same extent to a male sovereign. (The Earl of Pembroke offered to attend Her Majesty with 300 horses and 500 foot armed at his own cost; a Dorset regiment was said to have offered five hundred pounds to form part of the Queen's Guard.)[51] Now, as she passed, the men actually fell on their knees as though in prayer to her. Aske, whose descriptive poem of the whole wondrous occasion was aptly titled *Elizabetha Triumphans*, described her passage thus:

> They couch their pikes and bow their ensigns down
> When as their sacred royal Queen passed by
> In token of their loyal bearèd hearts
> To her alone, and none but only she...

It was ironic that at one point the cries of the kneeling soldiers as they called out blessings upon her name became so enthusiastic that the Protestant Queen sent messengers of reproof. Officially at least Elizabeth frowned upon such 'idolatrous reverence'. However much her subjects might happily sublimate their feelings for the banished Virgin Mary of the old Catholic religion in their adoration of their female sovereign, this was not to be a conscious process. Deafening cries of 'God Save the Queen' were one thing, prayers quite another. The Queen's behaviour looked forward not back: for her particular stance, 'cheerfully her body bending' and 'waving her royal hand', prefigured royal behaviour on ceremonial occasions up to and including the present day.

The Queen spent the night at Saffron Garden.[52] The next day – 9 August – she returned to the camp, and with her princely image cunningly enhanced by the expedient of abandoning her customary female attendants – 'her ladies she did leave behind her', wrote Aske – she reviewed her troops and made that speech which would make of her the female equivalent of King Arthur, a symbol of a nation's proud defiance of danger. Furthermore, for once it is gratifying to relate that mythology has not burnished the event, for Queen Elizabeth i *did* deliver the famous speech – we have the evidence of the Earl of Leicester's chaplain, Leonel Sharp, who was present at Tilbury, was summoned to record it the next day and related her words later to the Duke of Buckingham: 'This I thought would delight your Grace...'.[53] (It should be further noted that its contents, far from being unusual, were, as we have seen, at the very core of her utterances concerning her 'sexly weakness' from beginning to end of her reign.)

The Queen was dressed in white velvet, with a silver cuirass over her dress, to symbolize once more – to those who might have missed it – the ever-present danger to her person: 'the most dainty and sacred thing we have in this world to care for', as Leicester expressed it.[54] A page walked behind her holding a helmet adorned with white plumes: but this Bellona-like helmet was never actually put on, lest one iota of the contrast between the Queen's fragile femininity of person and the bold masculinity of her demeanour be missed by her audience. Part of the review was conducted on foot. But for the speech itself the Queen was, in Aske's words, 'most bravely mounted on a stately steed': the steed in question being a stout white gelding which could be trusted to behave itself, specially imported for the occasion. Nevertheless the presence of the white horse – which could be a mettlesome charge in the eye of an adoring beholder – was, like the armour and helmet, another piece of careful planning; these were the sumptuous trappings for the message which was to follow.

She had come among them, said Queen Elizabeth, as they could see, 'not for my recreation and disport, but being resolved, in the midst and heat of the battle, to live or die amongst you all, to lay down for my God, and for my kingdom, and for my people, my honour and my blood, even in the dust'. She continued with that deathless declaration, the very watchword of Elizabeth I as a Warrior Queen: 'I know I have the body of a weak and feeble woman, but I have the heart and stomach of a King, and of a King of England too, and think foul scorn that Parma or Spain or any Prince of Europe should invade the borders of my realm...'. Aske, paraphrasing that section of her speech in his verse tribute, fails, unlike the Queen, at the last fence of inspiration:

> Although she be by Nature weak
> Because her sex no otherwise can be
> Yet wants she not the courage of her sire.

'Rather than any Dishonour shall grow by me,' went on Elizabeth, 'I myself will take up arms ... In the meantime my Lieutenant General shall be in my stead.' The latter sentiment is almost an afterthought compared to the thrilling – but frightening – possibilities of the former.

How far distant the Queen on her white steed had now removed herself from the rest of the lowly female race! Dazzled by the matchless words, it is difficult even to bear in mind that the so-called weaker sex actually played an important if subservient role in European armies of the time. 'As woman was created to be a helper to man, so women are great helpers to armies, to their husbands, especially those of the lower condition . . .', Sir James Turner would write in the next century. In the army, as outside it, women provided what has been called 'the warp of the social fabric' by giving sexual favours and by childbearing, quite apart from their ceaseless cooking and nursing which was taken for granted. Three years before Tilbury, Leicester himself in the Netherlands had drawn up a list of 'sundry disorders and horrible abuses' among his troops. These included the presence of 'many vagrant idle women in an army'. But he deliberately excluded from their number the many lawful wives 'to tend the sick and serve as launderers'.[55]

Elizabetha Triumphans simply did not belong to the same gender as these inferior but essential workers. Or if she did, it was only to enhance still further the measure of her own kind of military glory, far from the sweaty field of battle, close to the minds and hearts of her people.

CHAPTER FOURTEEN

JINGA AT THE GATES

Rome for empire far renown'd
Tramples on a thousand states
Soon her pride shall kiss the ground, –
Hark! the Gaul is at her gates.

William Cowper, 'Boadicea'

When Queen Christina of Sweden, daughter of the warrior Gustavus Adolphus, expressed a wish to abdicate in 1651, it was to make room for her first cousin Charles Gustavus. She did so, she declared, in the best interests of her country: 'The realm would be granted a man and a champion who when war threatened could ride with his people to battle, while a woman could not.' (As we shall see, this passive estimate of a woman leader's role in wartime was not shared at this date by Warrior Queens in other continents, where the thrilling or menacing practical involvement of the female in her country's cause by one such as Jinga of Angola continued.) Although Christina was persuaded not to abdicate in 1651, three years later the eccentric scholarly creature, a convert to Catholicism, who had worn man's clothing not with martial intent but for the freedom it gave her, departed for Rome. For all the legends which have her wearing Amazonian costume on this occasion, she and her ladies actually wore plain grey gowns to enter the Holy City.[1]

The particular intellectual temperament of Queen Christina – 'You know how it distresses me to lend my time to matters other than studying', she wrote – did not prevent her from taking part in various political intrigues in her new life in the south. But like many European queens regnant, she expressed the notion that participation in war was a masculine business. It is of this period that Joan Kelly has written of the phenomenon of the 'disarmed lady'.[2] Queen Elizabeth i, gamely acting the Warrior Queen at Tilbury despite a prudent natural pacifism, belonged to a vanished age. Then there were still relics of feudalism in the national unconscious, a vague expectation that the chief must personally wave the sword. Now a female ruler had no need to issue the fake if exciting threat that 'I myself will take up arms' in order to shore up her authority. A queen, no longer posing as an honorary male, could give vent to perceived natural feminine dislike of the actual battlefield, leaving the sword to be grasped by the nearest male. Queen Christina, publicly encouraging the trained soldier Charles Gustavus to take the sword away altogether, was merely carrying this trend to the extreme. He did so, incidentally, with alacrity, initiating a series of carnivorous campaigns of conquest.

'Oh Lord, when will all this dreadful bloodshed cease?' Thus with fervour exclaimed Queen Anne, reigning over Great Britain a century after the death of her kinswoman Elizabeth, a Britain in full spate of Marlborough's victories. 'I have no liking for war,' she observed on another occasion, 'and shall end it as soon as possible.' She was indeed improbable even as a symbolic Warrior Queen, as has been noted with regard to her 'Amazonian' display at Bath. 'Though this great Queen had made a very glorious figure in Europe by her arms and fleets abroad,' wrote Sir John Clerk, 'she appeared to me the most despicable mortal I had ever seen in any station.'[3] Yet the time when the sad private spectacle would have fatally negated the glamour of the glorious public figure had passed.

At the battle of Oudenarde in 1708, the young Prince George of Hanover, the Queen's distant cousin and eventual heir (the future King George ii), took part. His courage in fighting on when his horse was shot under him was celebrated by Swift:

> Full firmly he stood as became his high blood
> Which runs in his veins so blue
> For this gallant young man, being a-kin to Queen Anne,
> Did as, were she a man, she would do.[4]

Were the Queen a man ... the Warrior Queen, no longer

pretending to have the heart and stomach of a king, now admits freely to her very different (female) nature. On the other hand, *were* the Queen a man, she would undoubtedly be a very brave one; the behaviour of her gallant young male relation epitomizes this. She might of course under certain circumstances show herself to be a great deal braver than the timorous men surrounding her. This – an aspect of the Shame Syndrome – received its most famous manifestation in the expostulation of Queen Victoria to Disraeli in 1878. 'Oh if the Queen were a man', she wrote furiously, 'she would like to go and give those horrid Russians whose word one cannot trust such a beating.'[5] It is a wonderful expression of unreality; but the Queen's frustrated sentiments are not purely comic. The ageing Queen Victoria (fifty-eight to Queen Elizabeth's fifty-four at Tilbury) has no intention of deserting her bonnet and shawl even for white plumes and silver armour. The limitations of her sex are thoroughly accepted.

Boadicea herself, in English literature, begins to float away from the historic queen of Tacitus and Dio, wronged in her situation and bloodthirsty in her behaviour, the one justifying the other: she enters some other idealized sphere of womanhood. At first her character merely underwent a subtle transformation from the appropriate Elizabethan heroine to someone representing the much lower estimate of women in Jacobean times; 'women's worth', as Anne Bradstreet had it, having departed 'with our Queen'. Fletcher's *Bonduca*, first performed in about 1614, has as its centre a hero not a heroine: the British Caratach (for Caratacus, whose historic involvement was of course with Cartimandua, not Boadicea). Even the goddess Andraste emerges here as a god: Andate, who inspires the British Queen proudly to roll her 'swarty [iniquitous] chariot wheels over the heaps of wounds and carcasses sailing through seas of blood'.[6]

Bonduca herself is a distinctly unheroic figure, for all her chariot wheels and her 'armed cart'. She is for example sharply ticked off by her ally Caratach for being boastful. After her first victory, Bonduca exults: 'A woman beat 'em ... a weak woman, a woman beat these Romans!' To which Caratach replies sardonically: 'So it seems.' Then he adds: 'A man would shame to talk so.' Throughout the play, indeed, Caratach the trained soldier, shows more respect for the Romans – professionals like himself – than he does for

Bonduca or her daughters. He will not let the Queen deride their 'weight and worth'. As he confesses at one point: 'I love an enemy, I was born a soldier.'

Most powerfully of all, Caratach saves some Roman soldiers from torture at the daughters' hands, since they have been captured by treachery. It matters not to Caratach that these are the soldiers responsible for the British princesses' brutal violation (his language will sound a sombre but not unevocative note to modern ears):

> Caratach: A woman's wisdom in our triumphs? Out, out, ye sluts, ye follies, from our swords filch our revenges basely? [To the Romans] Arm again, Gentlemen. [To the Britons] Soldiers, I charge ye help 'em.
> Daughter 2: By ——— Uncle, we will have vengeance for our rapes.
> Caratach: By ——— ye should have kept your legs closed then.

Caratach's best advice to his nieces is to 'Learn to spin, and curse your knotted hemp.'

Throughout the play, a Jacobean misogyny prevails. It is Fletcher's Bonduca – unlike Spenser's betrayed heroine – who brings about the defeat of the Britons by a military mistake. This elicits from Caratach the violent condemnation, 'O woman, scurvie woman, beastly woman', before the Queen in her turn is told to go home and spin. For the Romans equally, Bonduca is 'woman, woman, unnatural woman' when she urges her daughters to kill themselves rather than face the Roman depredation (that fate so coarsely dismissed by their uncle) a second time. Only Bonduca's patriotic Britishness – her final refusal to plead for mercy with the noble words 'I am unacquainted with that language' – is still admired; her sex is scorned.

The floating away of Boadicea from this human, if despised figure into some gauzier sphere is well illustrated by the changes which have taken place to Fletcher's play by the time it emerges in an adaptation, with music by Henry Purcell, performed in 1695.[7] Fletcher's original is referred to in the Prologue to the printed play book as 'so ingenious a Relick' of time past; in this new 'fighting age' – that of William III's continental campaigns against Louis XIV – it is appropriate that 'proud Bonduca', played here by Mrs

Frances Knight, should once more tread the British stage. But proud Bonduca is a figure much chastened by the passage of a century, a period in which even the official lustful energy of women has been stripped from them in the public estimation.

Purcell's score has been described as ranking 'among his finest' with the invocation 'Divine Andate, President of War', an exquisite tenor recitative; although *Bonduca* has been generally overshadowed in reputation by *The Indian Queen*, written about the same time.[8] But the drama lacks all the violence which once made it a savage but effective piece. The language has been generally softened with Fletcher's lusty expletives omitted. The daughters' characters have been made tender, languishing, even sentimental, and since they no longer take rebellious action against their unpleasant fate, Caratach is no longer compelled to castigate them. As for Bonduca herself, this is the meek fashion in which she now addresses Caratach:

> My Fortune wound my Female Soul too high
> And lifted me above myself; but thou
> Hast kindly work'd down all my Towering Thoughts...

This was an opinion – and language – more calculated to appeal to John Knox than to Queen Elizabeth I.

It was not that scholarly interest in the ancient Britons waned in the course of the seventeenth century: very much to the contrary. The 'discovery' of the North American Indians by the West Europeans led to a happy obsession with the concept of the so-called noble savage. In many cases, antiquarian accounts of the ancient Britons borrowed characteristics observed in the Indians. On her arrival in England as the wife of an Englishman, John Rolfe, in 1616 Pocahontas, daughter of the chief Powhatan, caused a sensation as a member of the Sioux tribe, who were all about six feet tall with 'the cleanest and most exact limbs in the world'. But the 'Nonpareil of Virginia', as she was known, had turned gracefully into 'the Lady Rebecca' on her Christian baptism.[9] Nor was Pocahontas in any sense a Warrior Queen; she was the biblical Ruth, not Judith, a well-treated Madam Butterfly, not a Boadicea. Originally she had twice saved the life of an Englishman, John Smith, preferring his welfare to that of her own tribe; peace not war had followed her marriage to Rolfe.

Among antiquarians destined to feel interest in the ancient Britons, another happy obsession which emerged in the seventeenth century concerning the origins of Stonehenge focused particular interest on Boadicea. As has been mentioned in Chapter Seven, Edmund Bolton in 1624 proposed Stonehenge as her missing tomb (where, according to Dio, she had been given that rich burial by her tribe). Thomas Heywood, in his *Exemplary Lives* of 1640, followed suit. His Boadicea, duly buried at Stonehenge – 'that admirable monument of the stones upon Salisbury Plain' – is illustrated in the plumes and pearls of the day, a Caroline court lady dressing up, one breast tastefully exposed in something which may have been designed to resemble the Amazon's chiton, but certainly does not. She is also described as a 'Mother and nurse of magnanimity', a description which surely fits Pocahontas more closely than the first-century Queen.[10]

Outside history, Boadicea as a name gradually developed into a useful generic term for a heroine. It was employed for example when the making of lists of such became common in the second half of the century, figuring with severe Judith but also with peace-loving Deborah, the prophetess Hannah and the learned Abbess Hilda of Whitby; these lists themselves, generally compiled by women, being a form of protest against the prevalent denigration of their sex's 'worth'. To term someone a Boadicea was to make of her a heroine, but was not even necessarily to connect her to military feats. The petition of the Leveller women for the release of John Lilburne in 1649 pointed to the various 'deliverances' wrought by God by women's 'weak hands', as Boadicea had helped the Britons to defeat the Danes (a well-meant if inaccurate historical comparison).[11] A great lady such as Charlotte Countess of Derby, who defended her castle against siege in the Civil War, might be compared to the British Queen; but so might the spirited playwright Aphra Behn, the first professional woman writer, whose fortitude was evidently in another sphere than that of the battlefield.

Historians and antiquarians similarly began to make of Boadicea more of a generic figure of patriotic intent, than a rounded female character. Aylett Sammes, in his *Britannia Antiqua Illustrata* of 1676,

relies heavily on Tacitus for his account of 'those insufferable Inso-
lences' (towards the royal women) which caused the British revolt.
But he discounts the idea that Boadicea's death could have dis-
couraged her people, and salutes her with a laudatory verse beneath
her portrait:

> To War, this Queen doth with her Daughters move
> She for her Wisdom, followed, they for Love...
> But they being ravisht, made her understand
> 'Tis harder beauty to secure than Land.
> Yet her example teaching them to dye,
> Virtue, the room of Honour did supply.[12]

This 'Thrice Happy' Princess is as stylized, no more real than
Purcell's Bonduca. Her portrait (engraved by W. Fairthorne) shows
her voluptuous rather than brawny. Here is the characteristic
oval face, small curly mouth, dimpled chin and long nose of
the late Stuart beauty; her long rippling hair has a tiny little crown
set on top of it; the low-cut gown sets off her 'torc', in fact
a double-stranded necklace; on her feet are a pair of elegant
sandals. With her toy spear and its pretty tassel, she too is a lady
in fancy dress, but with the march of time she has become a
professional actress rather than a court lady: one of the stately
Marshall sisters perhaps, who specialized in tragedy, playing
Zempoalla, Dryden's tempestuous Indian queen who fell in love
with Montezuma.

Two courtly episodes illustrate this increasingly 'fancy dress'
aspect of Boadicea. In 1669 the Honourable Edward Howard printed
'An Heroick Poem', dedicated to his aristocratic friends, including
the poet Rochester, in order to elicit their comments.[13] Rochester
himself took advantage of this opportunity to designate the poem
as 'incomparable' but also 'incomprehensible'; Thomas Hobbes, on
the other hand, from the library at Chatsworth, with more reason
to appreciate the demands of aristocratic friendship, responded that
it was a virtue in any poet 'to advance the honour of his remote
Ancestors' while murmuring encouraging names like Homer and
Virgil.

After the statutory hesitation over his heroine's name – and finally going for Bonduca* – Howard launched himself into a description of a paragon of beauty and virtue. Everyone, it seems, wants to marry this peerless maid, including notably Albanius, son of King Arthur, and the British chieftain Vortiger. Bonduca herself, although courageous – 'she dares, above her blushing Sex's gentle fears' – is hardly a brash Warrior Queen. For one thing her voice – that perennial test – is 'too soft to accent the rough Laws of War', and in any case 'Wars' stern horrors her soft Soul affright'. Seated as she is on a white charger, with auburn tresses 'softer than gossamer', in a robe embroidered with the dawn stars, surrounded by fellow virgins compared to Spring and Morning, it is hardly surprising that, after the taking of London, this Boadicea goes about the city tenderly nursing the wounded, Britons and Romans alike.

In the end Bonduca virtually dies of modesty, so far as one can make out. Since in her 'bashful accents' she is unable to choose between Albanius and Vortiger, they fight it out in a tournament at which both perish; Bonduca temporarily dies too or at least faints into death, until Merlin resurrects her:

> The Queen's soft life so far were fled
> His Art must now recall her from the Dead.

One cannot resist observing that the bold Celtic Warrior Queen who led her armies to Colchester, to London, to St Albans and beyond, must have been turning in her grave at this amiable travesty – wherever that grave happened to be.

The Society of Roman Knights, which was formed in 1722 and lasted for three years, was the brainchild of William Stukeley, the first Secretary of the Society of Antiquaries founded in 1718.[15] Stukeley was a man of an unconventional cast of mind, with a passion for Druids which finally overwhelmed his archaeological good sense – he did much valuable fieldwork at Avebury for example. Members of the Society, whose aim was to 'search for and illustrate' Roman monuments in Britain, took their titles from Celtic

---

* Bonduca is the name usually, but not invariably, employed in the seventeenth century, following Dio's Greek; but frequent references to Boadicea, in all its rich variety of spellings, following Tacitus, also continue. (Howard himself cites both Voadicia and Boadicia before plumping for Bonduca.) To John Horsley in his *Britannia Romana* of 1732 has been ascribed the honour of settling the spelling generally in favour of Boadicea.[14]

princes and other notables associated with the Roman Conquest, such as Cingetorix (Lord Winchelsea), Prasutagus and Venutius (Maurice Johnson and Roger Gale, fellow antiquaries) and Agricola (adopted by Sir John Clerk, author of that unflattering portrait of Queen Anne quoted earlier). Stukeley himself was Chyndonax, then believed to be an authentic Druid's name.

The constitution actually allowed for members of both sexes – doubtless part of Stukeley's scorn for the conventions, since this was two hundred years before the Society of Antiquaries admitted its first women fellows. At some point Stukeley's wife Frances was admitted as Cartimandua, a development which, with members sticking closely to nomenclature in their frequent correspondence, led to laments like this from Cunobelinus (Samuel Gale): 'Having been inform'd since the arrival of Prasutagus . . . of the never enough to be lamented Miscarriage of the incomparable Cartimandua, a Misfortune which not only myself but all Albion must be seriously touch'd with, since without doubt we have lost a second Chyndonax, or at least another Boadicea.'[16]

Boadicea herself was chosen by Frances Thynne, Countess of Hertford (later Duchess of Somerset). In one sense it could be argued that this wealthy and well-born patroness of writers was an admirable incarnation of the British heroine. Lady Hertford, who would have been in her twenties at the time of her induction into the Society, acted as Lady of the Bedchamber to Queen Caroline both as Princess of Wales and Queen Consort. It was Lady Hertford who pleaded for Richard Savage, convicted of homicide, and secured his pardon. Other writers upon whom she looked with favour included Watts, Shenstone and James Thomson, author of 'Rule Britannia', who dedicated his 'Spring' to her and in another poem, 'Liberty', written later, featured Boadicea herself 'with her raging troops' – although once Thomson was admitted to her circle, according to naughty Horace Walpole, he took more pleasure in the aristocratic but unintellectual conversation of her husband than in her ladyship's 'poetical operations'.[17]

In another sense, the character of Frances Countess of Hertford, the philanthropic court lady and poetaster, was about as far from the patriotic and partisan Celtic Warrior Queen as it would be possible to imagine. (An equally inappropriate sobriquet was that of 'Veleda, Archdruidess of Kew' – a reference to Tacitus' tower-dwelling prophetess – applied to the Dowager Princess Augusta, mother of George III, by William Stukeley in 1753, when dedicating a book about Druids to her.) The final accolade for misplaced use of the Boadicean myth must however be reserved for William Cowper in his eponymous ode of 1780.[18]

Cowper's 'Boadicea' begins, apparently, in fine historical fettle:

> When the British warrior queen,
>   Bleeding from the Roman rods
> Sought with an indignant mien
>   Counsel of her country's Gods
>
> Sage beneath a spreading oak
>   Sat the Druid, hoary chief,
> Every burning word he spoke
>   Full of rage and full of grief.

Here is a picture both plausible and poetic, without too much licence, one feels, in its details. It is only when one realizes that Cowper, no friend to the American patriots currently engaged in the War of Independence, is actually casting the Americans as the *Romans*, that the full extent of the transference emerges. For Cowper devoutly hoped for the triumph of the British forces. And he uses the story of Boadicea as a text on which to hang the British right to empire; Boadicea herself may be defeated but the future belongs to Britain – not the Romans (or the Americans).

> Regions Caesar never knew
>   Thy posterity shall sway
> Where his eagles never flew
>   None invincible as they.

The ode ends:

> Ruffians! pitiless as proud
>   Heaven awards the vengeance due;
> Empire is on us bestow'd
>   Shame and ruin wait for you.

For Boadicea, the British Warrior Queen who attempted to throw

off the Roman yoke, to be regarded as a symbol of Britain's inalien-
able right to its own imperialism – towards America – is indeed an
audacious use of patriotic legend.

About the time Christina of Sweden was formally granted power as
'king' – only to surrender it voluntarily a few years later – another
genuine Warrior Queen was giving the Portuguese in Angola good
reason to regret the persistent tradition of African female leadership
in war. An eccentric, intellectually inclined female, a woefully insipid
princess as Boadicea had become in certain literary works: these
would certainly have provided riper targets for the seventeenth-
century Portuguese. Instead they faced Jinga Mbandi. This at least
was her tribal name, but since the rich variety of its spellings
approaches that of Boadicea, including Nzinga, Singa and Zhinga,
she will here be described by the name invariably used by the
Portuguese then, and dignified by widespread popular usage in the
People's Republic of Angola today: Queen Jinga.[19]

Unlike Queen Elizabeth I, for example, with her private pacifism
and her artificial creation of a Warrior Queen persona, Queen Jinga
followed in the bold tradition of Boadicea as she actually was (so
far as we can tell about the British leader). That is, the Angolan
Queen, described by a European with much truth as 'a Cunning
Virago', led her people in war against the forces of an alien would-
be occupying power, failing in the end to throw off their yoke. As
a result, there is another parallel with Boadicea. Jinga's story, too,
has survived down the centuries in its own emolliated form, to make
her a patriotic heroine in her country today.

The Queen as a symbol of national resistance is of course a
category into which female rulers can fall without necessarily displaying the sheer belligerence of a Boadicea or a Jinga. As we shall
see, both Maria Theresa and Catherine the Great shared Elizabeth
I's prudent love of peace not war; a preference which in Europe
and its environs was fast becoming the hallmark of an intelligent
female leader, and, one might argue, has remained so ever since. On
the other hand, there is always a special niche for the Boadicean
type of Warrior Queen in her country's pantheon, which does at
least suggest a lingering connection in the popular consciousness to
the ancient goddesses of war.

Within the confines of this book, the nineteenth-century Rani of

Jhansi will also be found to come into that category: but examples are found in many different civilizations throughout the world and straddle history. In AD 39, twenty-odd years before Boadicea led her own uprising, two Vietnamese sisters, Trung Trac and Trung Nhi, led the first rising in their country against the domination of the Chinese.[20] The parallels between the story of Trung Trac and that of Boadicea are even more exact than those of Queen Jinga; Trung Trac was a lady of title, the widow of a man murdered by the Chinese, and she herself was raped by them. Together with her sister, she mustered an army of vassals to avenge her husband's death. Hers was not the only female heroism attached to her cause: of Trung Trac's supporters, Phung Thi Chinh, who was heavily pregnant, did not hesitate to plunge into the middle of the fray and, when she actually gave birth, paused merely to strap her baby on her back before hacking her way out. The kingdom of the battling Trungs, extending south to Hué and north to southern China, lasted only three years: finally defeated by the Chinese, the sisters flung themselves into a river and drowned.

Like the Trungs, Trieu Au in the third century has survived in Vietnamese myth as a female war leader who stood out against Chinese oppression. Trieu Au's story is the stuff of Western fairy tales as well as Vietnamese myth: an orphan who was cruelly treated by her brother and sister-in-law, she killed the latter and escaped to the mountains. A virgin warrior (she is sometimes known as the 'Vietnamese Joan of Arc'), she raised a thousand troops to liberate her country from the Chinese in 248. When her brother tried to remonstrate with her, Trieu Au answered him boldly in words which have become enshrined at the heart of her legend: 'I want to rail against wind and tide, kill the whales in the ocean, sweep the whole country to save people from slavery, and I have no desire to take abuse.' Trieu Au's story too ended in defeat and suicide: but the Vietnamese prints which show her in her golden armour, a sword in either hand, riding upon an elephant, give a better impression of the undying quality of her reputation as a patriotic Vietnamese heroine (a reputation only enhanced in Vietnam today where she is regarded as an early resister against Vietnam's modern enemy: China).

It is the oppression of an imperialist power – the Romans, Portuguese, British and Chinese respectively – which not only links the fortunes of Boadicea, Jinga, the Rani of Jhansi and the Vietnamese heroines, but is also half responsible for their immortality. The other essential element is of course the subsequent resurgence of the defeated people in question, without which their heroines' martial reputations might have perished with them. (A street in Luanda was named after Queen Jinga immediately after Angolan independence.) Cowper's ode was written to justify Britain against America – 'empire is on us bestow'd' – in an age when a queen no longer needed to be overtly militaristic, and Boadicea had become a mere waxwork figure of generalized patriotism. Yet ironically its lines could have been taken as rallying cries for these other far more genuine 'Boadiceas'.

Jinga Mbandi was born in the 1580s and lived until 1663, an extraordinary span for any human being at that time. But then Queen Jinga *was* extraordinary, the mere facts of her career, ungarnished by propaganda, causing wonder. As in the case of Queen Tamara of Georgia, the swirling legends of creation which wreathed so many African societies were not inimical to the idea of a powerful, even all-powerful woman. These legends included a tradition of female semi-deities, such as the two mighty queens of the Mpororo of central East Africa, priestesses to their people, carried round in baskets by their ministers. In the Hausa lands of northern Nigeria (where creation was said to have begun with a woman going out and founding a kingdom), a queen known as Amina ruled in Katsina in the first half of the fifteenth century; south of Zaria, a woman, Bazao-Turunku, led another warrior tribe. There were feats of arms by the women of the Nilotic Lango.[21]

Nor did this tradition die away with Jinga's own death. Livingstone and Stanley encountered independent queens ruling the Fanti in Ghani; the 'King's Amazons' of Dahomey were not so much notorious in the eyes of their opponents as celebrated. During the course of King Gueso's disastrous war against Abeokuta, they stood their ground while the men fled, or, as Captain Duncan of the Life Guards expressed it, 'On a campaign I would prefer the women of that country, as soldiers, to the men.' *Sarraounia*, a recent film directed by Med Hondo of Mauritius from a novel by Aboulaye Mamani of Niger, was based on real events that occurred in Central Africa at the end of the nineteenth century. It tells the story of an African queen, half-warrior, half-sorceress, who leads her people

to victory against the oppressive French colonial power in true
Boadicean style, a towering figure of matriarchal strength as she
shakes her spear and invokes the tribal gods before battle. Nor
have such manifestations died away in the present century: popular
uprisings in Uganda in 1987 were headed by a woman, Alice
Lakwena, a self-styled high priestess of magic who inspired her
Holy Spirit Movement to battle.[22]

Jinga herself operated in central West Africa, where the two
principal kingdoms were those of Kongo and Ndongo. She was
probably the daughter of the King – the Ngola – of Ndongo, with
a mother from a vassal tribe. Until a few years before Jinga's
birth, the Portuguese presence in Ndongo had consisted of friendly
missionaries; but its geographical situation made it an ideal base for
the growing Portuguese slave trade. With that in mind, Luanda was
founded in 1576, and given its first Portuguese governor. It is from
the century of conflict which followed – ending in the Portuguese
victory – that Jinga's name has emerged as a heroic national figure.

We first hear of her, however, as an official negotiator with the
Portuguese on behalf of her brother, the new Ngola, in the early
1620s. By the beginning of the seventeenth century, the slave
markets based in Angola were rapidly expanding: an enthusiastic
official wrote that the huge interior population would provide slaves
enough 'until the end of the world'.[23] Ten thousand of them annually
were already being exported from Luanda. It was a trade from which
the African chiefs (like the Arabs) did not flinch when it suited their
local purposes. Their selling members of rival or hostile tribes for
a good price was one part of the process which enabled the Portuguese to build up such a gargantuan and horrifying trade, in order
to satisfy the greedy labour demands of the Brazilian plantations
and mines. But the Africans wanted co-operation to be on their own
terms: and they also naturally wished to preserve their independence.
Thus the aggressive new Portuguese Governor of Luanda – João
Mendes de Vasconcelos – had exiled the Ngola of Ndongo to the
Kwanza Islands.

Jinga's task was to negotiate the independence of Ndongo from
the Portuguese, and at the same time to enlist their help in expelling
the Imbangalas from the Ndongo kingdom. It is generally agreed
that Jinga conducted these negotiations skilfully although certainly
not as one raising her voice 'for suppliant humanity' (as that watered-

down Zenobia was purported to do in the eighteenth century: the real Zenobia had much more in common with Queen Jinga). Perceiving for example, in the desire of the Portuguese to baptize her, a possible entry into their favour, she allowed herself to add to her armoury of names with that of Anna de Sousa (in honour of the incoming Governor Correira de Sousa). Her sisters, who would show themselves, like Jinga, wily and intelligent characters, became the Ladies Grace and Barbara respectively.

In 1624 Jinga's brother the Ngola died under mysterious circumstances: possibly he committed suicide, but possibly also Jinga had him killed.[24] Whatever the truth – and legend credited Jinga with another murder at the same time, that of her nephew, with the additional titillating accusation that she subsequently ate his heart – it was certainly Jinga who benefited from these demises, since she now assumed power. Unlike Pocahontas, who remained 'the Lady Rebecca', the Angolan princess now renounced her convenient Christianity. Anna de Sousa was no more; Queen Jinga was born.

The next important stage in the story of this 'redoubtable Amazon', as C. R. Boxer has called her, was reached when the Portuguese declared war upon her.[25] They did so reluctantly. A tacit peaceful alliance in the business of producing and shipping slaves was infinitely more desirable. Queen Jinga however played by her own rules. In the end the Portuguese preferred to set up a puppet chief from another tribe on the Ndongo throne, and Jinga was driven out. The loyalty of her Mbandi people however remained steadfast: the puppet kings were scorned as the sons of slaves on the one hand, inadequate rainmakers on the other. And in 1630 Queen Jinga made an alliance with the neighbouring Kasanje kingdom, which had the effect of closing the vital slave routes to the Portuguese.

The Queen then led her people further east to the kingdom of Matamba, where she conquered the indigenous Jaga tribe, acquiring not only a useful base, but also the ferocious rituals associated with its members. The Jagas themselves have been described as indulging in cannibalism 'not merely as a ritual sacrifice, but as a matter of habit, convenience and conviction'. They also indulged in deliberate infanticide, in order to preserve the hardy nature of the tribe, turning for replenishments of their population to the children of their conquered enemies.[26]

Queen Jinga, following her take-over of the Jagas, indulged in the first practice, at least in public and at least for ritual effect. As it happens, we have an eyewitness account of the Queen as she appeared to the Dutch captain of her bodyguard, during her wars against the Portuguese in the late 1640s.[27] Captain Fuller, who was in command of sixty men put at the Queen's service for a period of years, referred to the deep importance attached to her by people: rumours of her death – the death of the Holy Figurehead – were always concealed from the Portuguese lest they take too much heart from them.

More crucially, he also witnessed Queen Jinga performing a ritual sacrifice. She wore, as she always did, 'man's apparel' for the occasion. She was also hung about with 'the skins of Beasts, before and behind', had a sword about her neck, an axe at her girdle and a bow and arrows in her hand. This awesome figure proceeded to leap 'according to the custom, now here, now there, as nimbly as the most active among her attendants' (Queen Jinga would by this date have been well over sixty). All the while she continued to strike the two iron bells which she used instead of drums. 'When she thinks she has made a show long enough, in a masculine manner ... then she takes a broad feather and flicks it through the holes of her bored Nose, for a Sign of War.' This sinister gesture was the prelude to the first sacrifice: Queen Jinga selected the first victim, cut off his head and drank 'a great draught of his blood'.

As for male company, the Queen had evidently adopted that second practice of the Jagas: infanticide. According to Fuller, she kept fifty or sixty young men instead of husbands, who were in turn allowed as many wives as they pleased, 'with the proviso that if any became with child, they must kill the infant'. Jinga was also described as going further and clothing selected young men in women's clothes (shades of Radegunde, Spenser's Queen of the Amazons, with her 'unnatural order' of knights holding distaffs!). The clothing of her obedient favourites, in the pretence that they had become women, as she herself had been transformed by her 'man's apparel', enabled them to move freely among the other women of her household: 'and if they fail in their obligations, they seldom escape to tell further news'.

It is a vivid if intimidating picture. Yet as with the head-hunting of the Celts, and as with Boadicea's chilling sacrifices to Andraste, one must be wary of condemning the Jagas and Queen Jinga outside the standards of their own time and society; one should bear in mind also the slave trading which was the quite open practice of the alternative officially 'Christian' cultures of the Portuguese and Dutch.

In terms of the outside world at this date, Angola was indeed a mere pawn in the game played out between these two nations, each eager to supply much-needed slaves to the colonies of the New World. Its inhabitants were estimated as something lower than pawns: pieces without any significance so long as the supply was sufficient. About this time the captured Negroes destined for the slave ships and death, or a tormented exile of drudgery at best, were casually described by those responsible for their fate as 'brutes without intelligent understanding'.[28] That was not a description which anyone could or would have applied to Queen Jinga in the years of raiding against the Portuguese, aided by other tribes such as the Congolese and the Dembos, which followed.

Nor was she herself a pawn. Whatever the cruelties of her own practice, like Boadicea Jinga did at least stand for the independence of her race in the person of at least one individual (a female, as it happened). 'Every kind of display and power is necessary when dealing with this heathen', wrote Antonio de Oliveira Cadornego, about twenty years after Jinga's death;[29] but the reverse was of course also true for the Africans dealing with the European 'heathen'. In the late-twentieth-century meaning of the word, among so-called Mafia business organizations, Queen Jinga demanded and received 'respect'.

Captain Fuller's verdict on her, for all her 'Devilish Superstition and Idolatry', her ritual sacrifices and bizarre sexual habits, is fundamentally a respectful one. She was, he wrote, 'a cunning and prudent Virago, so much addicted to arms that she hardly uses other exercises; and withal so generously valiant that she never hurt a Portuguese after quarter given, and commanded all her slaves and soldiers alike'.[30] This is perceptibly the tone of the British Caratach praising his Roman enemy as a comrade-soldier in Fletcher's *Bonduca*; it is certainly not that of Caratach denouncing the Warrior Queen herself as a weak, boastful and shameless woman.

In the end the Queen was responsible, if indirectly, for the defeat of the Portuguese at the hands of the Dutch, by which Luanda fell to the latter in 1641. Her tactical withdrawal to the interior had obliged the Portuguese to penetrate too far from their own base in search of their slave-prey. Queen Jinga was now pleased to make allies of the Dutch. She set up camp on the Dande river. From this vantage point she could both despatch caravans to the Dutch at Luanda – selling them her prisoners of war – and conduct a series of short campaigns on her own account, notably against the puppet monarch of Ndongo, Ngola Ari, and his Portuguese sponsors.

In 1643 Queen Jinga's forces routed the Portuguese outside Mbaka and there were further victories in 1647 and 1648. Unfortunately an intervening defeat inflicted by the Portuguese resulted in the capture of Jinga's sister Mukumbu (to them the Lady Barbara), a considerable blow to one who had none of Queen Elizabeth I's dislike of her own sex, but rather relied on the matriarchal family network. Jinga's other sister Kifunji (the Lady Grace), long a captive of the Portuguese, had justified the Queen's faith in this network by supplying her with intelligence: in October 1647, Kifunji was drowned by the Portuguese as they retreated, either out of fear of her efforts or in retaliation.

On 10 August 1648, in a reversal of the events which had led to the seizing of Luanda by the Dutch, the daring Brazilian landowner Salvador de Sá recaptured the town for the Portuguese. This time it was the presence of two hundred Dutch soldiers at Jinga's side in her last victory of 1648 which had fatally weakened the garrison. With the return of Portuguese mastery to Luanda, Queen Jinga's finest hour was over. Yet even now, where the Kongo state made peace on humiliating terms, Jinga herself was able to retreat back to her Matamba heartlands. Here she was able to lie low for a few years; since the prime concern of the Portuguese remained their slave trade, and that depended on milking the interior, finally they had more to gain from negotiating with Jinga than battling against her. It was however the continued captivity of Mukumbu at the hands of the Portuguese which ultimately persuaded Jinga to agree to an official peace in October 1656.

One hundred and thirty slaves were formally exchanged for the person of 'the Lady Barbara', to be restored to her Mbundu *persona* for good. Other conditions imposed by the Portuguese were the establishment of 'trade fairs' along the borders of their Portuguese territories, and the introduction of a Christian mission into Matamba. In return 'the ancient Virago' – now in her seventies – was to receive military help when she required it. Lastly, in a settlement which was certainly to the advantage of most of the parties concerned, the Jagas were to abandon their notoriously savage habits: there was to be no more infanticide, for example, and although the women of the tribe were still compelled to give birth outside the war-camp, at least they could now bring up their offspring.

This peace lasted until Queen Jinga's death in 1663. After her death her corpse, still richly arrayed in the royal robes encrusted with precious stones, still clutching a bow and arrow in its hand, as though to symbolize the majesty and ferocity which were Jinga's dominant qualities, was formally displayed to her subjects.[31] They viewed it with a mixture of apprehension, awe and sorrow. All three reactions can surely be justified.

Even in the short term, the effect of Queen Jinga's rule was beneficial to the prosperity of Matamba – compared for example to the puppet kingdom of Ndongo, whose fortunes went rapidly downhill and which was eliminated altogether as an independent entity in 1671.[32] Matamba benefited from the trade and the missions, and did not suffer direct European authority. In addition, there were the many long-term legacies of her career. The first of these was the undeniable 'respect' she had earned by her own capabilities. 'History furnishes very few instances of bravery, intelligence and per-severance equal to the famous Zhinga, the Negro queen of Angola': thus wrote Mrs Child in 1833, at the beginning of the American movement for the emancipation of slaves. Mrs Child, a liberal writer, issued *An Appeal in Favor of that Class of Americans called Africans*.[33] She was concerned in particular to refute one contemporary argu-ment against such an emancipation, that the Negroes lacked the natural ability of the white race. Although Mrs Child granted that Queen Jinga had been a despot, and granted that she had committed murderous acts, she still cited the Queen's story as part of her impassioned plea, since her ability could hardly be doubted.

Then there is the 'pan-African' element to Jinga's rule, the fact that she did at certain points combine various tribes other than her own under her leadership (a leadership which in itself, being female, acts as an inspiration to a growing women's movement). Lastly, of course, and most importantly, in the People's Republic of Angola (established in 1975), there is the legacy of Jinga as the Warrior Queen who attempted gloriously but in vain to oust the Portuguese. Modern Angolan school textbooks naturally stress both of these aspects of Queen Jinga's heroic career.* 'She tried to unite the different peoples in the struggle against the foreign threat ... After a few years of effort she succeeded in her aims, which were to unite the people of Ndongo, Matamba, Congo, Casnje, Dembos, Kissama and the Central Planalto. This was the greatest alliance ever formed to fight against the foreign colonialists.' Even if Queen Jinga was not successful then, her 'great dream did not disappear. Her idea of a union of the Angolan people in its struggle against colonialism is today realized.'

Some modern Angolan students of history are beginning to assess Queen Jinga's contribution more critically: such matters as her alliance with the Dutch, her co-operation at various stages with the Portuguese, her own involvement in the slave trade, even her own claim to the throne, are being subjected at least to scrutiny. On the other hand the best known of all the legends about the Queen explains the deathless quality of her popular image, and why it is not likely to be widely superseded.

There are many variants of this story, but they unite in taking place in the course of that visit by Queen Jinga to the Portuguese Governor Correira de Sousa in the early 1620s in which her public career was inaugurated. They also unite in having the Governor seated on his throne, while Jinga was required to remain standing; whereupon Jinga, in a gesture at once characteristically bold and characteristically imperious, ordered one of her slaves to kneel on all fours to form a seat. After that she sat down. Did she refuse to take the slave away when she left the Governor's mansion, saying that she would not remove the Governor's furniture? Or did she refuse to remove the slave on the ground that she never sat on the same chair twice? Was the slave actually a maidservant? In one version, she even went as far as to have the slave (or maidservant) executed on the same ground: 'I have no further use for him [or her].'

The clear message of the story is the same in all its versions: even

* These quotations (originally in Portuguese) are taken from a fourth-form history textbook in use in an elementary school in Luanda in 1987.

in her enforced national subjection, Queen Jinga's personal pride was equal, even superior, to that of the Portuguese Governor. And this pride proved to be prophetic:

> Rome for empire far renown'd
> Tramples on a thousand states
> Soon her pride shall kiss the ground, –
> Hark! the Gaul is at her gates.

Once again Cowper's lines for a British Boadicea are more appropriate to another Warrior Queen in another country than they were to Britain – and British women – in the age in which he wrote them.

CHAPTER FIFTEEN

QUEEN
VERSUS MONSTER

Let us fight the Monster, let us beat the Monster down
Queen Louise of Prussia on Napoleon

A woman with a pretty face, but little intelligence and quite incapable of foreseeing the consequences of what she does
Napoleon on Queen Louise of Prussia

Butterflies are not associated with battlefields (although they may actually be found there, fluttering incongruously amid the trampled corn and wildflowers of a long hot bloodstained summer's day). Napoleon Bonaparte thought that women did not belong there either: he had a profound dislike of anything approaching the Amazon in womankind, and theoretically even intriguing women met with his censure. As he assured his first wife Josephine, he liked women to be *'bonnes, douces et conciliantes'* and on another occasion *'bonnes, naïves et douces'*; adding, with more tact than accuracy, that that was because such good, sweet, naïve, soothing women resembled her.[1]

The object of Napoleon's disapproval was Queen Louise of Prussia. Ironically enough, she was by nature quite as gentle and submissive as the most exigent male could require, as well as being as lovely a princess as ever won the heart of a king. It was cruel destiny – a destiny incarnated by Napoleon himself – which transformed this harmless and iridescent creature into a Warrior Queen 'dressed as an Amazon' as Napoleon termed her in 1806, in the uniform of her regiment of dragoons: writing twenty incendiary letters every day, 'an Armida in her madness destroying her own palace with fire'. The reference was to Gluck's opera *Armide*, popular with both French and Prussian audiences: it was in fact performed in Berlin for Louise's own wedding day. The eponymous heroine was a princess of Damascus at the time of the First Crusade, founded on Tasso's 'wily witch' in *Jerusalem Delivered* who, foiled of her lover, ended by calling on demons: 'destroy this palace!'[2]

Queen Louise's tragedy, in one sense, lay in the fact that she found herself matched against a man whom the Queen and her circle were inclined to sum up in one simple expression of horror as the 'Monster'. This was of course too simple a judgement: the real threat was not so much in Napoleon's perceived monstrosity of nature as in the brilliance of his military talent. Even one of Louise's staunchest confidantes ruefully admitted that war was Napoleon's trade: 'he understands it and we do not'.[3]

But there was another deeper layer to Louise's tragedy, which made of her a genuine martyr to her people's own zeal at the time, as well as a patriotic heroine and martyr to the generations which followed. If Napoleon was indeed a monster, then it was optimistic at best to match the frail Queen Louise against him. Why did the fact that she emerged crushed from the encounter, failing to save Prussia from his depredations, generate surprise as well as despair? This was a development which must always have been expected along a level of common sense. The answer lies in the false but exciting expectations sometimes aroused in the human breast by the sight of one type of Warrior Queen: 'sainted' and 'possessed of angelic goodness' – descriptions freely applied to Queen Louise – this Holy Figurehead of the Prussian armies must surely bless her people with victory over the forces of evil.

It is true that the Queen did have, apart from her beauty, the natural appeal of a female in distress, to which male soldiers traditionally reply by springing to arms. It is a point of view most famously expressed by Edmund Burke in his lament for another tragic queen, Marie Antoinette: 'I thought ten thousand swords must have leaped from their scabbards to avenge even a look that threatened her with insult'. In similar if less exotic terms Robert Wilson, a young British envoy at the Prussian court, wrote movingly of the spectacle of Louise's melancholy following the defeat at Jena in 1806: 'but soldiers must not reflect, and a beautiful woman in misfortune should animate to enterprise'. Besides, Louise's grief was a potent symbol of her nation's woe, for which reason 'a queen in distress is universally acknowledged to be a more tragical sight than the more disastrous and general calamities of the commonalty'.[4]

Despite this inspiration, Queen Louise's own powers as a Warrior Queen were, if challenged by the brutal reality of conflict and disaster, a mere illusion, vanishing into the mists of romance and chivalry from whence they came. Her story illustrates how the 'fancy dress' aspect of a Warrior Queen, so brilliantly developed by Elizabeth I at Tilbury to mask the possible weaknesses of her position as a female ruler in time of war, might come to be mistaken for the real thing: a passive queen allows herself to be used, ignorant of the true hollowness of her position because she has been trained by upbringing to female impotence, just as Boadicea, a doughty battling queen in literature at the end of the sixteenth century, becomes a modest and delicate princess two hundred years later, who conquers with a blush not a spear, rides in a litter not a chariot.

Under different circumstances – and with a different character involved – the 'distress' of a queen could indeed be used to good effect. Robert Wilson, suggesting that Louise's misfortunes should spur her supporters to military action on her behalf, recalled the example of Maria Theresa sixty years before: 'So thought and felt the nobles of Hungary, and Maria Theresa retrieved the fortunes of her house.' The reigns of two great empresses, Maria Theresa of Austria and Catherine the Great of Russia, spanned altogether over seventy years, 1740 to 1780 and 1762 to 1796 respectively. Gibbon was well able to write in his *Decline and Fall*, first printed in 1776, of those 'illustrious women' able to bear the weight of empire: 'nor is our own age destitute'.[5]

These great tracts of time were matched by the vast tracts of land over which each woman presided. At first sight, however, the resemblance between the two stops there; not only their characters but the circumstances which brought them to power were certainly very different. The Archduchess Maria Theresa was a young married woman of twenty-three when the death of her father the Emperor Charles VI brought the male Habsburg succession to an end; but by that treaty of 1713 known as the Pragmatic Sanction, the right of his eldest daughter to succeed had been theoretically accepted. Sophie-Auguste of Anhalt-Zerbst, born in 1729 and thus twelve years younger than Maria Theresa, was on the other hand an obscure German princess before her marriage to the Grand Duke Peter, heir to the Tsarina Elisabeth of Russia. By this union she was transformed first into the Grand Duchess Catherine, and then, following a dramatic coup in which her doltish husband was deposed, into the Tsarina Catherine II; she was by now in her early thirties, someone who could claim to have contributed strongly to her own surprising exaltation.

When time and various military endeavours had combined to establish Maria Theresa securely on her hereditary throne of Hungary, with her husband Francis of Lorraine beside her as the elected Holy Roman Emperor, she displayed in private a love of cosy royal family life with her apparent infinity of children. Personally chaste, she also showed an austerity, even puritanism of temperament which recalls the 'sainted' Isabella of Spain. The pleasures of Catherine II were, notoriously, rather different. This was Voltaire's 'Semiramis of the North', the Warrior Queen with a taste for magnificently strong guards officers as lovers, who in her day created a sensation for her debauchery: 'excesses which would dishonour any woman whatever her station in life' in the disapproving opinion of the British Ambassador to her court. She herself actually believed, engagingly enough, in frequent (and incidentally straightforward) sexual activity as a means to health; but she never denied that it was also enjoyable, and as such should be welcomed. 'Nothing in my opinion is more difficult to resist than what gives us pleasure', wrote Catherine. 'All arguments to the contrary are prudery.' It was a hedonistic point of view shared in no way by the pious and self-abnegatory Maria Theresa.[6]

Yet there *was* a further interesting resemblance between the two rulers despite their opposing personal morality. Both the Queen–Empress and the Tsarina encountered that familiar problem for a reigning female, the need to exert military leadership, or at least some kind of leadership in war (although the Russian Empire, unlike Austria, had known the rule of other women autocrats, including Catherine's own mother-in-law Elisabeth). In both cases, they made use of the skilful technique of Elizabeth I, putting on a show of glory, in which the appealing femininity was artfully contrasted with stern and indeed noble patriotic resolve. And neither of them, despite presiding over military victories, had that heroic love of war for its own sake which has marked so many male rulers: Louis XIV, who boasted in 1662 that glory was the principal aim of all his actions, recommended his great-grandson on his deathbed half a century later, 'Do not imitate my love of war.'[7]

The first challenge to Maria Theresa occurred when Frederick the Great of Prussia snatched her province of Silesia only seven weeks after her father's death. To Carlyle, this act of territorial rape, contrary to Frederick's promised word, was merely the Prussian King grabbing bravely at Opportunity as at a wild horse: 'rushing hitherward, swift, terrible, clothed with lightning like a courser of the gods; dare you catch *him* by the thunder-mane and fling yourself upon him ... '. Many may prefer the cooler estimate of Macaulay concerning the War of the Austrian Succession: 'The selfish rapacity of the King of Prussia gave the signal to his neighbours. The whole world sprang to arms ... '. (We might forgive Carlyle for his blithe cruelty towards one Warrior Queen, for the sake of that bright suggestion made to the young Miss Jane Welsh that Boadicea would be the ideal subject for her initial 'literary effort', with the comforting rider that 'she need not be "big" or "grim" unless you like' – except for the fact that bigness and grimness were the qualities that Carlyle evidently admired.)[8]

The young Maria Theresa was hailed as Queen of Hungary by her loyal subjects in that country, or rather by an oxymoron of a title – *domina et rex noster* (our mistress and our king), another variant of that familiar theme of gender transference. In her beleaguered state, the *domina–rex* was at least armed with one important weapon in the shape of an infant male heir; and she was quick to play upon the appealing possibilities of the image of the Warrior Queen as Young Mother. Sending a picture of herself and the child to General Khevenmüller in 1742 just after he had taken Munich on her behalf, Maria Theresa wrote this accompanying letter: 'Dear and faithful Khevenmüller – Here you behold a queen who knows what it is to be forsaken by the whole world. And here also is the heir to her throne. What do you think will become of this child?'[9] The next day the troops at Linz were shown both the picture and the letter, amid outbursts of wild enthusiasm.

At her coronation at Pressburg (Bratislava) in Hungary Maria

Theresa mounted a huge black charger, and according to immemorial custom drew her sword to the four points of the compass, to signify her role as Hungary's protector. This was once again Elizabeth I at Tilbury, making the show stand for the substance, especially as Maria Theresa had to learn to ride astride specially for the event: furthermore, she had only just over a month in which to do so (following the invitation to Pressburg) and was in the process of recovering from the birth of her first son. Thereafter Maria Theresa continued to enjoy all the spectacles of military life such as reviews, parades and manoeuvres in which she could similarly display herself. She designed a uniform for herself and her ladies on these occasions which combined the practical chamois leather breeches and boots of the *rex* beneath, with the voluminous skirts of the *domina* above.

None of this amounted to a predilection for warmongering. The frequent battles she had to fight were more likely to be in defence of her own inheritance than in pursuit of others'. Indeed the Queen (in her own right) and Empress (by virtue of her husband's election) displayed on occasion a consciousness of the sheer immorality of national aggression which seems to have been rooted in her own personal piety. When the Polish Partition of 1772 was first suggested, Maria Theresa protested against the robbing of an innocent nation 'that it has hitherto been our boast to protect and support', adding 'The greatness and strength of a state will not be taken into consideration when we are called to render our final account.' Towards the end of her life the Empress protested vehemently against Austria's attempt to annex Bavaria: 'Let them call me a coward, a weakling, a dotard if they like [she was approaching sixty], nothing shall prevent me from extricating Europe from this perilous situation.' Afterwards she said: 'For me it is an inexpressible happiness to have prevented a great effusion of blood.'

More symbolic of her personal style than the image of the young Queen on the black charger at the beginning of the reign, is that presented by the statue erected in the nineteenth century opposite the Hofburg in Vienna. Here the Empress – 'the General and first Mother of the said Dominions', as she described herself – is seen presiding like an enormous benevolent muffin in her long dress and ceremonial robes (there is no glimpse of those practical chamois leather breeches and boots).[10] All about her, at the four corners of the statue, prance on horses, her male generals and ministers, both smaller and more active.

Unlike Maria Theresa, Catherine the Great did have, it is true, a penchant towards glory. When she told her adoring correspondent Voltaire in 1771 that 'the nation's glory is my own, that is my principle',[11] she summed up an intelligent philosophy which explained how she had come to rule the unwieldy Russias so successfully for the last nine years. This little German Princess had loved rough games as a child, hating to be fobbed off with dolls and cots instead of riding and shooting birds with the local children. As the unheeded bride of the Grand Duke Peter – their marriage was not consummated for nine years – she took her chief pleasure in riding, even in bed, by her own account, where she galloped away her frustration as 'a postilion on my pillow'.[12] When the Tsarina Elisabeth protested that riding like a man on a flat saddle led to sterility, the neglected wife replied pointedly that the more violent the exercise, the more she liked it. As Tsarina herself, Catherine put this caged energy to good use.

The coup against Catherine's husband, who had succeeded as the Tsar Peter III at the beginning of 1762, took place six months later. It was ten o'clock of the light northern night on 29 June, according to the Russian style of dating; there was thus scarcely any darkness to shroud the startling spectacle of the Grand Duchess Catherine, dressed in uniform, at the head of the rebel regiments whose members included prominently her current lover Grigory Orlov and his brother. When these rebels – disgusted by the Tsar's pro-German policies – had come for Catherine, she had borrowed the green and red uniform of a young officer, Captain Talietzin, in the Semeonovsky regiment, who was slight enough for his clothes to fit her. Her lady-in-waiting Princess Dashkova took the uniform of another young officer, Lieutenant Poushkin. According to the Princess's memoirs, it was she, Dashkova, who suggested that her mistress should now substitute the Order of St Andrew for that of St Catherine worn over her uniform: the order of St Andrew was theoretically worn only by the reigning sovereign, and the substitution was thus a dramatic gesture indicating the assumption of command.[13]

'For a man's work, you needed a man's outfit' was Catherine's official explanation for her masculine attire[14] (although since she had been accustomed to steal out of her palace in man's costume to meet her lover Stanislaus Poniatowski, it could clearly be used for a woman's work as well). The former tomboy easily mounted the mettlesome grey stallion brought for her use and mastered it. With her drawn sword and her long flowing hair beneath her black three-cornered hat lined with sable and decorated with oak leaves, the symbols of victory, Catherine now presented a very passable goddess of war at the head of her troops. The loyalty inspired by the sight was epitomized when a young NCO rushed forward to present her with a pennant for her naked sword. His name was Grigory Potemkin.

During her long reign, her triumphant progress towards military victories galore – she listed seventy-eight of them – Catherine never failed to present herself wherever possible in the same heroic light. When the French diplomat the Comte de Ségur first saw her in 1785, he found her 'richly attired, her hand resting on a column'. Her majestic air, the pride in her expression and her 'slightly theatrical pose' so took him aback that he forgot his speech of welcome. So successful was this projection that the portrait painter Madame Vigée Le Brun, meeting her during a tour of Russia, was amazed to discover that the Tsarina was actually very short: 'I had fancied her prodigiously tall, as high as her grandeur'.[15]

Ségur described her in the course of that triumphal procession to Kiev of 1787 arranged by Potemkin, following the defeat of Turkey and Russia's annexation of the Crimea, which brought her both the fruitful steppes of the south and an invaluable access to the Black Sea. Stout and tiny in her military uniform, she was nevertheless 'a conquering empress'. The descendants of the Tartars who had once swept across this territory (putting an end to the Georgian empire of Tamara) now prostrated themselves before 'a woman and a Christian'.[16] When a Georgian prince from Colchis brought presents to the foot of the Russian Tsarina Catherine's throne, it might be argued that the memory of Queen Tamara, in her sex if not her nationality, had been avenged.

Catherine, like Tamara six centuries before, understood how to make use of that deep mystical Slavic feeling towards the mother goddess, as well as the conquering goddess of war. To Orlov she was 'little mother' as well as 'most merciful sovereign lady'. To the later lover Potemkin she was 'Mother Tsarina Catherine . . . far more than a mother to me . . . my benefactress and my mother'. On the other hand, like Queen Elizabeth I, she did not consider that she belonged (unlike most mothers) to the 'weak, frivolous, whining species of women'; in this respect she was certainly the Warrior Queen as an honorary male. When Catherine founded an orphanage, for example, she ordered that the girls should learn to cook and make bread, following the much praised women of the Bible and those hard-working ones celebrated by Homer[17] (by which she definitely did not mean the Bible's sword-wielding Judith or Homer's flashing-eyed Athene, felling the war-god Ares with a stone).

At her accession, in fact, Catherine suffered from the same prudent dislike of war as Elizabeth I and for the same reason: the debts incurred by Russia during the Seven Years' War, which ended a year later in 1763. Even in 1770, after a successful campaign against the Turks, Catherine believed peace to be a fine thing, though she now admitted that war also had its 'fine moments'.[18]

Voltaire's correspondence with Catherine concerning the Turks was on a far more rambunctious level and there is a nice flavour of chivalry too: 'these barbarians deserve to be punished by a heroine for the lack of respect they have hitherto had for ladies', he wrote to the Tsarina in November 1768, a month after war had been declared by the Turks. 'Clearly, people who neglect all the fine arts and who lock up women, deserve to be exterminated.' A year later he was admonishing his 'Semiramis' and his 'Northern Star' in still more ardent terms: 'Come now, heir to the Caesars, head of the Holy Roman Empire, defender of the Latin Church, come now, this is your chance.' When there was news of a victory, he described himself as jumping out of bed in ecstasy: 'Your Imperial Majesty has brought me back to life by killing the Turks.' Voltaire's subsequent salute was a weird parody of the language of religion: for he began by crying 'Allah! Catherine!' and went on to sing 'Te Catharinam laudamus, te dominam confitemur'.[19]

Catherine herself had a more controlled appreciation of these tumultuous events. Did they serve the interest of Russian greatness (with which of course she identified herself)? That was her persistent concern. She had her own well-developed sense of Russian national pride – Russia, the country she had so successfully adopted. Not only did she display a taste for operas which celebrated Russian history, she also littered the imperial grounds at Tsarskoe Selo with monumental reminders of Russian military triumphs including obelisks and marble columns as well as war memorials. In 1771 she agreed with Voltaire that 'this army will win Russia a name for herself'. But when she declared that 'great events have never displeased me and great conquests have never tempted me', the second half of her statement was not quite as disingenuous as the list of her achievements and territorial acquisitions might indicate.[20]

Her own nominee on the throne of Poland and some of its territory annexed by Russia, further acquisitions on the Alaskan coast, to say nothing of the defeat of Turkey and Russia's surge into the Crimea, her revenues mightily increased: all this was brought about by only six years of war in her twenty-five-year reign. Nor, in all this, was Catherine a mere glittering figurehead of a Warrior Queen. Where military and naval matters were concerned, she played an active directing part. Attending twice-weekly meetings of the seven-man council which directed the war during the Crimean campaign, she herself was probably the originator of the daredevil plan whereby the Russian fleet in the Baltic sailed five thousand miles round the coasts of Western Europe to engage the Turks.

The results of this brilliantly executed expansionist policy for Russia were extraordinary: twenty million subjects owed Catherine loyalty at her coronation, compared to thirty-six million in 1795 shortly before her death. It was however expansion, not war itself with its manufactured heroics, which interested her, even if she could manufacture heroics herself with a will, where necessary. 'We need population not devastation': that was her philosophy. In short, as she herself declared, 'peace is necessary to this vast empire':[21] a perceptive comment on the vast Russian 'empire' at any stage of its history.

Where Warrior Queens are concerned, we return from the users – Maria Theresa and Catherine – to the used – Louise of Prussia. Although described by Napoleon as an 'Armida', there was by temperament nothing of Tasso's 'wily witch' and Gluck's destructive enchantress about Queen Louise of Prussia. 'Every day I realize that I am a weak woman,' she wrote during her early carefree years, 'and I am weak because I am kindhearted. I want everyone to be

Canossa in 1077; Countess Matilda of Tuscany extends a supplicating hand to Pope Gregory VII, on behalf of the kneeling, penitent Emperor Henry IV; from Donizo's contemporary *Vita Mathildis*.

Fifteenth-century depiction of the Empress Maud (Matilda), claimant to the throne of England, from a history of England written by monks at St. Albans.

A nineteenth-century Belgian evocation of Countess Matilda at Canossa, painted by Alfred Cluysenaar.

Queen Tamara of Georgia; an engraving published in 1859.

The monogram of Queen Tamara, formed from the letters TAMAR in the Georgian knightly hand, and employed in the copper coinage of her reign.

Queen Isabella of Spain; a detail from the painting *The Madonna of the Catholic Kings.*

Medal (*c.* 1480) showing Caterina Sforza, the spirited daughter of the Duke of Milan; her fate, as a would-be female ruler of Forlì, contrasted unhappily with that of Isabella of Spain.

Triumphal entry of Ferdinand and Isabella, 'the Catholic kings' of Spain, into Granada in January 1492 following the conquest of the last Moorish kingdom; a bas-relief on the altar of the Royal Chapel in the Cathedral.

The earliest loose popular print of Queen Elizabeth I: William Rogers' *Eliza, Triumphans* of 1589 (the year following the defeat of the Spanish Armada) shows the Queen as Peace, with an olive branch in her hand, while Victory and Plenty proffer her their crowns.

Opposite above: *Queen Elizabeth and the Three Goddesses* (Juno, Pallas Athene and Venus seen against a background of Windsor Castle), attributed to Joris Hoefnagel, 1569; it has been suggested that this allegorical picture refers to the Queen's suppression of the Northern Rebellion, the first military initiative of her reign. Opposite below: Panel from St Faith's Church, King's Lynn, showing Queen Elizabeth reviewing her troops at Tilbury in 1588.

A group of illustrations of the life of Jinga Mbandi, the seventeenth-century Queen of Angola, from *Relation Historique de l'Ethiopie Occidentale* by Father J. P. Labat, 1732.

Top: Queen Jinga being received by the Portuguese Governor, Correira de Sousa, in about 1622; according to the best-known legend about her, she commanded one of her servants to form a seat when the Governor failed to offer her a chair. Center: Queen Jinga receives Christian baptism as the Lady Anna de Sousa (in honour of the Governor); she subsequently returned to her tribal name, variously given as Zhinga, Nzinga and Jinga. Left: Queen Jinga venerates the bones of her brother, whom she succeeded as ruler. (Some stories hold that she had him murdered.)

Statue of Queen Anne by Rysbrack at Blenheim Palace; the reality of her appearance was very different from this august image.

Below: The Empress Catherine II of Russia, after a portrait by V. Erichsen painted in 1762, the year of her coronation; this followed the coup by which, at the head of the rebel regiments, she supplanted her husband Tsar Peter III. She borrowed a uniform to do so: 'For a man's work, you needed a man's outfit', she wrote.

The Empress Maria Theresa of Austria at her coronation as Queen of Hungary at Pressburg in 1742; she mounted a charger and drew her sword to the four points of the compass to signify her role as Hungary's protector, according to the ancient tradition of the Hungarian kings.

Nineteenth-century monument to Maria Theresa opposite the Hofburg in Vienna, showing her towering majestically above her male ministers and generals.

Queen Louise of Prussia, painted by Grassi in 1802 when she was twenty-six. 'There prevails a feeling of chivalrous devotion towards her', wrote an English diplomat at her court; 'a glance of her bright laughing eyes is a mark of favour eagerly sought for'.

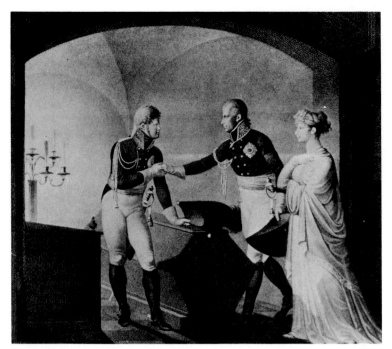

The celebrated print of King Frederick William III of Prussia and the Tsar
Alexander I swearing brotherhood over the tomb of Frederick the Great,
watched by Queen Louise; after Napoleon's occupation of Berlin a cruel
caricature of the same print was issued, with the Tsar as Nelson and Louise
as Lady Hamilton, currently notorious in Europe as Nelson's mistress.

Napoleon receiving Queen Louise at Tilsit, 6 July 1807; the Queen is supported by
her husband and watched by the Tsar. A detail from a picture by N. L. F. Gosse.

The Rani of Jhansi, a watercolour from Kalighat, 1890.

Contemporary painting, by an unknown artist, of Lakshmi Bai, the Rani of Jhansi; both Indian and British sources bear witness to her striking appearance.

Below: The site of the massacre of Europeans at Jhansi on 7 July 1857; the Rani was subsequently blamed — unjustly — for betraying them.

Hindu mythology contains several warrior goddesses; here Durga, wife of Siva, is seen, seated on her tiger, slaying the demon Mahesasura with the aid of her ten arms; unlike Kali, another of Siva's wives and the goddess of destruction, Durga (to whom both the Rani and Mrs Gandhi were compared) is portrayed as beautiful and basically benevolent, despite her capacity for aggression.

Statue of the Rani of Jhansi at Gwalior; she was killed here on or about 17 June 1858, leading her men in a battle to defend the fortress from the British assault under Sir Hugh Rose.

Mrs Golda Meir salutes the detachment commander of Israeli paratroops; her own 'grandmotherly' uniform includes a handbag.

Well-wishers present garlands to Mrs Indira Gandhi, Prime Minister of India and Leader of the Congress Party. (The newspaper caption to this photograph read 'Garlands for Mother Indira'.)

Mrs Margaret Thatcher with a
model of a Chieftain tank in 1987.

Her Majesty Queen Elizabeth II
in military uniform at the Trooping of the Colour, enacting the
purely ceremonial role of the
'Armed Figurehead'.

Mrs Thatcher at the dinner held on 26 January 1988 to celebrate her record as the longest-serving Prime Minister in twentieth-century Britain; she is surrounded by members of her Cabinet (her husband Denis Thatcher is on her left); it is noticeable that there are no female Cabinet ministers to distract attention from the central figure in her glittering brocade costume, amid the attendant dinner-jacketed males.

A June 1982 cartoon of Mrs Thatcher in Boadicean breastplates and driving a chariot (Ronald Reagan is seen, somewhat smaller, as a cowboy). It was published in the *Daily Express* following Mrs Thatcher's appearance on American television after the conclusion of the Falklands War, in which she described herself as having the 'reputation of being the Iron Lady'.

happy, and so I forgive, forget, and fail to scold when I should . . . '.[22]

Like Catherine a minor German princess, Louise of Mecklenburg-Strelitz possessed, apart from this sweet feminine pliancy, the gift of beauty. On Louise's exquisite looks there is a remarkable agreement of testimony. In 1793, when she was seventeen, her ravishing appearance captured the heart of Frederick William, the shy young heir to the throne of Prussia: 'it is she, and if not she, no other creature in the world', he is reputed to have exclaimed at the mere sight of her (much as Isabella of Castile is supposed to have greeted Ferdinand). A decade later, seeing the Prussian Queen dressed as Statira, the Persian bride of Alexander the Great at a fête in Berlin, Madame de Staël was 'struck dumb by her beauty'. In 1801 Madame Vigée Le Brun, whose observant painter's eye was disappointed in the stature of Catherine the Great, alleged that her pen failed her in trying to describe Louise. The Queen happened to be in deep mourning on their first encounter, but her coronet of black jet served only to set off the dazzling whiteness of her complexion; as for the beauty of her 'heavenly' face Madame Vigée Le Brun compared it to that of a sixteen-year-old girl, with the perfect regularity and delicacy of the features, the grace of figure, neck and arms: 'all was enchanting beyond anything imaginable!'[23]

In life this perfect regularity of feature and the supple slender figure often led to Queen Louise being compared to a Greek statue. For once, the art by which later generations must judge confirms and does not disappoint: there is something neo-Hellenic about the many representations of her which have survived, enhanced naturally by the clinging Grecian style of contemporary fashion which suited her so well. We can accept with relief the verdict of the English diplomat Sir George Jackson that the Queen was 'really a beauty and would be thought so even if she did not sit upon a throne'. The chivalry she inspired is equally easy to understand: 'among the younger men especially', wrote Jackson, 'there prevails a feeling of chivalrous devotion towards her; and a sunny smile, or glance of her bright laughing eyes, is a mark of favour eagerly sought for'.[24]

At first it was all lightness at the Prussian court, Frederick William succeeding his father in 1797, four years after his marriage. Perhaps the Queen – who was after all young – danced a little too much (she danced at a court ball in 1803 within hours of giving birth) and she was also lightheartedly unpunctual. There are unpublished passages in the diary of Countess Sophie von Voss, Louise's battleaxe of a lady-in-waiting (already in her seventies, with a father who fought against Marlborough at Malplaquet) that criticize the Queen's frivolity and even her petulance in these early years; but Countess Voss's final verdict was to be very different: 'all the loveliest virtues of woman and the most pleasing to God'.[25]

On the other hand Louise's surely admirable attempts at enlarging her perfunctory education with a study of German literature, to which more intellectual ladies-in-waiting introduced her, were greeted with boorish mockery by Frederick William. He described one of these intellectuals, Caroline von Berg, as 'vain, trivial ... and forever gushing poetry'. Nor was the reputation of Goethe sacred to the Prussian King. 'Wha's 'is name, t'great man from Weimar?' Frederick William would enquire, aping the local dialect. Another of these ladies, Marie von Kleist, aunt by marriage to the poet and playwright Heinrich von Kleist, persuaded the Queen to patronize her nephew; he received an honorarium under oath of secrecy.[26] Schiller became a special favourite: the Queen wanted him as Poet Laureate. She also read Shakespeare in translation.

The Queen's tentative efforts at intellectual independence had however little in common with that kind of Amazonian behaviour described with all the richness of sexual violence in Kleist's *Penthesilea*: 'A nation has arisen, a nation of women, Bound to no overlord...'.[27] Louise's submissiveness, her wifely wish to please, was most notably demonstrated by the continuous procession of children that she bore. Ten years after her marriage she had already born seven; two of the children had died and there were also various miscarriages. Louise gave birth to a total of nine children in fourteen years, the last of them less than a year before her death.

When Madame Vigée Le Brun met the Queen in 1801, she could not make an appointment before noon because, as Louise explained, 'the King reviews the troops at ten every morning and likes me to attend'. The only blight on this picture of domestic and marital bliss appeared to be the plain looks of Louise's numerous children. 'They are not pretty', murmured the Queen sadly. 'Their faces have a great deal of character', was the painter's tactful comment. Privately, she thought the youthful princes and princesses of Prussia downright ugly.[28]

But for Prussia and its king – if not yet its queen – already problems existed along more serious lines than those of a military review or a homely royal family. The rise of Napoleonic France had placed Prussia in a quandary: neutrality? And if not neutrality, alliance with which of the various great powers involved? It was a profound Prussian conviction of the time that its army, built up by Frederick William's great-uncle Frederick the Great, remained the finest in Europe. Time would test the validity of that belief. In the meantime Frederick William's indecisive nature led him to see his fine army as a bastion of Prussia's neutrality rather than as anything more aggressive.

The King's personal quandary however – neutrality versus alliance – remained. And it was this quandary, finally, which brought Louise to play the role of Warrior Queen. In 1803 the French forces occupied Hanover, a state which on the one hand Prussia was pledged to protect as a neutral zone, and on the other coveted for itself. Prussia was offered Hanover in return for a treaty with France. Frederick William hesitated unhappily. Napoleon made good use of his dilemma of conscience. The French judicial murder of the young Bourbon Prince the Duc d'Enghien on 21 March 1804 for alleged conspiracy horrified all royal Europe: but Louise was persuaded not to wear mourning for the Duc by the new Prussian Foreign Minister, the veteran statesman Carl-August von Hardenberg, who hoped to secure Hanover peaceably.

Louise's martial instincts were still nascent. Placatory gifts of dresses from the newly created Empress Josephine (Napoleon assumed the title of Emperor on 18 May) were accepted: pale grey satin magnificently embroidered with steel, and white satin embroidered with gold thread, further adorned with Alençon lace and Brussels point. The Queen's attempts at influencing the King towards war were dated nearly a year later by Sir George Jackson to February 1805. It was not until September of the same year that she was generally reputed to head the 'war party'.[29]

What brought about the transformation? Napoleon himself angrily and publicly ascribed the change to another charismatic man: the Tsar Alexander I. There had been that magic summer at the Baltic coastal resort of Memel in 1802, the year following the accession of the young Tsar. The grandson of Catherine the Great, Alexander was an intensely attractive figure: even the crabby

Countess Voss found him at this stage 'irresistible', with his handsome appearance and striking fair colouring (he was of course genetically far more German than Slav, his mother like his grandmother having been born a German princess).[30] Memel, symbolically enough, was not only on the Baltic, but also on the borders of Prussia and Russia: here the two courts mingled and the two youthful royal families – already interrelated – relaxed together.

Louise flowered. 'She was today more beautiful than ever', wrote Countess Voss of one particular June evening. There was dancing every night, and presents for Louise from the Tsar including earrings of her favourite pearls (even Countess Voss got a pearl necklace). No wonder the Countess wrote that she was 'quite grieved that these pleasant days should come to an end'.[31] But further delightful co-celebrations were planned by Alexander, such as a pageant based on the happy days at Memel for Louise's birthday the following March; Louise's current baby would be named Alexandrina with the Tsar as her godfather.

For all Napoleon's subsequent excoriations in which he vowed that the Prussian Queen had been 'so good, so gentle' until the Tsar's baleful influence made her desert 'the serious occupation of her dressing-table' for politics,[32] the story of an actual affair between Alexander and Louise was certainly a calumny. That primitive desire to find a Warrior Queen either preternaturally lustful or preternaturally chaste (Louise came in for both charges) may have played its part. The truth of Louise's feelings for Alexander was probably subtler. What a contrast the romantic young Tsar – born in 1777, he was a year younger than Louise – presented to the vacillating and uncultured Frederick William! For Louise, well knowing her duty both as a wife and a queen, her unacknowledged sentimental devotion to the Tsar could be safely expressed in a public admiration for his policies and a trust in his political objectives. 'I believe in you as I believe in God', she wrote to Alexander at one point:[33] this idolatry was not the outburst of a voluptuous and satisfied woman.

The late summer of 1805 brought persistent murmurs of war in the Prussian capital of Berlin. How could Prussia stand aloof while the French devoured half Europe? Frederick William reflected gloomily concerning his impossible position on 12 September: 'Many a king has fallen because he loved war too well, but I may fall because I am in love with peace.'[34] There was no doubt that the general Prussian mood veered towards war. Napoleon's enemy the Tsar was cheered wildly at the opera in Berlin (the performance incidentally was of *Armide*). And when a secret pact was finally concluded between Russia and Prussia, agreeing to send an ultimatum to Napoleon, Louise's influence over Frederick William was generally believed by those in the know to have brought it about. The treaty was signed on 3 November 1805. That night the three friends – Alexander, Louise and Frederick William – went secretly together to visit the tomb of Frederick the Great at the Tsar's request (a popular contemporary print would depict them standing reverently beside the historic sepulchre). The episode represented the romantic culmination of Louise's hopes that war would not only stop the unstoppable Napoleon, but bring honour to the Prussian King at last, by uniting him with the brave and honourable Tsar of Russia.

At the beginning of the next month it was Louise's turn to be cheered wildly as she stood on the palace balcony to watch the Prussian troops leaving Berlin, the banners dipping as they passed. Her popularity with the army at this point knew no bounds. Here was their beloved patroness, she who had in peacetime attended those morning parades, danced at their balls, befriended young officers in trouble; now she was to be not only their queen but their goddess of victory. Moreover Louise herself had always reciprocated these feelings. When the Tsar praised her good relationships with the military, the Queen replied that 'such a respected estate, whose vocation brought such toil and changes of fortune could not be admired enough'.[35]

Unknown to the Queen on her balcony, one of those swift changes of fortune which would affect the destiny of the bonny Prussian soldiers beneath her had already taken place. In late October Napoleon had secured the capitulation of the Austrians at Ulm; on 13 November he entered Vienna; on 2 December, in a brilliant striking manoeuvre, he had utterly crushed the Austrian and Russian forces at Austerlitz. When the news reached the Queen in Berlin, she exclaimed that 'no one who is a German can hear of this and not be moved'. She was right to see the chilling significance of the defeat. Prussia for her part was simply told she must accept the territorial changes imposed: Hanover for example could be retained, but Ausbach ('the cradle of the Hohenzollern race' as Louise tear-fully told Frederick William), Neuchâtel and Cleves with its fortress of Wesel must be given up. In June 1806 the Holy Roman Empire would be brutally ended, the Confederation of the Rhine put in its place.

The Queen, passionately opposed to the ratification of this Treaty, wrote: 'There is only one thing to be done, let us fight the Monster, let us beat the Monster down, and then we can talk of worries!'[36] Her words became a patriotic slogan for the party still resolutely opposed to dealing with Napoleon, just as the Queen herself was increasingly credited with all the qualities of inspiration the King so signally lacked. Prince Louis Ferdinand, Frederick William's clever raffish cousin, remarked that if the people knew how much Louise had done, they would raise altars to her everywhere. Even without the benefit of altars, popular admiration expressed itself in a thousand ways. One unit demanded that its name be changed to the Queen's Cuirassiers! Let Louise lead them!

With a weak king and a valiant queen, there was the inevitable emergence of the Better-Man Syndrome. After this period of debate and anxiety was over, Hardenberg would quote the famous words of Catherine de Foix to her husband Jean d'Albret: 'If we had been born, you Catherine and I Don Jean, we would not have lost our kingdom.' Queen Louise, he said, had an equal right to address her husband thus.[37]

It was not until the autumn of 1806 that the Prussian King's hopes of treating with France were formally abandoned; he agreed at last to combine with the allies including Russia, Austria and England, to try to beat the 'Monster'. By this time Queen Louise's personal fixation against Napoleon as the source of all their woes had begun to be matched by the anger of the Emperor at what the Prussians considered her patriotic fervour but he deemed her womanly interference in dragging Prussia away from France. The Bulletin of the Army, an official propaganda publication, printed a conversation Napoleon was said to have had with Marshal Berthier: 'a beautiful queen wants to see a battle, so let us be gallant. Let us march off at once to Saxony.' It went on to report Napoleon's outburst quoted earlier concerning the Queen with her army 'dressed as an Amazon'. On another occasion: 'So – Mademoiselle de Mecklenburg [an allusion to Louise's birth outside Prussia] wants to make war on me, does she? Let her come! I am not afraid of women.'[38]

This elevation of Queen Louise to something more than a pretty woman attired from time to time in a becoming adaptation of military uniform suited both sides, in fact. But the Queen's true intentions were probably better interpreted by Thomas Hardy later in his poetic drama *The Dynasts*, than by Napoleon. Here Hardy has the loyal Berliners protest against Napoleon's insulting epithet of Amazon: 'Her whose each act Shows but a mettled modest woman's zeal ... To fend off ill from home!'[39] Alas, the mettled but modest Louise, like Armida, but for very different reasons, would all too soon find that very home laid low.

The French victory over Prussia at the double battle Jena–Auerstädt on 14 October 1806 virtually obliterated the Prussian army, that force which had, under Frederick the Great – dead only twenty years before – terrorized Europe. In the wake of the general destruction, the Queen found herself enquiring wildly for her husband: 'Where is the King?' 'I don't know, Your Majesty.' 'But, my God, isn't the King with the army?' 'The army? It no longer exists.'[40] The Prussian army, Prussia itself and for that matter Queen Louise were none of them ever to be quite the same after this ghastly day of national humiliation. (The French Marshal Davout would be made Duc d'Auerstädt for defeating an army twice his own strength.) A week before the battle, Frederick von Gentz, the philosopher–politician, had an interview with the Queen at the Prussian war camp in which she expressed herself 'with a precision, a firmness and energy, and at the same time with a restraint and wisdom, that would have enchanted me in a man'.[41] Afterwards, the Queen was transformed into both a fugitive and an invalid.

Her flight from the French was real enough. Napoleon had hoped that the Queen who had defied him would be captured. Although he was cross that she had escaped, he was at least able to exult in the Bulletin of the Army: 'She has been driven headlong from danger to danger ... she wanted to see blood, and the most precious blood in the kingdom has been shed.' As for Louise's health, that finally collapsed as she made her painful way via Berlin and Königsberg to Memel, safe on the borders of Russia but already wrapped in the Baltic winter. Snow was falling in heavy flakes as her husband's cousin Princess Anton Radziwill watched Louise depart from Königsberg, lying down in her coach, barely able to wave a hand in farewell.[42]

What was the Queen doing at the war camp in the first place? The Duke of Brunswick, the Commander-in-Chief of the army, was appalled to find her there, on the scene of battle, in her little carriage. 'What are you doing here, Madame? For God's sake, what are you doing here?' he exclaimed. Then he pointed at the fortress occupied by the French: 'Tomorrow we will have a bloody decisive day.' The Queen departed very early the next morning with the noise of the cannonades in her ears: already the French could distinctly perceive her amid the Prussian lines, and in the event missed capturing her by a mere hour. (Later the Queen would remark wryly that the Duke of Brunswick's order to retreat was the first time she ever heard him express himself either positively or energetically.)[43]

Queen Louise's official explanation for her presence was the King's need of her support; Gentz at least accepted this, as did General Kalkreuth. She propped up the King's waning confidence, he believed, and besides her presence had its usual encouraging effect on the soldiers. Kalkreuth's reasoning was undoubtedly correct. Yet the grim truth was that on a battlefield, for the Prussians, King and soldiers alike, the encouragement of their goddess could avail little against the superior French. And a fancy-dress Warrior Queen, however patriotic, had little place there, when she might have been captured and given cause for still further exultation on the part of her enemies.

Queen Louise's tribulations were not at an end with her flight to Memel. How freezing, how forlorn and how horribly crowded with refugees was beloved Memel now, compared to that sweet summer place where she had danced with the Tsar four years earlier! The Queen herself was ill most of the time. She was still recovering from typhus, while that combination of a weak heart and congestion of the lungs which would finally kill her was beginning to take its toll. Diplomatic negotiations to save something for Prussia from the wreck of its defeat caused her further anguish, as the Prussian King and his advisers struggled to conciliate France while not antagonizing Russia. Perhaps the Queen derived some ironic amusement from her riposte to the hated French Marshal Bertrand who asked her to use her influence to bring about a proper peace between

France and Prussia. 'Women have no voice in the making of war and peace', replied the Queen, with dignity. When Frederick William sent her a soldier's pigtail, to indicate that the sacred but old-fashioned costume of the Prussian army was at last being modernized, Louise both laughed and wept. But by June tears were constantly dripping down the Queen's cheeks, 'despite her brave little games' as the British envoy, Lord Granville Leveson-Gower, noted.[44]

Meanwhile the 'Monster', in the Queen's own room at Weimar, gloated over the notes and reports which he found in her drawers, mixed with the other more delicate objects of her toilette, still perfumed by the musk which was used to scent them. 'It seems as if what they say of her is true', he noted. 'She was here to fan the flames of war.' Then he dismissed Louise as 'a woman with a pretty face, but little intelligence and quite incapable of foreseeing the consequences of what she does'. He even managed a kind of compassion: 'Now she is to be pitied rather than blamed, for she must be suffering agonies of remorse for all the evil she has done to her country and to her husband, who, everyone agrees, is an honourable man, wanting only the peace and welfare of his subjects.'[45]

But at the City Hall in Berlin, Napoleon ranted on concerning the excellent example of the Turks who kept women out of politics (shades of Voltaire's salute to that 'woman and a Christian', Catherine the Great!) and would not listen to two elderly ecclesiastics who praised their queen's kindness and goodness. When the wife of Prince Hatzfeld pleaded on her knees for her husband's life, on the other hand, Napoleon was pleased to grant the request and issued a picture commemorating the incident; that presumably was the proper position for a woman. Queen Louise was already suffering furious humiliation at Napoleon's insinuations concerning her relationship with the Tsar. She burst out in a letter otherwise written in French: '*Und man lebt und kann die Schmach nicht rächen*' (And one lives and cannot take revenge for the humiliation).[46] She was now further punished by the issue of a very different picture. At the tomb of Frederick the Great, in a caricature of that secret night visit and its vows depicted in the popular print, Louise was shown in the guise of Lady Hamilton to the Tsar's Nelson. Since Lady Hamilton was then notorious in Europe as the late Nelson's mistress, the implication was clear.

It was at this time that Queen Louise was traditionally supposed to have transcribed this harpist's song (set by Schubert) from Goethe's *Wilhelm Meister*, with its mournful quatrain:

> Who never ate his bread in sorrow
> Who never spent the darksome hours
> Weeping and watching for the morrow
> He knows ye not, ye heavenly powers![47]

But the greatest humiliation lay ahead. Its prelude was another crushing defeat: that of the Russian army under General Bennigsen at Friedland, twenty-seven miles south of Königsberg, on 15 June 1807. A week later it was the Tsar Alexander's turn to negotiate a truce. This was the prayer of Louise to Alexander before the battle: 'You are our only hope: do not abandon us, not for my sake, but for my husband's sake, for the sake of my children, their future and their destiny.' Her prayer would go for nothing compared to the crudeness of *Realpolitik*. Louise's 'only hope' was indeed about to abandon them, as she would shortly discover.

At Tilsit, while the Emperor Napoleon of France and the Tsar Alexander of Russia met on an island in the middle of the river, King Frederick William of Prussia was condemned to await their summons standing in the pouring rain, on the shore. His unhappy stance perfectly illustrated the comment of the Austrian Prince Metternich: at Tilsit Prussia descended from the first rank 'to be ranged among powers of the Third Order'.[48] What was Prussia's fate likely to be – what territorial sacrifices, what financial reparations would be demanded at a treaty negotiated under such unpromising circumstances?

It was at this point that someone at the Prussian court, convinced that the Queen's 'fascinating affability' would win over 'this Monster vomited from hell' (the King's phrase on this occasion), had the idea of sending for Louise. One German biographer suggests that it was Hardenberg and General Kalkreuth who decided to use the Queen. Another name proposed is that of Murat, working on Frederick William. But on the French side Talleyrand was certainly very much against it and, accepting Louise's putative powers as an enchantress, enquired of Napoleon angrily: 'Sire, will you jeopardize your greatest conquest for a pair of beautiful eyes?'[49]

We know from the testimony of those young British diplomats stationed at Memel – all of them half in love with the Queen – how reluctant she was to go. Her health alone might have precluded such an ordeal. To the King, however, Louise wrote that her arrival would be a proof of her love for him: for as she confided to her diary, 'this burden is demanded', whatever it might cost her to be pleasant and courteous towards Napoleon.[50] Louise was condemned to the 'burden' by the romantic Prussian belief, which she herself obviously shared, that she could succeed where male diplomacy failed. Furthermore, hopeful signs elicited, as it seemed, from the 'Monster' only underlined the general atmosphere of expectation: he drank the Queen's health and asked with some tenderness after her family's welfare.

Perhaps it was as well that the Prussian courtiers could not read Napoleon's reassuring letter to Josephine on the subject of the Prussian Queen's 'coquetting': 'I am like cere-cloth, along which everything of this sort slides without penetrating. It would cost me too dear to play the gallant on this subject.' The Queen herself might have been more affronted by the merry gossip of the time in London where bets were being taken on whether she would get Napoleon to fall in love with her. The playwright Sheridan took, on the other hand, the cynical line that Louise would fall in love with Napoleon: from an empress to a housemaid, 'all women are dazzled by glory, and sure to be in love with a Man whom they begin by hating and who has treated them ill . . .'.[51]

In the event what happened satisfied neither the optimists, the romantics nor the cynics. The Queen arrived in Tilsit on 6 July.[52] Napoleon behaved extremely courteously all along, ending dinner especially early out of regard for her delicate health. When the Queen gently taxed him, 'Sire, I know you accuse me of meddling in politics', Napoleon responded gallantly, 'Ah, Madame, you must not believe that I listen only to malicious gossip' (thus splendidly ignoring the subject of his own Bulletins of the Army). Nor did Louise herself find the 'Monster' as odious as she had expected (although she certainly did not fall in love with him).

But while Louise saw it as her role to plead with him, as the traditional Queen-in-distress – 'I am a wife and mother and it is by these titles that I appeal for your mercy on behalf of Prussia' – Napoleon responded blandly with compliments on her white embroidered crêpe de Chine dress made in Breslau, and the superb collar she wore of her favourite pearls. After Louise's death, Countess Voss would comment sadly on the Queen's love of pearls, with their connotation of tears, as opposed to diamonds, which stood for prosperity; certainly there were tears enough to be shed on this occasion. Again and again the Queen tried to steer the conversation away from clothes back to the fate of Prussia itself. Privately, Napoleon rather admired her for her polite tenacity, how she always got back to her subject: 'perhaps even too much so, and yet with perfect propriety and in a manner that aroused no antagonism'. He even went as far to admit that 'In truth, the matter was an important one to her...'. Publicly, he would have none of it.

There is a celebrated story concerning the occasion following the dinner when Napoleon went to call on Louise in her Tilsit lodgings; like many celebrated stories which sum up the popular image of a particular character (or characters) – the story of Queen Jinga and her royal 'chair' is another noted example – it has several variants. It seems that the Queen pleaded with Napoleon to exclude certain Prussian possessions from the confiscation which was planned as part of the peace treaty. Those to be reallocated included all the Prussian territories west of the Elbe, not omitting Magdeburg itself, on the river, most of Prussian Poland (to be reconstituted as the Napoleonic Duchy of Warsaw) and the Silesian fortresses. It is not known for certain exactly which provinces the Queen named to Napoleon, but attention has generally focused on Magdeburg.

The most colourful version of the story has Napoleon asking for a single rose from the Queen's arrangement of flowers. In reply, the Queen asked for an exchange: 'A rose for Magdeburg, Sire.' Some biographers have found this behaviour on the part of the Queen to be uncharacteristically arch. In another version (which accords better with Napoleon's own description of Louise as relentless – but dignified – in pursuit of her aims) the Queen struck a tragic note more or less on Napoleon's arrival: 'Sire, Justice! Justice! Magdeburg! Magdeburg!' There is no dispute however about the Queen's lack of success in securing from Napoleon even the slightest diminution of the harsh terms imposed upon Prussia, including an enormous bill of financial reparation. (Ironically enough, her reproaches to the Tsar for abandoning them did move him guiltily to plead for an alleviation of the Prussian punishment;[53] Louise, however, had been brought to Tilsit to woo Napoleon, not to reproach the Tsar.)

Everyone had been wrong: Frederick William, Hardenberg, General Kalkreuth, all those who had pinned their hopes on the 'fascinating affability' of their Queen. Three years before, seeing Louise dressed as Statira, wife of Alexander the Great (on that same occasion when she had struck Madame de Staël dumb with her beauty), Sir George Jackson had reflected that 'our queen of beauty' too would have conquered Alexander, 'had the hero the happiness of seeing her'. But the Queen of beauty had not conquered the Alexander of the hour: Napoleon. Much later, on St Helena, Napoleon referred to her 'winning ways' as well as her attempts to win him over. The Queen on the other hand wept bitterly and continuously afterwards, according to Countess Voss, referring over and over again to her 'deception' and reading her favourite Schiller (*The Thirty Years' War*) for comfort. 'In that house', she told one of the young Englishmen at Memel, referring to Tilsit, 'I was cruelly deceived.'[54] Napoleon had become once more the 'Monster', 'this inhuman being' who must be beaten down for the sake of the future of Prussia, of her husband and of her children.

Queen Louise did not survive to see the 'Monster' beaten down, although Frederick William did. She died of a pulmonary embolism in July 1810, having given birth to two more children, on 1 February 1808 – she must have been once again in the early stages of pregnancy at Tilsit – and 4 October 1809. But it was widely thought that she had died of a broken heart, to which her humiliation at Tilsit, symbolizing the humiliation of Prussia, had contributed. Her last years were marked by the inevitable sorrow of Prussia's grievous political situation, as well as by her persistent attempts to bolster up Frederick William. Heinrich von Kleist gives a moving picture of her at this time: 'She has developed a truly royal character ... She, who a short time ago had nothing better to do than amuse herself with dancing or riding horseback, has gathered about her all our great men whom the King neglects and who alone can bring us salvation. Yes, it is she who sustains what has not collapsed.'[55]

The Queen also made earnest attempts to study history – Hume, Robertson and Gibbon – as though to try to make sense of the great if tragic events she had lived through. As with the whole of Louise's brief life – she was thirty-four when she died – there is a touching quality about the enterprise. 'I am so stupid and I hate the stupidity', she exclaimed. 'What was the Punic War? Was it against Carthage? Who were the Gracchi and what were their troubles? What does hierarchy mean?' Even here, patriotism was never forgotten: Louise admired Theodoric for instance as 'a genuine *German*', with his love of justice, his upright character and his magnanimity.[56]

Like Queen Jinga of Angola, however – albeit a very different kind of Warrior Queen – Queen Louise of Prussia was to have another whole life as a national heroine, far more enduring than her actual life on earth. To the grieving King, she quickly became his 'sainted Louise', while he was always firm against charges of political interference: she had 'never quitted her own sphere of feminine usefulness'. Her popularity with the army was deliberately invoked when he instituted the order of the Iron Cross for military valour on the anniversary of her birth in 1813. (The *Luisenorde* for ladies, on the other hand, instituted on his own birthday – 'we are determined to do honour to the female sex' – concentrated on women who relieved suffering, not warriors; and the medal showed the late Queen in silver on a pale blue background, with a crown of stars – not in military uniform). When the 'Monster' was despatched to Elba, a hymn was composed in the Queen's honour beginning: 'Oh Saint in bliss ... Thy tears are dried at last' and ending with the refrain:

> Louise, the protectress of our right,
> Louise, still the watchword of our fight.[57]

Classically, the ordinary soldiers in the Prussian army refused to believe in their beloved Queen's death for years afterwards; as for the rest of the nation, Princess Anton Radziwill wrote that twenty-five years later 'still the same regrets are given to the memory of that angel of goodness!' And an English author, Mrs Charles Richardson, who toured Prussia in the 1840s, subsequently dedicating her biography of Louise to Queen Victoria as another one distinguished 'for pre-eminence in female excellence', found many local traditions of the Queen as a guardian angel in time of war, 'a lovely vision' who appeared and then disappeared back to heaven.[58]

Nor did the cult of the holy and patriotic Warrior Queen stop there. Queen Louise may claim to have possessed a genuine sense of Prussia's importance as part of the German whole: she was not after all born a Prussian, and throughout Prussia's troubles retained a conviction that its triumph or defeat should be seen as affecting Germany itself (her remark concerning Theodoric was not uncharacteristic). It was therefore not inappropriate that in the late nineteenth century, continuing into the twentieth, she should come to be regarded as the Holy (departed) Figurehead of the resurgent and mighty Prussian-led Germany. On the sixtieth anniversary of her death, 19 July 1870, her son, then still King William of Prussia, went to pray at her grave; this was the day on which war was declared against France, that war from which he would return as German Emperor. Louise's son was convinced that he had thus fulfilled her dearest dreams and hopes, she who could be viewed 'as a martyr to her love for the Fatherland'.[59]

The Queen's verdict on herself was both more modest and more poignant.[60] 'If posterity will not place my name amongst those of celebrated women [she might have instanced Maria Theresa or Catherine the Great] yet those who were acquainted with the troubles of these times, will know what I have gone through and will say "She suffered much and endured with patience".'

CHAPTER SIXTEEN

THE
VALIANT RANI

On every parapet a gun she set
Raining fire of hell,
How well like a man fought the Rani of Jhansi
How valiantly and well!

Indian folk song of '1857'

The story of the Rani of Jhansi, which ended with her death leading her men in the course of the Indian Rebellion, or 'Mutiny', began like that of Boadicea, with an injustice. In this case, however, the injustice was British, not Roman.

In Britain itself – two or three months away even by steamer – preparations were already under way for that huge ceremonial sculpture commemorating Boadicea and her daughters which stands today on the Embankment of the Thames. The sculptor Thomas Thornycroft and his wife – also a sculptress – were favourites of the British royal family. She had immortalized the young Princess Alice as 'Spring' and the Prince of Wales as 'Winter'; he had produced public pieces such as 'Alfred the Great encouraged to the pursuit of learning by his mother' and an equestrian statue of the Queen. In 1856, under the patronage of Albert, the Prince Consort, who lent horses from his own stable as models and often visited the sculptor's studio to measure progress, Thornycroft embarked on the Boadicean group.[1]

Although, as we shall see, it was to be half a century before Boadicea, her daughters and her chariot achieved their present resting place (the Prince Consort had envisaged the central arch of the entrance to Hyde Park) the accession of another queen regnant in the shape of Victoria had had its predictable effect in drawing attention to Boadicea's fortunes. In the winter of 1859 the Poet Laureate Lord Tennyson read aloud to his wife what he described as 'a fiercely brilliant poem', constructed in an unusual and extremely difficult metre adapted from the Latin of Catullus.[2] That poem was *Boädicea*:

> So the Queen Boädicéa, standing loftily charioted,
> Brandishing in her hand a dart and rolling glances lioness-like,
> Yell'd and shriek'd between her daughters in her fierce volubility
> Till her people all around the royal chariot agitated . . .

The poem ended with a sombre picture of the Roman colony awaiting the British holocaust and reflecting in silence on their misdeeds which had brought it about:

> Out of evil evil flourishes, out of tyranny tyranny buds.
> Ran the land with Roman slaughter, multitudinous agonies.
> Perish'd many a maid and matron, many a valorous legionary,
> Fell the colony, city, and citadel, London, Verulam, Cámulodúne.

In truth, there was little real parallel to be drawn between Tennyson's 'loftily charioted', yelling and shrieking Boadicea, and Victoria, whose own conception of being a Warrior Queen was more that of Maria Theresa. On the one hand Queen Victoria displayed throughout her long reign a real affection for her ordinary soldiers and devotion to what she perceived as their interests; on the other hand, despite bursts of emotion – 'Oh, if the Queen were a man!' – she was in no sense a warmonger. When she urged on Mr Gladstone in 1871 over the Franco–Prussian war 'the necessity for great prudence and for not departing from our neutral position',[3] above all not to take action alone, one can sense the cautious shade of Queen Elizabeth I at her shoulder.

Yet ironically enough, within Queen Victoria's increasingly vast dominions – that 'empire . . . on us bestow'd' celebrated by Cowper – a situation had arisen which did parallel, almost exactly, that of Boadicea and the Romans. At the time the Rani of Jhansi was

compared, not to Boadicea, but to another very different warrior–
woman, Joan of Arc. Sir Hugh Rose, the British commander who
finally defeated her at Gwalior, himself used the phrase 'a sort of
Indian Joan of Arc' to the Commander-in-Chief of the army, the
Duke of Cambridge.[4] Since Boadicea had now become a patriotic
symbol of British rule on the one hand and an established queen
regnant on the other, it was perhaps scarcely surprising that British
contemporaries of the Rani did not note the similarities of their two
stories.

The parallels however were and remain remarkable. The injustice
with which the story of the Rani of Jhansi began was not only dealt
out to her by a dominant 'occupying' power of another race, but
was also dealt out to her as a young or youngish widow. (As with
Boadicea, the Rani's exact date of birth is unknown.) This was not
a case of physical brutality – scourging or rape; but there was a clear
element of violation, according to Hindu law, in the way the Rani's
claims to rule Jhansi in the name of her late husband's adopted son
were ignored.

'I have always considered Jhansi among the native states of the
Bundelkhand as a kind of oasis in the desert': this was the verdict
(in his memoirs) of Sir William Sleeman, long stationed at the court
of the Rani's husband, Gangadhar Rao.[5] It is important to realize
that the small Mahratta principality of Jhansi, in the Bundelkhand
hill country of northern India, had a history of friendship towards
the British interest, just as the Iceni's resentment at their treatment
was fuelled by memories of their voluntary submission to Caesar.
Jhansi had been raised by the British to princely status by that treaty
of 1817 which brought the Mahratta Confederacy to an end although
its dynasty had in fact been sovereign for nearly a hundred years.
Thereafter the Rajah of Jhansi considered himself to be its independent and hereditary ruler; but he also inherited a tradition of
benevolence towards and dependence upon the British government.
In 1825 Gangadhar Rao's grandfather, Ramachandra Rao, was
granted the title of maharajah and 'devoted servant of the glorious
King of England' (George IV) for aiding the British against some
rebels. When Gangadhar Rao's own succession in 1838 was disputed
within the family, the British backed his claim.[6]

Prosperity and peace followed for Jhansi, in both cases assured
by the efficient supervision of British officials. Gangadhar Rao

himself liked to spend his time in the theatre, both directing and acting: he played female parts and was reputed to wear female dress offstage as well. Not necessarily for these reasons alone, Gangadhar Rao was believed to be homosexual. Be that as it might, it was more to the point that he did not manage to produce an heir: his first wife died childless. In 1842 Gangadhar Rao married again. His bride was she who would be known to history as Lakshmi Bai, the Rani of Jhansi.

Lakshmi Bai was probably born in about 1830: estimates vary between 1827 and 1835, with the British authorities tending to go for the earlier and the Indians for the later figure.[7] Her original name was Manukarnika – one of the many names of the holy river Ganges – and she was brought up in the wing of a palace in Benares on the south bank of the great river itself. This was because her father, Moropant Tambe, a brahmin official, acted as chief political adviser to the brother of the last Peshwa of Bithur, whose court had come to rest in Benares after his deposition.

A web of legends surrounds the childhood of little 'Manu'. Her horoscope is said to have indicated an important marriage. It is also scarcely surprising to find that many of these legends feature her one way or another as a tomboy. Here once again are the familiar stories of the future Warrior Queen wrestling with boys and disdaining the company of girls (except to insist on always playing the role of leader among them). A favourite if probably apocryphal tale has 'Manu' demanding a seat on the howdah of an elephant when playing with the adopted son of the Peshwa, Dhondu Pant, later known as Nana Sahib (he was surely too old to have acted as her playmate in childhood, despite the dramatic destiny which would one day link their names). The little girl was rebuked for her presumption: 'You were not born to ride on an elephant.' At which the future Rani shouted at the future Nana Sahib: 'I'll show you! For your one elephant, I will have ten. Remember my words.'

On a more elevated level, Lakshmi Bai's convenient birth in the very 'lap of Mother Ganges' meant that her birth could later be imbued with a religious significance: here was the pure incarnation of the sacred river, come to save India by destroying the heathen British. On this level, she was said to have been an assiduous attender at the Temple of Vishweshwar with her parents. Future places of pilgrimage were being provided, her pride in the Hindu religion underlined. A typical story, told of the Rani at the height of her triumph, had her encountering a brahmin by a well and, in spite of her thirst, refusing to let him pull up the clay pot for her: 'You are a learned brahmin and it does not befit you to do this. I will do it myself.' Concerning the Hindu religion, she informed the brahmin: 'for this I have sacrificed all attachment for wealth, life, everything'.[8]

For all the curtailed freedoms – both sexual and social – of the female in the Hindu religion, as laid down by its brahmin lawgivers, little 'Manu', she who had boldly demanded a seat upon the elephant, came from a culture where powerful intelligent women were not unknown.[9] Some of these belonged to history: there were folk memories of well-educated Hindu princesses and intrepid women at the Indian courts in the past who had ridden armed with the men. After her death, the Rani would indeed be described to Queen Victoria by Lady Canning, her former lady-in-waiting, now wife of the Governor-General of India, as having kept up the tradition of the Mahratta women for being both 'brave and clever' (although this particular Mahratta woman had been 'wicked' as well).[10]

Even within the confines of the Hindu religion itself, there were sundry menacing goddesses, whose mythical behaviour hinted at a very different female nature from that of the gentle and unselfish Sita. This was the heroine of the Ramayana epic who, having been abducted forcibly, was repudiated by her husband, only to prove her continuing love for him (and her virtue) by immolating herself in fire.[11] The goddess Durga, for example, wife of Siva, although seen as basically benevolent and maternal and endowed with a serenely beautiful face, also displayed a remarkable capacity for aggression, with the help of her ten arms, each bearing a different weapon, and her eight accompanying demonesses. (It was to Durga, riding on her tiger, that Mrs Ghandi in her turn would sometimes be picturesquely compared.) As for another version of Siva's wife, the much-venerated goddess Kali, the black one, here was the force of destruction represented in its most terrifying form: four arms ending in bloodstained hands, fang-like teeth and protruding blood-dripping tongue.

Where the powers of women were concerned, the unconscious influence of Hindu mythology was underlined by public Indian example. Moreover, roughly contemporary with the Rani herself were two remarkable Indian Muslim female rulers. One of these, the Begum of Bhopal, was described to Queen Victoria by Lady Canning in 1861 as 'A really clever upright character': she looked after the affairs of her country herself and ruled it admirably. 'No one disputes her power or her justice.' When the Order of the Star of India was founded, the Begum of Bhopal was one of the twenty-five 'Knights' appointed to it.

Hazrat Mahal, the Begum of Oudh, on the other hand, was also formidably clever – but not morally upright. John Low of the East India Company called her 'one of those tigress women, more virile than their husbands, who when finding themselves in a position to gratify their lust for power, have played a considerable part in oriental history'. Yet the courageous part played by the Begum as Queen Regent, in the defence of Lucknow against British attack, could not be denied. The *Times* correspondent, W. H. Russell, referred to her as 'Penthesilea', an Amazonian image confirmed by the female sepoys who guarded the entrance to the Begum's harem, wearing military jackets and white duck trousers, with muskets and bayonets, cross-belts and cartridge boxes. Russell reflected: 'it appears from the energetic characters of these Ranees and Begums that they acquire in their zenanas and harems a considerable amount of actual mental power . . . '.[12]

After her enthronement, the Begum of Oudh was received by Queen Victoria in England. It was a development greeted with angry cynicism by Ernest Jones, the Chartist poet and leader (whose father, in contrast or perhaps in explanation, had been a royal equerry). Despite the Begum's notorious 'peccadilloes', once she had been dethroned, he exclaimed, moral scruples had been thrown out of the window in face of her rank: 'and the dusky royalty hob-nobs with the pallid'.[13] One might look at it from another angle and see in Queen Victoria's persistent welcome to various Indian royalties her attractive lack of racism, in the sense that so many British people of the time practised it.

There is yet another possible angle. The career of Hazrat Mahal, long-reigning Queen Cartimandua to the Rani's more dramatic Boadicea, reminds one how differently matters might have gone for Lakshmi Bai . . . Given her energy, courage and determination, given that female rule was not of its nature inimical at this point to the British, how might she not have fared under another set of stars – another horoscope? As it was, Manukarnika, who took on her marriage the name of Lakshmi, the lovely goddess of fortune and prosperity, would one day be transformed further into powerful Durga riding upon her tiger – and even, maybe, bloodstained Kali herself.

One legend concerns Lakshmi Bai's actual wedding day. When the priest – according to tradition – tied the ends of her various gowns together, the bride shocked those present with her boldness. 'Make the knot very firm', she said. But whatever the state of the knot, the new Rani did not succeed in presenting Gangadhar Rao with an heir, although a baby boy was said to have died at the age of three months. Then in 1853 Gangadhar Rao fell seriously ill. In the absence of an existing heir, one was adopted. Damodar Rao, as he became known, was five years old: a descendant of Gangadhar's grandfather and thus a member of the royal family.

The ruler now proceeded to dictate his will and have it read aloud to Major Ellis, the British Political Agent in Jhansi: 'Should I not survive, I trust that in consideration of the fidelity I have evinced towards the British government, favour may be shown to this child and that my widow during her lifetime may be considered the Regent of the State (*Malika*) and mother of this child, and that she may not be molested in any way.' Major Ellis replied that he would do everything possible to bring this about. The substance of this will was then repeated in a letter to Major Malcolm, the Political Agent for Gwalior and the Bundelkhand, in which Gangadhar Rao referred once more to that treaty which had guaranteed the throne of Jhansi to Ramachandra Rao 'and his heirs and successors'.[14]

Gangadhar Rao died on 21 November 1853. Not long afterwards the Governor-General of India, the Marquess of Dalhousie, announced that under the policy of 'lapse', Jhansi was to be annexed by the British government. That is, since Gangadhar Rao had left no heir or successor – adoption did not count – the state of Jhansi reverted by treaty to the East India Company (no longer an independent corporation but largely under governmental control).

The only possible defence of Dalhousie's 'policy of lapse', in this instance, is that of expediency, if defence it be. Certainly expediency had long been the watchword of the East India Company when the possibility of annexation arose; to that extent it could be argued that Dalhousie was only implementing a policy which others had conceived.[15] But if Dalhousie's policy had its roots in the past, it was also to cast its black shadow upon the future.

Dalhousie had already annexed Satara in 1848, the year of his arrival in India, on the same grounds of 'lapse' (once again there was the question of an adopted heir). This move too had aroused deep resentment – and also bewilderment. The resentment was due to the unfair prohibition of a practice – adoption – allowed by Hindu law. The bewilderment sprang from the known religious significance of adoption in the Hindu religion. The sacrifices of a son were an essential duty, if the father was not to be condemned to punishment – the hell called Put – after death. But an adopted son could perform these vital sacrifices equally with a natural one.

Colonel, later Major-General Sir John Low, who had been Political Agent at Gwalior and Lucknow, reported in his memoirs this general anguish which followed the annexation of Satara. 'What crime did the late Rajah commit that his country should be seized by the Company?' was the one question which every Indian put to him.[16] Similarly in Jhansi in 1853 little Damodar Rao was unarguably the late ruler's 'son' in Hindu law; as such he was surely his 'successor' under the terms of the earlier treaty. To regard him otherwise was 'so ungenerous, and being so ungenerous, so unwise'. These were the terms which would be used by the distinguished British military historian Sir John Kaye (who worked for the East India Company and later the India Office) in his *History of the Sepoy War in India 1857–1858*, published in 1880.[17] Significantly, Dalhousie's wiser successor Lord Canning – derisively nicknamed 'Clemency' at the time, a name he has since borne with honour in the roll of history – explicitly stressed the Indian rulers' right of adoption at his healing durbar of 1859.[18]

Meanwhile in 1856, the year of his own departure from India, Dalhousie would go further and annex the much larger state of Oudh: as early as 1848 he had described it as being 'on the high-road to be taken under our management'. On this occasion, the pretext was not the lack of heirs to the Nawab – there was an heir – but the Nawab's numerous transgressions against his subjects. It was a rather more sympathetic excuse. Nevertheless an Indian ruler had once again been removed. A leading Indian historian of the events of 1857 has judged Dalhousie's policy of annexation as one of the main contributory facts to the rebellion and 'perhaps the decisive one'.[19]

We return to Lakshmi Bai, she who had expected to rule Jhansi during the boyhood of Damodar Rao and was now consigned to the unenviable fate of a childless Hindu widow. Was she perhaps inadequate to the task of the regency, at least in the view of the British? But only a week after Gangadhar Rao's death, the Political Agent Major Malcolm wrote that his widow, 'in whose hands he has expressed a wish that the government should be placed during her lifetime, is a woman highly respected and esteemed, and I believe fully capable of doing justice to such a charge'. Other witnesses confirm that the Rani comported herself as 'a brave-minded woman had to do in her position', being in herself 'quite capable of discussing her affairs with a Committee or a government'.[20]

Moreover her behaviour was perfectly discreet: she kept purdah where the British were concerned, although not at home (later she would indeed encourage women to take part in the defence of Jhansi). Her life was disciplined in the extreme: she would rise at 3 a.m., supervise work in the political and military offices, and then at her court listen to religious readings. One is reminded indeed of the application and austerity of another female ruler called from a secluded life to greatness: Isabella of Spain.

All this time, the Rani was hoping – even perhaps expecting – that the terms of Gangadhar Rao's will would be allowed to prevail. Two petitions appealing against Dalhousie's decision were sent, in late 1853 and early 1854, the Rani herself being credited with composing them.[21] Attention was drawn to the position of the adopted son in the Hindu religion, his ability to make sacrifices on behalf of his late father, equal to that of a natural son. In the second petition, the difference between 'heirs' and 'successors' in the original treaty was argued; for if Damodar Rao was not one, he was certainly the other. It was significant of the justice of the Rani's case that Major Ellis, the Political Agent at Jhansi, himself endorsed her petition. Unfortunately – or possibly due to malevolence – this vital letter was not forwarded to Dalhousie. For Major Malcolm, who did not choose to forward it, now believed the petition should be refused. Dalhousie's decision was dated 27 February 1854. Adoption, he considered, was valid only in the case of sovereign princes, and he held firmly to Jhansi's dependent status (an argument which has since been convincingly demolished by Indian writers).

When the document was read to the Rani on 15 March 1854, she cried out loudly: '*Mera Jhansi Nahin Denge.*' (I will not give up my Jhansi.) Then she shut herself away, refusing food or water. But if the Rani despaired, it was only a temporary state. With remarkable pertinacity, she continued to argue her cause, employing a British counsel, John Lang, who advised her to appeal to London. It was not until 1854 that the appeal too was turned down. At Malcolm's suggestion, the Rani was granted a pension of five thousand rupees monthly from the Treasury at Jhansi; the palace and the state jewels and funds which her husband had willed to her were also to be handed over. Even at this point, the British administration managed to arouse further resentment: with what Sir John Kaye described as 'extraordinary meanness', it was now laid down that the Rani should pay her husband's debts before receiving her emoluments.[22]

So the Rani, with no other choice before her, fell back for the next three years into private life. Dalhousie left India. He once told a correspondent in England – whom he termed his 'safety valve' – of his feelings about the great subcontinent he ruled: 'I don't deny that I detest the country and many of the people in it. I don't proclaim it; but I don't doubt that my face does not conceal it from those I have to do with.' It was not likely that such a man – one who would come out of his dying coma in order to learn the score in the Eton and Harrow cricket match – would spare much thought for the feelings or resolves of an obscure Hindu widow.[23]

Jhansi itself, like its Rani, was judged unimportant for the future. Its prosperity inevitably declined with the disappearance of the princely court. Another brisk British judgement from the centre was the discontinuance of the state revenues paid to the Temple of Lakshmi, just outside the city; although once again Major Ellis, the man on the spot, had suggested that the practice should be maintained. As to the garrison of such an important place, a few hundred soldiers were surely all that were necessary nowadays. A safe farewell could be bidden to the thousands of troops who had once added to the lustre of Jhansi's princely ruler – could it not?

In 1855, the year before Lord Canning arrived in India to replace Dalhousie, he gave a speech in London to the Court of Directors of the East India Company. It contained this remarkably prophetic passage: 'We must not forget that in the sky of India, serene as it is, a cloud may arise, at first no bigger than a man's hand, but which growing bigger and bigger, may at last threaten to overwhelm us with ruin.'[24] By the summer of 1857, that cloud had indeed arisen.

The causes of the Indian Rebellion – or Mutiny – are not the subject of the present work; suffice it to say that on the Indian side, the case of the Rani of Jhansi, the mixture of injustice, insensitivity and indifference displayed by the British administration towards entrenched Indian customs and interests, might perhaps stand as a microcosm of the whole. On the British side, the case of Jhansi itself, the unexpected uprising of supposedly loyal troops, coupled with the treacherous slaughter of British women and children (as well as soldiers and officials) might equally stand for what was most dreadful in India wherever the Mutiny occurred.

Canning's words were prophetic. They had not however prepared him for the event itself. In April 1857 Lady Canning was happily telling Queen Victoria of the 'ridiculous stories' being circulated that the Governor-General had signed a bond saying that he would make all the Indians into Christians within three years. She added that there was 'an odd mysterious thing going on, still unexplained', by which she referred to the circulation of some native chupatties or biscuits from district to district (a strange episode whose precise relevance to the events of 1857 – were the chupatties coded signals? – has never been totally explained). Only five months later Queen Victoria would write in her turn to the King of the Belgians, 'we are in sad anxiety about India, which engrosses all our attention'; although even now, characteristically, she spared a thought for the feelings of her protégé, the dispossessed Indian Prince Duleep Singh, who had been virtually raised with her own sons: 'What can it be for him to hear his fellow countrymen called *fiends* and *monsters*?'[25]

In keeping with its reputation for pro-British tranquillity, Jhansi was not in the forefront of the rebellion. As late as 18 May, following the first weeks of disruption elsewhere, Captain Skene, the Political and Administrative Officer of Jhansi, was able to write, 'I do not think there is any cause for alarm about this neighbourhood.'[26] It was not until 4 June that some of the garrison at Jhansi (drawn from the Twelfth Bengal Native Infantry and the Fourteenth Irregular Cavalry and commanded by a Captain Gordon) actually mutinied. Under a rebel sergeant, Gurbash Singh, they invaded the Star Fort;

in the battle to seize it, they killed all the British officers they found there except a Lieutenant Taylor, who, despite being badly wounded, managed to escape to the City Fort. This was the place appointed by Captain Skene for some British and Eurasians in Jhansi – some sixty people all told, over half of them women and children – to take refuge.

With the mutineers seemingly impregnable in the vastly superior Star Fort (which contained Jhansi's magazine as well as its treasure chest), who would now come to the aid of this vulnerable fragment of humanity? Ironically enough, the only possible bastion for the Europeans at this point against the rage of the sepoys was none other than the deposed Rani herself. She had earlier been allowed a few troops of her own as security against the disturbances which were sweeping across India. Now Captain Gordon appealed to her in the following terms. Given the extreme danger to the European and Eurasian community, who might all be killed by the mutineers the next day, 'we suggest', he wrote, 'that you take your kingdom [*sic* – shades of Lord Dalhousie] and hold it, along with the adjoining territory, until the British authority is established'. He added, 'We shall be eternally grateful if you will also protect our lives.'[27]

It cannot be known for certain what if anything the Rani replied to this appeal. The most plausible version, given her circumstances, has her answering, 'What can I do? ... If you wish to save yourself, abandon the fort, no one will injure you.' The most damning version has the Rani promising a safe conduct which she had no intention of carrying out.[28] Whatever the Rani's reactions – for there are numerous contradictory versions, mainly based on hearsay – the tragedy which followed is not in dispute.

On 7 July the City Fort was duly besieged by the mutineers, and Captain Gordon, the commander of the garrison, killed in the assault. Captain Skene, the Political Agent, then gave the signal of surrender. A safe retreat from the fort itself was now promised to the remaining Europeans inside if they would lay down their arms. This they agreed to do. So the British, defenceless but hopeful, filed out of the City Fort. A little column was just outside the walls of Jhansi itself, when the rebel leader, Risaldar Kala Khan, ordered them all to be killed. One of the Europeans still surviving in Jhansi (who had not gone to the fort) was a Mrs Mutlow, who by her own account was concealed by her Indian ayah in the native quarter, and by another account was able to adopt Indian dress successfully since she was herself a Eurasian, although her husband and brother went to the fort and were killed. (We shall return to the testimony of Mrs Mutlow.) For the moment it is enough to say that a frightful massacre had just been carried out by the rebel sepoys: their victims were mainly civilians, and the majority of them of course women or children.

It is inconceivable that the Rani encouraged this piece of wanton mayhem. Leaving aside her actions at a later stage, the Rani in these first days of mutiny at Jhansi rightly considered the sepoys to be a frightening force outside her own control, and indeed outside anyone else's. It may well be that she did give the rebels money – 35,000 rupees – as well as two elephants and five horses. She probably had little choice. According to one report, the rebels threatened to execute her if she did not comply. The charge of aiding the sepoys in this manner was made against the Rani by Mr Thornton, the Deputy-Collector of Jhansi, on 18 August, and it does have a ring of truth; but in the wake of the bloodbath Thornton went further and added the *post hoc propter hoc* remark that the slaughter had taken place 'wholly at the instigation' of the Rani of Jhansi. It was this statement, incorporated in the official British report of 20 November 1858, which was to prove damaging to the Rani's reputation in the estimates of British historians (some of whom further embellished Thornton's statement to make the Rani responsible for the *original* mutiny of 5/6 June – which Thornton had not even suggested).[29]

An important part of this myth of the Rani's responsibility for the Jhansi massacre was the treachery she was said to have displayed in that false promise of a safe conduct. But the existence of this safe conduct rests either on hearsay or on the testimony of Mrs Mutlow; as has been pointed out by Dr Surendra Nath Sen, who sifted through the mass of evidence in the National Archives of India for his authoritative centenary study *1857*, the document which Mrs Mutlow is supposed to have seen, written in the first person and signed by the Rani personally, is quite implausible.[30]

Although Mrs Mutlow would not have known this, the Rani, as an Indian ruler, would never write in the first person and in any case invariably signed her official documents with a seal. Another colourful piece of the myth had the Rani exclaiming that she would have nothing to do with those 'swine' the British, when Captain Skene implored her protection. But as the (nameless) clerk who provided the evidence obviously did not know, the Rani's language was Maratti, not English, and in Maratti the word 'swine' was not one of abuse. Thirty years after these bloodstained happenings, one T. A. Martin, a resident of Jhansi who escaped the siege, wrote a letter to the Rani's adopted son Damodar Rao in the Rani's defence: 'Your poor mother was very unjustly and cruelly dealt with – and no one knows her true case as I do.'[31] Unfortunately – by a further piece of irony in a career already marked by such – it was the Rani's alleged implication in the massacre, her guilt in the eyes of the British authorities which finally persuaded her many months later that she had nothing to lose by siding against the British.

For the moment however the Rani in Jhansi was seen – including by the British – as bringing order into a disorderly situation. She formed a government which included her own father. She also wrote an account of the whole ghastly business of the massacre to Major Erskine, the Commissioner at Sagar, in two letters of 12 and 14 June. The Rani roundly condemned the 'faithlessness, cruelty and violence' which the troops had displayed towards the Europeans and regretted that she had not had sufficient soldiers and guns of her own to help them (thanks, of course, to the withdrawal of the previous strong garrison). The Rani explained that the sepoys had threatened to blow up her own palace and for this, to save her 'life and honour', she had given them sums of money to depart. Since then, in the absence of any British officer (they had all been killed, although some civilians survived by one means and another in the town) she had taken over the government.[32]

There is no reason to doubt the truth of this account nor did Erskine himself do so. He forwarded the letters to the central government with the covering note that their content 'agrees with what I have heard from other sources'. On 2 July he asked the Rani to continue to manage the district including collecting revenues and recruiting police, until a new supervisor should arrive.[33] For a few halcyon months, interrupted only by certain successful military campaigns against the neighbouring states (in which all parties claimed to be supporting the British in paying off old scores), the Rani was able at last to enjoy what she had so long desired, the rulership of 'my Jhansi'.

Her court was conducted with traditional splendour and dignity. The Rani herself would be seated behind a curtain on a raised seat. Previously she had worn a plain white muslin dress drawn about her tightly to reveal her figure: 'and a remarkably fine figure she had', commented her lawyer John Lang. Now, somewhat stouter – 'but not too stout' – she adopted a costume which symbolically combined the elements of a warrior with those of a queen: jodhpurs, a silk blouse with a low-cut bodice, a red silk cap with a loose turban (or puggree) round it. She wore diamond bangles and large diamond rings on her small hands: but a short bejewelled sword and two silver pistols were stuck into her cummerbund.[34]

'A woman of about middle size', the Rani must have been quite beautiful when she was younger, thought Lang: she was at this point around thirty. Even now her 'particularly fine' expressive eyes and a nose 'very delicately shaped' gave her countenance many charms. Lang added: what spoiled her was her voice. This was later described as 'somewhere between a whine and a croak' – but then, as has been noted, Warrior Queens have always had trouble with their voices, either from their enemies or from those of another race (to her fellow Indians, the Rani's voice was on the contrary 'melodious'). Other estimates described the Rani without qualification as 'a very handsome woman', although her complexion ('not very fair but far from black', according to Lang) had been marred by smallpox. Her grace in particular impressed the British.[35]

For the moment the Rani – with her diamonds but also her pistols – was free to enact Lakshmi, rather than Durga or Kali. A library was formed, plays once more encouraged. But either from natural inclination since her tomboy childhood or from prescience, she also studied the martial arts. Her daily round included shooting at a target with a rifle and a pistol, and of course riding. Lady Canning heard later that her riding was 'wonderful'. In an interesting link with history, one Turab Ali, who was then in Jhansi and who died in 1943 aged 113, survived long enough to tell tales of his youth when he had watched the Rani practising the art of managing her horse with the reins in her teeth and two swords in her hands.[36]

There was however a cloud on the Rani's horizon, as there had once been on the horizon of the British in India. As the latter gradually pressed back the rebels into submission, recapturing Delhi and Oudh, still no official proclamation had come to Jhansi confirming that the Rani had been put in charge of the district in July. The arrival of Sir Robert Hamilton from England, to resume his work as Political Agent for Central India, prompted the Rani to write to him on 1 January 1858, giving once again her side of the story. This was a nervous communication; the Rani was well aware that the recapture of Delhi and Oudh meant that Jhansi would not be tolerated much longer as a kind of unofficial rebel state – or was it? She was anxious to make it clear that it was not. On the other hand she was equally anxious to maintain her own position of power.

In any case it was too late; perhaps it had always been too late. Despite Erskine's judgement, despite the Rani's own pleas, despite Sir Robert Hamilton's confidence in the veracity of one of the rebels under sentence of death – 'she was obliged to yield' – the Rani was already believed to be guilty of complicity in the massacre. Her official guilt was even now in the process of being established. (One of the pieces of damning evidence cited to Erskine, who was 'forgiven' for originally crediting the Rani's story, was a telegraphic message from Major Ellis, dated 26 June; but he actually referred to the mutineers as 'having at last forced the Ranee to assist them with Guns and Elephants' – evidence surely of duress rather than complicity.)[37]

There is cause to believe that the Rani's reputation also suffered from guilt by association. Later, as we shall see, she would join forces with 'that fiend' Nana Sahib, he who was held responsible for another frightful massacre, that of Cawnpore, which took place on 27 June.[38] Nana Sahib was another with a grievance against the British: as the adopted son of the last Peshwa of Bithur, he was allowed to be styled maharajah as a courtesy, but not to enjoy the Peshwa's pension.

It is not clear exactly at what point the Nana joined forces with the rebels within Cawnpore, a wealthy city lying about 260 miles east of Delhi, guarding the road to Lucknow; subsequently many of the British would believe that the Nana had been 'at the races and sipping coffee etc. with our officers and all the time planning the mutiny'. That may not be quite how it happened. Possibly a character of mysterious origins who went under the pseudonym Tatya Tope was actually the 'master butcher', as one later British investigation suggested, the Nana being offered an even starker choice than was the Rani by the sepoys: a kingdom if he joined them, death if he didn't.[39] But if that was the case, Nana Sahib certainly did not hesitate. The massacre of Europeans and Eurasians at Cawnpore took place in roughly similar circumstances to that of Jhansi, with all the indications of treachery, captives going trusting and all unknowing to their deaths.

It is impossible to exaggerate the feelings of horror aroused by this grisly episode in the hearts and minds of the British community not only then but long afterwards; quite regardless of the fact, as Indian historians have pointed out, that in the meantime they themselves had performed acts of equal savagery in retaliation. For the Indian men, women and children who died subsequently in Cawnpore, ten times the number of the slaughtered Europeans, are hardly registered in the British consciousness.[40] A parallel may once again be drawn between the Britons' rampant slaughter of the Romans at Colchester – vividly reported by the Roman Tacitus – and his bald account of the extinction of the Britons, including their womenfolk, at the final battle.

Many years later the British Field-Marshal, Lord Roberts, described his feelings as a young soldier on returning to Cawnpore in the autumn of 1857. As ever, the small things were the most poignant: 'tresses of hair, pieces of ladies' dresses, books crumpled and torn, bits of work and scraps of music, just as they had been left that fatal morning...'. It is easy to believe Roberts's verdict: 'the sights which met our eyes, and the reflections they gave rise to, were quite maddening'. In vain Queen Victoria spoke out against 'any retribution' which 'I should deeply deprecate': officers and men, by abandoning the prospect, should show 'the difference between Christians and Hindoos or Musselmen'. G. O. Trevelyan, in a study, *Cawnpore*, published in 1865, compared the British soldiers' behaviour to that of Telemachus slaughtering his mother's maids and he added the comment that it was 'curious' that this 'Pagan' act should be revived by 'a Christian warrior' (Brigadier-General Neill) after twenty-five centuries.[41]

The recapture of Jhansi lay ahead; but it was not to be expected that the British behaviour there would be marked by any 'maudlin clemency'. These were the words with which Dr Thomas Lowe, who was present as the Medical Officer to the Corps of Sappers and Miners, would choose to dismiss the quality of mercy, *pace* his sovereign, in an account of it all published in 1860. As for the Rani herself, once officially implicated in the Jhansi massacre, her likely fate, were she to be captured, was death (her father, who was captured, was hanged). To Lowe, as to many others not imbued with the spirit of Queen Victoria, the Rani had become 'the Jezebel of India ... the young, energetic, proud, unbending, uncompromising Ranee, and upon her head rested the blood of the slain, and a punishment as awful awaited her'.[42]

Perhaps Tennyson's sad verdict in *Boädicea* is the fairest on the state of India during the frenzied months of the Rebellion, when the land certainly ran with slaughter – Indian as well as British – and 'many a maid and matron' of both races did suffer 'multitudinous agonies' before perishing: 'Out of evil evil flourishes, out of tyranny tyranny buds.'

In the new year, Sir Hugh Rose, in the process of mopping up the remaining rebel encampments, set off for Jhansi. It was time for the Rani to put aside the peaceful mien of Lakshmi and mount the tiger of Durga. To this end she began to recruit a large army of her own, securing fourteen thousand volunteers from a population of some two hundred and twenty thousand, as well as fifteen hundred sepoys. She also strengthened the defences of the city itself. The siege of Jhansi began on 20 March 1858. One eyewitness, an Indian, told of the fierce British fire, including 'red-hot balls' which thundered over the city walls 'like the rains in autumn'.[43]

An attempt by Tatya Tope to relieve Jhansi from Kalpi, ended in a disastrous defeat at the Betwa river, with many Indian casualties, or as Thomas Lowe put it: 'a bloody day for not a man of the enemy asked for quarter or received it'.[44] Jhansi, it seemed, stood alone, with Rose determined not to allow the rebels to escape (as had happened at certain other fortresses *en route*) and the Rani, supported by the inhabitants, determined not to surrender.

On the British side, the energetic quality of the defence, Indian soldiers scurrying about with more vigour than they had ever been seen to display under British orders, was especially noted. 'They worked like bees', wrote Lowe, apparently surprised. The women of Jhansi, organized by the Rani, joined in; they were seen by the British working the batteries, carrying ammunition and otherwise bringing food and water to the soldiers.[45]

As for the Rani herself, whose standard flew proudly from one white turret, she was constantly visible both to her own followers and to the enemy. To the one she was a source of encouragement, to the other not entirely a source of abhorrence for all the mutterings of 'Jezebel': for already the strange double standard which could sometimes protect a Warrior Queen, where it would not protect her male counterpart, was in operation. There was wonderment and even admiration there too.

It is said that one of the bombardiers told Rose that 'he had covered the Queen and her ladies with his gun'; he asked permission to fire. To this Rose chivalrously replied that he did not approve of that kind of warfare.[46] Yet this was a woman who, it is suggested, would have been executed if she had been captured. There is certainly, from this point on, a dichotomy between the reactions of the soldiers who fought against her – who, in sum, admired her for her pluck, 'a perfect Amazon in bravery ... just the sort of daredevil woman soldiers admire', as the historical records of the 14th Light Dragoons described her[47] – and those who preferred to write about her in the vivid terms of the Voracity Syndrome, recalling those charges of sexual licence which Semiramis, Cleopatra and other Warrior Queens in the past had incurred. Both these types of judgement were of course directly inspired by her sex, and for better or for worse would not have been applied to a man.

Afterwards Sir John Kaye summarily dismissed the tradition of the Rani's 'intemperance', as he phrased it, as 'a myth' based on contemporary prejudice. It is true that tales of the hot-blooded Indian, avid to lay his fingers upon Anglo-Saxon womanhood, widely embellished the true horrors of the Mutiny with further not-quite-unspeakable (and untrue) details. For the coming of the white womenfolk to British India had brought to an end those jolly eighteenth-century days when a young Englishman would happily set his heart on 'A lass and a lakh a day' – to adapt the conventional lament – a lakh being 100,000 rupees and the lass being Indian. As the races drew apart, the customs of child marriage and polygamy seemed to give credence to the notion of Indian lustfulness.[48] Once again the Rani, for all the discretion of her personal behaviour, suffered by association.

A typical comment was that of Ellen C. Clayton (author of *Celebrated Women, Notable Women*, etc.) in her omnibus study *Female*

Warriors published in 1879, the year before Sir John's own more judicious work: 'All agreed as to the extreme licentiousness and immorality of her [the Rani's] habits; and the rooms in her palace are said to have been hung with pictures "such as pleased Tiberius at Capri"' – the delicate Victorian allusion is to pornographic art, although the Rani's keen detractor Lowe, who actually saw her apartments, mentioned no such titillatory detail in his own full description. One of the most damning – but equally quite unsupported – judgements was that of George W. Forrest in *A History of the Indian Mutiny*, published between 1904 and 1912, since his former position as the Director of Records for the government of India naturally carried weight. Picking eagerly on the phrase 'the Jezebel of India', he wrote that 'to speak of her [the Rani], as some have done, as "The Indian Joan of Arc" is indeed a libel on the fair name of the Maid of Orleans'. (Given Forrest's nationality, a somewhat self-righteous comment in any case.)[49]

He who had so described her – Sir Hugh Rose in two letters back to his royal Commander-in-Chief, the Duke of Cambridge – and had just spared her life, was granted no similar mercy by the lady in question. He watched the Rani first firing in his direction and then peering through a telescope to see what harm she had done. 'Like the 3rd Europeans and the 86th she requires a good deal of drilling,' commented Rose sardonically, 'nobody having been able to discover where the Ranee's shot went.'[50] But these days of mutual observation and raining fire could not last forever. The British assault upon Jhansi, which was to be both fierce and final, took place on 3 April. It may have been prompted by knowledge of a weakness in the defence supplied from inside: all accounts agree that the Rani herself was in the thick of the fighting.

At some point that night, however, the Rani escaped with about four followers, including her father. It is sometimes supposed that Rose laid a trap for her by allowing her to escape: but if there was a trap, she certainly eluded that too.[51] Riding hard, outdistancing her pursuers, in particular one Lieutenant Bowker, she succeeded by stages in reaching the fortress of Kalpi. She had travelled over one hundred miles in twenty-four hours. Here were congregated, among Indian rulers who had joined the rebels, not only Nana Sahib but the Nana's nephew, Pandurang Rao, known as Rao Sahib, as well as Tatya Tope.

Lieutenant Bowker's own story has him perceiving the Rani aloft on her celebrated grey (or white) horse and pursuing her with Rose's permission. A shot – possibly but not certainly fired by the Rani herself – disabled him, and so 'the lady escaped for the time being'. Indian sources have the Rani wounding the Lieutenant in a sword fight at Bhander, a small village where she stopped for food; some of these accounts take on already the heady quality of incantation, as in this one written by a barrister and published in Calcutta in 1930: 'But Lakshmi, put your horse now into a gallop. For Lieutenant Bowker is galloping behind, followed by select horsemen, in order to capture you. And you, O Horse, fortunate on account of the sacred treasure you carry, gallop on! ... The dawn has now broken. So, heroic goddess, flying all night on the wings of the wind, test thee!'[52]

There can be no question that Lakshmi Bai was right to escape both from her own point of view and that of her cause. The vengeance taken in Jhansi was frightful by any standards; some British historians have suggested that while four to five thousand died in battle, the civilians were spared. But Vishnu Godse, a priest from Bombay who was present, recalled four days of fire, pillage, murder and looting without distinction; it was difficult to breathe, he wrote, for the stink of burning flesh. Lowe's words, that the enemy were slain in their 'puffed up thousands ... such was the retribution meted out to this Jezebel Ranee and her people...' do not suggest there was much of a distinction between soldiers and civilians.[53]

In his description of the vanished Rani's personal apartments, however, Lowe dipped his pen into the ink of Sir Walter Scott, as he described the palace doors inlaid with plate-glass, mirrors, chandeliers, velvet and satin beds, bedsteads with silver feet, velvet cushioned chairs, brazen throne, gold- and silver-handled tulwars, spears, silver bird cages, ivory footstools, dozens of shawls, silver candlesticks 'and a thousand other things such as a luxurious woman would have' (although there is no mention of pictures 'such as pleased Tiberius'). All these accoutrements, as well as the works of Horace, Longfellow and Browning said to have belonged to the dead officers, 'lay here and there in chaotic confusion in every part of the building'. 'The soldiery went to and fro tramping over and through these things and kicking them about as they would any heap of rubbish', wrote Lowe, 'until order was somewhat restored.' Meanwhile the rebels fought like tigers 'so the bayonetting went on till after sunset'. The fate of the Rani might not have been so summary as that of her luxurious belongings but it is difficult to believe she would in the end have fared much better.[54]

While the Union Jack flew once more over Jhansi, in Kalpi, in contrast, the Rani was given an honoured reception by Rao Sahib, with a special parade of his soldiers. The next engagement which followed, that of Kalpi itself, to which Sir Hugh Rose and his army patiently slogged their way in heat so great that big tears trickled down the cheeks of the patient elephants and the very camels groaned. It is sometimes suggested that if Rao Sahib had given the command to the Rani, not to Tatya Tope, the result of the battle – another total defeat for the Indians – might have been different.[55] Another expression of the general admiration for the Rani is the widespread belief that she was responsible, as 'their most determined, spirited and influential head', for the Indians' next plan, one of extreme daring, to seize the fortress of Gwalior (although Tatya Tope, with contacts inside Gwalior, is perhaps a more likely author).[56] As a manoeuvre it was certainly remarkably successful, at a time when the rebel fortunes were badly in need of some coup to rally them. Gwalior was seized, and there the coronation of Rao Sahib took place. From the great regalia of Scindia, which resided in the Treasury at Gwalior, the Rani was granted by Rao Sahib a fabulous pearl necklace. Like the torc of Boadicea, it was to prove an ornament of ritual significance.

For all the daring which had attended its seizure, Gwalior could not expect to remain long immune from reprisal. When that attack came, the Rani was said to have been put in charge of the eastern side of the defence. She wore her armour, her sword with its jewelled scabbard – and her wonderful new acquisition, the pearl necklace. According to tradition, she took as her motto on this occasion, the celebrated verse: 'If killed in battle we enter the heaven and if victorious, we rule the earth.'

Of the two alternatives, it seemed that the Rani of Jhansi was not destined to rule the earth. She was killed at some point in the fierce but ultimately unsuccessful battle to defend Gwalior: the most likely date being 17 June – the second day of the fighting. As Boadicea's daughters traditionally died with their mother, two of the Rani's 'maids of honour' – in the British phrase – were said to have died with her: Indian sources give their names as Mandar and Kashi. One was described as 'most beautiful' and in her last agony stripped off her clothes.[57]

The exact manner of the Rani's death is not known for certain, nor who actually killed her. The British clearly took some trouble afterwards to find out. Three independent accounts written within a week of her death agree that she was mortally wounded as a result of a blow received during hand-to-hand fighting.[58] As J. Henry Sylvester, who was present, wrote: 'the gallant Queen of Jhansi fell from a carbine wound, and was carried to the rear, where she expired, and was burnt according to the custom of the Hindoos'. This is probably the truth although some local Indian ballads and songs have the Rani carried by faithful servants to the nearby monastery of Baba Gangadas and whispering to the Baba as he put the Ganges water in her mouth: 'I leave my [son] Damodar in your charge.'

A small locked notebook was found among Lord Canning's papers after his death (in 1862: like Lord Dalhousie, who died in 1860, he did not long survive his Indian experience). Canning had jotted down the following observations:[59] '*Ranee of Jhansi.* Killed by a trooper of 8th Hussars, who was never discovered. Shot in the back, her horse baulked. She then fired at the man and he passed his sword through her ... She used to wear gold anklets, and Sindia's pearl necklace, plundered from Gwalior. (Sindia says its value is untold.) These when dying she distributed among the soldiery, when taken to die under the mango clump.' (Sir Hugh Rose told the Duke of Cambridge, apropos 'these ornaments', that Tatya Tope had 'intercepted' the necklace.)[60]

Lord Canning went on: 'The army mourned her for two days.' But even in this terse report he paid tribute by implication to the Rani's gallantry – and to her continued femininity: 'The Infantry attacked the Cavalry for allowing her to be killed. The Cavalry said she would ride too far in front.' He added: 'Her tent was very coquettish.'

At the time, Sir Hugh Rose's report back to the Duke of Cambridge in England confirmed the story of the Rani's speedy immolation. After burning, she was buried 'with great ceremony, under a tamarind tree under the Rock of Gwalior, where I saw her bones and ashes'. His own epitaph contained the generous tribute of one soldier to another: 'The Ranee was remarkable for her bravery, cleverness and perseverance; her generosity to her Subordinates was unbounded. These qualities, combined with her rank, rendered her the most dangerous of all the rebel leaders.' In its regimental history, the 8th Hussars, at whose hands the Rani probably died (the squadron commander was granted a VC for his conduct in the course of that charge) reiterated Sir Hugh Rose's praise: 'in her death the rebels lost their bravest and best military leader'.[61]

The Rani's epitaph at the hands of her own people was to be nobler yet. The verdict of Colonel Malleson, who continued the work of Sir John Kaye in his own history of the mutiny published in 1896, proved correct: 'Whatever her [the Rani's] faults in British eyes may have been, her countrymen will ever remember that she was driven by ill-treatment into rebellion and that she lived and died for her country.'[62]

Nana Sahib, that master of 'ferocity and slaughter', escaped to Nepal where his legendary adventures as a wandering fakir inspired Jules Verne. Since his exact date of death was unknown, false Nanas were to reappear throughout the nineteenth century.[63] The Rani's adopted son Damodar Rao had a more prosaic but happier fate: he surrendered to the British in March 1860 and was subsequently granted a pension.* But the Rani's reputation passed into the airy world of ballad and song. There are statues of the Rani – at Gwalior as well as Jhansi – and nowadays innumerable highly coloured pictorial representations of the celebrated Warrior Queen. Nevertheless, it is by the ballads that the Rani of Jhansi is preserved in the Indian folk memory. A study by P. C. Joshi – *Folk Songs of '1857'* – published as part of a symposium in 1957 to mark the centenary,[65] explains why: 'The Rani's noble example and supreme sacrifice have blazed the path for countless sons and daughters of India to join the freedom struggle. She is one of the immortals of our national movement and such songs have kept her alive in our memory.'

> The song of joy, the song of freedom rises
> In every corner of the land this song is heard
> Here fought Lakshmi Bai and Peshwa Nana...[66]

---

* In 1957, to mark the centenary, his descendant was also given a symbolic monetary reward by the Indian state.[64]

Some of these songs have a fairy-tale quality: the Rani moulds her army from clay and stones, she makes swords from mere wood. Others dwell on the loyalty of her followers: the chief gunner guarding the main gates of Jhansi who tells his companion that 'we have to die one day, brother' and 'I shall choose today, For our Queen I shall lay down my life'. The old names ride again, but in a different guise. Here is 'Proud Hugh Rose' begging for 'one pot of water' to quench his thirst. The heroism of the Rani is however a constant element:

Old India was filled again with the bloom of youth...

wrote Subhadra Kumari Chauhan,

> The old sword flashed once more in fifty-seven
> This is the story we have heard
> From the Bundelas who worship Shiva
> The Rani of Jhansi fought valorously and well.

One popular ballad in particular calls attention to the salient characteristic of a heroine who, like Boadicea, will never be forgotten by her own people: that, for all the apparent weakness of her sex, she was in fact in courage the equivalent of any hero:

> How valiantly like a man fought she,
>> The Rani of Jhansi
> On every parapet a gun she set
>> Raining fire of hell,
> How well like a man fought the Rani of Jhansi
>> How valiantly and well!

CHAPTER SEVENTEEN

IRON LADIES

The Iron Lady of the Western World! Me? A Cold Warrior?
Well, yes – if that is how they wish to interpret my defence
of values and freedoms fundamental to our way of life.

Margaret Thatcher (1976)

When Queen Boadicea, courtesy of the sculptor Thornycroft, did finally take up her position upon the Thames Embankment in 1902, it was as an embodiment of the age of empire. Lest the message be missed, Cowper's proud lines of prophecy were inscribed upon the plinth:*

> Regions Caesar never knew
> Thy Posterity shall sway.

Queen Victoria had died early in the previous year, at the ripe age of eighty-one. The role of the female ruler, provided it did not involve the actual battlefield, appeared to be conducive to longevity. In 1900 a very different kind of Warrior Queen, Tz'u-Hsi, the so-called Dragon Empress of China, had the impudence to solicit support from Queen Victoria during the Boxer Rebellion which she

---

* It was not missed. As late as the Second World War, Prime Minister Churchill's Private Secretary, John Colville, strolling through London in the Blitz to inspect landmarks he might not see again, described Boadicea's statue as 'a monument to successful imperialism'.[1]

herself had done much to foment on this very basis: 'two old women', so ran her telegram, should understand each other's difficulties.[2] (Born in 1835, an approximate contemporary of the Rani of Jhansi, the Dragon Empress was sixteen years younger than Victoria.) Nevertheless even in 1902 the erection of the Boadicean monument should still be seen as celebrating the kind of maternal imperialism – indistinguishable to its practitioners from patriotism – personified by Victoria herself.

Curiously enough, the Embankment site was a second, or if one remembers Prince Albert's original suggestion of the Hyde Park Arch nearly a half century before, a third choice.[3] Thornycroft's project had passed through various vicissitudes following the Prince's premature death in 1861. To be sure, there was a melancholy bonus in a series of equestrian portraits of his former patron; but Thornycroft had toiled on the Boadicean group for fifteen years before a favourable review of it in *The Times* in 1871 suggested the possibility of a government commission. The sculptor resumed work in 1883, but died two years later, at which point his family offered the group to the public, together with a contribution to the heavy cost of casting.

It was a spurt of interest in the supposed burial place of Boadicea near the end of the century which was responsible for the final step. The London County Council proposed to erect the statue at the top of Parliament Fields, on the grounds that a tumulus there was the traditional site; a subscription of £2,800 was raised to have Thornycroft's statue cast in bronze, with a further £1,500 for a pedestal by J. G. Jackson. Intervention from the Society of Antiquaries, who rejected the Parliament Fields tradition, left the Boadicean group once more siteless, until 1902 when it reached its present resting place, near Westminster Bridge, and within sight of the Houses of Parliament.

Beyond Cowper's significant lines, the inscription beneath the statue kept various other options open. The subject of the monument was described as 'Boadicea (Boudicca) Queen of the Iceni Who died AD 61 after leading her people against the Roman invader'. Boadicea's daughters, however, although shown as part of the group – two strapping females, bare-breasted as Amazons for the fight – suffered from their usual official disregard and were not named or even mentioned. As for the Iceni Queen herself (her hair in a neat pageboy style rather than flowing), 'One really must admire her sang-froid', wrote Lord Edward Gleichen in 1928 in a study of London's open-air statuary. For the horses, modelled – not too closely one hopes – on those of Prince Albert's stables, are galloping wildly, but Boadicea has no reins with which to control them, as she stands coolly aloft with her spear.[4]

This belief in the nobility of empire, attached to the idealized character of a patriotic woman, was to be one important element in the survival of the Boadicean legend.[5] The year 1900 for example saw the publication of *Britain's Greatness Foretold*, the story of Boadicea by Marie Trevelyan, which traced the foundations of 'our present freedom' back to those ancient struggles against the Romans.[6] (The South African War against the Boers had begun while Marie Trevelyan was in the process of writing.) The book is redolent with direct comparisons between Boadicea and Queen Victoria: also characteristic of the time is the general emphasis placed upon the inspiring femininity of both queens.

British colonization, Marie Trevelyan pointed out, was the task of families, not soldiers, 'just as it was the woman Boadicea who rallied all the tribes of Britain round her in her day'. Led by Queen Victoria, it was the women of Great Britain who had materially helped to spread and maintain the British Empire. As for Marie Trevelyan's Boadicea, even in war she never surrendered her natural tenderness: at the last battle indeed the 'majestic queen' was described as being 'lost in the weeping woman'. On the other hand, when Boadicea's men responded loudly to her speech with the rallying cry 'For Britain, Boadicea and freedom', they were of course intent on making aggressive war rather than domestic peace.

So Boadicea, aided both by late Victorian perceptions concerning women and empire, and by the image of Queen Victoria herself, passed into the pantheon of idealized patriotic women. It is a place she has not lost in the odd ninety years since the erection of her statue and is not likely to lose, so long as national crises arise, demanding reference to comforting historic symbols of courage and endurance.

Patriotic fervour helped to make up one part of the modern Boadicean plinth. At the same time, as women stirred in their struggle for general recognition as a sex (rather than as privileged individuals)

Boadicea's protean legend began to be employed in quite a different connection. Pageants had become increasingly popular in late Victorian and Edwardian times; in this manner the British aristocracy was able to show off both its adequate historical knowledge and its more than adequate historical fancy dress, in a pleasurable real-life example of zeugma. But *The Pageant of Great Women*, first performed on 10 November 1909 at the Scala Theatre, London, was a pageant with a difference, since it was performed in the suffragette cause.[7] This was two months after the Prime Minister, Asquith, had instructed the prison doctors to feed suffragette hunger-strikers forcibly. Originally produced by the play department of the Actresses' Franchise League, written by Cicely Hamilton, designed and directed by Edith Craig, the pageant subsequently toured the country.

Boadicea, 'a Briton in arms', was one of the most prominent characters. When she appeared, spectators were adjured to 'look on her who stood ... and spat defiance at the hosts of Rome!' A photograph of the event in the *Daily Mirror* shows what they saw: a stalwart Boadicea, towering over her companions and got up more or less according to Dio Cassius' instructions, with flowing tresses over a barbaric robe, a torc and other jewels, and an enormous spear in her hand (another possible comparison, to Ellen Terry's famous portrait as Lady Macbeth, reminds one that Edith Craig was Ellen Terry's daughter).

The character of Prejudice was played by a man. Otherwise the familiar stage army – in this case literally so – of great women was paraded in categories which included 'Learned Women', 'Artists' and 'Saintly Women' as well as 'Rulers' and 'Warriors'. Here Queen Zenobia 'of the hero's heart' was placed among the Rulers; but the Rani of Jhansi – 'though but a child in years' – found her place among the Warriors together with Boadicea, Joan of Arc and the fourteenth-century Scot Agnes Dunbar. It was intended by this appeal to the rich past to draw public attention to the 'physical, intellectual, creative and ethical' strengths of women, in contrast to Prejudice's contemptuous declaration that Woman's innate stupidity made her incapable of thought. Fifty-two actresses took part.

In order to facilitate touring, it was Edith Craig's plan that such a pageant should contain only three speaking parts, all allegorical; these were performed by professionals. Otherwise members of suffragette societies on the spot would supply the colourful heroines, Edith Craig arriving to dress them. This ingenious arrangement was not without its little local difficulties: the extreme popularity of the role of Joan of Arc constituted one of them. Another of a rather different nature was encountered when the members of a suffrage society in a university town thought they knew enough for no one to be anxious to play Catherine the Great: who, 'whatever may have been her merits as a ruler, was renowned for the scandals of her private life'. Finally a girl was found who presumably shared Edith Craig's view that a good part was a good part for all that.

The pageant ended with Prejudice taking his stand on force as 'the last and ultimate judge', and claiming that force for man alone 'who takes the sword – The sword that must decide!' Woman on the other hand, declared Prejudice, 'Fears the white glint of it and cowers away'. It was at this point that the Warriors, led by Boadicea, were paraded in rebuttal. The stage directions read: 'Then Prejudice slinks away.'

But Prejudice, if he left the stage of the Scala Theatre, did not slink far, let alone slink away altogether, even with the winning of the vote for women at various dates in various countries across the world. Seventy years after the *Pageant of Great Women* an extraordinary exhibition was shown in San Francisco for the first time before embarking upon a worldwide tour to packed attendance.*

The Dinner Party was conceived by the American artist and craftswoman Judy Chicago and executed by her over five years with 'a working community of women and men'.[8] The exhibition consisted of thirty-nine 'place settings' upon a large open triangular banqueting table, which in turn rested upon a porcelain 'Heritage Floor', bearing the names of 999 women, grouped into categories. Its aim – an avowedly feminist one – was not only to 'symbolize the long history of female achievement' but also to remind its audience that 'the history of Western civilization, as we have understood it, has failed to represent the experience of half the human race'.

The Dinner Party's categories include 'Primordial Goddess' and 'Fertile Goddess' but also 'Kali', a category described as a 'traditionally positive view of female power misrepresented as a

* There were, for example, long queues in London when it was shown at a converted warehouse in White Lion Street, Islington, in the spring of 1986.

destructive force' (such as Celtic Britain's Rhiannon). 'Boadaceia d. 62 AD' (*sic*) is, like 'Kali', the name which heads a category standing for 'the tradition of warrior queens extending back to legendary times'. Other Boadiceas include Cartimandua, Artemisia, Cleopatra, defined as a 'Ruler–Deity', Medb of Connacht, Tomyris and Zenobia, given the full panoply of description as 'Queen, warrior, military strategist and scholar'.

Give or take changes in the language of female protest between 1909 and 1979, there is an obvious and significant similarity between the suffragette pageant and the feminist exhibition in method of execution. It is not just that certain devaluations of the nature of women – her innate stupidity and cowardice for example as denounced by the pageant's male figure of Prejudice – are clearly still perceived to need rebuttal in the late twentieth century, as they have been rebutted by bold spirits throughout history. Further than that, the appeal in both cases to 'Triumphant Women' of the past bears witness once again to the enduring importance of heroines such as Boadicea, mythical or actual, to women combating their own inferior status; and this despite the passionate desire of many women to help forward *all* their sex, not merely the potential leaders.

With the coming of the Women's Movement, such heroines naturally take on new guises. In *The Dinner Party*, for example, 'Elizabeth R', like 'Boadaceia d. 62 AD', constitutes a category: the first Elizabeth is described as 'One of the greatest female rulers who ever lived, distinguished stateswoman and scholar.' While not dissenting from the verdict, one cannot help wondering what Elizabetha Triumphans herself would have made of the all-female company, she who was accustomed to pikes being couched and ensigns lowered in devotion as she passed, 'to she alone and none but only she'; to say nothing of her calculated boast of having the heart and stomach of a *man*. Boadicea, on the other hand, has come to symbolize a kind of female freedom and even sexual liberation.

The discovery by the feminist poet Judy Grahn – to her own satisfaction – that the name Boadicea (in its original Boudica form) was the origin of the word 'bulldike', may stand as an extreme example of this.[9] Grahn, in an article of 1980 entitled 'The Queens of Bulldikery', described how in years past the mystery of the word 'bulldike' had 'burbled and thickened' in her mind; deciding that it stemmed from Old English, she therefore searched for a historical

people who once worshipped and valued bulls. From here to Boadicea ('Bo' means 'cow' in Irish while English friends assured her
that 'bull' was pronounced 'Boa') and thence happily to Boudica,
was a short leap of Grahn's creative imagination.

'Boudica was a barbarian and a Celt,' wrote Grahn, 'and her
pudenda would have been active, unashamed, and radiating with
female power all her life ... Considering Celtic customs it would
have been unnatural of Queen Boudica *not* to be a lesbian. She was,
after all, a queen and a military leader of her people.' With an even
greater leap of the imagination, Grahn also drew attention to the
large number of puns surrounding Boadicea's name, such as the
soldiers' *dikes* which they made in AD 61, and her statue called
'Boadicea on the Embankment', embankment being a synonym for
dike.

Grahn however derided Dio Cassius' description of the atrocities
committed under Boadicea's command – the laceration of the
women's breasts in particular – as being 'too much like the typical
patriarchal response to women warriors in general to be believed'.
(This point of view, incidentally, provides Grahn with an ally in
the shape of Milton, however unlikely the combination; he too
dismissed such invented details by which historians hoped to
'embellish' their work.)[10] The next leap is to transfer the word
'bulldike' to the United States: Grahn's explanation lies in the slang
of Newgate Prison, from which many indentured criminals proceeded westwards, a high percentage of them, according to Grahn,
Celts, who remembered their ancestors as homosexual 'as a matter
of course'.

It is too easy to dismiss all this as ludicrously unhistorical (which
of course it is). For one might observe with truth that Grahn's
imaginative reconstruction is really no more ludicrous than some
of the other theories which have been proposed about Boadicea in
the past, including, famously, her 'rich burial' at Stonehenge, actually erected nearly two millennia before, but believed as an article
of faith in the early seventeenth century. Nor is Grahn's bold lesbian
Celt, 'radiating with female power all her life', necessarily further
away from the original than Purcell's meekly apologetic late-seven-
teenth-century princess ('My Fortune wound my Female Soul too
high And lifted me above myself').[11]

Be that as it may, Grahn's alluring but fantastical theory has its own importance: for it draws attention to the Warrior Queen, here epitomized by Boadicea, as a symbol of sexual freedom as well as female independence. At the same time, such an image looks back to the remote past. Grahn's poem, written in 1972, 'She Who', acts as the epigraph of her article:

> I am the wall at the lip of the water
> I am the rock that refused to be battered
> I am the dyke in the matter, the other . . .
> and I have been many a wicked grandmother
> and I shall be many a wicked daughter . . .

This is once again the language, proud, mystical and ferocious, of the Ptolemaic creed of Isis, invoked to adorn the image of Cleopatra: 'I am she that rises in the Dog star, she who is called Goddess by women . . . I am the queen of war, I am the queen of the thunderbolt . . . '.[12]

Liberated sexuality in general − not merely homosexuality − contributes to the modern image of the Warrior Queen. *Boadicea: A Tragedy of War* by Robert Reynolds, issued by the Poets Press in New York in 1941, has a heroine who is seldom mentioned without a reference to her heavy breasts 'like pillows . . . ' and her frank sexual desires characteristic of Celtic women: 'Yet she attracted the younger tribesmen. She was the eternal, fecund woman of their songs and stories, and their myths.' Henry Treece's heroine, in an English novel of 1958, *Red Queen, White Queen*, has not only Boadicea but her daughters (Gwynedd and Siara), all three of them plump and buxom and blonde, sleeping with whoever pleases them 'in the old fashion'. In 1986 a British television programme on 'Imaginary Women' conducted by Marina Warner, showed Toyah Wilcox, twenty-five-year-old rock singer turned actress and film star, driving a chariot; her hair − an appropriate modern version of Dio's 'tawny' − was a violent punk red.[13] Toyah Wilcox, who had accepted the role of Boadicea − 'a character I greatly admire' − in a film the year before, now described her heroine as a 'free liberated sexual woman'.

Such a picture of a free-wheeling female rebel against patriarchal attitudes may seem in quaint contrast to the statuesque image inherited from late Victorian times, gravely maternal, deeply imperialist. Yet once again, as in the case of Grahn, the idea of the rebel, give or take her sexuality (the true nature of Boadicea's sexuality is one of the many things about her which are likely to remain forever obscure), is, of the two, the more in keeping with the few known facts of Boadicea's career.

There is still a further element in the mythology of Boadicea which has ensured the survival of interest in her image into modern times. That is the emergence of the political female leader. At first sight an elected woman Prime Minister may seem to have little in common with a Warrior Queen of ancient or even more recent times. Yet there is still an equivocal relationship perceived to exist between women and force which can rise to a head whenever a woman is voted into power, or even (significantly in modern democracies) *might* be voted into power. This equivocal relationship brings the notion of Boadicea, or some other legendary Warrior Queen, into play once more.

In the suffragette pageant of 1909, Prejudice had claimed force for Man alone, on the grounds that Woman traditionally cowered away from 'the white glint' of the sword; he also claimed force as 'the last and ultimate judge', effectively debarring timorous Woman from the exercise of power. Or in General de Gaulle's nobler version of the same sentiment, quoted in Chapter One, force was described as watching over civilization and ruling empires, 'the fighting spirit' being an integral part of man's inheritance. On the stage in 1909 Prejudice had been easily routed by the appearance of the defiant Boadicea, epitomizing Woman's ability to handle any martial matter. But the reality was very different and remains so. The question of what Kleist in *Penthesilea* called 'Fate's iron tongue, the sword' will not go away.[14]

Can women, if voted into power, handle the great issues of war (and death) and peace? Are they not too tender, if not actually too timid? Female leaders of the second half of the twentieth century have conspicuously found themselves having to prove their credentials in this respect by one means or another, not only after election but during the process leading up to it. Geraldine Ferraro was the Democratic Vice-Presidential candidate in the United States presidential election of 1984: the first woman to figure in such an outstanding position (and at the time of writing – 1988 – the year of the next round of presidential elections, the only one). Her account of her experiences campaigning, as related in *My Story*, published in 1986, makes illuminating reading. For it shows clearly that deep, primitive fears of women's potential timidity or weakness lurked in certain quarters of her country. Nothing in the political development of women elsewhere or even in America's own vigorous Women's Movement had affected this.[15]

Such fears were not exactly nursed in secret. In her confrontation on nationwide television with her opposite number, the sitting Republican Vice-President George Bush, on 11 October 1984, Geraldine Ferraro described herself facing 'the final and inevitable question'. Thus Vice-President Bush: 'Congresswoman Ferraro, you have had little or no experience in military matters and yet you might some day find yourself Commander-in-Chief of the armed forces. How can you convince the American people and the potential enemy that you would know what to do to protect this nation's security, and do you think in any way that the Soviets might be tempted to try to take advantage of you simply because you are a woman?' (This question was posed incidentally five years after Mrs Thatcher had become Prime Minister of Great Britain, hardly a good example of a woman of whom the Soviets had successfully taken advantage!)

'I didn't hesitate', wrote Geraldine Ferraro. ' "Are you saying that I would have to have fought in a war in order to love peace?" I shot back . . . '. And she did of course assure the questioner of her confidence in her own ability to handle such a situation. But she admitted that it was a terribly important question 'and I had thought a great deal about how to answer it'. George Bush for his part emphasized his own combat experience in the Second World War – for which Geraldine Ferraro, born in 1934, would of course have been too young, quite apart from her gender: 'Yes, I did serve in combat, I was shot down when I was a young kid, scared to death. And all that . . . heightened my convictions about peace.'

Marvin Kalb on *Meet the Press* put the question to Geraldine Ferraro in an even simpler form: 'Are you strong enough to push the button?' (Another legitimate question – to candidates of both sexes – might be: Are you strong enough *not* to push the button? But this was not posed.) Although Ferraro gave the obvious reply that she could do whatever was necessary for the protection of her country, privately she found it endlessly annoying to be presumed weak and indecisive just because she was a woman. There was a bigger underlying issue: if her candidacy was really being judged on the same level as a man's, she would hardly be asked to answer questions like that. Nor indeed was this question asked of any other candidates, other than members of Congress who were religious ministers.

But of course Geraldine Ferraro's candidacy – in the event unsuccessful since the election was won by the Republicans in a landslide – was not being judged on the same level as a man's. And those elected female leaders who have emerged triumphant have needed to pull the mantle of the Warrior Queen about them, where appropriate, and use it to lend further mythic authority to the role of mere Prime Minister: sex has had to be made a subtle advantage, instead of a crude disadvantage.

Indira Gandhi became Prime Minister of India on 24 January 1966 at the age of forty-eight. She was not in fact the first woman in the world to occupy the position: that honour had already gone to Mrs Gandhi's contemporary, Sirimavo Bandaraneike of Sri Lanka, who was elected in July 1960. Interestingly enough, at their inception, the careers of both Mrs Gandhi and Mrs Bandaraneike indicate that the Appendage Syndrome common to so many Warrior Queens continued to operate under elective conditions as it had done under the hereditary system in the past. That is to say, although the London *Evening News* wrote concerning Mrs Bandaraneike of the need for a new word – 'Presumably we shall have to call her a Stateswoman' – the comment of the *News Chronicle* was considerably more apt: 'Gentle widow heads for job as premier'.[16]

For Mrs Bandaraneike, Rani-like, was the widow of the veteran Sri Lankan statesman Solomon W. R. D. Bandaraneike, eighteen years her senior, who had acted as premier for three and a half years before he was assassinated in 1959 by a Buddhist monk. An inconclusive political election the following March was followed by an invitation to Mrs Bandaraneike to head the government: 'she was the symbol, the figurehead that was necessary; the spark to ignite the flame', in the words of her biographer.[17] (There is an obvious modern comparison to be made with Mrs Corazon Aquino, grieving widow of an assassinated opposition Filipino leader, whose symbolic presence heading a political party, at a time when her remarkable personal qualities were largely unknown, provided the spark to sweep away President Marcos in 1986.)

As for Indira Gandhi, coming from a Kashmiri brahmin family, the only child of Pandit Nehru, she could in a sense be said to have been born to rule: a princess who inherited from her parent, as Matilda of Tuscany inherited from her father Boniface II, or Tamara of Georgia from Giorgi III. Prior to her election, Indira Gandhi, the shy child of a brilliant father, absent much of her childhood in prison, and of an uneducated mother of lower social standing, had indeed held only one political position: she had been President of the Congress Party in 1959, but resigned after less than a year in favour of her maternal duties. Indira Gandhi actually became Prime Minister when Lal Bahadour Shastri died suddenly in office of a heart attack. In this uneasy situation, it was a symbol of that same continuity which Queen Elizabeth I constantly sought to establish with references to her sire 'Great Harry', that the crowds in 1966 shouted not only *'Indira ki jai!'* (Long live Indira!) but also *'Jawaharlal ki jai!'* (Long live Nehru!).[18]

Mrs Gandhi, the beneficiary of the Appendage Syndrome, quickly became part of another familiar syndrome – that of the Better-Man: in her first year of office, for example, she was described as 'the only man in the cabinet of old women'. She also received much of the same 'heroic' treatment concerning her youth from her admiring biographers, as well as herself stressing such early heroic self-identifications in what was surely a calculated manner. An early girlhood identification with Joan of Arc for example is frequently mentioned even by her family, and confirmed by Mrs Gandhi herself in a letter to her lifelong friend Dorothy Norman: she was 'a great heroine of mine ... one of the first people I read about with enthusiasm'.[19]

In other interviews, as with the celebrated Italian journalist Oriana Fallaci, Mrs Gandhi underlined a tomboy past: she revealed that her very doll play had been militarily oriented: 'I had many dolls. And I played with them, not necessarily seeing them as babies to feed. In fact I used them as men and women to perform insurrections, battles and so on.' She told a would-be biographer that sometimes her dolls were arranged to perform a struggle between the Satyagrahis and the police, with the bridegroom doll playing the Satyagrahi leader, while the little Indira shouted slogans such as '*Mahatma*

Gandhi ki jai!' Mrs Gandhi's 'male' aggressive role was by her own account encouraged by her mother, who had resented the constrictions on her own life, as well as by her father: 'I was brought up as a boy when I was small. I climbed trees, I ran and I never had any feeling of inferiority or weakness.'[20]

It was politically adroit of Mrs Gandhi, faced with the problem of being a woman premier in a country which was 83 per cent Hindu, to hint at the honorary male in such statements about herself. Officially however she took a slightly different stance: 'As Prime Minister, I am not a woman. I am a human being.' (Although her confidence to Dorothy Norman – 'I am in no sense a feminist but I believe in women being able to do everything' – may have come nearer to representing her real feelings on this complicated subject.) Again she stated: 'I do not regard myself as a woman but as a person with a job to do.' Golda Meir's version of this, incidentally, when asked how it felt to be a female Foreign Minister, was to crack back, 'I don't know, I've never been a male Foreign Minister.' A short biography of Mrs Gandhi 'for young boys and girls' by R. Sundara Raju, published in New Delhi in 1980, begins with the prophecy of a dying old man, Sarojini Naidu, at her birth that she would be the 'Nightingale (the new soul) of India'. Later Indira Gandhi declared that 'Being a woman has neither helped nor hindered me. During the struggle for independence, nobody was concerned about being beaten up or shot at or anything. Nobody said: "This is a woman and we won't shoot." It would be unfair if, later on, this question were to crop up.'[21]

Yet since inevitably it did crop up and would always do so, Mrs Gandhi also employed that other expedient of the Warrior Queen by which she made a virtue of necessity with wonderful dexterity. That is to say, she assumed the role, even the title, of 'The Mother', so deeply embedded in the Hindu consciousness, with the aura of those goddesses bright and dark, Durga and Kali, rulers of fertility and destruction, hovering about her. History, or folk memories of history as described in Chapter Sixteen with regard to the Rani of Jhansi, could be said to be on her side, to make of her in the minds of the less educated the last in a long line of queens and empresses, rather than the first woman Prime Minister. Moreover in 1966 Mrs Gandhi possessed to the simple mind the hopeful imperial quality of being the mother of sons – Rajiv Gandhi, later Prime Minister of India in his turn after his mother's assassination in 1986, was twenty-two at the time. One remembers Isabella of Spain, bolstered up in authority by the birth of an heir during the civil war.

It was however war – the successful Indian war against Pakistan of 1971 – which gave Mrs Gandhi her ultimate prestige and also her ultimate kind of deification, as Durga on the one hand, an imposing leader of her country on the other. Afterwards, as Dom Moraes wrote, 'She had achieved the status of a myth. She was Joan [of Arc] without the inconvenience of prison, fire and cross.'[22] It was not a war of Mrs Gandhi's seeking (in fact it can be argued that the female premiers of the twentieth century, like the eighteenth- and nineteenth-century queens regnant, have not been of their nature belligerent – merely determined to do their belligerent best in war when it comes – that is to say, to be as good as men if not better). Yet following the first Pakistani air raids against India in December 1971, no one could ever again ask, in India at least: how will this woman react in a crisis? Will she be too timid, or if not too timid, too tender?

Golda Meir, born in 1898, and thus nearly twenty years older than Indira Gandhi, became Prime Minister of Israel in 1969, having served as Minister for Foreign Affairs from 1956 to 1965. She had previously been the first Israeli Ambassador to the Soviet Union and Minister of Labour and would also serve as Secretary-General of the Labour Party. Early in her career Golda Meir had also shown herself capable of oratory on the (imagined) Boadicean scale. On 21 January 1948 she spoke eloquently to the Council of Jewish Federations in Chicago, appealing for funds without which the future state could not survive. It was a speech subsequently praised by the first premier of Israel, David Ben-Gurion: 'Some day when history will be written, it will be said that there was a Jewish woman who got the money which made the state possible.'[23] To British ears, at least, it has a Churchillian ring: 'I am not exaggerating when I say that the Yishiv in Palestine will fight in the Negev and will fight in Galilee and will fight on the outskirts of Jerusalem till the very end. You cannot decide whether we should fight or not. We will ... You can only decide one thing: whether we shall be victorious in this fight or whether the Mufti will be victorious. That decision American Jews can make. It has to be made quickly within hours, within days...'. Golda Meir returned to Palestine with promises of fifty million dollars.

As with Mrs Bandaraneike, the choice of Mrs Meir was intended to be a healing one, in view of the rival claims of Moshe Dayan and Yigel Allon; and once again Mrs Meir's elevation followed an unexpected death, that of the premier Levi Eshkol. Otherwise, there was one very important difference: here at last was a female leader who owed nothing to the Appendage Syndrome, one who was neither the daughter or widow of a famous man, nor the regent–mother for some form of infant princeling. To secure her place without the benefit of any specific male connection was in itself a remarkable achievement on the part of Golda Meir; and one far rarer in the history of women than is generally supposed. One can appreciate the judgement of Mrs Meir's political adviser Simcha Dinitz, later Director-General of the Prime Minister's Office (and Ambassador to Washington 1973 to 1978), that she had 'the best qualities of a woman – intuition, insight, sensitivity, compassion – plus the best qualities of a man – strength, determination, practicality, purposefulness'.[24]

Nevertheless for all the self-made quality of her position, the kind of questions – sometimes innocent, sometimes not – which Mrs Meir faced concerning the implications of her reaching high office have as ever a familiar ring. In *My Life*, published in 1975, Golda Meir described a visit to the National Press Club in Washington when she was Foreign Minister: 'there were only two queries that were at all new'. The first concerned Israel's intention – or otherwise – to employ nuclear weapons if its survival was in jeopardy. The second went as follows: 'Mrs Meir, your grandson Gideon says you make the best *gefilte* fish in the world. Would you reveal your recipe to us?' This was naïve behaviour at worst, and it made Mrs Meir laugh at the time. On the other hand the Jordanian newspaper which mocked Mrs Meir in 1969 for asking for negotiations before war, as 'a grandmother, telling bedtime stories to her grandchildren' (she was indeed a grandmother at this point, not surprisingly for a woman in her early seventies), was not naïve but calculating.[25] Once again, it is impossible to envisage a male leader being subject to this particular diatribe.

And yet the ambiguity at the centre of the whole subject of the Warrior Queen remains. Mrs Meir also derived strength, surely, from her 'grandmotherly' image, not least among her own strongly matriarchal people. It was after all perfectly possible that the president of the Washington Press Club genuinely wanted that recipe, and admired Mrs Meir for her alleged skill: months later in Los Angeles, when she answered a question on television about her chicken soup, 40,000 people wrote in for the recipe! That juxtaposition of Israel's survival with a recipe could have been evinced only by the sight of a woman minister. And there was indeed something matriarchal – grandmotherly even – about the way she ran her government. To quote Chaim Herzog (later President of Israel), another who knew her well and worked under her, Golda Meir had a particular style of government in which her personality was the deciding factor: and that personality was very much that of 'the overbearing mother who ruled the roost with her iron hand'.[26]

This was not always, in his opinion, to the benefit of her government. With little idea of orderly administration, she preferred to work closely with cronies in an *ad hoc* framework that soon came to be known as her 'kitchen' – so named for good reason, since Golda Meir was wont to make coffee and tea there for her associates throughout the long night hours (as well as making coffee at 4 a.m. for her guards). At the same time one might most easily rebut the Jordanian sneer by observing that in the Arab–Israeli War of 1973 – the War of Atonement – the 'grandmother' acquitted herself both gallantly and expertly. To quote Chaim Herzog again on her conduct during the war: 'on many occasions she [Golda Meir], a woman who had reached seventy-five, found herself thrust into a position where she had to decide between differing military options proposed by professionals. She decided, and invariably decided well, drawing on a large measure of common sense which had stood her in good stead.'[27] Her stubborn decisiveness proved a national asset during the war, even if her doctrinaire approach to problems and to the operation of government contributed to the failings of that government before it.

And then there was that special rapport which Golda Meir had with the ordinary soldiers of Israel, something bringing her close to Isabella of Spain or Tamara of Georgia. When Golda Meir wept at the Wailing Wall on the fifth day of the Six Day War for the sacrifices of Israel's youth, the soldiers watched her and wept too.[28]

· · ·

There is however one twentieth-century female political leader who has had to be extremely cautious at any overt suggestion of queen-ship – warrior or otherwise. That is not to say that the subject in all its emotive strength does not arise. Margaret Thatcher, then aged fifty-three, became Prime Minister of Great Britain in May 1979, the first woman to occupy the position, as five years earlier she had been the first woman to lead any British political party. By this date, Queen Elizabeth II, a mere six months younger than the new Prime Minister, had already been on the throne for over twenty-seven years.

'This nation loves a monarch', a committee of the House of Commons had advised Lord Protector Oliver Cromwell in 1657, suggesting that he should regularize his position by accepting a crown himself. In the words of Secretary Thurloe advocating the same course: 'it's the office which is known to the laws and this people. They know their duty to a King and his to them.'[29] Certainly the British love their monarchy, and certainly they love their present monarch, Queen Elizabeth II, who regularly tops polls as the most admired British woman. They also know their duty to her: just as she knows hers to them, the Queen's conspicuous sense of duty being among the qualities which have endeared her to her subjects in the course of a reign whose span, in 1988, is already approaching that of her illustrious predecessor, the first Elizabeth. It is Queen Elizabeth II who enacts the role of the Holy (Armed) Figurehead to her people in her frequent ceremonial appearances at military parades, naval reviews and so forth; of which her presence for many years in uniform and on horseback at the Trooping of the Colour is probably the best-known.

Under the circumstances one can understand the alarm, both public and private, which Mrs Thatcher has displayed at any sugges-tion of encroachment on the royal role on her own part. She is obviously well aware of the resentment she might unleash.[30] 'You don't do that to me, my dear, I'm only in politics', she observed hastily to an unwary Spanish tourist who curtseyed to her, when the Prime Minister was glimpsed on a shopping tour in 1987.[31]

But, once again, the issue is not so simple. The existence of queens regnant in British history, and the tradition of national prosperity under two of them, the long-reigning Elizabeth I and Victoria, means that every British schoolchild – the one who knows about the knives on the wheels of Boadicea's chariot – also knows that it is not out of the question for a woman to rule Britain, much as Mrs Gandhi benefited from Hindu traditions of powerful women in religion, literature and history, despite the theoretically inferior position of women in Hindu society.

In January 1988, when Mrs Thatcher became the longest-serving Prime Minister in twentieth-century Britain, there was a plethora of commentaries and comparisons: but after lip-service had been paid to Prime Minister Asquith – whose record she had just beaten – the main comparisons were made unashamedly to British reigning queens. As Robert Harris wrote rather despairingly in the *Observer*: 'It is not sexist to use a regal analogy to describe her impact on the country. It is not particularly facetious. It is simply the nearest thing we have to an historical parallel.' Lord Hailsham, Lord Chancellor in Mrs Thatcher's government for eight years, openly described his premier as being in the same category as Mary Tudor, Elizabeth I, Queen Anne and Queen Victoria, favouring Elizabeth I especially 'in her handling of men'.[32]

So Mrs Thatcher, without visibly seeking it – rather to the contrary – did benefit from that tradition expressed long ago by Tacitus concerning the Britons and Boadicea: 'they did not discriminate against women in matters of command'. There is a kind of justice in this. For Mrs Thatcher also had to contend with many of those problems special to the Warrior Queen – or Queen Regnant – which have been mentioned throughout this book.

The female voice of command, which grates on the male ear for reasons which are as much psychological as physiological, is one of these problems, from Boadicea's allegedly 'harsh' voice onwards. The disadvantage to Mrs Thatcher of her female lightly timbred voice in a massively male-dominated House of Commons – which means of course deep-male-voice-dominated – is not one to be dismissed lightly, since it has entailed exactly that kind of screeching in making herself heard most disliked by men (and many women).

Mrs Thatcher has acknowledged this herself: 'Yes, I do have to shout to make myself heard,' she admitted in an interview in 1986, 'and sometimes I say, "I am not going to shout any more like I did last time, I will just stand there until they are quiet".' In the same year the Labour Shadow Minister Gerald Kaufman drew attention to what he called Mrs Thatcher's 'fishwife' act in the House of

Commons: 'screaming away in a shrill, strident voice, with her face absolutely contorted'. The Liberal leader David Steel made the same point – and independently used the same epithet: 'I don't personally like her House of Commons style. I don't think that the "fishwife" approach ... is at all effective or impressive.' It was however in vain that Kaufman hoped his own comment was made 'in an unsexist way': for the point is indeed a sexist one, whether intended as such or not, in that no man could possibly be subject to the same criticism. (One cannot help recalling Leonardi Bruno's quattrocento advice to Battista Malatesta about a woman who 'increases the volume of her speech with greater forcefulness': she will appear 'threateningly insane and requiring restraint'.)[33] A man bellowing to make himself heard in the House of Commons, as many men do, does not sound either to his own side or to his opponents like a 'fishwife' – that traditional English misogynist term of abuse going back to the fourteenth century – let alone as though requiring restraint.

There is no obvious solution to this particular problem of the female leader's voice except of course more women members of Parliament – after the 1987 general election, there were forty-one women to six hundred and nine men. But another lingering problem, the problem which will not go away (to judge from Geraldine Ferraro's experience) – how resolute can a female leader be expected to show herself against a nation's enemies? – was solved for Mrs Thatcher from an unexpected quarter: the Soviet Union, ironically enough the most likely candidate at the time for the title of Britain's enemy.

In January 1976, just under a year after she had been elected leader of the Conservative Party, Mrs Thatcher made a major speech in London which described the Soviet Union as a serious threat, both military and political, to which threat it was vital that the West should respond with strength and confidence. It was the Soviet Union's response, attacking her as the 'Iron Lady' in *Red Star*, the official journal of the Red Army, which presented Mrs Thatcher with what rapidly became, for good tactical reasons, her favourite sobriquet. It was immediately given wide prominence, not only in the Western Press, but by the victorious victim herself. 'I have the reputation of being the Iron Lady', she would say on US television at the time of the Falklands War. 'I have great resolve.' (A cartoon in the *Daily Express* of her visit to the United States on this occasion showed Mrs Thatcher as Boadicea, long sword raised, iron breast-plates prominent, with President Reagan at her chariot wheels in a cowboy hat.)[34]

Even if Mrs Thatcher had been variously dubbed 'Iron Maiden' and 'Iron Lady' by Marjorie Proops in the London *Daily Mirror* as early as 1973, it was the Soviet Union's adoption (or spontaneous invention) of the phrase which gave it exactly the endorsement which Mrs Thatcher needed to emerge as a Warrior Queen, at any rate in the estimation of Britain's 'enemies'. As Bruce Arnold wrote in a hostile work, *Margaret Thatcher: A Study in Power*, published in 1984 (that memorable line 'the female of the species is more deadly than the male' acts as the epigraph), Mrs Thatcher's baptism as the Iron Lady 'effectively created the political reputation on inter-national affairs which, by their dismissal, her Labour opponents had denied her, up to that point'.[35] 'The Iron Lady of the Western World! Me? A Cold Warrior?' she was able to riposte publicly. 'Well, yes – if that is how *they* [the Russians] wish to interpret my defence of values and freedoms fundamental to our way of life.'[36]

What propaganda had so felicitously – from Mrs Thatcher's point of view – begun, war itself was to confirm. Certainly the fact that the Falklands campaign would be the crucible of Mrs Thatcher's reputation as a leader was appreciated in advance. In the House of Commons in the opening debate following the Argentinian invasion, on 3 April 1982, Enoch Powell (no longer a member of the Conservative Party) actually referred to the phrase 'Iron Lady' in order to add: 'In the next week or two this House, the nation and the Right Honourable Lady herself will learn of what metal she is made.' It is said that Mrs Thatcher nodded her head in agreement.[37]

Another observer of the political spectrum hostile to Mrs That-cher, Anthony Barnett, author of *Iron Britannia: Why Parliament Waged its Falklands War* (the epigraph this time was merely the biblical name JUDITH in heavy black type) wrote cogently that Mrs Thatcher remained 'a misfit' until the 3 April debate 'elevated her into the war-leader of a bipartisan consensus'. An important inside testimony, on the other hand, is that of Patrick Cosgrave, the author of three successive biographical studies of Mrs Thatcher, since he worked for her as her Special Adviser for four years. In 1985 Cosgrave wrote that not only did the period between 2 April and 14 June 1982 show the Prime Minister at her most typically daring and resolute, but 'the war in the South Atlantic will undoubtedly be seen in the future, as it was at the time, as bearing witness to Margaret Thatcher as most truly herself'.[38]

As a result the British campaign in the South Atlantic to recover the Falkland Islands from the Argentine invader saw Mrs Thatcher's personal popularity as a leader jump from 36 per cent approval in March 1982 to 59 per cent after the war – a staggering leap. There can be no starker illustration of the continuing potency of the image of the Warrior Queen in a nation's consciousness. As for the armed forces themselves, and the men who lead them, they have been described as responding to her as a war-leader 'in a way that hasn't been known since the time of Elizabeth I, with a passion and loyalty that few male generals have ever inspired or commanded'. For the army at least Mrs Thatcher has begun to have her own *mana* as a goddess: an apparition transcending that of the Armed Figurehead, for example, holy or otherwise, because of its sheer personal strength. It was suggested (by Selina Hastings in the *Sunday Telegraph*) that in view of 'the aphrodisiac pull of power itself ... for the armed forces she is far and away the favourite object of sexual fantasy'.[39]

Equally, for those for whom power is not necessarily thrilling (Mrs Thatcher being the most powerful woman in the world), she sometimes seems like Kali, 'the grim Indian goddess of destruction', as she ruthlessly demolishes 'old ideas, policies and personalities', while at the same time exercising her other talents as 'the great creative stateswoman, the Blessed Margaret'. This remarkable double-headed comparison to the goddess–destroyer on the one hand and the sainted female was that of the historian and political journalist Paul Johnson on the eve of the Conservative Party Conference in 1987. He warned discontented Tories: 'Don't get caught under the wheels of the juggernaut. Blessed Margaret the creative–radical is driving it, but Kali–Thatcher the Destroyer is at hand – if required.'[40]

Opinions vary about what use Mrs Thatcher has actually made of her own unavoidable femininity, consciously or unconsciously, and what difference the whole intricate topic has made to her premiership. Commentators of both sexes and all shades of political opinion have gazed at her with fascinated awe: some seeing in Mrs Thatcher that Medusa on the 'snaky-headed Gorgon shield' wielded by 'wise Minerva', which froze her foes to stone; others viewing her with more admiration as wise Minerva herself, whose own 'rigid looks of chaste austerity and noble grace', as Milton pointed out in *Comus*, were enough to dash 'brute violence' without need of any Gorgon shield. But there has been remarkable unanimity among commentators and biographers that it has made *some* difference. Hugo Young and Anne Sloman, for example, in *The Thatcher Phenomenon* of 1986, agreed that her style of leadership turns heavily on her being a woman – without being sure how.[41]

While the independent-minded Conservative MP Julian Critchley described her as deploying her feminine qualities 'like artillery pieces', one biographer summed it up more ambivalently thus: 'she has played the matter of being a woman, and that of woman's place in modern society, in a variety of not always very clear-cut ways'.[42] The explanation for this lack of clear-cutness lies surely in Mrs Thatcher's own intuition concerning her situation. As the brilliantly instinctive politician she undoubtedly is, Mrs Thatcher has realized either consciously or unconsciously (the effect is the same) that if the issue were to be clear-cut, it would be to rob her of a great deal of support on the one hand, a good deal of manoeuvrability on the other.

On the one hand she has played the role of the 'honorary male' with all the aplomb of Queen Elizabeth I, as when in 1979 on a visit to Northern Ireland following the murder of Lord Mountbatten and a number of British soldiers, Mrs Thatcher adopted the red beret and flak jacket of the Parachute Regiment (thus pleasing the regiment itself but not the Northern Ireland Office). This can be directly compared to Queen Elizabeth I's choice of a silver cuirass and plumed helmet for her appearance at Tilbury, since neither lady actually intended to take to the battlefield. There have been numerous other carefully organized sightings of Mrs Thatcher in military situations, particularly in the early days of her premiership, where her symbolic presence as a Warrior Queen was hard to miss.

Like Queen Elizabeth again, Mrs Thatcher has displayed another interesting characteristic of the honorary male; she has no visible preference for the advancement of her own sex. After nine years of Mrs Thatcher's premiership, only one other woman has been appointed to the Cabinet, and she incidentally a member of the non-competitive House of Lords, not Commons: Baroness (Janet) Young's two-year stint, in her capacity as Leader of the House of Lords, included the period of the Falklands War, a fact which Mrs Thatcher either had temporarily forgotten, or chose grandly to ignore, when she told her Cabinet on 2 April 1982: 'Gentlemen, we shall have to fight.' It ended when Baroness Young was demoted to a minor role in the Government outside the Cabinet. It has been percipiently observed that the presence of *another* woman in the Cabinet photograph spoils the radiance which the leader alone possesses in photographic terms, making her so clearly unmistakable in her visible female dress.[43] At some very primitive level, did Mrs Thatcher resent Baroness Young's presence?

For there is the element of chivalry which the woman in a man's world traditionally evokes (an honorary male perhaps, but not sacrificing any of the prerequisites allowed by society to the female). At Mrs Thatcher's first Party Conference as Conservative leader, in October 1975, Barbara Castle, a prominent Labour politician in the Wilson government who had yet to see her own party elect a female leader, confided to her diary, possibly not without a small jealous pang, that Mrs Thatcher now displayed a special bloom, produced by 'the vitamin of power'. In March she had written, 'Margaret's election has stirred up her own side wonderfully: all her back-benchers perform like knights jousting a tourney for a lady's favours, showing off their paces by making an unholy row at every opportunity over everything that the [Labour] Government does.' Thirteen years later, the official photograph to commemorate Mrs Thatcher's long-serving record certainly did give her a remarkable air of a Tudor sovereign, in her long gold brocade dress, surrounded by males including Cabinet ministers, top civil servants and her own husband: twenty-six black-and-white (dinner-jacketed) knights.[44]

Then there is Mrs Thatcher's celebrated reaction to a question concerning Women's Liberation, at her first press conference as Conservative leader: 'What's it ever done for me?' Queen Victoria, among past female rulers, might have approved of this disdain, with her well-known antipathy to Women's Rights in principle and professional women in practice. But in her own time such contempt has earned Mrs Thatcher the justified dislike and disapproval of the Women's Movement. An editorial of August 1982 in *Spare Rib*, a leading feminist magazine, criticized the way 'masculinity' had been propagated throughout the whole Falklands crisis, military and sexual powers mixed up together as glorious, most notably by the (female) Prime Minister: 'We are not saying women should avoid positions of power, but that unless we direct our efforts to the good of all women ... we are likely to promote rather than challenge the current notions of masculinity.' In short, there is the 'very real danger of leading to more Margaret Thatchers'.[45]

On the other hand, with Mrs Thatcher's denial of any specifically female qualities has gone an ability to capitalize on them where necessary – once again, probably successful just because it is instinctive. (One has to admit that even her reaction to Women's Liberation may, fortunately or unfortunately depending upon one's view of the subject, have gained her far more support than she lost in Britain in 1975.) Nor can Mrs Thatcher fairly be blamed for capitalizing on her sex, since she has had to suffer a good many slings and arrows on the subject, from the first moment when Labour supporters shouted 'Ditch the bitch!' until honourably restrained by women members of the Labour movement.

During the Falklands campaign, insults in the Argentine Press varied from 'chicken brain' (because she was a woman) to 'go back to knitting' and 'stay in the kitchen'. Although such outbursts were smoothly dismissed by President Galtieri of Argentina in an interview, once more with Oriana Fallaci, on the grounds that 'humour and caricature belong to the Latin temperament', the area of attack chosen was surely significant.* [47] Under the circumstances, Mrs Thatcher was well entitled to use that metaphorical knitting needle, to which she was told to return, as an offensive weapon.

As early as 1979, on the eve of her first general election as Conservative leader, Mrs Thatcher emphasized the practical value of her female domesticity: 'I know what it is to run a home and a job...' and quoted the recent example of Golda Meir for authority, that characteristic technique of the female leader through history, back to Zenobia stressing her descent from Cleopatra. In an important and prominent interview with George Gale in the *Daily Express*, shortly after the Falklands War was over, Mrs Thatcher directly

---

* Nor was the 'kitchen' reference confined to the Latin temperament. The puppet Iron Lady, as depicted by Luck and Flaw, the British cartoonists, on television in November 1976, had her breastplate and armour created out of colanders and other pieces of kitchen equipment.[46]

compared the running of the campaign to household management – something on which she, as a woman, could be presumed to be an expert, or at least by implication more expert than the men surrounding her.[48] This was in answer to the question: 'Did being a woman make any difference?' 'It may just be that many, many women make naturally good managers and organizers. You might not think of it that way, George,' she went on sweetly, 'but each woman who runs a house is a manager and an organizer. We thought forward each day, and we did it in a routine way and we were on the job twenty-four hours a day.'

Mrs Thatcher's reaction to George Gale's next topic is however a perfect illustration of the kind of manoeuvrability she has allowed herself. 'Was it difficult for a woman to issue orders involving blood being shed?' he asked. 'We were thinking in terms of saving lives,' she answered (without directly replying to the question), 'but bearing in mind that our people had been invaded by a pretty awful dictatorship. One lived with the agony of the troops who were going down on the supply line on ships. One lived with the agony of the soldiers. But we didn't look only at the agony: we also looked at the professionalism, the loyalty and the devotion of our troops.' In a trice, the cosy super-feminine housekeeper has become the dedicated Warrior Queen, the 'singular exception' in Gibbon's phrase, the woman ruling proudly in the man's world.

So Boadicea marches on in her third modern personification, not the abstract patriotic symbol of empire, not the independent woman, free of shackles which may be political or sexual, but the elected female Prime Minister and occasional war-leader, whose existence continues to enrage, fascinate and inspire, in equal quantities, beyond any capacity of her male contemporaries to do these same three things. The innumerable allusions and comparisons to Boadicea during Mrs Thatcher's premiership, far from being monolithically favourable in intention (or unfavourable), in fact illustrate just this many-sided aspect of her own image, as well as that of Boadicea herself.

At the time of the Falklands campaign, the left-wing *New Statesman* in a critical editorial called Mrs Thatcher 'this Boadicea' who would have to come back into 'the real world' when the war was over. Adam Raphael in the *Observer* also called her Boadicea at roughly the same date (late May): 'every time she opens her mouth she castrates one of her ministers'. When the action was over, however, she would need 'to pipe down'. In 1985 however *Woman's Own* magazine interviewed a lady who had just been voted 'the most feminine woman of the year' for believing that a woman's place is not in the office but to stay at home having babies. The happy winner also professed herself a great admirer of Mrs Thatcher. When it was pointed out that this was a contradiction in view of Mrs Thatcher's manifest career as Prime Minister, 'the most feminine woman' was at first nonplussed; then she took refuge in a safe historical comparison: 'Well, ideally she shouldn't be there [in office], but she is an extremely exceptional woman and the exceptions will always find their way to the top. Look at Boadicea...'.[49]

The most potent image is a visual one, that of the cartoonist Gale in the *Daily Telegraph* (the foremost newspaper of Conservative sympathies) on polling day, 11 June 1987. Mrs Thatcher is seen dressed as Boadicea, late-twentieth-century version, in a Celtic robe but with pearl necklace and stud earrings (as Thomas Heywood's seventeenth-century heroine wore the lambent pearls of her own day). As the leader urges forward her chariot towards the third-term Conservative victory – which would in fact resoundingly be hers by the next day – the huge knives set in its wheels dominate the foreground of the picture. Meanwhile sundry small male figures in chains from other political parties drag behind; even Mrs Thatcher's own recognizable jubilant supporters are tiny in stature compared to the dominant figure of the Warrior Queen.

CHAPTER EIGHTEEN

UNBECOMING
IN A WOMAN?

Fell, from those funeral flames
A golden mist; which token is, from high gods
Of their unending glory to endure.

Charles Doughty on the funeral pyre of Boadicea
and her daughters, *The Dawn in Britain*, 1906

'Tis no less unbecoming [in] a Woman ... to conduct an
Army, to give a Signal to the Battle, than it is for a
Man to tease Wool, to handle the Distaff ...

George Buchanan, *History of Scotland*, 1571

Boudica of the Iceni was not a savage and she was a patriotic leader; that is to answer two of the questions originally posed about her in Chapter One. A courageous widow, she led her oppressed people in an uprising against a foreign occupation, having herself – and her daughters – been foully treated at the hands of the conqueror. The details of the uprising were not pretty, as such things seldom are. At the end of it, following a last battle, Boudica met her death, most probably at her own hand and again most probably carrying her daughters with her. She is buried in an unknown grave. All this – the known or supposed facts about Boudica – took place around AD 60.

Queen Boadicea on the other hand has had a far longer and more varied history. If not all female things to all men, she has certainly been a good many of them, and recently she has also represented a good many different things to many very different women. To the sixth-century monk Gildas, for example, Boadicea, far from being a patriot, was a 'deceitful lioness' for daring to oppose her morally superior Roman rulers.[1] Falling soon after that into a long sleep of obscurity, due to the vanishing of the Classical records, Boadicea awakened to the kiss of humanist scholarship in the sixteenth century to find herself a patriot once more, and on a far grander scale than that of a mere tribal queen.

For now she was the heroic leader of the *Britons* in their resolve to recover 'their old liberty', in Camden's phrase. Most importantly, Boadicea as a woman valorous had become a prefiguration of the patriot currently on the English throne, Elizabetha Triumphans: one of those rare women lifted, according to Spenser, to 'lawful sovereignty', as opposed to all the rest of her sex, whose destiny from birth to death was 'base humility'.[2] The long fruitful inter-relationship of Boadicea with the queens regnant (or female leaders) of this country had begun.

Alas for the all-British heroine! It was not only as Camden's high-minded patriot that Boadicea would survive. The seventeenth-century Queen, in accordance with the general estimate of women at that time, veered from Fletcher's boastful venal creature at the beginning (described by her ally Caratach as 'beastly' and by the Romans as 'unnatural') to a fragile blossom, whose very voice was too soft 'to accent the rough Laws of War'.[3]

At least these very differing Warrior Queens had some kind of human character, however inappropriate to the truth. The idealized Boadiceas of eighteenth-century poetry stood for a special kind of national pride, rather than anything more personal. In the case of James Thomson, whose 'Liberty' was written around 1730, his was nostalgia for 'a stubborn isle, disputed hard and never quite subdued' by the Romans. Thomson was one of the several men of letters patronized by the 'Patriot King' movement centred round Frederick Prince of Wales. When he went on to praise Boadicea for her 'Sparkling ardent flame' of rebellion, and ended with a vision of the Goddess of Liberty, he wished to show how ill all this accorded with the times in which he lived. Cowper, half a century later, looked to the past in order to issue a hymn to the British Empire.[4] But in both cases the woman herself had departed for that allegorical sphere where her feminine gender made her suitable for such an inspiring role, not unsuitable, as it would otherwise have done in real life.

Nor did the nineteenth-century growth of empire – and imperial values – rescue Boadicea from such an idealization, although the increase in historical novel-writing in the reign of Victoria did bring an inevitable crop of 'womanly' Boadiceas, a tribute to the sovereign if not the art. These were in keeping with that belief in the sweetness of feminine influence enunciated by Mrs Matthew Hall in her preface to *The Queens Before the Conquest* of 1854: 'Woman has thrown a bright light over the dark history of the first eleven centuries of our annals.'[5] (Although according to Victorian rules for women's conduct neither Boadicea nor Cartimandua really cast much bright light on Britain's dark first-century history.)

It was the suffragette movement first, and the Women's Movement generally, which created a demand for a new kind of heroine, an independent woman operating successfully in what was generally held to be a man's sphere. Queen Boadicea, still trailing her clouds of patriotic endeavour, fitted neatly into such a mould, just as her imagined Celtic free living made her for others an exciting figure with which to combat the perpetual encroachments of patriarchy.

Such a brief summary of the fortunes of the legendary Boadicea does not however of itself explain the persistence of the legend. For on one level these fortunes have merely echoed intriguingly the fortunes of 'women's worth', in Anne Bradstreet's eloquent phrase. The endurance of the story is another matter.

> High ride the flames, now giddy bowering wave;
> Which licks, with golden throat, the Summer woods,
> Surging to heaven; wherein ascend their spirits,
> Like unto like: whence now, immortal pure,
> They look from stars.

This is the 'timeless death' of Boadicea and her daughters, described by Charles Doughty in *The Dawn in Britain*. He recounts her story at length under the name of Boudicca – 'commonly but *mendosè* written Boadicea' – in an epic poem, full of strange imagery. It was written between 1866 and 1875, but first published in 1906. It was also reissued in 1943 when a British wartime generation read again of 'a furious scour of [British] women warriors' defying Rome: at a time when women were an integral and essential part in the defence of the nation, or in the words of a spirited 'woman warrior' of that period, 'it had to be done and women were as good at it as men'.[6]

Having taken poison, Doughty's three royal women fall upon a huge funeral pyre as the menacing Romans under Suetonius approach; soon their dead bodies are seen by the mourning Britons to 'wreathe' like holly in a herdsman's fire. The scene of the immolation is one to which Wagner might have done justice in music and setting; certainly Doughty, far more than Tennyson, whose own *Boädicea* was written roughly a decade earlier, captures that magical and mythical quality of the legend. He concludes:

> Fell, from those funeral flames
> A golden mist; which token is, from high gods
> Of their unending glory to endure.

For it is finally to her presence in the great pantheon of Valkyries, rather than to her actual historic significance (about which so little is known for certain), that the British Brünnhilde owes her own 'unending glory' or at least her enduring reputation. In order to comprehend her survival further it is time to try to catch hold of this shimmering phenomenon of the Warrior Queen.

At the heart of the matter lies the feeling, almost if not entirely universal in history, that war itself is 'conduct unbecoming' in a woman. When George Buchanan attacked female government, especially in time of war, in the late sixteenth century, he explicitly contrasted the established roles of the two sexes. "'Tis no less unbecoming [in] a Woman', he wrote, 'to levy Forces, to conduct an Army, to give a Signal to the Battle, than it is for a Man to tease Wool, to handle the Distaff, to Spin or Card, and to perform the other Services of the Weaker Sex.' When a woman did take part in such unnatural (to her sex) procedures, the effects were dire: for that which was reckoned 'Fortitude and Severity' in a man, was liable to turn to 'Madness and Cruelty' in a woman.[7]

It is not difficult to see why this philosophy should be widely held. 'The act of giving birth itself' has been considered throughout history to be 'profoundly incompatible with the act of dealing death';

thus wrote Nancy Huston in a 1986 symposium of 'contemporary perspectives' entitled *The Female Body in Western Culture*.[8] Biology alone – or by extension let us call it chivalry – provides an obvious explanation: if women, as the mothers of the race, need physical protection which they in turn extend to their young, then surely it is unreasonable, even unkind, to expect them to take part in war as well. From women's weaker physical strength, a more or less universal estimate, springs the concept of their tenderness, again an almost if not entirely universally held opinion; an extension of this is their timidity. (Why not be timid if physically so much weaker than a potential aggressor? It is a reasonable reaction.) And from their tenderness in one sense is derived another sense of their tenderness: woman the nurse, the nurturer, the succourer...

The epitaph to Pocahontas in St George's churchyard, Gravesend, on the outskirts of London, where she lies buried, is a perfect case in point: 'Gentle and humane, she was the friend of the earliest struggling English colonists whom she boldly rescued, protected and helped.' It was an early American feminist writer, Margaret Fuller, who commented on the universal appeal of the American Indian Princess: 'All men love Pocahontas for the angelic impulse of tenderness and pity that impelled her to the rescue of Smith', she wrote in *The Great Lawsuit: Man v. Woman*, first published in *The Dial*, Boston, in 1843; while women pity her for 'being thus made a main agent in the destruction of her own people'.[9] Compared to Boadicea, with those threatening knives on the wheels of her chariot, Pocahontas is a heroine who fulfils the highest expectations concerning her sex in general.

The problems of 'masculinity' in a woman – inevitable in some sense in a woman who leads in war – were argued by Helene Deutsch, one of the first four women to be analysed by Freud. *The Psychology of Women* was a comprehensive study of the female lifecycle and emotional life, which extended and modified Freud's own postulates. In it, Helene Deutsch devoted considerable discussion to what she called 'The "Active" Woman' and her 'Masculinity Complex' which 'originates in a surplus of aggressive forces that were not subjected to inhibition and that lack the possibility of an outlet such as is open to man. For this reason the masculine woman is also the aggressive woman.' This view stretches back at least as far as the wild, untamed and basically anarchic conception of the female in Athenian drama, at a time when woman's physical nature was itself thought to be unstable (based on the demands of her reproductive system).[10]

Although *The Psychology of Women* was published in 1944 (in the United States whither Helene Deutsch had fled in 1933), time and political events have not diminished the strong perceived connection between 'masculinity' – activity – in a woman and an 'aggression' felt by many to be unsuitable in one of her sex.

It is the leading role upon the stage which is felt to be unnatural in a woman, as opposed to any role. Many men all through history have after all been content to accept and even approve the ambitions of Fulvia, wife to Antony, as described by Plutarch: 'her desire was to govern those who governed or to command a commander-in-chief'. Cleopatra the dominatrix (and the seducer) is another matter. Boadicea herself may have acted the Fulvia before the death of her husband Prasutagus: we cannot know, *pace* Judy Grahn's free-wheeling lesbian Celt. When women have been compelled by circumstances to take a dominating role, they are expected to surrender it gracefully afterwards; the 'natural' behaviour is that of Spenser's Britomart, the chaste warrior–maid who finally dropped her shield when her purpose was fulfilled and became 'a gentle courteous Dame'. As for the unnatural Amazons whom Britomart subdued, 'that liberty' being removed from them, which they as women had wrongfully usurped, they were returned to 'men's subjection'.[11]

The strong contention of many theorists of the Women's Movement that war itself is the product of aggressive *masculine* values, and might even be eliminated if 'the whole wide world' were under 'a woman's hand' (one of the Sibylline prophecies linked to Cleopatra), meshes of course with these more primitive feelings.[12] *Spare Rib*'s denunciation of Mrs Thatcher following the Falklands War for promoting such values will be recalled, but the point is inclined to emerge whenever women, outraged by the depredations of war, manage to find a voice.

Militarism versus Feminism was written in 1915, the anguished product of feminist pacifism in response to the first terrible months of carnage in the First World War.[13] It was in effect a plea for internationalism – the Hague Women's Peace Conference of that year – in the cause of peace. The three authors, Mary Sargent Florence, Catherine E. Marshall and C. K. Ogden, argued not only that war was man's creation (as opposed to woman's) but also that man used war as a weapon in order to keep the other sex in perpetual subjection, since in time of war he was the manifest ruler. Catherine Marshall in particular, a prime mover behind the setting up of the conference, referred to the 'deep horror of war' which had entered into the soul of the organized Women's Movement, adding her belief that 'women's experience as mothers and heads of households' had given them 'just the outlook on human affairs' which was needed in such a process of international and creative reconstruction. (This is the argument which Mrs Thatcher, following the Falklands War, stood on its head by announcing that it was just her practical feminine abilities as a homemaker which had enabled her to keep going in the direction of military affairs.)

'But if woman climbed up to the clearer air above the battlefield', wrote Catherine Marshall in 1915, 'and cried aloud in her anguish to her sisters afar off: "These things must not be, they shall never be again!", would man indeed say, "Down with her!" Would he not allow her prerogative? Would he not even wish to climb up, too?' Once again, the experience of women sixty or seventy years later protesting at Greenham Common against nuclear weapons in the cause of peace does not suggest that man necessarily allows woman her prerogative in this respect. Nor does it propose that all men (any more than all women) wish to climb up to the clearer air above the battlefield.

Nevertheless the sheer appalling magnitude of the disaster to humankind inherent in any actual use of nuclear weapons suggests an interesting possibility. John Keegan, at the end of *The Mask of Command* (1987), a study in heroic leadership, calls for a new 'Post-heroic leadership'; he points out that the old inspiring 'heroic' leader, at the forefront of the battle itself, has been rendered obsolete and even dangerous by the advent of nuclear weapons. 'Today the best must find convictions to play the hero no more'; leaders should now be chosen for 'intellectuality' and the capacity for making decisions.[14] Women might now make more suitable political leaders than men (being strong enough *not* to press the button), provided of course that the conventional view of woman the peacemaker is accepted.

Certainly for many feminists the connection between women and peace remains 'some sort of "given"' – the phrase is that of the more sceptical Lynne Segal. As Petra Kelly for example wrote in 1984 in *Fighting for Hope*: 'Woman must lead the efforts in education for peace awareness, because only she can ... go back to her womb, her roots, her natural rhythms, her inner search for harmony and peace...'. Woman's pacific nature can however only be taken as some sort of given so long as any outstanding woman who does not seem to suffer from conspicuously peaceful inclinations is treated as an honorary male. According to this argument, which has a circular quality, Tomyris, issuing her plea to Cyrus of Persia, 'Rule your own people, and try to bear the sight of me ruling mine', is acting in accordance with her true feminist nature, whereas the same Queen Tomyris who had Cyrus put bloodily to death was acting as a man.[15] In the absence of an all-female-ruled state (with all-female-ruled neighbours) the thesis must remain unproved. But the importance of the argument from the point of view of a study of Warrior Queens is that it represents the meeting point of visionary feminism and its direct opposite: war is an unnatural occupation for a woman.

We return to the question of motherhood, at the source of this unease. The idea of female dominion, that authority posed in childhood from which happy infants must one day escape for the sake of their own maturity, is surely also at the source of the implicit threat posed by the notion of the Warrior Queen. Many percipient women writers and activists have drawn attention to this phenomenon, from Margaret Fuller in 1843 who wrote, 'Man is of Woman born and her face bends over him in infancy with an expression he can never quite forget', to Gloria Steinem in 1987 who suggested that part of the antagonism towards Mrs Thatcher 'may be because, in a deep sense, we fear women having power in the world because we associate that with childhood'.[16]

Dorothy Dinnerstein, in a classic of feminist psychological analysis first published in the United States in 1976, drew attention to woman's primary role in infant care as being responsible for early memories of her domination. For while woman continues to be the parent who is the 'first [remembered] boss' in most societies in the world, her relationship to other adults will be unfavourably affected by these memories. 'The right to be straightforwardly bossy – the right to exercise will head-on ... – cannot reside as comfortably in a woman as a man', wrote Dorothy Dinnerstein.[17]

That this is true at least in some measure is indicated most recently by the innumerable references to Mrs Thatcher as 'Nanny', one famed for her 'bossiness'. (The equivalent words used for a male prime minister might be 'autocrat' and 'authoritativeness'.) It is therefore fascinating to observe the ways in which the Warrior Queens in history have felt their way to a solution to the problem. At the same time, these solutions, universally adopted, also do suggest that there was (and is) such a universal problem.

Adopting the role of an honorary male has been only one among the expedients employed by the Warrior Queens with instinctive or calculated cunning, a quality which they have certainly needed in order to survive in what has always been realistically a man's world. It has however been one of the most successful – to act the King of Kartli as Tamara did, the Catholic King of Spain like Isabella, a mighty prince like Elizabeth I, *rex noster* of Hungary like Maria Theresa. The frequency with which the Tomboy Syndrome is found in accounts of the childhood of a given Warrior Queen testifies to the same deliberate process. The type of Camilla of the Volsci ('her girl's hands had never been trained to Minerva's distaff') occurs again and again, be it in the young Catherine the Great who never cared to play with girlish dolls, or in Mrs Gandhi who employed her own dolls in creating Indian nationalist battles. The message put across is that an 'honorary boy' has been the father to the honorary man.

Fortunately adopting the role of the honorary male has not precluded the Warrior Queen from appealing at the same time to the chivalrous instincts of her compeers, the real males. Rather the reverse has been found to be the case, as the Warrior Queen, so clearly marked out by her femininity in a man's world, has employed another successful series of expedients based on this evidently singular fact. The use of masculine uniform or military accoutrements which set off rather than conceal her sex is one of them. The concept of chivalry due towards the tender woman is also responsible for the Shame Syndrome whereby the Warrior Queen is able to contrast her own willed courage with that lassitude of the supposedly courageous-by-nature males around her. Thus Queen Isabella's grandees were sufficiently 'mortified' at being outdone in zeal for the holy war by a woman to renew their energies.[18]

The Shame Syndrome can in turn lead on to the popular estimate of the Warrior Queen as being the 'Better-Man' (of the two: if a husband such as Frederick of Prussia and a wife such as Louise is involved). Or it can lead to the Warrior Queen's own protestations of being 'Only-a-Weak-Woman': 'just a lady and timid too' as the beautiful, bold Caterina Sforza declared herself, in order to show up her superior strategic skill. This pose of being 'Only-a-Weak-Woman' is of course also convenient when trouble looms: for the Warrior Queen can hope to avoid responsibility at the same time. Hence wily Zenobia was able to live on in her Roman villa, swift female dromedary forgotten, on the grounds that 'many persons', i.e. her male advisers, 'had seduced her as a simple woman' into mounting her campaigns.[19]

Since none of these poses, attitudes or expedients would be possible without the existence of the masculine audience at which they are aimed, all of them merely serve to emphasize the Appendage Syndrome. Very few outstanding women in history have achieved or been granted their place without the benefit of some kind of male-derived privilege, generally that of descent, whatever glorious destiny has ensued. This is certainly true of the Warrior Queens, up to the second half of the twentieth century.

Understandably, most Warrior Queens have underlined their claims as honorary males by emphasizing such connections. 'I am descended from mighty *men*!': thus Boadicea boasted in her last speech, at least according to Tacitus.[20] It is a pattern – that of Elizabeth I, 'Great Harry's daughter' still, to the end of her long reign – which has been pursued. For such emphasis, like the pose of being an honorary male, once again enables the Warrior Queen to preserve her place within the natural order. She must never forget that the original importance of the Amazon tribe to the Greeks was as a tribe of unnatural as well as belligerent females, unnatural because they were outside the control of men, and nobody's appendage.

It is however in the confrontation with the whole treacherous theme of motherhood and the unsuitability of the mother to do battle, that the wits of the Warrior Queen have had to be most subtly exercised. In this connection it is significant how many successful Warrior Queens – in the eyes of the world – have been seen to be acting on behalf of their children. Even Cleopatra drew about her the authority of co-rulership, according to Ptolemaic custom, with her infant son. This is one extension of the Appendage Syndrome which carries with it considerable allure. For there is nothing in the slightest bit unnatural about the mother's defence of her young, which can even be quite blatantly aggressive without incurring the taint of 'masculinity'. The rape of Boadicea's daughters, the imagined agonies of the mother as a result, provide after all the most sympathetic explanation for the atrocities which followed her uprising.

Otherwise a protective and appealing maternity casts a pleasant gloss on what might be the harsh picture of a Warrior Queen, as Maria Theresa realized when she sent a picture of herself with her son to General Khevenmüller with the poignant question: 'What do you think will become of this child?' No wonder the troops the next day at Linz, shown the picture and read the letter, roared their enthusiasm! The persistent legends concerning the Rani of Jhansi riding into battle with her adopted son Damodar on the horse behind her, and similar depictions, even if not accurate, belong to the same tradition as does the legend of her dying words 'Look after Damodar', spoken in a temple (although, as has been seen, a variety of independent witnesses confirm that she died in the heat of battle). In the nineteenth century Agnes Strickland summed up a widespread feeling of approval for the Mother–Warrior when she described Stephen's wife, 'good Queen Matilda', as avoiding 'all Amazonian display' by acting in the name of her son.[21]

There is another way of handling the whole matter of war and woman's maternal role in terms of war and that is – triumphantly ignoring the 'unnatural' taint – to make of it something boldly transcendent. It is this which accounts for the palpitating thrill which the idea of the Warrior Queen arouses, threat as she may be. The most successful Warrior Queens have always been those who pre-empted the obvious disadvantage of their sex in this field by turning it into an apparent advantage; and biological motherhood is after all the one role which is totally closed to man. Thus the role of the fighting mother in wartime can be put across as primordially patriotic, instead of primitively distasteful, that of Catherine the Great for example, being hailed by her troops as the 'Little Mother' of Russia. Soon the 'Mother of her Country' begins to be seen in a supernatural rather than an unnatural light: a goddess, a Mother–

Goddess perhaps, and by extension a Goddess of War.

The supernatural aura of the Warrior Queen has the further effect of sanctifying the nation's struggle in its own eyes: and all through history it is always good for morale to be fighting a holy war. When Judith struck off the head of Holofernes, according to the tenth-century poem, she 'ascribed the glory of all that to the Lord of Hosts'. A kind of pious patriotism, like the stance of outraged motherhood, gives moral authority to many a Warrior Queen, enabling her to become a Holy Figurehead of her nation's aspir-ations, as the Arab Lady of Victory with her long hair and her lute in the forefront of the battle embodied an appeal to valour, honour and passion.[22] When the Warrior Queen is successful in her dominion, the way is paved for the idea of the golden age of the nation – especially golden since over it presides a goddess.

The type of goddess most usefully personified by a given Warrior Queen alters, of course, from country to country, age to age and civilization to civilization. If Boadicea represented some kind of Celtic war-goddess and Queen Jinga of Angola an ancient African mother–deity, then Isabella the Catholic was elevated as 'the new Eve', the madonna of her country. This is a conspiracy into which the male population enters willingly: given that circumstances have brought about some form of female rule in war, a supernatural woman leader is infinitely better than an unnatural one.

There is certainly a sexuality at the heart of this conspiracy, as the ancient goddesses, those creations of the universal subconscious, were generally creatures of human sexual feeling and appetite if of divine power and strength. Very few Warrior Queens, whatever the true facts of their lives, have been allowed to enjoy an ordinary female sexuality in terms of the propaganda spread about them. The Chaste Syndrome being marked, the Warrior Queen has been depicted, where possible, as a virgin by her supporters (and some-times where not possible, as in the case of Zenobia and Matilda of Tuscany): virginity too having its own connotations of sanctity. For Gibbon, for example, Zenobia's 'chastity' meant that her 'valour' surpassed that of Cleopatra: an interesting argument if not exactly a logical one. Conversely by the Voracity Syndrome, accusations of lust (so much more exciting in a queen regnant than in a king, where prodigious amours tend to be taken rather wearily for granted) are used to vicious political purpose, as in the case of Caterina Sforza, denounced by the same ruler – the Pope – who wanted her possessions for his son Cesare Borgia.[23] It was axiomatic to many of the nineteenth-century British that the Rani of Jhansi *must* be 'the Jezebel of India', just because she was an outstanding warrior leader: another interesting if once again illogical argument.

Yet the overriding impression of the personal lives of the Warrior Queens, if one may generalize for a moment, is of austerity, even puritanism, Tamara of Georgia, Isabella of Spain and the real Rani being far more typical in this respect than the admitted exceptions such as Caterina herself, Catherine the Great and Semiramis; details of the latter's life are however sufficiently veiled in time for it to be quite possible that she never actually possessed the rampant voracity which has enabled her legend to survive. That overriding impression may be put against another subtler one, to which it is most likely to be connected: there is no lack of personal ambition among these Warrior Queens, whatever the fluttering protestations which contemporary social standards may have called forth from some of them. And ambitious women have seldom so far had much time to spare to be *grandes amoureuses,* with so many more demanding problems to tax their time: preferring to bond men to them by a more ethereal kind of loyalty (in short, acting out their own version of the goddess).

Is it not just this appreciation of the Warrior Queen which continues to make her an inspiration to women as well as a source of threat and excitement to men? Whether or not woman's nature is in truth more pacific and more tender than that of the other sex, the Warrior Queen is secretly seen by women as one who has made a dazzling job of a position so seldom granted to one of her own sex. Boadicea *is* a heroine, cruel knives on her chariot notwithstanding: and it can be argued that women need heroines even more than men need heroes because their expectations of independence, fortitude and valour have generally speaking been so much lower.

So Queen Boadicea still towers above her reckless horses on the banks of the Thames. In her case the hand that once rocked the cradle now drives the chariot and shakes the spear and 'yet though overcome in hapless fight' she does so in manifest victory. Secure within her monument constructed equally of Thornycroft's bronze and history's myth, her conduct is no longer unnatural but triumphant. Her glory may be expected to endure.

REFERENCE NOTES

Bibliographical details of each book or article are given at its first point of entry (the place of publication is London unless otherwise stated). Thereafter, only a short entry is given, with a note indicating where the first full reference can be found in brackets, i.e. in Chapter Four, note 6, 'Tacitus (III–1), p. 265' refers back to Chapter Three, note 1, Tacitus, *The Annals of Imperial Rome*, translated and with an Introduction by Michael Grant (revised edn 1977 pbk).

CHAPTER ONE: *A Singular Exception*

'Flashes afresh . . . ' is a quotation from Philip Larkin's poem 'Aubade'.

1 Research carried out at the Colindale Newspaper Library fully confirms this.

2 Jonson, Ben, *The Masque of Queenes*, with the designs of Inigo Jones (1930), p. 35.

3 Cit. Dudley, Donald R. and Webster, Graham, *The Rebellion of Boudicca* (1962), p. 130; Webster, Graham, *Boudica: The British Revolt against Rome AD 60* (1978), p. 15.

4 See Courteault, Paul, 'An Inscription Recently Found at Bordeaux', *Journal of Roman Studies*, Vol. XI (1921), pp. 102f. for a votive altar to Tutela Boudiga; Webster (1–3), p. 15.

5 Ubaldini, Petruccio, *Le vite delle Donne illustri del regno d'Inghilterra, e del regno di Scotia . . .* (1591); 'Le Vite e i Fatti di sei Donne Illustri', British Library MS 14A XIX. Translated by Angus Clarke.

6 Ogilby, John, *Africa etc . . . Collected and translated from the most authentic authors* (founded mainly on the work of O. Dapper), 2 vols (1670), Vol. II, pp. 564–5.

7 'Joan Kelly's Cancer Journal,' cit. Kelly, Joan, *Women, History and Theory: The Essays of Joan Kelly* (Chicago 1985), p. xv; interview with Graham Turner, 'Feminists Count the Cost', *Sunday Telegraph*, 22 February 1987.

8 Pisan, Christine de, *The Treasure of the City of Ladies, or The Book of the Three Virtues*, translated and with an Introduction by Sarah Lawson (1985 pbk), p. 51.

9 Tocqueville, Alexis de, *Democracy in America*, 2 vols (1875), Vol. II, p. 179; Gibbon, Edward, *The History of the Decline and Fall of the Roman Empire*, edited by J. B. Bury, 7 vols, Vol. I (1896), p. 27.

10 E.g. Hacker, Barton C., 'Women and Military Institutions in Early Modern Europe', *Signs*, Summer 1981.

11 Cit. Abbott, Nabia, *Aishah: The Beloved of Mohammed*, Preface by Sarah Graham-Brown (1985), p. 176.

12 Gibbon (1–9), I, p. 149.

13 De Gaulle, Charles, *The Edge of the Sword*, translated by Gerard Hopkins (1960), pp. 13–14.

14 Tacitus, *Germania*, Chs 13–14, cit. Keen, Maurice, *Chivalry* (1984), p. 55.

15 de Beauvoir, Simone, *The Second Sex* (1972 pbk), p. 21.

16 Troyat, Henri, *Catherine the Great*, translated by Emily Read (1979), p. 183.

17 *A Comment on Boadicia* by W. Rider AB, late Scholar of Jesus College, Oxon (1754); Wapshott, Nicholas and Brock, George, *Thatcher* (1983 pbk), p. 240; Mrs Thatcher, by substituting the word 'failure' for 'defeat', slightly misquoted Queen Victoria.

18 Young, Hugo and Sloman, Anne, *The Thatcher Phenomenon* (BBC Publications, 1986), p. 40; Denis Healey returned to the charge in the 1987 election (13 May), calling Mrs Thatcher 'the Catherine the Great of Finchley'.

19 Boccaccio, Giovanni, *Concerning Famous Women*, translated with an Introduction by Guido A. Guarmio (1964), p. 5.

20 Campbell, Joseph, *The Masks of God: Creative Mythology* (1974), p. 519 note; Leigh Fermor, Patrick, *A Traveller's Tree: A Journey through the Caribbean Islands* (1950), p. 374.

21 Carras, Mary C., *Indira Gandhi: In the Crucible of Leadership. A Political Biography* (Bombay 1980), p. 47; Breisach, Ernst, *Caterina Sforza: A Renaissance Virago* (Chicago 1967), p. 24; cit. Duff, Nora, *Matilda of Tuscany* (1909), p. 77.

22 King, Betty, *Boadicea* (1975), p. 9.

CHAPTER TWO: *Antique Glories*

1 See Ross, Anne, *Pagan Celtic Britain: Studies in Iconography and Tradition* (1967), Ch. V, pp. 204f.

2 *The Mabinogion*, translated with an Introduction by Jeffrey Gantz (1976 pbk), p. 52.

3 Ross, *Pagan* (11–1), pp. 219, 152.

4 *The Tain*, translated from the Irish epic by Thomas Kinsella (Oxford 1970 pbk), pp. 52f.; I have preferred this lively unbowdlerized translation.

5 Spenser, Edmund, *The Faerie Queene*, Introduction by J. W. Hales, 2 vols (1910), Vol. I, p. 381.

6 Diner, Helen, *Mothers and Amazons* (New York 1965), p. 27.

7 Lefkowitz, Mary R., *Woman in Greek Myth* (1986), p. 177 and 'Influential Women' in *Images of Women in Antiquity*, edited by Averil Cameron and Amélie Kuhrt (1983), pp. 49–64; Pomeroy, Sarah B., *Goddesses, Whores, Wives and Slaves: Women in Classical Antiquity* (1976), p. 13 and 'A Classical Scholar's Perspective on Matriarchy' in *Liberating Women's History: Theoretical and Critical Essays*, edited by Berenice A. Carroll (Chicago 1976), pp. 217–24.

8 Todd, Malcolm, *Roman Britain 55 BC – AD 400: The Province beyond the Ocean* (1981 pbk), p. 36.

9 Sobol, Donald J., *The Amazons of Greek Mythology* (South Brunswick and New York, 1972), pp. 90f.; Warner, Marina, *Joan of Arc: The Image of Female Heroism* (1981), Ch. x, pp. 198f.; see also Briffault, R., *The Mothers*, 3 vols (1927), Vol. ii, p. 457 note 2 for a convenient list of references on this subject.

10 Lefkowitz (ii–7), p. 133.

11 The *Bibliotheca Historica* of Diodorus Siculus, 2 vols (1956–7), Vol. i, pp. 199–203; Virgil, *The Aeneid*, translated into English prose by W. F. Jackson Knight (revised edn 1958 pbk), pp. 299, 200.

12 Heywood, Thomas, *Gynaekeion or Nine Bookes of Various History Concerning Women* (1624), p. 226.

13 Knox, John, *The First Blast of the Trumpet against the monstrous regiment of Women*, edited by Edward Arber (1880), p. 13; for the *mignons* see Davis, N. Z., *Society and Culture in Early Modern France* (1975), p. 133.

14 *Correspondance de Napoléon Ier*, Vol. xiii (Paris 1863), p. 326.

15 Kelly, Amy, *Eleanor of Aquitaine and the Four Kings* (Cambridge, Massachusetts 1950), p. 34.

16 Cit. Kelly, *Eleanor* (ii–15), p. 38.

17 Green, David, *Queen Anne* (1970), p. 101.

18 Green (ii–17), pp. 109, 154.

19 London *Independent*, 10 December 1986.

20 Duff (i–21), p. 274.

CHAPTER THREE: *The Queen of War*

1 Tacitus, *The Annals of Imperial Rome*, translated and with an Introduction by Michael Grant (revised edn 1977 pbk), p. 330.

2 *Encyclopaedia Britannica* (15th edn 1974), Vol. 11, p. 983.

3 Herodotus, *The Histories*, translated by Aubrey de Sélincourt, revised by A. R. Burn (1972 pbk), p. 115; *The Elegies of Propertius in a Reconditioned Text*, translated by S. G. Tremenheere (1932), p. 229.

4 *The Works of Voltaire*, 22 vols (New York 1927), Vol. ix, p. 173; Diodorus Siculus (ii–11), p. 153.

5 Herodotus (iii–3), pp. 123f.; Dewald, Caroline, 'Women and Culture in Herodotus' Histories', in Foley, Helene B., *Reflections of Women in Antiquity* (New York 1981), pp. 91–125.

6 Boccaccio (i–19), p. 104.

7 Herodotus (iii–3), pp. 8, 14, 475f., 554.

8 Moraes, Dom, *Mrs Gandhi* (1980), p. 133; George Brown, cit. *Observer*, 24 April 1988.

9 Aylmer, John, *An Harborowe for Faithfull and Trewe Subjectes against the late blown Blast...* (1559).

10 Heywood (ii–12), p. 204.

11 See Grant, Michael, *Cleopatra* (revised edn 1974 pbk), *passim*, which is the basis of these dates and also much of the following passage.

12 Grant (III–11), p. 37.

13 Lefkowitz (II–7), p. 57.

14 Plutarch, *Fall of the Roman Empire: Six Lives*, translated by Rex Warner (1972 pbk), p. 290.

15 Cicero, *Letters to Atticus*, translated by E. O. Winstedt, 3 vols, Vol. III (1918), pp. 337–9.

16 Cit. Grant (III–11), pp. 184–5.

17 Cit. Grant (III–11), p. 261.

18 Grant (III–11), p. 208.

19 Horace, *Odes*, translated by James Michie (1964), 1, 37, p. 87.

20 *Nine Lives by Plutarch*, 'Makers of Rome,' translated and with an Introduction by Ian Scott-Kilvert (1972 pbk reprint), p. 280.

21 Propertius (III–3), p. 231.

22 Horace (III–19), 1, 37, p. 89; *Antony and Cleopatra*, Act v, scene ii.

23 *Dio's Roman History*, with an English translation by Earnest Cary, 9 vols, Vol. VIII (1925), pp. 83–105; Wright, F. A., *Marcus Agrippa* (1937), pp. 251–3; *Cambridge Ancient History*, Vol. x (Cambridge 1934), pp. 266–70; Macurdy, Grace H., *Vassal-Queens and Some Contemporary Women in the Roman Empire* (Baltimore 1937), p. 2.

24 Virgil (II–11), p. 173.

CHAPTER FOUR: *Iceni: this Powerful Tribe*

The principal sources for the following four chapters are Dudley and Webster, *The Rebellion of Boudicca* (1–3); Webster, *Boudica* (1–3); also Frere, *Britannia* (IV–15); Salway, *Roman Britain* (IV–7); and Todd, *Roman Britain* (II–8).

1 Caesar, *De Bello Gallico*, 5, 21, in 'War Commentaries of Caesar', translated by Rex Warner (New York 1960), p. 97; Allen, D. F., 'The Coins of the Iceni', *Britannia*, Vol. 1 (1970), p. 1 note 4, writes: 'with little doubt'; but Todd (II–8), p. 24: 'Cenimagni *might* later appear as the Iceni'.

2 Ekwall, Eilert, *Concise Oxford Dictionary of English Place-Names* (4th edn Oxford 1959), pp. 267, 268; Dudley and Webster (1–3), Appendix II p. 143.

3 The famous judgement of Gibbon on Abyssinia, actually a quotation from Alexander Pope, *Eloisa to Abelard*, (1717), l. 207.

4 Allen, 'Coins' (IV–1), p. 1.

5 Tacitus (III–1), p. 265; Todd (II–8), p. 83 note 8.

6 Tacitus (III–1), p. 265.

7 Salway, Peter, *Roman Britain* (Oxford 1984 pbk), p. 101; Allen, 'Coins' (IV–1), p. 2; Todd (II–8), p. 53.

8 See Ross, Anne, *Everyday Life of the Pagan Celts* (1970); Ross, *Pagan* (II–1); Powell, T. G. E., *The Celts* (1958), *passim*.

9 Clarke, R. Rainbird, *East Anglia* (1960), p. 110; Piggott, Stuart, *The Druids* (1974 pbk), p. 36.

10 *The Geography of Strabo*, translated by H. L. Jones, 8 vols, Vol. II (1923), pp. 237, 247.

11 Fox, Sir Cyril, *Pattern and Purpose: A Survey of Early Celtic Art in Britain* (Cardiff 1958), p. 59 and illustration p. 58; Salway (IV–7), p. 76; Powell (IV–8), p. 109: 'no archaeological evidence' for scythed chariots.

12 Cit. Piggott (IV–9), p. 136; Clarke (IV–9), p. 99.

13 Fox (IV–11), p. 70; Allen, 'Coins' (IV–1), p. 14.

14 Allen, 'Coins' (IV–1), p. 3 and fig. 1; Tony Gregory, Norfolk Archaeological Unit, to the author, 1985.

15 Frere, Sheppard, *Britannia: A History of Roman Britain* (revised edn 1978), p. 40; Todd (II–8), p. 53; Webster (I–3), p. 24.

16 Spratling, Dr Mansel, 'Note on Santon, Norfolk, Hoard', *Britannia*, Vol. 6 (1975); Fox (IV–11), p. 84.

17 'Very heavy and uncomfortable' were the terms used to the author by one individual who tried on a torc; see Clarke, R. Rainbird, 'The Early Iron Age Treasure from Snettisham, Norfolk', *Proceedings of the Prehistoric Society* (1954); and Brailsford, John and Stapley, J. E., 'The Ipswich Torcs', *Proceedings of the Prehistoric Society* (1972).

18 Brailsford and Stapley (IV–17), p. 227; alternatively if the Snettisham torcs come from further south, the Ipswich torcs may be local.

19 Reynolds, Peter, 'Experimental Archaeology and the Butser Ancient Farm Research Project' in Collis, J., *The Iron Age in Britain* (1977), p. 37.

20 Thetford, *Current Archaeology*, no. 81 (1981), pp. 294–7; Gregory (IV–14) to author.

21 Dio (III–23), VII, pp. 414–15.

22 Gardner, Jane F., *Women in Roman Law and Society* (1986), p. 5; and Balsdon, J. P. V. D., *Roman Women: Their History and Habits* (1962), *passim*.

23 Wells, Colin, *The Roman Empire* (1984 pbk), p. 271.

24 Ross, *Everyday* (IV–8), p. 146.

25 Caesar cit. Ross, *Everyday* (IV–8), p. 133; Ross, *Pagan* (II–1), pp. 62f.; Webster (I–3), p. 82.

26 Livy cit. Ross, *Everyday* (IV–8), p. 154; Strabo (IV–10), II, p. 247.

27 Tacitus (III–1), p. 266.

28 See Richmond, I. A., 'Queen Cartimandua', *Journal of Roman Studies*, Vol. 44 (1954), pp. 43–52.

29 Tacitus (III–1), p. 269.

30 Tacitus, *The Histories*, translated by Kenneth Wellesley (revised edn, 1986 pbk), p. 172; Webster, Graham, *Rome against Caractacus: The Roman Campaigns in Britain AD 48–58* (1981), p. 14.

31 Richmond (IV–28), p. 52.

32 Ubaldini, *Donne* (I–5); Milton, John, *The History of Britain . . . continu'd to the Norman Conquest* (1670), p. 60.

33 Tacitus, *The Agricola and the Germania*, translated by H. Mattingly, revised by S. A. Handford (1970 pbk), p. 66.

34 Syme, Sir Ronald, *Tacitus*, 2 vols (Oxford 1958), Vol. I, p. v.

35 Tacitus (III–1), pp. 327–32; Tacitus, *Agricola* (IV–33), pp. 65–7; Dio (III–23), VIII, pp. 83–105.

36 Syme (IV–34), I, pp. 270f.; II, p. 763.

37 Millar, Fergus, *A Study of Cassius Dio* (Oxford 1964), pp. 32f.

38 Webster (I–3), p. 105.

39 In 1962 Dudley and Webster (III–1), pp. 144f., wrote of 'a strong presumption in favour of 60 ... with 61 not disposed of completely'; Syme (IV–34), I, p. 20 note 8 chooses 60; but in 1981 Salway (IV–7) referred to 'more recent opinion' returning to 61; i.e. Carroll, Kevin J., 'The Date of Boudicca's Revolt', *Britannia*, Vol. x (1979), pp. 197–202, who argues for 61; however Webster (III–1) sticks to 60, as do Frere (IV–15) and Clarke (IV–9).

40 Salway (IV–7), p. 90 and note 2.

41 See Braund, David C., *Rome and the Friendly King: The Character of the Client Kingship* (1984), Part III, 'Royal Wills', p. 144 where the point is made that 'we simply do not know how Nero and the King's daughters were to divide the inheritance, for Tacitus does not tell us'.

CHAPTER FIVE: *Ruin by a Woman*

1 Tacitus trans. Dudley and Webster (I–3), p. 137; Tacitus, *Agricola* (IV–33), p. 66; Dio (III–23), VIII, p. 85.

2 Bulst, Christoph, 'The Revolt of Queen Boudicca in AD 60: Roman Politics and the Iceni', *Historia*, Vol. 10 (1961), p. 499.

3 Dio (III–23), VIII, p. 85; cit. Powell (IV–8), p. 76; cit. Chadwick, Nora, *The Celts* (1970), p. 50.

4 Cit. Jardine, Lisa, 'Isotta Nogarola: Women Humanists, Education for What?', *History of Education*, Vol. 12, no. 4 (1983), p. 233.

5 Donizo cit. Huddy, Mary E., *Matilda, Countess of Tuscany* (1905), p. 76; cit. Hibbert, Christopher, *The Great Mutiny, India 1857* (1978), p. 378; *The Scriptores Historiae Augustae*, with an English translation by David Magie, 3 vols (1922–32), Vol. III, p. 139; Gibbon (I–9), I, p. 302.

6 *Johnsonian Miscellanies*, ed. G. B. Hill, 2 vols (Oxford 1897), Vol. I, p. 118; Dudley and Webster (I–3), p. 46.

7 Salway (IV–7), p. 113; Braund (IV–41), p. 144.

8 Graham Webster in the *London Archaeologist*, Vol. 4, no. 15 (1984) p. 411 suggests 'Boudica and her household' may have misunderstood what was an accounting process; alternatively Catus saw an opportunity for personal gain; Tacitus (III–1), p. 328.

9 Cit. Salway (IV–7), p. 146; Brownmiller, Susan, *Against our will: Men, Women and Rape* (1975), p. 14.

10 Breisach (I–21), p. 341.

11 I.e. Salway (IV–7), p. 114.

12 Cit. Balsdon (IV–22), p. 33.

13 Dio (III–23), VIII, p. 83.

14 Salway (IV–7), p. 115.

15 See Richmond, I. A., 'The Four *Coloniae* of the Roman Empire', *Archaeological Journal*, Vol. 103 (1947), p. 57.

16 Frere (IV–15), pp. 104–5.

17 Fishwick, Duncan, 'Templum Divo Claudium Constitutum', *Britannia*, Vol. 3 (1972), pp. 168f.; Webster (1–3), p. 89.

18 See Wheeler, R. E. M. and Laver, P. G., 'Roman Colchester', *Journal of Roman Studies*, IX (1919), pp. 139–69; Crummy, Philip, 'Colchester: The Roman Fortress and the Development of the Colonia', *Britannia*, Vol. 8 (1977), pp. 65–106.

19 Dudley and Webster (1–3), p. 49.

20 Ross, *Pagan* (II–1), p. 53; also Piggott (IV–9), *passim* for the Druids.

21 Todd (II–8), p. 257; Salway (IV–7), p. 24.

22 Gibbon (1–9), I, p. 29.

23 Laing, Lloyd, *Celtic Britain* (1979), p. 81; Piggott (IV–9), p. 99; Powell (IV–8), p. 153; Ross, *Everyday* (IV–8), p. 151; Syme, Sir Ronald, *Ten Studies in Tacitus* (Oxford 1970), p. 25 and note 2.

24 Cit. Holmes, Richard, *Footsteps* (1984), p. 263.

25 Strongly argued by Webster (1–3), pp. 63f.; Richmond, I. A., *Roman Britain* (2nd edn 1963 pbk), p. 28, agrees, as does Frere (IV–15), p. 76; but see Todd (II–8), Appendix pp. 255–6 for contrary view and Dyson, Stephen L., 'Native Revolts in the Roman Empire', *History*, Vol. XX (1971), p. 260: the Druids' role has been 'exaggerated'.

26 Fox (IV–11), p. 145.

27 *Holinshed's Chronicles of England, Scotland and Ireland*, 6 vols, Vol. 1 (1807), p. 496; Milton (IV–32), p. 65; Syme (IV–34), I, p. 763 and note 6; Overbeck, John C., 'Tacitus and Dio on Boudicca's Rebellion', *American Journal of Philology*, Vol. XL (1969), p. 136 note 27.

28 See Layard, John, *The Lady and the Hare* (1944), *passim*; Ross, *Pagan* (II–1), pp. 349–50.

29 Note by Dr Anne Ross, Dudley and Webster (1–3), p. 151; Briffault (II–9), II, p. 70 note 12; Ross, *Everyday* (IV–8), p. 159; cit. Fox (IV–11), p. 139 and plate 80 no. 19.

30 Tacitus, *Histories* (IV–30), p. 247; Powell (IV–8), p. 195.

31 Dyson (V–25), p. 265.

32 Dudley and Webster (1–3), p. 57.

33 Crummy (V–18), p. 81.

34 Crummy, Philip, *Colchester, Recent Excavations and Research* (Colchester 1974).

35 Philip Crummy, Colchester Archaeological Trust, to the author, Colchester, 1985.

36 Dudley and Webster (1–3), pp. 106–7.

37 Webster (1–3), p. 117.

CHAPTER SIX: *The Red Layer*

1 Todd (11–8), p. 90.
2 Tacitus, *Agricola* (1v–33), p. 63.
3 Webster (1–3), pp. 90–1.
4 See Frere, S. S. and Joseph, J. K. St., 'The Roman Fortress at Longthorpe', *Britannia*, Vol. 5 (1974).
5 Ogilvie, R. M. and Richmond, Sir Ian (eds), *Cornelii Taciti De Vita Agricolae* (Oxford 1967), p. 198 note to '*universi*'.
6 Webster (1–3), p. 90.
7 Webster (1–3), p. 93; Firth, C. H., *Cromwell's Army*, with a new Introduction by P. H. Hardacre (1967 pbk), p. 106.
8 See Merrifield, Ralph, *London: City of the Romans* (1983), pp. 41–6 and notes 1 and 2 p. 274 for a concise summary.
9 Hall, Jenny and Merrifield, Ralph, *Roman London* (HMSO 1986), p. 6.
10 Merrifield (v1–8), pp. 26–7 suggests a military origin; but see Marsden, Peter, *Roman London* (1980), pp. 22–4 for a theory of civil trading settlement.
11 Marsden (v1–10), p. 24 for acreage; Frere (1v–15), p. 296 for population, if Tacitus' figures are accepted, since his language suggests 'an official source'.
12 Merrifield (v1–8), p. 42.
13 Marsden (v1–10), p. 26.
14 Marsden (v1–10), p. 25.
15 Webster (1–3), p. 94.
16 Dudley and Webster (1–3), p. 55.
17 See Lambert, Frank, 'Some Recent Excavations in London', *Archaeologia*, Vol. LXXI (1921), pp. 55–8; Dunning, G. C., 'Two Fires of Roman London', *Antiquaries Journal*, Vol. XXV (1945), pp. 48–50 and fig. 3.
18 Marsden (v1–10), p. 33; Report by the Police President of Hamburg, 1 December 1943, Appendix 30, *German Documents, 1943–45*, p. 311.
19 Marsden (v1–10), p. 31.
20 Merrifield (v1–8), p. 57.
21 But Marsh, Geoff and West, Barbara, 'Skulduggery in Roman London?', London and Middlesex Archaeological Society, *Transactions*, XXXII (1981) reject 'the events of AD 60' in connection with the skulls, in favour of 'Celtic religious practices connected with water'.
22 Fraser, Antonia, *Cromwell, Our Chief of Men* (1973), p. 338.
23 Tacitus, *Agricola* (1v–33), p. 66; Tacitus (111–1), p. 329; Dio (111–23), VIII, p. 95.
24 Grimal, Pierre, *The Dictionary of Classical Mythology* (1986), pp. 75–6.
25 I.e. Salway (1v–7), pp. 65–7; Wells (1v–23), pp. 276–8.
26 Pete Rowsome, site supervisor for Museum of London, quoted in *New Scientist*, 29 August 1985.
27 Clive, Thomas, *The Complete Works of Lord Macaulay*, 12 vols (1898), Vol. VII, p. 362.

CHAPTER SEVEN: *Eighty Thousand Dead*

1 See Frere, Sheppard, *Verulamium Excavations*, Vol. 1, Reports of the Research Committee of the Society of Antiquaries of London no. XXVIII (Oxford 1972); Webster (1–3), p. 124.

2 Tacitus (III–1), pp. 328–9; Dio (III–23), VIII, p. 95; Webster (1–3), p. 124.

3 Todd (II–8), p. 91 for ten thousand; Webster, Graham, *The Roman Imperial Army of the First and Second Centuries AD* (2nd edn reprinted with corrections 1981), p. 229 for 15,000–20,000.

4 See Fuentes, Nicholas, 'Boudicca re-visited', *London Archaeologist*, Vol. 4, no. 12 (1983); Webster, Graham, 'The Site of Boudica's Last Battle: A Comment', and Nicholas Fuentes' response to Graham Webster, *London Archaeologist*, Vol. 4, no. 15 (1984).

5 See Webster, 'The Site' (VII–4).

6 Spence, Lewis, *Boadicea: Warrior Queen of the Britons* (1937), p. 248.

7 See Fuentes (VII–4).

8 See *Transactions of the Birmingham Archaeological Society* (Oxford), Vol. 79 (1964), pp. 117–20 for Adrian Oswald on coins and an earthenwork from Mancetter; Vol. 84 (1971), pp. 18–44 for evidence of a first-century ditch; Vol. 85 (1973), pp. 211–13 for possible importance of the site in association with the great revolt of AD 60; Dudley and Webster (1–3), p. 111; Webster (1–3), p. 97 and fig. 5, p. 98. Other sources: Frere (IV–15), p. 107, 'reasonable guesses' have placed the site close to Watling Street, north-west of Towcester or near Mancetter; Salway (IV–7), p. 120: 'somewhere in the Midlands', Todd (II–8), p. 91: 'may not have been far to the north-west of Verulamium'.

9 Salway (IV–7), p. 77.

10 See Webster, *Army* (VII–3), pp. 122–32.

11 *The Tragedie of Bonduca* in *Comedies and Tragedies written by Francis Beaumont and John Fletcher, Gentlemen* ... (1647), Act V, scene iv.

12 Bolton, Edmund, cit. Piggott (IV–9), p. 136; Jones, Inigo, *The Most Notable Antiquity of Great Britain, Vulgarly called Stone-Heng, on Salisbury Plain Restored* (2nd edn 1725), pp. 34–5.

13 Scott, J. M., *Boadicea* (1975), pp. 31f.; Spence (VII–5), p. 260; *The Times*, 23 February 1988; Nicholas Fuentes, letter to *The Times*, 27 February 1988 thought Platform 8 – 'who knows' – not impossible.

14 Gibbon (1–9), I, p. 39.

15 Tacitus, *Agricola* (IV–33), p. 67; Tacitus (III–1), p. 331; Bulst (V–2), p. 506; Overbeck (V–27), pp. 141–2.

16 Bulst (V–2), p. 506; Clarke (IV–9), p. 114.

17 Clarke (IV–9), p. 114; Bulst (V–2), p. 506 and note 80; Tacitus, *Agricola* (IV–33), p. 81.

18 Todd (II–8), p. 91; Salway (IV–7), Appendix IV p. 751.

19 Cit. Nieng Cheng, *Life in Shanghai* (1986), p. 203.

CHAPTER EIGHT: *O Zenobia!*

1 *Historia Augusta* (v–5), III, p. 247; Dio (III–23), VIII, p. 83.

2 See Février, J. G., *Essai sur l'histoire politique et économique de Palmyre* (Paris 1931); Tlass, Moustapha, *Zénobie Reine de Palmyre: Oeuvre adaptée en français par Athanase Vantchev de Thracy* (Damascus 1986), *passim*.

3 I.e. Oliver Cromwell in seventeenth-century England, Fraser (VI–22), p. 564; Février, J. G., *La Religion des Palmyréniens* (Paris 1931), p. 222.

4 Cameron, Alan, 'The Date of Porphyry's KATA KRISTIANON', *Classical Quarterly*, XVII (1967), pp. 382–4.

5 *Historia Augusta* (v–5), III, p. 135.

6 See Abbott, Nabia, 'Pre-Islamic Arab Queens', *American Journal of Semitic Languages and Literature*, Vol. LVIII (1941), pp. 1–22.

7 Gibbon (1–9), I, p. 150.

8 Abbott, Nabia, 'Women and the State on the Eve of Islam', *American Journal of Semitic Languages and Literature*, Vol. LVIII (1941), pp. 269–78; Abbott, *Aishah* (1–11), p. x.

9 Abbott, 'Women' (VIII–8), p. 262; Beard, Mary R., *Women as Force in History: A Study in Traditions and Realities* (New York 1946), p. 290; Clayton, Ellen C., *Female Warriors: Memorials of Female Valour and Heroism, from the Mythological Ages to the Present Era*, 2 vols (1879), Vol. 1, p. 88.

10 Février (VIII–2), pp. 59–62; Fedden, Robin, *Syria: An Historical Appreciation* (revised edn 1956), p. 87.

11 Février, *Religion* (VIII–3), p. 235.

12 *The History of Count Zosimus, Sometime Advocate and Chancellor of the Roman Empire* (1814), pp. 21f.; Février (VIII–2), p. 75.

13 Février (VIII–2), p. 85; *Historia Augusta* (v–5), III, p. 104 note 1.

14 See *Historia Augusta* (v–5), III, pp. 135f., 193f., but nothing is known of the various authors to whom the biographies are attributed: see *Oxford Companion to Classical Literature*, compiled by Sir Paul Harvey (Oxford 1984), p. 210.

15 *Historia Augusta* (v–5), III, pp. 135–43 for 'Trebellius Pollio's' description of Zenobia.

16 Gibbon (1–9), I, p. 302 and note 62; Boccaccio (1–19), p. 226; Jonson (1–2).

17 *Historia Augusta* (v–5), III, p. 109, for theory of Zenobia's conspiracy; Février (VIII–2), p. 90 believes in the possibility of Zenobia's guilt only because Herodianus' death helped her; a modern Arab writer, Moustapha Tlass (VIII–2), describes the accusations as 'gratuitous', since there is no proof of her complicity; Abbott, 'Queens' (VIII–6), p. 13 for Roman guilt.

18 *Historia Augusta* (v–5), III, p. 135; *Cambridge Ancient History*, Vol. XII (Cambridge 1939), p. 302.

19 Février, *Religion* (VIII–3), p. 241; *Cambridge Ancient History* (VIII–18), XII, p. 302.

20 Février (VIII–2), pp. 113–14; *Cambridge Ancient History* (VIII–18), XII, p. 302.

21 Février (VIII–2), p. 103.

22 Mommsen, Theodor, *The Provinces of the Roman Empire from Caesar to Diocletian*, Vol. II (1909), pp. 106–7 note 5.

23 Zosimus (VIII–12), p. 29.

24 Zosimus (VIII–12), pp. 25f.

25 *Historia Augusta* (V–5), III, pp. 243–4; Zosimus (VIII–12), p. 25.

26 Zosimus (VIII–12), p. 27; although the exchanges may well, of course, be fictional.

27 *Cambridge Ancient History* (VIII–18), XII, p. 306.

28 *Historia Augusta* (V–5), III, p. 137.

29 Zosimus (VIII–12), p. 29; *Historia Augusta* (V–5), III, p. 249.

30 Gibbon (I–9), I, pp. 311–12; *Historia Augusta* (V–5), III, pp. 141, 259; *Cambridge Ancient History* (VIII–18), XII, p. 305 note 1: 'Zosimus should be rejected'.

31 Perceval, A. P. Caussin de, *Essai sur l'histoire des Arabes avant l'Islamisme, pendant l'époque de Mahomet*..., Vol. II (Paris 1897), pp. 30 note 4, 192–8; Abbott, 'Queens' (VIII–6), p. 13.

32 Mommsen (VIII–22), p. 110; Gibbon (I–9), I, p. 308.

33 See Tlass (VIII–2), p. 169 note 1 for another Queen Al-Zabba, part of the royal family of Al-Hyra, sometimes confused with Zenobia.

34 *Zénobie* by Assi and Mansour Al-Rahbani, cit. Tlass (VIII–2), pp. 254–60.

35 *Zenobia: A Tragedy*, 'As it is performed at the Theatre Royal in Drury-Lane. By the Author of the Orphan of China [Arthur Murphy]' (1768).

CHAPTER NINE: *Matilda, Daughter of Peter*

1 The '*Epistolae Vagantes*' of *Pope Gregory VII*, edited and translated by H. E. J. Cowdrey (Oxford 1972), p. 13.

2 Dudley and Webster (I–3), p. 115.

3 Cit. Briey, Comte Renaud de, *Mathilde, Duchesse de Toscane, Comtesse de Briey, Fondatrice de l'Abbaye d'Orval (1046–1115): Une Jeanne d'Arc Italienne* (Brussels 1934), p. 50.

4 See Overmann, A., *Gräfin Mathilde von Tuscien* (Innsbruck 1895) for *Regesta* of her life pp. 123–90; also Tondelli, Leone, *Matilda di Canossa – profilo storico* (3rd edn Reggio 1969); Duff (I–21), for biographical details.

5 Vedriani and Paluda, cit. Duff (I–21), p. 77; Tondelli (IX–4), pp. 30–1.

6 Huddy (V–5), p. 104.

7 See Colucci, G., *Un nuovo poema latina dello IX secolo* (Rome 1895), pp. 132–3.

8 Villani, Giovanni, *Istorie Fiorentine*, Vol. I (Milan 1802), pp. 201f.

9 Tondelli (IX–4), pp. 5, 144–5; Schevill, Ferdinand, *History of Florence from the Founding of the City through the Renaissance* (New York 1961), p. 54.

10 Erra, C. A., *Memorie storico–critiche della gran contessa Matilda* (Rome 1768), p. xiii.

11 Dante, *De Monarchia*, translated by P. H. Wicksteed, Book III (1896), pp. 277–8.

12 Cit. Duff (I–21), p. 91.

13 Tondelli (IX–4), pp. 30–1.

14 Cit. Duff (I–21), p. 127.

15 Cit. Briey (IX–3), p. 53.

16 See Gregory VII, *Epistolae* (IX–1) *passim* and biographies of Matilda, esp. Briey (IX–3), Duff (I–21) and Tondelli (IX–4).

17 Briey (IX–3), p. 56.

18 Donizo's *Vita Comitissae Mathildis* – in two books of Latin verse – is the principal source for events at Canossa (1734) BL:12 f.6; see also the latest Italian translation by G. Marzi and V. Bellocchi (Modena 1970).

19 Gregory VII's letter in Duff (I–21), Appendix D pp. 290–1.

20 Donizo, I, 2, v. 203 cit. Briey (IX–3), p. 127.

21 Cit. Briey (IX–3), p. 151.

22 Schenetti, Matteo, 'La vittoria de Matilde di Canossa su Arrigo IV', *Studi Matildici*, Reggio 7–9 ottobre 1972 (Modena 1978), pp. 238–9.

23 Cit. Duff (I–21), p. 204.

24 Schevill (IX–9), pp. 58f.

25 See Rough, Robert H., *The Reformist Illuminations in the Gospels of Matilda Countess of Tuscany: A Study in the Art of the Age of Gregory VII* (The Hague 1973).

26 Inscriptions given in Duff (I–21), pp. 275–6.

27 Cit. Stephan, Rt. Hon. Sir James, *Essays in Ecclesiastical Biography*, Vol. I (1907), pp. 35f.

28 *The Vision of Purgatory and Paradise* by Dante Alighieri, translated by Rev. H. F. Cary (1893), Cantos XXVIII, XIX, XXXI and XXXII, and p. 120 note 1. Tasso's *Jerusalem Delivered*, translated by Edward Fairfax, The Carisbrooke Library, Vol. VII (1890), Book XVII, p. 352.

29 Nencioni, G., *Matilde di Canosse* (Milan 1937), p. 190.

30 Tondelli (IX–4), Preface.

CHAPTER TEN: *England's Domina*

1 For the Empress Maud see *Dictionary of National Biography* entry by Kate Norgate (1908–9); Onslow, the Earl of, *The Empress Maud* (1939) and Pain, Nesta, *Empress Matilda: Uncrowned Queen of England* (1978); for the period generally, Chibnall, Marjorie, *Anglo-Norman England, 1066–1166* (Oxford 1986) is the principal source.

2 *DNB* (X–1).

3 *The Works of Gildas, in Six Old English Chronicles*, edited by J. A. Giles (1878), p. 301.

4 See Dudley and Webster (I–3), p. 114.

5 Ruskin, *Mornings in Florence*, cit. Purdie, Edna, *The Story of Judith in German and English Literature* (Paris 1927).

6 *William of Malmesbury, The History of the Kings of England . . .*, Vol. III, Part 1 (The Church Historians of England 1854), p. 109.

7 *Judith*, edited by B. J. Timmer (1966), p. 7.

8 *Anglo-Saxon Poetry*, selected and translated by Professor R. K. Gordon (revised edn 1954), pp. 320–6.

9 See Chibnall (x–1), pp. 83–5.

10 Cit. Chibnall (x–1), p. 67 note 33.

11 *The Idea of a perfect Princesse, in The Life of St Margaret Queen of Scotland. With Elogiums on her children David and Mathilda Queen of England. Now englished* (Paris 1661).

12 Chibnall (x–1), p. 68.

13 *The Historia Novella by William of Malmesbury*, edited by K. R. Potter (1955), pp. 3–5.

14 See Gillingham, John, *The Angevin Empire* (1984 pbk), p. 9 for the view that Henry had Geoffrey in mind as his successor at the time of the betrothal; Chibnall (x–1), p. 85: 'no reliable evidence that he ever changed his mind about his heir'.

15 Cit. Strickland, Agnes, *Lives of the Queens of England*, Vol. 1 (reprint 1972), p. 203.

16 Gillingham (x–14), pp. 10–11.

17 *Gesta Stephani*, edited and translated from the Latin by K. R. Potter, with a new Introduction and Notes by R. H. C. Davis (Oxford 1976), p. 5; William of Malmesbury (x–6), III, Part I, p. 389.

18 Fell, Christine, Clark, Cecily and Williams, Elizabeth, *Women in Anglo-Saxon England and the Impact of 1066* (1984), p. 170.

19 Strickland (x–15), p. 1 where the quotations are given in Latin, slightly mixed up.

20 Geoffrey of Monmouth, *Histories of the Kings of Britain*, translated by Sebastian Evans, introduction by Lucy Anne Paton (1934), p. 34.

21 See Reilly, Bernard F., *The Kingdom of León-Castilla under Queen Urraca 1109–1126* (Princeton, New Jersey 1982), especially Ch. 12, pp. 352f.

22 *DNB* (x–1); Chibnall (x–1), p. 94 note 103.

23 *Gesta Stephani* (x–17), pp. 179–84.

24 *The Anglo-Saxon Chronicle*, edited and translated by D. Whitelock, D. C. Douglas and S. I. Tucker (1961), p. 200.

25 Cit. *DNB* (x–1).

26 Strickland (x–15), p. 225 gives the various contemporary references; *Gesta Stephani* (x–17), pp. 94–5; William of Malmesbury (x–6), III, Part I, pp. 421–2.

27 Onslow (x–1), p. 106; Pain (x–1), p. 102.

28 Cit. Pain (x–1), pp. 85, 91.

29 *Matthaei Parisiensis, Monachi Sancti Albani, Chronica Majora*, edited by H. R. Luard (part of *Rerum Britannicarum Medii Aevi Scriptores or, Chronicles and Memorials of Great Britain and Ireland during The Middle Ages*), Vol. II (1874), p. 324; *DNB* (x–1).

CHAPTER ELEVEN: *Lion of the Caucasus*

The principal sources for this chapter are W. E. D. Allen's *History of the Georgian People* (xi–3) and D. M. Lang's *The Georgians* (xi–7).

1 Professor Mariam Lordkipanidze, communication to the author; Kelly, Lawrence, *Lermontov: Tragedy in the Caucasus* (1983 pbk), p. 78.
2 'The Demon' translated by Robert Burness (Edinburgh 1918), cit. Kelly (XI–1), p. 79.
3 Thubron, Colin, *Among the Russians* (1985 pbk), p. 165; Allen, W. E. D., *A History of the Georgian People: From the Beginning down to the Russian Conquest in the Nineteenth Century* (1932), pp. 40, 103.
4 Allen (XI–3), p. 2.
5 Shota Rustaveli, *The Knight in Panther's Skin*, a free translation in prose by Katharine Vivian, Foreword by David Lang (1977), p. 39.
6 Allen (XI–3), pp. 39–40.
7 Cit. Lang, D. M., *The Georgians* (1966), pp. 112, 28.
8 Lang (XI–7), pp. 64f. gives a good summary.
9 Cit. Allen (XI–3), p. 107.
10 Cit. Maclean, Sir Fitzroy, *To Caucasus* (1976), p. 20.
11 Allen (XI–3), p. 102.
12 d'Auriac, Eugène, *Thamar Reine de Géorgie* (Paris 1892), p. 2.
13 Allen (XI–3), p. 103.
14 Lang (XI–7), p. 225.
15 Allen (XI–3), p. 106.
16 d'Auriac (XI–12), pp. 9, 12.
17 Cit. Katharine Vivian to author.
18 d'Auriac (XI–12), p. 12.
19 Allen (XI–3), p. 103.
20 *Titus Andronicus*, Act v, scene iii; *Georgian Shakespeariana*, III, edited and with a Foreword and notes by Nico Kiasashvili (seminar in Georgia to celebrate the 400th anniversary of Shakespeare's birth) (Tbilisi 1964), p. 336.
21 Rustaveli (XI–5), p. 9.
22 Rustaveli (XI–5), p. 11.
23 *The Georgian Chronicle*, cit. David Lang's Foreword to Rustaveli (XI–5), p. 18.
24 Urushadze, Venera, *Shota Rustaveli's The Knight in Panther's Skin*, translated from the Georgian, Introduction by David M. Lang (Tbilisi 1979), p. 11.
25 Bowra, C. M., *Inspiration and Poetry* (1955), pp. 45–67.
26 Allen (XI–3), p. 244: his own translation.

CHAPTER TWELVE: *Isabella with her Prayers*

The principal modern sources consulted for this chapter are J. H. Elliott's *Imperial Spain 1469–1716* (XII–1), J. N. Hillgarth's *The Spanish Kingdoms 1250–1516* (XII–4) and F. Fernández-Armesto's joint biography of Ferdinand and Isabella (XII–2).
1 J. H. Elliott's *Imperial Spain 1469–1716* (1963), p. 65.
2 Cit. Fernández-Armesto, F., *Ferdinand and Isabella* (1975), p. 96.
3 Fernández-Armesto (XII–2), p. 149.
4 Bernáldez cit. Hillgarth, J. N., *The Spanish Kingdoms 1250–1516* (Oxford 1978), p. 451.

5 Hillgarth (XII–4), p. 483.
6 Cit. Fernández-Armesto (XII–2), p. 53.
7 See Elliott (XII–1), p. 11: 'a consideration lately gives her the benefit of the doubt'.
8 Elliott (XII–1), pp. 10, 66.
9 Walsh, W. T., *Isabella of Spain* (1931), p. 137.
10 Fernández-Armesto (XII–2), p. 83.
11 Fernández-Armesto (XII–2), p. 27.
12 Prescott, W. H., *History of the Reign of Ferdinand and Isabella the Catholic* (new and revised edition 1885), p. 592 note 3.
13 Fernández-Armesto (XII–2), p. 64.
14 Fernández-Armesto (XII–2), p. 41.
15 Prescott (XII–12), pp. 591f.; Fernández-Armesto (XII–2), pp. 106f.
16 Hillgarth (XII–4), p. 363; and see Walsh (XII–9), p. 616 note 2 writing in 1931: 'The canonization of Isabel as a saint has been urged strongly in Spain during the past year.'
17 Elliott (XII–1), p. 11.
18 Viaggio cit. Prescott (XII–12), p. 596.
19 Prescott (XII–12), p. 240.
20 Laffin, John, *Women in Battle* (1967), pp. 20–1.
21 Walsh (XII–9), p. 365.
22 Prescott (XII–12), p. 244.
23 Fernández-Armesto (XII–2), p. 90.
24 Elliott (XII–1), p. 20.
25 Prescott (XII–12), p. 240; Walsh (XII–9), p. 325.
26 Nervo, Baron de, *Isabella the Catholic: Queen of Spain. Her Life, Reign and Times 1451–1504* (1897), p. 203.
27 Nervo (XII–26), p. 195.
28 Fernández-Armesto (XII–2), p. 49; Walsh (XII–9), p. 22.
29 See Colby, Kenneth Mark, 'Gentlemen, the Queen', *Psychoanalytic Review*, Vol. 40 (1953), pp. 144–8.
30 Fernández-Armesto (XII–2), p. 136.
31 Ernst Breisach's biography of Caterina Sforza (I–21) is the basis of the ensuing pages; see also Kelly (I–7), pp. 31f.
32 See Breisach (I–21), p. 296 note 99 for sources of the various versions.
33 Fernández-Armesto (XII–2), p. 55.
34 Elliott (XII–1), p. 42; Walsh (XII–9), p. 605.

CHAPTER THIRTEEN: *Elizabetha Triumphans*

1 *Harborowe* (III–9).
2 Knox (II–13), p. 12.
3 Knox (II–13), pp. 31f.
4 Knox, John, *History of the Church of Scotland*, cit. Knox (II–13), Appendix.
5 Abbott, *Aishah* (I–11), p. 176; see Phillips, James E., Jr, 'The Background of

Spenser's Attitude Toward Women Rulers', *Huntington Library Quarterly* (1941–2), pp. 5f.

6 Knox (II–13), pp. xvii, 31.

7 Knox (II–13), Appendix; Phillips, (XIII–5), *passim.*

8 *Harborowe* (III–9), *passim.*

9 Ridley, Jasper, *Elizabeth I* (1987), pp. 25–6, 85.

10 Prescott, H. F. M., *Mary Tudor* (1953), p. 164.

11 Erickson, Carolly, *Bloody Mary* (1978), p. 56.

12 Waldman, Milton, *The Lady Mary: A Biography of Mary Tudor 1516–1558* (1972), p. 204.

13 Neale, J. E., *Queen Elizabeth I* (1960 pbk), p. 69.

14 Williams, Neville, *Elizabeth I: Queen of England* (1971 pbk), pp. 48, 70.

15 Fraser, Antonia, *Mary Queen of Scots* (1969), p. 163; *Jewels and Plate of Queen Elizabeth I: the Inventory of 1574*, edited by A. Jefferies Collins (1955), p. 112; Neale (XIII–13), p. 288.

16 Cit. Erickson (XIII–11), p. 388.

17 *The Works of Anne Bradstreet in Prose and Verse*, edited by John H. Ellis (Charlestown 1867), p. 361.

18 Heisch, Allison, 'Queen Elizabeth I and the Persistence of Patriarchy', *Feminist Review*, February 1980, pp. 45–55.

19 Longford, Elizabeth, *Victoria RI* (1964), p. 395.

20 Cit. Erickson (XIII–11), p. 390.

21 *The Memoirs of Sir James Melville of Halhill*, edited and with an Introduction by Gordon Donaldson (1969), p. 37.

22 Buchanan cit. Phillips, James E., Jr, 'The Woman Ruler in Spenser's *Faerie Queene*', *Huntington Library Quarterly* (1941–2), p. 220.

23 Strong, Roy, *The Cult of Elizabeth: Elizabethan Portraiture and Pageantry* (1977), p. 50.

24 Williams (XIII–14), p. 168.

25 Williams (XIII–14), p. 324.

26 Palliser, D. M., *The Age of Elizabeth: England under the Later Tudors 1547–1603* (1983), pp. 12, 107f.; Adams, Simon, 'The Queen Embattled: Elizabeth I and the Conduct of Foreign Policy' in *Queen Elizabeth I: Most Politick Princess*, edited by Simon Adams, *History Today* special issue (1984).

27 Cit. Fraser, *Mary* (XIII–15), p. 344; Palliser (XIII–26), p. 108.

28 Creighton, Rev. Mandell, *Queen Elizabeth* (1896), p. 179.

29 Nichols, John (ed.), *Bibliotheca Topographica Britannica*, 2 vols (1780–90), Vol. I, Appendix vii pp. 525–6.

30 Williams (XIII–14), p. 290.

31 Williams (XIII–14), pp. 279, 347.

32 See Strong, *Cult* (XIII–23), *passim*; most recently Strong, Roy, *Gloriana: The Portraits of Queen Elizabeth I* (1987).

33 Strong, *Cult* (XIII–23), p. 47.

34 *Jewels* (XIII–15), p. 112; Williams (XIII–14), pp. 350–1.

35 Dunlop, Ian, *Palaces and Progresses of Elizabeth I* (1962), p. 85; Williams (XIII–14), p. 250.

36 Chambers, Anne, *Granuaile: The Life and Times of Grace O'Malley, c.1530–1603* (Dublin 1983 pbk), Ch. VI, pp. 127f.

37 Dunlop (XIII–35), p. 32; cit. Erickson (XIII–11), p. 276.

38 *Henry VI Part III*, Act I, scene iv.

39 Savile, Henry, *The Ende of Nero and the beginning of Galba. Fower bookes of the histories of Cornelius Tacitus. The life of Agricola* (1591), Preface.

40 Dudley and Webster (1–3), p. 115; *Polydore Vergil's English History*, Vol. I, edited by Sir Henry Ellis (1846), pp. 17, 70–2.

41 *The Chronicles of Scotland*, compiled by Hector Boëce, translated into Scots by John Bellenden 1531, edited by R. W. Chambers and Edith Batho, Vol. I (Edinburgh 1938), pp. 141–5.

42 Holinshed (V–27), I, pp. 43–8.

43 Ubaldini, *Donne* (1–5).

44 Ubaldini, 'Fatti' (1–5).

45 *Camden's Britannia*, Introduction by Stuart Piggott (1971 facsimile), pp. 311, 347, 366; Dudley and Webster (1–3), pp. 117, 156 note 10.

46 Spenser (II–5), Vol. I, p. 297.

47 Spenser (II–5), Vol. II, p. 199.

48 Williams (XIII–14), pp. 307, 311; Camden (XIII–45), p. 10.

49 'Elizabetha Triumphans' in Nichols, John, *The Progresses, and Public Processions, of Queen Elizabeth...*, Vol. II (1788), p. 22.

50 This account is based on Christy, Miller, 'Queen Elizabeth's Visit to Tilbury in 1588', *English Historical Review* (1919), pp. 43–61; Mattingly, Garrett, *The Defeat of the Spanish Armada* (1959), pp. 290–7; also *The Queenes visiting of the Campe at Tilburie with her entertainement there*, BL c. 18 l. 2 (64) (1588); 'Elizabetha Triumphans' (XIII–49); Ridley (XIII–9), p. 285 and note.

51 Calendar of State Papers Domestic 1581–90, p. 516; Neale (XIII–13), p. 301.

52 See Barker, Felix, 'If Parma had Landed', *History Today* (May 1988), p. 40. Recent research dismisses Arden Hall as the Queen's residence.

53 Barker (XIII–52), p. 38 questions the text because Aske reports the speech differently; but Sharp would have been closer to the Queen than Aske and, as Leicester's chaplain, closer to court circles. Letter to *The Times*, 12 May 1988.

54 CSP Domestic (XIII–51), p. 514.

55 Hacker (1–10), p. 653.

CHAPTER FOURTEEN: *Jinga at the Gates*

1 Oakley, Stewart, *The Story of Sweden* (1966), p. 82.

2 Kelly (1–7), p. 86.

3 Cit. Green (II–17), p. 187.

4 Swift, *Jack Frenchman's Lamentation*, cit. Green (II–17), pp. 191, 360 note 28.

5 Blake, Robert, *Disraeli* (1966), p. 637.

6 *Bonduca* (VII–11), Act III, scene i; Fletcher, John, *Bonduca* (Malone Society reprint Oxford 1951) suggests it is 'hardly open to doubt' that the play is 'substantially Fletcher's'.

7 *Bonduca or, The British Heroine*, A Tragedy Acted at the Theatre Royal by his Majesty's Servants (1696); Price, C. A., *Henry Purcell and the London Stage* (Cambridge 1984), pp. 97, 117–25.

8 Price (XIV–7), p. 117.

9 Piggott (IV–9), p. 81; Mossiker, Frances, *Pocahontas: The Life and the Legend* (1977), pp. 43, 157, 166.

10 Piggott (IV–9), p. 136; Heywood (II–12), p. 72.

11 Petition of Women, BL E551 (14) (1649); Shepherd, Simon, *Amazons and Warrior Women: Varieties of Feminism in Seventeenth-Century Drama* (Brighton 1981), pp. 87f.

12 Sammes, Aylett, *Britannia Antiqua Illustrata, or, The Antiquities of Ancient Britain*, Vol. 1 (1676), pp. 223–9.

13 *The British Princes*, An Heroick Poem Written by the Honourable Edward Howard Esq. (1669).

14 Dudley and Webster (1–3), p. 125.

15 See Piggott, Stuart, *William Stukeley: An Eighteenth-Century Antiquary* (Oxford 1950), *passim*, especially pp. 54–5 and note 1; *Lincolnshire Notes – Queries*, MS in the possession of W. A. Cragg of Threckingham, Vol. 10 (1909), pp. 177–80.

16 Piggott, *Stukeley* (XIV–15), p. 56.

17 G. E. C. (Cokayne), *The Complete Peerage* (reprint 1981), XII/1, p. 81; *The Complete Poetical Works of James Thomson*, edited by J. Logie Robertson (1908), p. 413.

18 *The Works of William Cowper*, 8 vols (1853–5), Vol. V, pp. 265–6.

19 Information supplied to the author from resident in Angola in 1987.

20 Buttinger, Joseph, *Vietnam: A Dragon Embattled*, Vol. II: *Vietnam at War* (New York 1970), pp. 54–6. Karnow, Stanley, *Vietnam: A History* (New York 1983), p. 100.

21 Ladner, Joyce A., 'Racism and Tradition: Black Womanhood in Perspective' in Carroll (II–7), pp. 179–93; Diner (II–6), pp. 221–7; Laffin (XII–20), pp. 47–51.

22 Diner (II–6), pp. 223; *Spectator* (London), 29 October 1987.

23 The main sources for the life of Queen Jinga are: Birmingham, David, *Trade and Conflict in Angola: The Mbundu and their Neighbours under the Influence of the Portuguese 1483–1790* (Oxford 1966); Boxer, C. R., *Race Relations in the Portuguese Colonial Empire 1415–1825* (Oxford 1963) and *Salvador de Sá and the Struggle for Brazil and Angola 1602–1686* (1952); Chilcote, B., *Portuguese Africa* (1967); Duffy, James, *Portuguese Africa* (1959).

24 Birmingham (XIV–23), pp. 92–5.

25 Boxer, *Salvador* (XIV–23), p. 243.

26 Boxer, *Race* (XIV–23), p. 25.

27 Ogilby (1–6), II, pp. 563–5.

28 Cit. Boxer, *Race* (XIV–23), p. 29.

29 Cit. Boxer, *Race* (XIV–23), p. 30.

30 Ogilby (1–6), II, p. 563.

31 Child, Mrs, *An Appeal in Favor of that Class of Americans called Africans* (Boston 1833), p. 161.

32 Birmingham (XIV–23), p. 125.

33 Child (XIV–31), p. 161.

CHAPTER FIFTEEN: *Queen versus Monster*

1 Napoleon (11–14), p. 488.

2 Napoleon (11–14), p. 326; Gluck's *Armide*: libretto by Philippe Quenault, Act v, scene v.

3 Voss, Sophie Marie Countess von, *Sixty-Nine Years at the Court of Prussia: From the recollections of the Mistress of the Household*, 2 vols (1876), Vol. II, p. 42.

4 Burke, Edmund, *Reflections on the Revolution in France . . .*, edited and with an Introduction by Conor Cruise O'Brien (1969 pbk), p. 170; *Life of General Sir Robert Wilson*, edited by Rev. Herbert Randolph, Vol. II (1862), p. 53.

5 Wilson (XV–4), p. 53; Gibbon (1–9), I, p. 302.

6 Biographies consulted for Maria Theresa and Catherine respectively are: Crankshaw, Edward, *Maria Theresa* (1971 pbk); Cronin, Vincent, *Catherine Empress of all the Russias* (1978); Gooch, G. P., *Catherine the Great and Other Studies* (1954); Troyat, Henri, *Catherine the Great* (1–16).

7 *Saint Simon at Versailles*, selected and translated by Lucy Norton. With a preface by Nancy Mitford (1985 pbk edn), p. 241.

8 Cit. Crankshaw (XV–6), pp. 59, 61; *The Love Letters of Thomas Carlyle and Jane Welsh*, edited by Alexander Carlyle, 2 vols (1909), Vol. I, p. 41.

9 Crankshaw (XV–6), p. 78.

10 Crankshaw (XV–6), pp. 308f.; *c.*1749 cit. *Maria Theresia's Politisches Testament*, edited by J. Kalbrunner and C. Biener (Vienna 1959).

11 Voltaire (III–4), IX, p. 32.

12 *Memoirs of Catherine the Great*, translated by Katharine Anthony (New York 1927), p. 15.

13 *Memoirs of the Princess Daschkaw [Dashkova], Lady of Honour to Catherine II, Empress of all the Russias, Written by Herself*, edited by Mrs W. Bradford, 2 vols (1840), Vol. I, pp. 78f.

14 Catherine's *Memoirs* (XV–12), p. 266.

15 Troyat (1–16), p. 187; Gooch (XV–6), p. 95.

16 Troyat (1–16), p. 270.

17 Gooch (XV–6), p. 18; Troyat (1–16), p. 166.

18 Voltaire (III–4), IX, p. 84.

19 Voltaire (III–4), IX, *passim*, esp. pp. 51, 68.

20 Voltaire (III–4), IX, p. 84.

21 Cronin (XV–6), p. 183.

22 Wright, Constance, *Louise, Queen of Prussia* (1970), p. 47.

23 Wright (XV–22), p. 18; *Memoirs of Madame Vigée Le Brun*, translated by Lionel Strachey, 2 vols (1904), Vol. II, p. 167.

24 *The Diaries and Letters of Sir George Jackson*, KCH, *from the Peace of Amiens to the Battle of Talavera*, edited by Lady Jackson, 2 vols (1872), Vol. I, p. 126.

25 Voss (xv–3).

26 Taack, Merete von, *Königin Luise: Eine Biographie* (Tübigen 1978), pp. 226–7; Delbrück, Hans, 'Von der Königin Luise, dem Minister v. Stein und dem deutschen Nationalgedanken', *Preussische Jahrbücher*, Vol. 136 (1909), p. 452; Maass, Joachim, *Kleist: A Biography* (1983), pp. 88, 122, 206.

27 Kleist, Heinrich von, *Penthesilea: A Tragedy*, English version by Humphrey Trevelyan (1959), Act I, scene xv.

28 Vigée Le Brun (xv–23), II, pp. 168–9.

29 Jackson (xv–24), I, pp. 153, 241; Klett, Tessa, *Königin Luise von Preussen in der Zeit der Napoleonischen Kriege* (Berlin 1937), p. 131.

30 Voss (xv–3), II, pp. 29–30.

31 Voss (xv–3), II, p. 30.

32 Napoleon (11–14), p. 425.

33 Klett (xv–29), p. 72.

34 Wright (xv–22), p. 81.

35 Krieger, Bogdan, 'Russischer Besuch am preussischen Hof vor 100 Jahren', *Deutsche Revue*, Vol. 29 (1904), p. 348.

36 Aretz, Gertrude, *Queen Louise of Prussia 1776–1810* (New York 1929), p. 144.

37 Wright, (xv–22), p. 141.

38 Napoleon (11–14), p. 324; Delbrück (xv–26), p. 520.

39 Hardy, Thomas, *The Dynasts: An Epic Drama* (1920), p. 155.

40 Taack (xv–26), p. 371.

41 *Mémoires et lettres inédits du Chevalier de Gentz* (Stuttgart 1841), p. 296.

42 Napoleon (11–14), p. 363; Princess Louise of Prussia (Princess Anton Radziwill), *Forty-five Years of My Life 1770–1815* (1912), p. 228.

43 Taack (xv–26), p. 371; Bailleu, Paul, *Königin Luise: Ein Lebensbild* (Berlin and Leipzig 1908), p. 199.

44 Klett (xv–29), p. 145; Leveson-Gower, Lord Granville (First Earl Granville), *Private Correspondence 1781 to 1821*, edited by Castalia Countess Granville, 2 vols (1916), Vol. II, p. 265.

45 Napoleon (11–14), pp. 367–8.

46 Bailleu (xv–43), p. 210.

47 Taack (xv–26), p. 380.

48 *Memoirs of Prince Metternich (1773–1815)*, edited by Prince Richard Metternich, Vol. II (1880), p. 144.

49 Klett (xv–29), p. 154; Bailleu, Paul, 'Königin Luise in Tilsit', *Hohenzollern Jahrbuch*, 3 Jahrgang (1899), p. 224; Aretz (xv–36), p. 214.

50 Aretz (xv–36), p. 216; Granville (xv–44), II, p. 70; Jackson (xv–24), I, p. 163; Wilson (xv–4), p. 298.

51 Granville (xv–44), II, p. 271.

52 The best account in English is in Wright (xv–22), pp. 169–178, and in German in Taack (xv–26), pp. 398f.; see also Bailleu, 'Tilsit' (xv–49).

53 I.e. Taack (xv–26), p. 405; Palmer, Alan, *Alexander I: Tsar of War and Peace* (1974), p. 141.

54 Jackson (xv–24); Wilson (xv–4), p. 310.

55 Maass (xv–26), p. 111; Richardson, Mrs Charles, *Memoirs of the private life and opinions of Louisa, Queen of Prussia* (1847), p. 193.

56 Richardson (xv–55), p. 263.

57 Moffat, Mary Maxwell, *Queen Louisa of Prussia* (1906), p. 308.

58 Louise of Prussia (xv–42), p. 27; Richardson (xv–55), p. 1.

59 See Bellardi, Paul, *Königin Luise, ihr Leben und ihr Andenken in Berlin* (Berlin 1893), for a description of the many kinds of memorial to Queen Louise; Treitschke, Heinrich von, 'Königin Luise' in *Historische und Politische Aufsätze*, IV (Berlin 1897), pp. 310f.; Kelly, Rev. John, *Louisa of Prussia and other sketches* (1888), p. 93.

60 Richardson (xv–55), p. 291.

CHAPTER SIXTEEN: *The Valiant Rani*

1 Thornycroft, Elfrida, *Bronze and Steel: The Life of Thomas Thornycroft, Sculptor and Engineer* (Shipston-on-Stour 1932), pp. 51f.

2 Tennyson, Charles, *Alfred Tennyson* (1949), p. 323; Tennyson, Alfred, *Poetical Works Including the Plays* (1953), pp. 224–6.

3 *The Letters of Queen Victoria, 2nd Series, 1862–1878*, edited by G. E. Buckle, 2 vols, Vol. II (1926), p. 119.

4 Royal Archives, Windsor Castle, Vic. Add. EI/1048.

5 Tahmankar, D. V., *The Ranee of Jhansi* (1958), p. 19.

6 Tahmankar (xvi–5), pp. 13f.

7 See the most recent biography, Lebra-Chapman, Joyce, *The Rani of Jhansi: A Study in Female Heroism in India* (Honolulu 1986), pp. 15 and note 11, 168 for a discussion of the date, Indian sources mostly reporting 19 November 1835; also Tahmankar (xvi–5), p. 23: 'about 1827'; Smyth, Brigadier the Rt. Hon. Sir John, Bt. VC MC, *The Rebellious Rani* (1966), p. 11: 'about 1828'.

8 Shastiko, Pyotri, *Nana Sahib*, translated by Savitri Shahani (New Delhi 1980), p. 25.

9 See Agnew, Vijay, *Elite Women in Indian Politics* (New Delhi 1976), p. 3; Gaur, Albertine, *Women in India* (British Library Publications 1980), *passim*, esp. pp. 2–25; Gupta, A. R., *Women in Hindu Society: A Study in Tradition and Transition* (New Delhi 2nd edn 1980), pp. 6f.; Jacobson, Doranne and Wadley, Susan S., *Women in India: Two Perspectives* (New Delhi 1977), pp. 114f.

10 Royal Archives, Windsor Castle, RA Z502/49.

11 Allen, Charles, *A Glimpse of the Burning Plain: Leaves from the Indian Journals of Charlotte Canning* (1986), p. 149; Maclagan, Michael, '*Clemency Canning': Charles John, 1st Earl Canning. Governor-General and Viceroy of India, 1856–1862* (1962), p. 287.

12 Low, Ursula, *Fifty Years with John Company, From the Letters of General Sir John Low of Clatto, Fife: 1822–1858* (1936), p. 176; Russell, W. H., *My Diary in*

India in the year 1858/9, 2 vols (1860), Vol. II, p. 299.

13 Bryce, James, 'British Opinion and the Indian Revolt' in *Rebellion 1857* (XVI–65), p. 303.

14 Tahmankar (XVI–5), p. 28.

15 Maclagan (XVI–11), p. 32.

16 See Sinha, Shyam Narain, *Rani Lakshmi Bai of Jhansi*, with a Foreword by Bisheshwar Prasad (Allahabad 1980), pp. 13f. for a discussion of Hindu adoption law; Maclagan (XVI–11), p. 33 note A.

17 Kaye, J.W., *A History of the Sepoy War in India 1857–1858*, 3 vols (9th edn 1880), Vol. III, p. 360.

18 Maclagan (XVI–11), p. 316.

19 *Private Letters of the Marquess of Dalhousie*, edited by J.G.A. Baird (2nd imp. Edinburgh 1911), p. 33; Sen, Surendra Nath, *1857*, with a Foreword by Maulana Abul Kalam Azad (Calcutta 1958), p. xii.

20 Tahmankar (XVI–5), pp. 37–9.

21 Tahmankar (XVI–5), p. 39.

22 Kaye (XVI–17), III, p. 362.

23 Dalhousie (XVI–19), p. 427; Diver, Maud, *Honoria Lawrence: A Fragment of Indian History* (Boston and New York 1936), p. 371.

24 Maclagan (XVI–11), p. 21.

25 Surtees, Virginia, *Charlotte Canning, Lady-in-Waiting to Queen Victoria and Wife of the First Viceroy of India 1817–1861* (1975), p. 229; see Hibbert (V–5), pp. 59–60 and 404 note 5 for the evidence re the chupatties; *The Letters of Queen Victoria, 1837–1861*, edited by A.C. Benson and Viscount Esher, 3 vols (1907), Vol. II, p. 313.

26 Tahmankar (XVI–5), p. 54.

27 Tahmankar (XVI–5), p. 67.

28 See Sen (XVI–19), pp. 273–9 for the evidence and the pros and cons of the Rani's guilt/complicity; Rice Holmes, T., *A History of the Indian Mutiny* (5th edn 1898), pp. 491f., for a characteristically British view.

29 Tahmankar (XVI–5), pp. 70f.

30 Sen (XVI–19), p. 276; Sinha (XVI–16), p. 55.

31 Cit. Tahmankar (XVI–5), pp. 73–5; Sen (XVI–19), p. 279.

32 Sen (XVI–19), Appendix pp. 297–306 for Erskine and the Rani's letters.

33 Sen (XVI–19), p. 301.

34 Lang cit. Hibbert (V–5), p. 378.

35 Royal Archives, Windsor Castle, RA Z502/49; Hibbert (V–5), p. 378; Clayton (VIII–9), II, p. 180.

36 Royal Archives, Windsor Castle, RA Z502/49; Smyth (XVI–7), p. 195 note 2.

37 Tahmankar (XVI–5), pp. 84 note 1, 90f.

38 Gupta, Pratul Chandra, *Nana Sahib and the Rising at Cawnpore* (Oxford 1963), pp. 7, 71; Trevelyan, G.O., *Cawnpore* (1865) for details; Fitzmaurice, Lord Edmond, *The Life of Granville George Leveson Gower, Second Earl Granville 1815–1891*, 2 vols (1905), Vol. I, p. 253.

39 Gupta (XVI–38), p. 116.

40 See Thompson, Edward, *The Other Side of the Medal* (1925), p. 83, where it is pointed out that Forrest (XVI–49) avoids any reference to British excesses in three volumes of 1,500 pages, while the *Oxford History of India* (1919) merely writes (p. 719): 'the justly infuriated troops took a terrible vengeance'; Sen (XVI–19), p. xvi for British atrocities 'glossed over'; Tahmankar (XVI–5), p. 69 for Prof. R. C. Majumdar's point: 'very few' outside historians have 'any knowledge' of the 'massacre in cold blood' of the Indians, including women and children.

41 Roberts cit. Smyth (XVI–7), p. 54; Hare, Augustus J. C., *The Story of Two Noble Lives, being memorials of Charlotte, Countess Canning and Louisa, Marchioness of Waterford*, 3 vols (1893), Vol. II, p. 256 note 1; Maclagan (XVI–11), p. 141; Trevelyan (XVI–38), p. 359.

42 Lowe, Thomas, *Central India during the rebellion of 1857 and 1858* (1860), pp. 236–7.

43 Tahmankar (XVI–5), p. 120.

44 Lowe (XVI–42), p. 250.

45 Lowe (XVI–42), p. 233.

46 Burne, Major-General Sir Owen Tudor KCS, *Clyde and Strathnairn*, Rulers of India series (Oxford 1895), p. 116.

47 Smyth (XVI–7), p. 11.

48 Kaye (XVI–17), III, p. 362; Ballhatchet, Kenneth, *Race, Sex and Class under the Raj: Imperial Attitudes and Policies and their Critics, 1793–1905* (1980), pp. 2–5.

49 Clayton (VIII–9), II, p. 180; Forrest, G. W., Ex-Director of Records, Government of India, *A History of the Indian Mutiny*, 3 vols (1912), Vol. I, p. 282.

50 Royal Archives, Windsor Castle, Vic. Add. EI/1048.

51 Tahmankar (XVI–5), p. 130; Smyth (XVI–7), p. 135.

52 Savarkar, Barrister, *Indian War of Independence* (Calcutta 2nd edn 1930), p. 94.

53 Tahmankar (XVI–5), pp. 132, 134; Lowe (XVI–42), p. 259.

54 Lowe (XVI–42), p. 263.

55 Smyth (XVI–7), p. 148.

56 Lowe (XVI–42), p. 301; Tahmankar (XVI–5), p. 140.

57 Savarkar (XVI–52), p. 104; Royal Archives, Windsor Castle, Vic. Add. EI/1048.

58 Smyth (XVI–7), pp. 193f. summarizes the theories concerning the Rani's death and the sources.

59 Lord Canning's Notebook cit. Maclagan (XVI–11), p. 220.

60 Royal Archives, Windsor Castle, Vic. Add. EI/1070.

61 Royal Archives, Windsor Castle, Vic. Add. EI/1070; Smyth (XVI–7), p. 11.

62 Malleson, Col. G. B., CSI, *History of the Indian Mutiny 1857–1858*, 3 vols (1896), Vol. III, p. 221.

63 See Gupta (XVI–38), for the subsequent career of Nana Sahib.

64 Sinha (XVI–16), p. 102 note 11.

65 See Joshi, P. C. (ed.), *Rebellion 1857* (New Delhi 1957) for P. C. Gupta, '1857 and Hindi Literature', pp. 225f.; P. C. Joshi, 'Folk Songs on 1857' in *Rebellion 1857*, pp. 271f.

66 Joshi, 'Folk Songs' in *Rebellion 1857* (XVI–65), p. 277.

CHAPTER SEVENTEEN: *Iron Ladies*

1 Colville, John, *The Fringes of Power: Downing Street Diaries 1939–1955*, Vol. I 1939–41 (1986 pbk), p. 447, 20 April 1941.

2 Warner, Marina, *The Dragon Empress: Life and Times of Tz'u-Hsi, 1835–1908, Empress Dowager of China* (1972), p. 235.

3 Thornycroft (xvi–1), pp. 56–70.

4 Gleichen, Lord Edward, *London's Open-Air Statuary* (1928), p. 97.

5 See Warner, Marina, *Monuments and Maidens: The Allegory of the Female Form* (1985), pp. 49f.

6 Trevelyan, Marie, *Britain's Greatness Foretold: The Story of Boadicea, the British Warrior-Queen* (1900), pp. xi, lv, 369.

7 See Hamilton, Cicely, *A Pageant of Great Women* (1910); *Edy: Recollections of Edith Craig*, edited by Eleanor Adlard (1949), pp. 38–44; Holledge, Julie, *Innocent Flowers: Women in the Edwardian Theatre* (1981), pp. 69–71.

8 *The Dinner Party* (1979) Catalogue, Diehard Productions and Judy Chicago.

9 Grahn, Judy, 'The Queen of Bulldikery', *Chrysalis*, 1980.

10 Milton (iv–32), p. 60.

11 Piggott (iv–9), p. 136.

12 Cit. Grant (iii–11), pp. 184–5.

13 Reynolds, Robert, *Boadicea: A Tragedy of War* (New York 1941), p. 201; Treece, Henry, *Red Queen, White Queen* (1958), p. 24; Warner, Marina, *Imaginary Women*, Channel Four Television, 13 July 1986.

14 De Gaulle (1–13), pp. 13–14; Kleist (xv–27), Act I, scene xv.

15 Ferraro, Geraldine A. with Francke, Linda Bird, *My Story* (New York 1986), pp. 261f., 273, 314.

16 Seneviratne, Maureen, *Sirimavo Bandaranaike: The World's First Woman Prime Minister* (Colombo, Sri Lanka 1975), p. 178.

17 Seneviratne (xvii–16), p. xiv.

18 Carras (1–21), p. 245; Moraes, Dom, *Mrs Gandhi* (1980), p. 123.

19 *Indira Gandhi, Letters to a Friend 1950–1984*, Correspondence with Dorothy Norman (1986), p. 12.

20 Shoksi, M., *India's Indira* (Bombay 1975), p. 20; Carras (1–21), pp. 47f.

21 Carras (1–21), p. 48; Shoksi (xvii–20), p. 113; Mann, Peggy, *Golda: The Life of Israel's Prime Minister* (1972); Raju, R. Sundra, *Indira Gandhi: A Short Biography* (New Delhi 1980), pp. 5, 96.

22 Moraes (xvii–18), p. 193; Norman (xvii–19), p. 20.

23 *Golda Meir Speaks Out*, edited by Marie Syrkin (1973), p. 73.

24 Mann (xvii–21), p. 231.

25 Meir, Golda, *My Life* (1976 pbk), pp. 321, 329.

26 Herzog, Major-General Chaim, *The War of Atonement October 1973* (Boston 1975), p. 282.

27 Herzog (xvii–26), p. 282.

28 Mann (xvii–21).

29 Fraser, *Cromwell* (vi–22), p. 607.

30 Mrs Thatcher's acute anxiety not to be seen to encroach upon the Queen's

role has been confirmed to the author from a wide variety of sources.

31 *International Herald Tribune*, 5 November 1987.

32 *Observer*, 3 January 1988.

33 *Sunday Telegraph*, 27 July 1986; Young and Sloman (1–18), pp. 95, 52; Jardine (v–4), p. 233.

34 Cosgrave, Patrick, *Thatcher: The First Term* (1985), pp. 53, 57, 226 note 3; cartoon by Griffin, *Daily Express*, 24 June 1982.

35 Cosgrave (xvii–34), p. 226 note 3; Arnold, Bruce, *Margaret Thatcher: A Study in Power* (1984), p. 144.

36 Campbell, Beatrix, *The Iron Ladies: Why do Women Vote Tory?* (1987), p. 243.

37 Barnett, Anthony, *Iron Britannia: Why Parliament Waged its Falklands War* (1982 pbk), p. 19.

38 Barnett (xvii–37), p. 19; Cosgrave (xvii–34), pp. 209–10.

39 Wapshott and Brock (1–17), p. 251; Lord Lewin quoted in Young and Sloman (1–18), p. 119; author's conversation with John Keegan; *Sunday Telegraph*, 7 June 1987.

40 *Daily Mail*, 6 October 1987.

41 *Comus*, ll. 447–50, *The Poetical Works of John Milton*, edited by H. C. Beeching (new edn 1941), p. 60; Young and Sloman (1–18), p. 142.

42 Janet Watts quoting Julian Critchley, *Observer*, 24 April 1988; Cosgrave (xvii–34), p. 4.

43 Author's conversation with a former member of Mrs Thatcher's Cabinet.

44 Castle, Barbara, *The Castle Diaries 1974–76* (1980), pp. 518, 330; *The Times*, 27 January 1988; *Evening Standard Magazine*, 5 February 1988.

45 Cosgrave (xvii–34), p. 4; *Spare Rib*, August 1982.

46 Wapshott and Brock (1–17), illustration.

47 *The Times*, 12 June 1982.

48 Harris, Kenneth, 'Margaret Thatcher Talks to the *Observer*' (April 1979); *Daily Express*, 26 July 1982.

49 *New Statesman*, 28 May 1982; *Observer*, 23 May 1982; *Woman's Own* magazine, 15 June 1985.

CHAPTER EIGHTEEN: *Unbecoming in a Woman?*

1 Gildas (x–3), p. 301.

2 Camden (xiii–45), p. 117; Spenser (11–5), 1, p. 297.

3 *Bonduca* (vii–11), Act 1, scene i; Howard (xiv–13).

4 Thomson (xiv–17), pp. 375–6; Clark, J. E. D., *English Society 1688–1832: Ideology, Social Structure and Political Practice during the Ancien Régime* (Cambridge 1985), pp. 179–80.

5 Hall, Mrs Matthew, *The Queens Before the Conquest*, 2 vols (1854), Vol. 1, p. iv.

6 Doughty, Charles M., *The Dawn in Britain* (1943), pp. 9, 597, 346; Air Commodore Dame Felicity (Hanbury) Peake in conversation with the author, 1986.

7 Cit. Phillips, 'Woman Ruler' (xiii–22), p. 220.

8 Huston, Nancy, 'The Matrix of War: Mothers and Heroes' in *The Female Body*

in Western Culture: Contemporary Perspectives, edited by Susan Rubin Suleiman (1986), pp. 119–38.

9 Mossiker (xiv–9), p. 225; Fuller Ossoli, Margaret, *Women in the Nineteenth Century*, edited by Arthur B. Fuller (Boston 1874), p. 307.

10 Deutsch, Helene, MD, *The Psychology of Women: A Psychoanalytic Interpretation*, 2 vols (New York 1944), Vol. 1, Ch. 8, pp. 279–324; see Foley, Helene B., 'The conception of women in Athenian drama' in Foley (iii–5), p. 134.

11 Plutarch (iii–20), p. 280.

12 Grant (iii–11), p. 84.

13 Marshall, Catherine, Ogden, C. K. and Florence, Mary Sargent, *Militarism versus Feminism*, edited by Margaret Kamester and Jo Vellacott (1987 pbk reprint), pp. 40, 47, 96, 140.

14 Keegan, John, *The Mask of Command* (New York 1987), pp. 345–6, 351.

15 Segal, Lynne, *Is the Future Female? Troubled Thoughts on Contemporary Feminism* (1987 pbk), p. 198; Kelly, Petra, *Fighting for Hope* (1984), p. 104; Herodotus (iii–3), p. 123; Boccaccio (1–19), p. 104.

16 Fuller Ossoli (xviii–9), p. 307; Gloria Steinem quoted in Attallah, Naim, *Women* (1987), p. 543.

17 Dinnerstein, Dorothy, *The Rocking of the Cradle and the Ruling of the World* (1987 pbk), p. 124, 191, 28, 164, 177.

18 Prescott (xii–12), p. 240.

19 Février (viii–2), p. 36.

20 Tacitus (iii–1), p. 330.

21 Lebra-Chapman (xvi–7), p. 128; Strickland (x–15), p. 204.

22 *Anglo-Saxon Poetry* (x–8), p. 326; Abbott, 'Women' (viii–8), p. 262.

23 Gibbon (1–9), 1, p. 302; Breisach (1–21), p. 130.

INDEX

Abbott, Nabia, 110
Abeokuta, 238
Achilles, 20
Actium, Battle of, 30 BC, 40
Actresses' Franchise League, 300
Adad-nirari III, Assyrian King, 28
Adams, Simon, 211
Adela of Blois (daughter of William the Conqueror), 152, 156
Adeliza of Louvain, Queen of Henry 1 of England, 152
Aeneas, 20; *see also* Virgil
Aethelflaed (Ethelfleda), Lady of the Mercians, 154
Aethelred, Earlderman of Mercia, 154
Africa, 238–9; *see also* Jinga, Queen
Agnes, Empress, 134
Agrippa, Marcus, Governor of Jerusalem, 41
Agricola, 56, 62, 91, 93, 103; *see also* Tacitus
Ahenobarbus, 39
Aife (Irish woman warrior), 16
Ailill, King, 15–16
Aishah, wife of Muhammad the Prophet, 110

Albert, Prince Consort, 272–3, 298
Alexander, Roman Emperor, 110
Alexander II, Pope (*formerly* Anselm of Lucca), 137–9, 141, 145, 147–9
Alexander VI, Pope, 196–7, 200–1
Alexander I, Tsar of Russia, 259–61, 265–6, 268
Alexander Helios (son of Cleopatra), 38
Alexandria, Donations of, 38
Alexios Comnenos, Byzantine Emperor, 177
Alfonso (the Battler), King of Aragon, 160
Alfonso V, King of Portugal, 189, 191–2
Alfred, King of the West Saxons, 154
Allectus, 85
Allon, Yigel, 311
Al-Rahbani, Assi and Mansour, 127
Amazons: historical evidence for, 19–21; reputation, 21–3; in Spenser, 219; 'unnaturalness', 332

Ameinias, 33

Amina, Queen of Katsina, 238

Ammianus Marcellinus, 59

Anarchy, the (twelfth-century England), 152, 160, 162

Anchises, 41–2

Andate (Andarta, goddess), 71

Andraste (Andaste; goddess), 71, 86–7, 132, 228, 242

Andrew, Grand Prince of Suzdal, 174

Andronicus I, Byzantine Emperor, 178

Anglesey (Mona), 66–9, 77, 79

Anglo-Saxon Chronicle, 156, 163

Angola, 236, 239, 242, 245; *see also* Jinga, Queen

Annales Cambriae, 154

Anne, Queen of Great Britain, 24–5, 227

Anne Boleyn, Queen of Henry VIII, 206

Anselm of Lucca *see* Alexander II, Pope

Antioch: Synod of (268), 119; Zenobia and, 121–2

Antony, Mark, 37–40

Anu (goddess), 71

Apollo Sarpedonius, Seleucia (oracle), 121

Appendage Syndrome: in Warrior Queens, 12, 21, 32, 107, 332; Maud and, 155–6; Queen Elizabeth and, 21, 107, 212, 308, 332; and female political leaders, 307–8; and motherhood, 332–3

Aquino, Battle of, 1066, 139

Aquino, Mrs Corazon, 307

Arab–Israeli War, 1973, 312

Arago, 182, 184–6; *see also* Ferdinand, King of Aragon

Arc, Joan of, 8, 300–1, 309, 310

Ardabil, Emir of, 178

Arduino della Paluda, General, 135, 139

Aristotle, 22

Armed Saint *see* Holy Figurehead

Armida, 248

Arnold, Bruce, 316

Arnulf, Bishop of Lisieux, 166

Arsinoe (sister of Cleopatra), 34, 36

Artemisia, Queen Regent of Halicarnassus, 32–4, 205

Arthur, King of Britain, 3

Arthur, Prince of England, 202

Arundel, Henry Fitzalan, 12th Earl of, 218

Asander, King of Bosphorus, 40–1

Aske, James: *Elizabetha Triumphans*, 221–4

Aspurgus, 41

Asquith, Herbert Henry, 1st Earl of Oxford and Asquith, 300, 314

Astarte (Ishtar; goddess), 17, 29, 170

Atrebates (tribe), 95

Augusta, Dowager Princess, 235

Augustine, St, 170, 204

Augustus (Gaius Octavius), 38, 40, 87

Aulus Plautius, 45

Aurelian, Roman Emperor: war against Zenobia, 108, 120–4, 127; Triumph, 125; quells later Palmyrene rebellion, 126

Austerlitz, Battle of, 1805, 261

Austrian Succession, War of, 251

Avaricum (Bourges), 87

Aylmer, John: *An Harborowe for Faithfull and Trewe Subjectes against the late blown Blast*, 203, 205–6

Bachofen, J. S., 18

Bacon, Francis, 212

Badbh (Celtic figure), 15

Bagrat Bagrationi, King of Georgia, 172

Bagrationi dynasty, 168–9, 171, 174

Banda Nera, Giovanni della, 201

Bandaraneike, Sirimavo, 307, 311

Bandaraneike, Solomon W. R. D., 307

Barnett, Anthony: *Iron Britannia*, 316

Basiani, Battle of, 1205, 177–8

Baza (Spain), 194–5

Bazán, Alvaro, 188–9

Bazao-Turunku, 238

Beatrice, Margravine, Duchess of Lorraine, 133–5, 141, 143n

Beaumont, Francis and Fletcher, John: *Bonduca*, 99

Beauvoir, Simone de, 10

Becket, Thomas à, Archbishop of Canterbury, 165

Bede, Venerable, 153

Behn, Aphra, 231

Belgic peoples, 48

Bellona (goddess), 87

Beltrán de la Cueva, Don, 185

Ben-Gurion, David, 310

Bennigsen, General Levin August Gottlieb, Baron, 266

Berenice IV, Princess of Egypt, 34

Berg, Caroline von, 258

Bernáldez, Andrés, 183–4, 188, 190

Bernard of Clairvaux, Abbé, 23

Bernard, Archbishop of Toledo, 160

Bernard of Vallombrosa, 147–8

Bernardi, Giovambattista, 201

Berthier, Marshal Louis Alexandre, 262

Bertrand, Marshal Henri Gratien, 264

'Better-Man' Syndrome, 12, 115, 262, 308, 332

Bhopal, Hazrat Mahal, Begum of, 277

Bhutto, Benazir, 25

Blanche, Queen of France, 7

Boadbil (son of Mulay Hassan), 193–4

Boadicea (legendary figure): image and reputation, 3–6, 10–12, 61, 88, 169, 221, 231–2, 296, 299, 323–5, 335; name, 4–6, 218, 233n; as representative Warrior Queen, 13, 236–7; battle speech, 70, 332; burial, 100, 303; name vanishes from records, 153; and Elizabeth I, 203, 216, 221–2; represented in later literature, 216–17, 228–35, 238, 249, 273, 324–6; character of daughters, 217; pictured, 232; London statue, 272, 297–9, 335; Rani of Jhansi compared with, 273–4; and Women's Movement, 300–5, 325; and etymology of term 'bulldike', 302–3; and modern female political leaders, 305–6, 314, 316, 321–2; *for historical figure see* Boudica

Boccaccio, Giovanni, 11, 31, 116

Boëce, Hector, 217

Bolton, Edmund, 100, 231

Bonduca *see* Boadicea; Boudica

Boniface II, Margrave, 133–4, 155, 308

Borgia, Cesare, 62, 197, 200–1, 335

Bosphorus, kingdom of, 40–1

Botticelli, Sandro, 153

Boudica (historical figure): name, 4–6; date of rebellion, 5n, 56; and Celtic mother-goddesses, 17, 52, 69, 71–2, 87, 334; on victory or death, 27, 31; treatment by

Boudica—*cont.*
Romans, 43; life and career, 43–4, 55, 58–9; status as woman, 52, 55; regency, 55, 57; historical sources for life, 55–6; leads rebellion, 55, 63–4, 69, 77–8, 105–6, 323; daughters, 59; described, 59–60, 70, 96, 323; voice, 59–60, 314; flogged and daughters raped, 61–3, 333; addresses tribes, 70–1, 87; releases hare, 71–2, 121; and sack of Camulodunum, 72, 74, 76; vengeance and atrocities by, 88–9; destroys Verulamium, 90–2; size of army, 93; final battle and defeat, 94–6, 99; site of final battle, 94–5; death, 99, 101–2, 323; burial place, 100–1, 106, 231, 323; effect on Rome, 105–6; compared to Zenobia, 107–8; *for legendary figure see* Boadicea

Bowker, Lieutenant, 291–2
Bowra, Sir Maurice: *Inspiration and Poetry*, 179
Boxer, C. R., 240
Boxer Rebellion (China), 297
Bradstreet, Anne, 209, 228, 325
Breisach, Ernst, 198
Brigantes (tribes), 53–4, 58, 78
Brown Bull of Ulster (Donn Cuailnge), 16
Brown, George (*later* Lord George-Brown), 33
Brownmiller, Susan, 62
Bructeri (tribe), 72
Brünnhilde, 12, 141, 326
Bruno, Leonardo, 60, 315
Brunswick, Karl Wilhelm Ferdinand, Duke of, 264
Buchanan, George: *History of Scotland*, 210, 326

Buckingham, George Villiers, 1st Duke of, 223
Burke, Edmund, 248
Bush, George, 306
Butser Ancient Farm Project, Petersfield, Hampshire, 50–1
Byzantium, 177

Caesar, Julius: and Cleopatra, 36–7; on Iceni, 44; on Celts, 52, 71; on Druids, 68; on hare, 71; does not mention Londinium, 80; defeated by Vercingetorix, 83; and Caratacus, 101; executes Vercingetorix, 101
Caesarion (Cleopatra's son), 36
Calgacus, 62, 103
Callinicus Sutorius, 118
Calvin, John, 34, 204–6
Cambetch, Battle of, 1196, 177
Cambridge, George, 2nd Duke of, 274, 294
Camden, William: *Britannia*, 218, 220, 324
Camels, Battle of the, 656, 110
Camilla of the Volscians, 20–2, 116, 331
Camulodunum (Colchester): and Trinovantes, 44; as Roman *colonia* and site of temple, 64–6, 80; sacked by Iceni, 72–8, 85, 91, 96, 288
Canidius Crassus, 39–40
Canning, Charles John, Earl, 281–2, 294
Canning, Charlotte, Countess, 276–7, 282, 286
Canossa, 133–4, 141–4
Caratacus, 45, 53, 101; represented in later literature, 228–30
Carlyle, Jane Welsh, 251
Carlyle, Thomas, 251

Cartimandua, Queen of Brigantes, 53–5, 58, 83, 218, 234, 325

Cassivellaunus, 44

Castile: succession question, 182, 184–6; civil war in, 189–92; *see also* Isabella, Queen

Castle, Barbara, 319

Catherine of Aragon, Queen of Henry VIII, 187–8, 202

Catherine de Foix, 262

Catherine de' Medici, Queen of France, 204

Catherine II (the Great), Tsarina of Russia: Voltaire and, 10–11, 29, 255–6; love of peace, 236, 255; rule, 249–50, 255–6; licentiousness, 250, 335; character and style, 253–6, 331; as honorary male, 255; expansionist policy, 256; reputation, 271; in *Pageant of Great Women*, 301; patriotism, 333

Cato the Elder, 63

Catus Decianus, 61, 64, 73, 79, 102, 105

Catuvellauni (tribe), 91

Cawnpore, 287–8

Cecil, William, 1st Baron Burghley, 205

Celts: goddesses and Great Mothers, 13, 14–17, 71, 334; culture and customs, 19, 46–52, 170–1; physique and appearance, 47–8, 59; migrations, 48; women, 51, 55; religion, 51–2, 169; weapons, 97; and Georgians, 170–1; *see also* Iceni

Cethern (Celtic warrior), 16

Charlemagne, Emperor, 133

Charles V, Habsburg Emperor, 196

Charles VI, Emperor of Austria, 249

Charles X (Charles Gustavus), King of Sweden, 226–7

Chaste Syndrome: in Warrior Queens, 11–12, 168, 334; Zenobia and, 116; Matilda and, 131, 135; and Aethelflaed, 154

Chauhan, Subhadra Kumari, 296

Chicago, Judy, 301

Child, Mrs Lydia Maria: *An Appeal in Favor of that Class of Americans called Africans*, 244

Christina, Queen of Sweden, 226–7, 236

Christine de Pisan, 7

Churchill, Sir Winston S., 4

Cicero, 37

Cisneros, Francisco de *see* Ximenes, Cardinal

Claudius, Roman Emperor: in Britain, 45, 51, 53, 64, 84; temple and statues at Camulodunum (Colchester), 64–5, 75–6; clemency towards Caratacus, 101

Clayton, Ellen C., 290

Clement III, anti-Pope (Guibert of Ravenna), 145–7

Cleopatra V Tryphaena, 35

Cleopatra VI Tryphaena, 34

Cleopatra VII, Queen of Egypt: influence on Zenobia, 10, 109–10, 123, 125, 334; and Isis, 17, 37–8; and Appendage Syndrome, 21; treatment by Romans, 34, 40, 42, 62, 101; life and career, 34–40; in Spenser, 220; prophecies, 328; motherhood, 332

Cleopatra Selene, 38

Cleopatra Selene Cyrene, 38

Clerk, Sir John, 25, 227, 234

Cogidubnus, King of the Atrebates, 54, 83, 95

Colchester *see* Camulodunum

Colchis, 171

Columbus, Christopher, 182–3, 196

Colville, Sir John, 297n
Conrad II, Roman Emperor/
    German King, 133–4
Constantinople: falls (1453), 193
Corbulo, 67
Cordelia, Queen (Lear's daughter),
    160, 169
Coritani (tribe), 78
Cornovii (tribe), 78
Cosgrave, Patrick, 316
Cowper, William: 'Boadicea', 235,
    238, 246, 273, 297, 324
Craig, Edith, 300–1
Critchley, Julian, 318
Croesus the Lydian, 30
Cromwell, Oliver, 313
Crusades, 23–4, 172, 177
Cúchulainn (the Hound of Ulster),
    15–17, 97–8
Cyrus the Great, King of the Medes
    and Persians, 30–1, 330

Dahomey, 238
Dalhousie, James A. B. Ramsay, 1st
    Marquis of, 278–81, 294
Damodar Rao, 278–80, 285, 294–5,
    333
Dante Alighieri: *De Monarchia*, 137;
    Purgatorio, 149
Darnley, Henry Stewart, Earl of,
    207
Dashkova, Ekaterina Romanovna,
    Princess, 253
David II, the Restorer (or Builder),
    King of Georgia, 169, 172–3,
    178–9
David III, King of Georgia, 173
David Sosland, Consort of Queen
    Tamara, 175
Davout, Marshal (Duc d'Auer-
    stadt), 263
Dayan, Moshe, 311

Deborah (Biblical prophetess), 205,
    207, 212, 231
Dekker, Thomas, 214
Demna, King of Georgia, 173
Derby, Charlotte, Countess of, 231
Deutsch, Helene: *The Psychology of
    Women*, 327–8
Didgori, Battle of, 1121, 172
Dimitri, King of Georgia, 173
Dinitz, Simcha, 311
Dinner Party, The (exhibition), 301
Dinnerstein, Dorothy, 330
Dio Cassius: compares Boudica to
    Semiramis, 10; account of
    Boudica, 17, 55–6, 58–60, 71–2,
    300; on British rising, 61, 64, 69,
    78; on Boudica's speech, 70–1;
    on sack of Camulodunum, 76; on
    British atrocities, 86–9, 303; on
    sacking of cities, 93; and Sue-
    tonius' battle with rebels, 94, 96–
    7; and death of Boudica, 99–100;
    on Roman vengeance, 103; Poly-
    dore Vergil uses as source, 216;
    and burial of Boudica, 231
Diodorus Siculus, 19–20, 29, 59
'disarmed lady', 227
Disraeli, Benjamin, Earl of
    Beaconsfield, 228
Donizo: *Vita Comitissae Mathildis*,
    136–7, 142–3, 148
Doughty, Charles: *The Dawn in
    Britain*, 325–6
Drake, Sir Francis, 221
Drogheda: Cromwellian massacre,
    86
Druids, 52, 66–9, 100, 233
Dryden, John, 232
Dudley, Donald R. and Webster,
    Graham: *The Rebellion of Boudicca*,
    73
Duleep Singh, Prince, 282

Dunbar, Agnes, 300

Duncan, Captain (of Life Guards), 238

Durga (Hindu goddess), 276, 289, 309–10

Dynamis of Bosphorus, 40–2, 54

Edward the Confessor, King of the English, 156

Edward VI, King of England, 165, 206

Edward VII, King of Great Britain, 159, 173

Eleanor of Aquitaine, Queen of Louis VII of France, then of Henry II of England, 23–4

Elisabeth, Tsarina of Russia, 253

Elizabeth I, Queen of England: Ubaldini dedicates book to, 5, 218; and Golden Age, 9; in historical comparisons, 10, 54; daughterhood, 21, 107, 212–13, 308, 332; education and languages, 135, 187, 218; and succession, 165, 206, 208; attitude to war, 176, 210–12, 236, 255; dress, 188, 223, 318; appearance, 200; meets hostility to accession as woman, 203–6, 208–9; rivalry with Mary Queen of Scots, 205; as honorary male, 209; resists marriage, 207, 209; status as woman, 209–10, 212–14, 255; finances, 211–12; emphasises descent from Henry VIII, 212–13; presence and speech at Tilbury, 213, 220–4, 227, 249, 252, 318; self-presentation and image, 213–15, 220–1, 250; hunting, 215; in Spenser's *The Faerie Queene*, 220; and feminism, 302; authority, 331

Elizabeth II, Queen of Great Britain, 8, 173n, 313

Elizabeth of York, Queen of Henry VII, 206

Elliott, J. H., 192

Ellis, Major (Political Agent, Jhansi), 278, 280–1, 287

Emesa (now Homs), Battle of, AD 261, 113, 122–3

Encina, Juan del, 182

Enghien, Louis Antony Henry, Duc d', 259

Enobarbus *see* Ahenobarbus

Erskine, Major W. C., 285, 287

Erzerum, Sultan of, 175

Eshkol, Levi, 311

Essex, Robert Devereux, 2nd Earl of, 212, 214

Esther (biblical figure), 212

Euboea, Battle of, 487 BC, 32

Eustace (son of Stephen of Blois), 159

Fairthorne, W., 232

Falklands War, 1982, 4, 7, 11, 315–17, 320–1, 328–9

Fallaci, Oriana, 308, 320

Fanti people, 238

Faydide of Toulouse, 23

Female Body in Western Culture, The (symposium), 327

Feminist Review, 209

feminists, feminism: on non-aggressive matriarchies, 7; and Boadicea legend, 299–300, 302–5, 325; exhibitions and pageants, 300–2; Mrs Thatcher disdains, 319–20; on war and peace, 328–30

Feo, Giacomo, 199

Ferdinand, King of Aragon: and Columbus, 182–3; and Isabella,

Ferdinand—*cont.*
182–3, 185–6, 194; and throne of Castile, 185–6; infidelities, 188; and civil war in Castile, 189–90, 192; succeeds to throne of Aragon, 192; and Reconquista, 193, 195–6; overseas ambitions and claims, 196–7, 200, 202; and death of Isabella, 202
Fergus (Irish warrior), 16
Feria, Gomez de Figueroa, duque de, 207
Ferraro, Geraldine, 8, 305–7, 315; *My Story*, 306
Février, J. G., 119
Finnbenach (bull), 15
Fionni, Simone, 199
Flavius Vopiscus, 114
Fletcher, John: *Bonduca*, 229, 242, 324
Florence, Mary Sargent, Marshall, Catherine E. and Ogden, C. K.: *Militarism versus Feminism*, 328
Florine of Bourgogne, 23
Foix, Catherine de *see* Catherine de Foix
Forlì, 199–201
Forrest, George W.: *A History of the Indian Mutiny*, 291
Fox, Sir Cyril, 49, 69
Francis of Lorraine, Holy Roman Emperor, 250
Franco–Prussian War, 1870–1, 273
Frederick II (the Great), King of Prussia, 251, 259
Frederick William III, King of Prussia, 257–62, 264–7, 269
Frederick, Prince of Wales, 324
Frere, Sheppard, 91
Freud, Sigmund, 327
Friedland, Battle of, 1807, 266
Fuentes, Nicholas, 95

Fuller, Captain, 6, 241–2
Fuller, Margaret: *The Great Lawsuit*, 327, 330
Fulvia (wife of Mark Antony), 39, 328

Gale (cartoonist), 322
Gale, George, 320–1
Gale, Roger, 234
Gale, Samuel, 234
Gallienus, Roman Emperor, 113–14, 117, 123
Galtieri, General Leopoldo Fortunato, 320
Gandhi, Indira: as honorary man, 7, 33, 308–9; daughterhood, 107, 308; as Durga, 276; as Prime Minister, 307–10, 314; upbringing, 308–9, 331
Gandhi, Rajiv, 309
Gangadhar Rao, Rajah of Jhansi, 274–5, 278, 280
Gaulle, Charles de: *The Edge of the Sword*, 9–10, 305
Gauls, 83; *see also* Celts; Iceni
Genghis Khan, 181
Gentz, Frederick von, 263–4
Geoffrey, Count of Anjou, 157–8, 163–4, 166
Geoffrey of Monmouth, 80, 85, 153, 169; *Historia Regum Britanniae*, 160
George II, King of Great Britain (*formerly* Prince of Hanover), 25, 227
George, Prince of Denmark, Consort of Queen Anne, 24
George Bogolyubski, Prince Consort of Queen Tamara, 174–5
Georgia: folk memories, 168–70; geographical position, 169–70;

culture and society, 169; historical development, 170–3, 177–8; *see also* Tamara, Queen of Georgia

Gérard de Nerval, 68

Gergovia, Battle of, 52 BC, 83

Gibbon, Edward: on women rulers, 8–9, 249, 321; on Zenobia, 60, 116, 126, 150, 334; on Druids, 68; on captives, 101; on Mamaea, 110; *Decline and Fall of the Roman Empire*, 249

Gibo, Francescolotto, 200

Gildas, monk, 153, 218, 324

Giorgi II, King of Georgia, 173

Giorgi III, King of Georgia, 169, 173–5, 308

Giorgi IV, King of Georgia (*formerly* Prince; son of Tamara), 175, 178, 181

Gladstone, William Ewart, 273

Gleichen, Lord Edward, 299

Gluck, Christoph Willibald von: *Armide*, 248, 256, 261

Godfrey, Duke of Upper Lorraine, 134, 138–9

Godfrey the Hunchback (first husband of Matilda), 135, 137, 139–41

Godse, Vishnu, 291

Goethe, J.W. von, 258; *Wilhelm Meister*, 266

Goodman, Bishop, 220

Gordon, Captain (at Jhansi), 282–3

Grahn, Judy, 302–3, 306; 'She Who', 304

Granada, 190, 193, 195

Great Mother (Celtic), 13, 14–17, 71, 334

Greenham Common, 329

Gregory VII, Pope: relations with Matilda, 131–3, 140–1, 145;

struggle with Emperor Henry IV, 132, 137, 141–5; consecrated Pope, 139; prohibits lay investiture, 140; abducted, 140; death in exile, 145

Gregory, Augusta, Lady, 15

Gueso, King, 238

Guiscard, Robert, 145

Gurbash Singh, Sergeant, 282

Gustavus Adolphus, King of Sweden, 226

Gwalior, 293

Hadrian, Roman Emperor, 111

Hague Women's Peace Conference, 1915, 328

Hailsham of St Marylebone, Quintin Hogg, Baron, 314

Hairan (Herodianus; Odainat's father), 113

Hairan (heir of Odainat), 116–17

Hall, Mrs Matthew: *The Queens Before the Conquest*, 325

Hamilton, Cicely, 300

Hamilton, Emma, Lady, 265

Hamilton, Sir Robert, 287

Hannah (Prophetess), 231

Hardenberg, Carl August von, 259, 262, 266, 269

Hardy, Thomas: *The Dynasts*, 263

Harrington, Sir John, 214

Harris, Robert, 314

Hastings, Lady Selina, 317

Hatzfeld, Prince, 265

Healey, Denis, 11

Heath, Nicholas, Archbishop of York, 208

Heisch, Allison, 209

Henri III, King of France, 22

Henry IV, King of Castile, 185, 187

Henry I, King of England, 151–2, 155–8, 169, 173

Henry II, King of England ('Henry FitzEmpress'), 23–4, 157, 158, 160, 164–5, 191

Henry VII, King of England, 206

Henry VIII, King of England: and Elizabeth, 21; and succession, 165, 206n, 207, 212; marriage to Catherine of Aragon, 202; builds Tilbury fort, 221

Henry III, Holy Roman Emperor, 133–4, 140

Henry IV, Holy Roman Emperor: struggle with Pope Gregory VII, 132, 137–8; conflicts with Matilda, 134, 145–6; barefoot penitence at Canossa, 141–4; crowned at Rome, 145; death, 147; abdication, 151

Henry V, Holy Roman Emperor, 147–8, 151–2

Henry of Blois, Bishop of Winchester, 161

Hercules, 20

Hereti, Battle of, 1174, 173

Herodotus, 19, 28, 30–1, 32–3

Hertford, Frances Thynne, Countess of (*later* Duchess of Somerset), 234–5

Herzog, Dr Chaim (later President of Israel), 312

Heywood, Thomas: *Exemplary Lives*, 231; *Gynaekeion*, 22, 34

Hilda, St, Abbess of Whitby, 231

Hillgarth, J. N., 184n

Hind Al-Hunūd, Queen, 110

Hippolyta, Queen, 19–21

Hobbes, Thomas, 232

Holinshed, Ralph, 70, 217

Holofernes, 9, 154, 334

Holy (Armed) Figurehead: Warrior Queens as, 12, 72, 87, 111, 177, 334; Matilda as, 132; Maud as,

155; Isabella as, 189; Jinga as, 241; Louise as, 248, 271; Elizabeth II as, 313

Holy League, 197

Holy Roman Empire: ended, 262

Homer, 20

Hondo, Med, 238

Honorius II, anti-Pope (Caladus of Parma), 138–9

Hood, Thomas, 84

Horace, 39, 40

Horsley, John: *Britannia Romana*, 233n

Howard, the Hon. Edward, 232–3

Hugh, Abbot of Cluny, 143

Huldah (biblical figure), 205

Hunsdon, Henry Carey, 1st Baron, 211

Huntingdon, Henry Hastings, 3rd Earl of, 208

Huston, Nancy, 327

Iceni (tribe): nature and society, 43–6, 49–50; Romans and, 44–5, 52; rebellion, 45–6, 56–7, 63–4, 66, 69, 78, 87–8, 91; coins, 49; torcs, 49–50; houses, 50–1; plundered and punished, 61–4; famine, 102; repressed, 103; *see also* Boudica; Celts

Imola, 201

Indian Rebellion (or Mutiny), 1857, 282, 287–9

Ipswich hoard, 50

Iraq–Iran War: girls in, 18

Ireland: Warrior Queen in, 59

Irnerius, 147

Isabella, Queen of Castile: and Golden Age, 9; as Armed Figurehead, 12, 334; and Columbus, 182; and Ferdinand, 182–3, 186,

193–4; piety, 182–4, 187, 191, 193; expels Jews, 183; and Reconquista, 183–5, 190, 192–6; and Castile succession, 185–6; crowned, 185; education and training, 186–7; character and virtue, 186–8, 280; appearance and dress, 188, 194; in literature, 188–9; part in civil war, 189–91; and Shame Syndrome, 190, 331; pregnancy and birth of son, 191–2, 310; and Caterina Sforza, 196; dislike of bloodshed, 199; death and will, 202; authority, 331; austerity, 335
Isis (goddess), 17, 27, 37, 109, 304
Israel: women soldiers in, 18

Jackson, Sir George, 257, 259, 269
Jackson, J. G., 298
James I of England, VI of Scotland, King, 208
Jean d'Albret, 262
Jena, Battle of, 1806, 249, 263
Jerusalem: destroyed by Titus, 109
Jews: Zenobia and, 109, 118; in Palmyra, 112; Queen Isabella expels, 183–4
Jhansi (state): British policy on, 278–82; mutiny in, 282–3; massacre of Europeans in, 283–4, 287–8; British attack, 289–91; British retribution in, 291–2
Jhansi, Lakshmi Bai, Rani of: voice, 60, 286; widowhood, 107–8; seen as goddess of war, 236–8, 275–6, 278; reputation, 273–4, 277, 295; life, 275–6; wedding, 278; argues for regency, 280–2; and massacre of Europeans, 283–5, 287–9; rule, 285–7; appearance and dress, 286; riding, 286; in defence

of Jhansi, 289–91; accused of licentiousness, 290–1, 335; escapes to Kalpi, 291–3; killed in defence of Gwalior, 293–4; bravery, 295; tributes to and commemorations, 294–6; in *Pageant of Great Women*, 300; and adopted son, 333
Jinga, Queen of Angola (Jinga, Nzinga, Singa or Zhinga Mbandi): Fuller describes, 6, 241; and country's cause, 226; life and career, 236–46; legends about, 244–5, 268, 270; and slavery, 245; as goddess, 334
John II, King of Castile, 185
John, Prince of Castile (son of Isabella), 191–2; death, 201
John, King of England, 175
John, Hermit, 147
Johnson, Maurice, 234
Johnson, Paul, 317
Johnson, Samuel, 60
Jones, Ernest, 277
Jones, Inigo, 100
Jonson, Ben: *The Masque of Queenes*, 4, 116, 218
Josephine, Empress of France, 247, 259, 267
Joshi, P. C.: *Folk Songs of '1857'*, 295
Juana, Princess of Castile (Isabella's daughter), 201
Juana 'la Beltraneja', 185–7, 189, 192
Judith (biblical figure): as Warrior Queen, 9–10, 212, 334; portrayed, 153–4, 169; later reputation, 231
Judith (Old English poem), 154
Julia Domna, Empress of Septimius Severus, 110
Julia Maesa, 110

Julia Pacuta, 61
Julius Civilis, 77–8
Julius Classicianus, 61, 102

Kala Khan, Risaldar, 283
·Kalb, Marvin, 306
Kali (Hindu goddess), 276, 309, 317
Kalkreuth, General Friedrich Adolf, Count von, 264, 266, 269
Kalpi (India), 291–3
Kartli, 170–2; *see also* Georgia
Kashi (attendant to Rani of Jhansi), 294
Kaufman, Gerald, 314–15
Kaye, Sir John: *History of the Sepoy War in India*, 279, 281, 290
Keegan, John: *The Mask of Command*, 329
Kelly, Joan, 7, 227
Kelly, Laurence, 167
Kelly, Petra: *Fighting for Hope*, 330
Khevenmüller, General J. J., 251, 333
King, Betty: *Boadicea*, 13
Kleist, Heinrich von, 258, 269; *Penthesilea*, 258, 305
Kleist, Marie von, 258
Knight, Frances, 230
Knox, John, 22, 34; *The First Blast of the Trumpet against the monstrous regiment of Women*, 203–6, 212, 230

Lady of Victory, 12; *see also* Holy Figurehead
Lakwena, Alice, 239
Lambarde, William: *Pandecta*, 212
Lang, John, 281, 286
Lara, Count of, 160
Laver, P. G., 66
Lear, King, 160, 169
Legions (Roman): Augusta, IInd,

92–3; Hispana, IXth, 78–9; XIVth, 93, 95; XXth, 93
Leicester, Robert Dudley, Earl of, 208, 211, 214, 220–5
Lermontov, Mikhail: *The Demon*, 167–8, 170
Leveson-Gower, Lord Granville (*later* 1st Earl Granville), 265
Lilburne, John, 231
Livingstone, David, 238
Livy, 52, 63
Londinium: as Roman town, 79–82; Suetonius abandons, 82–3; sacked and burned, 83–6, 89, 91, 96
Longinus, Cassius, 118, 124, 127
Longinus Sdapezematygus, 75
Louis VII, King of France, 23
Louis XII, King of France, 200
Louis XIV, King of France, 24, 176, 229, 251
Louis Ferdinand, Prince of Prussia, 262
Louise, Queen of Prussia: as Warrior Queen, 22, 247–8, 259–60, 264; marriage and children, 191, 257–8, 269; and Napoleon, 247–9, 256, 259–63, 265–6; character and appearance, 256–8, 260, 268–9; and Tsar Alexander I, 259–60, 265; in alliance against France, 261; and French conquests, 261–2; flight and illness, 263–4; presence at battle, 264; meets Napoleon at Tilsit, 267–9; death, 269–70; as national heroine, 270
Low, Major-General Sir John, 277, 279
Lowe, Dr Thomas, 288–92
Lucca, 145, 147
Lucknow, 277, 287

Mabinogion, The, 14–15

Macaulay, Thomas Babington, 1st Baron, 89, 112, 251

Macha (Celtic figure), 15

Maeonius, 116

Maeve *see* Medb

Málaga, 194

Malatesta, Battista, 60, 315

Malcolm Canmore, King of Scotland, 156

Malcolm, Major (Political Agent, Gwalior), 278, 280–1

Malleson, George Bruce, 295

Malmesbury, William of, 154, 157–8, 164

Mamaea, 110

Mamani, Aboulaye, 238

Mamville of Roucy, 23

Mandar (attendant to Rani of Jhansi), 294

Mantua, 147

Manzikert, Battle of, 1071, 172

Mao Tse-tung, 105

Marcos, Ferdinand, 308

Marcus Favonius Facilis, 75

Mardonius (Persian General), 33

Margaret, St, Queen of Scotland, 156

Margaret of Anjou, Queen of Henry VI, 215, 219

Margaret of Flanders, 206

Maria, Queen of Portugal, 202

Maria Theresa, Empress of Austria: love of peace, 236; rule, 249–52, 331; dress and appearance, 252–3; reputation, 271; and motherhood, 333

Mariam Artsruni, Queen Dowager of Georgia, 172

Marie Antoinette, Queen of France, 248

Marlborough, John Churchill, 1st Duke of, 227

Mars Ultor (god), 87

Marsden, Peter, 85

Marshall, Catherine E., 328–9

Martha, Empress of Septimius Severus *see* Julia Domna

Martin, T. A., 285

Mary I (Tudor), Queen of England, 188, 204, 206–7

Mary II, Queen of England, Scotland and Ireland, 24

Mary, Queen of Scots: career, 36, 152; and Boadicea, 54; and succession to throne of England, 165, 208; Knox on, 204; rivalry with Elizabeth, 205; and Darnley, 207; eschews war, 212; in Spenser, 220

Mary of Guise, Regent of Scotland, 204

Mary of Scotland, 156

Matilda, Countess of Tuscany (or of Canossa): chastity and sex, 11, 131, 135–7, 154, 334; tombstone reference to as Amazon, 25–6, 148, 166; voice, 60; supports Gregory VII and papal cause, 131–3, 137–8, 140–2; character and background, 131; and inheritance, 133–5, 308; Tomboy Syndrome, 135; upbringing, 135; marriages, 135–7, 141, 146; battles, 138–9; piety, 140, 154, 196; and Henry IV at Canossa, 142–4; Henry IV punishes, 145; financial losses, 145; Sorbara victory, 146, 149; effect of struggles, 147; Henry V and, 147; death and burial, 148; wills, 148; tributes to, 149–50; legitimacy of succession, 155

Matilda of England, daughter of Henry I *see* Maud, Empress

Matilda of Boulogne, Queen of Stephen of Blois: marriage, 158; character and activities, 158–9; and capture of Stephen, 161, 163; supports Stephen's cause, 163; praised by Agnes Strickland, 333

Matilda of Ramsbury, 159

Matildine Gospels, 148

matriarchy, 17–19

Mau Mau rebellion, Kenya, 73

Maud (Matilda of England, daughter of Henry I), Empress: struggle with Stephen for English crown, 134, 152, 158, 161, 196, 205; marriage to Emperor Henry V, 151; character, 152, 155, 165–6; and succession question, 155–8, 169; marriage to Geoffrey of Anjou and sons by, 157–8, 191; crowned and made *Domina Anglorum*, 161; Londoners rise against, 162; accused of arrogance and harshness, 162–3; pursuit and escapes, 163–4; and accession of son (Henry II), 164–5; activities as Dowager Queen, 165; death, 166; Ubaldini on, 218

Mawia, Syrian Queen, 110

Medb (Maeve), Irish Queen, 15–17, 97–8

Medea (mythical figure), 171

Medici, Giovanni de', 201

Meir, Golda, 7, 309–12, 320; *My Life*, 311

Melville, Sir James, 210

Mendes de Vasconcelos, João, 239

Mendoza, Fray Inigo de, 189

Metternich, Clemens, Prince, 266

Miguel, Prince (son of Queen Maria), 202

Milton, John, 303; *Comus*, 187, 318; *History of Britain*, 54, 70

Mithraic religion, 51

Mommsen, Theodor, 126, 150

Mona *see* Anglesey

Monmouth, Geoffrey of *see* Geoffrey of Monmouth

Montmorency, Anne, Duc de, 214

Montoro (poet), 189

Moors: Isabella drives from Spain, 183–4, 192–3

Moraes, Dom, 310

Morant, Philip, 222

More, Sir Thomas, 216

Morrigan, the (Celtic figures), 15

mother-right *see* matriarchy

motherhood, 330, 332

Mountbatten of Burma, Admiral of the Fleet Louis, 1st Earl, 318

Mpororo people, 238

Muhammad the Prophet, 8, 204

Mukumbu (Jinga's sister), 243

Mulay Hassan, Nasrid King, 193

Munius Lupercus, 72

Murat, Marshal Joachim, King of Naples, 260

Mutlow, Mrs (of Jhansi), 283–4

Naidu, Sarojini, 309

Nana, Queen of Kartli, 170

Nana Sahib (Dhondu Pant), 275, 287–8, 291, 295

Napoleon I (Bonaparte), Emperor of the French: and Queen Louise of Prussia, 22, 247–8, 256, 259–66; on women in battle, 40, 247; assumes title of Emperor, 259; conquests, 261, 263–5; meets Louise at Tilsit, 267–9; Elba exile, 270

Nanny, wife of Old Cudjoe, chief of Maroons, 12

Ndongo (central West Africa), 239–40, 243–4
Neale, Sir John, 207
Nehru, Jawaharlal (Pandit), 308
Neill, Brigadier-General James George Smith, 288
Nelson, Vice-Admiral Horatio, Viscount, 265
Nelson, Thomas: *The History of Islington*, 94
Nemain (Celtic figure), 15
Nennius, 153
Nero, Roman Emperor, 101
New Statesman (journal), 321
Ngola Ari, 243
Nicetas, 23
Nicholas II, Pope, 138
Nicomachus, 124
Nino, St, 170–1
Ninus, King of Assyria, 28
Ninyas (son of Semiramis), 29
noble savage, 230
Norfolk, Emma, Countess of, 159
Norman, Dorothy, 308–9
Nzinga, Queen of Angola *see* Jinga

Octavia (wife of Mark Antony), 38–9
Octavius, Gaius *see* Augustus
Odainat (Septimius Odenaethus; husband of Zenobia), 113–15, 118–19, 124; death, 116–17; chariot, 125
Ogden, C. K., 328
Oliveira Cadornego, Antonio, 242
O'Malley, Grace, 214–15
Only-a-Weak-Woman Syndrome, 12, 127, 190, 198, 213, 332
Onslow, Richard William Alan Onslow, 5th Earl of, 165
Ordelaffi, Mario, 199
Orlov, Grigory, 253–4

Ornytus, 21
Orsi family, 198–9
Orsi, Andrea, 199
Ostorius Scapula, 45, 56
Oudenarde, Battle of, 1708, 227
Oudh: annexed, 279

Pageant of Great Women, 1909, 300–1
Pain, Nesta, 165
Palgrave, William, 111
Palmyra, 108–9, 111–14, 119–24, 126; *see also* Zenobia, Queen
Paul, St, 204
Paul of Samosata, Bishop of Antioch, 119
Pembroke, Henry Herbert, 2nd Earl of, 222
Penthesilea: as Warrior Queen, 10; leads Amazons, 19–20; Eleanor of Aquitaine imitates, 23; invoked for Matilda of Tuscany, 25–6, 148–9; Matilda compared with, 132; Begum of Oudh compared with, 277
Peredur (Welsh hero), 15
Peter III, Tsar of Russia (*formerly* Grand Duke), 250, 253
Peter Martyr of Anghiera, 202
Petilius Cerialis, 78–9, 82, 105, 217
Philip I, King of France, 145
Philip the Fair of Flanders, 202
Philip II, King of Spain, 207
Philippi, Battle of, 42 BC, 87
Phung Thi Chinh, 237
Piers of Langtoft, 157–8
Plutarch, 328
Pocahontas, 230–1, 240, 327
Poenius Postumus, 93, 104
Pole, Reginald, Cardinal, 207
Polemo, King of Pontus, 41

Polirone monastery, near Mantua, 147–8
Polish partition, 1772, 252
Polyclitus, 102
Polydore Vergil *see* Vergil, Polydore
Poniatowski, Stanislaus, 254
Potemkin, Grigory, 254–5
Powell, Enoch, 316
Pragmatic Sanction, 1713, 249
Prasutagus, King of the Iceni, 51, 55, 57–9, 61, 328
Prescott, W. H., 187, 193–4
Primrose, Lady Diana, 213
Probus, General, 120
Proops, Marjorie, 316
Propertius, 28, 40
Ptolemy XII Auletes, Pharaoh, 34–5
Ptolemy XIII, 35–6
Ptolemy XIV, 35–6
Ptolemy XV Caesar (Cleopatra's son), 36, 38
Ptolemy Philadelphus (Cleopatra's son), 38
Publius Petronius Turpillanus, 102
Purcell, Henry, 229–30, 232, 303

Radziwill, Princess Anton (Princess Louise of Prussia), 264, 270
Raju, R. Sundara *see* Sundara Raju, R.
Ramachandra Rao, Maharajah, 274, 278
Ramírez, Don Francisco (El Artillero), 190
Rangerius, 137, 145
Rao Sahib (Pandurang Rao), 291–2
Raphael, Adam, 321
Reagan, Ronald, 316
Reconquista (Spain), 183–5, 190–1, 192–4

Reynolds, Robert: *Boadicea: A Tragedy of War*, 304
Rhiannon (Welsh goddess), 14–15
Rhine, Confederation of the, 262
Riario, Girolamo, 197–8
Richard III, King of England, 173
Richardson, Mrs Charles, 270
Richmond, I. A., 54
Rigantona, 'Queen of the Demons' (Celtic), 15
Robert Curthose, 155
Robert, Earl of Gloucester, 163–4
Roberts, Field-Marshal Frederick Sleigh, 1st Earl, 288
Rochester, John Wilmot, 2nd Earl of, 232
Roger, Bishop of Salisbury, 159
Rolfe, John, 230–1
Rose, Sir Hugh, 274, 289–92, 294–6
Rossini, Gioacchino Antonio: *Semiramide*, 29
Rudolf of Swabia, King of Germany, 145
Rum, Sultan of, 177
Ruskin, John, 153–4
Russell, William Howard, 277
Rustaveli, Shota: *The Knight in Panther's Skin*, 169, 179–81
Rusudani, Princess (Tamara's aunt), 174–5
Rusudani, Princess (Tamara's daughter), 175, 181
Rutland, Edward Manners, 3rd Earl of, 214

Sá, Salvador de, 243
Salamis, Battle of, 480 BC, 31–3
Salic Law, 185–6
Sammes, Aylett: *Britannia Antiqua Illustrata*, 231
Samsi, Queen, 110

Samtzkhe, 176
Santon hoard (Norfolk), 49
Sapor I, King of Persia, 113
Sargis Mkhargrdzeli, 175
Sarmatia, 18
Sarraounia (film), 238
Sassanids, 112–13
Satara (Indian state), 279
Savage, Richard, 234
Savile, Sir Henry, 216
Scathach (Irish woman warrior), 16
Schiller, J. C. Friedrich von, 132, 258, 269
Scribonius, 40–1
Scriptores Historiae Augustae, 114, 118
Segal, Lynne: *Is the Future Female?*, 7, 330
Ségur, Louis Philippe, Comte de, 254
Seljuk Turks, 172
Sen, Surendra Nath: *1857*, 284
Semiramis: as Warrior Queen, 10–11; identified with Astarte, 17; historical origins and later writings on, 28, 220; sexual voracity, 28–9, 335; Zenobia and, 109
Septimius Severus, Roman Emperor, 110–11
Seven Years' War, 1756–63, 255
sexual licence *see* Voracity Syndrome
Sforza, Caterina: abused by Cesare Borgia, 62, 201; and Isabella, 183, 196–7; licentiousness, 197, 199–200, 334–5; background and life, 197–8; cruelty, 199; appearance, 200; fighting and campaigning, 200–1; death, 201; pose as 'Only-a-Weak-Woman', 332
Sforza, Galeazza Maria, Duke of Milan, 197–8

Sforza, Ludovico, 196, 198, 201
Shakespeare, William: on Cleopatra, 40, 101; uses Holinshed, 217; *Henry VI*, 215; *Titus Andronicus*, 178
Shame Syndrome: and Warrior Queens, 12, 331; Boudica and, 27; Cyrus the Great and, 30–1; Xerxes and, 33; and Zenobia, 108, 115; Aurelian and, 124; Isabella exploits, 190; Queen Victoria and, 228
Shamsi-Adad V, Assyrian King, 28
Sharp, Leonel, 223
Shastri, Lal Bahadour, 308
Sheba, Queen of, 110, 149
Shenstone, William, 234
Sheridan, Richard Brinsley, 267
Sidney, Sir Henry, 215
Silures (Welsh tribe), 53
Sixtus IV, Pope, 197
Sixtus V, Pope, 208
Skene, Captain Alexander, 282–3, 285
Sleeman, Sir William, 274
Smith, John, 230
Snettisham Treasure, 49–50
Society of Antiquaries, London, 233–4
Society of Roman Knights, 233
Solomon, King of Israel, 109–10
Soraya, Sultana, 194
Sorbara, Battle of, 1084, 139n, 146, 149
Sousa, Correira de, 240, 245
Spanish Armada, 220–1
Spare Rib (magazine), 319, 328
Spargapises (son of Tomyris), 31
Spence, Lewis: *Boadicea*, 94
Spenser, Edmund: *The Faerie Queene*, 18–19, 218–20, 229, 241, 324, 328

Staël, Germaine, Baronne de, 257, 269
Stanley, Sir Henry Morton, 238
Steel, David, 315
Steinem, Gloria, 330
Stephen ix, Pope, 138
Stephen (of Blois), King of England: struggle with Maud for English crown, 134, 152, 156, 158, 161–4, 205; coronation, 161–2; character, 158, 162; captured and imprisoned, 161; freed, 163; death, 164
Stonehenge, 100, 231, 303
Strabo: *Geographica*, 47–8, 106, 171
Strickland, Agnes: *Lives of the Queens of England*, 159, 164, 333
Strong, Sir Roy, 213
Stukeley, Frances, 234
Stukeley, William, 233–5
Suetonius Paulinus: and Iceni revolt, 66; on Mona (Anglesey), 66–7, 69; dash for Londinium, 79, 82; abandons Londinium, 82, 90; and Verulamium, 90; Boudica fails to surprise, 92; gathers reinforcements, 92–4; battle and defeat of Boudica, 94–7, 105–6, 122, 326; vengeance against Britons, 102
Sulla, 35
Sundara Raju, R., 309
Sutri, Council of, 1059, 138
Swift, Jonathan, 24, 227
Sybille, Countess of Flanders, 23
Sylvester, J. Henry, 294
Syme, Sir Ronald, 55, 70

Tacitus: on Boudica, 4, 55–6, 58–9, 70, 132, 159, 169, 332; on Germans, 10; on Iceni, 45; on Celts, 47; on Caratacus, 53; on Cartimandua, 54; on female rule, 55, 63; on abuse of Boudica and daughters, 62–3; on Iceni rebellion, 61, 63, 77; on Camulodunum, 65–6, 72–3, 208; on Mona, 67, 69; on women in German tribes, 71; on escape of Petilius, 78; on Suetonius, 79, 82; on Londinium, 81–3, 86; on Roman revenge, 87; on British atrocities and massacres, 87–8; on Verulamium, 90–2; on Suetonius' final defeat of Boudica, 93–6, 102; on British casualties, 99; on death of Boudica, 99, 101; on Julius Classicianus, 102; English translations, 216–17; as source for later writers, 218, 232; *Agricola*, 55–6, 58, 86, 102; *Annals*, 55–6, 86, 102
Talietzin, Captain (*later* Admiral) Ivan, 253
Tain, The (Celtic cycle), 15–16
Talleyrand, Charles Maurice, 266
Tamara (Thamar), Queen of Georgia: and Golden Age, 9; daughterhood, 107; reign, 167, 175, 331; legends and literature on, 167–8, 178–80; succeeds to throne, 167, 173–4, 308; and Voracity Syndrome, 167–8; character, 168; titles, 174; marriage and children, 174–5; hunting, 174; and revolts, 175–6; campaigns and conquests, 176–7; death, 181; and Catherine the Great, 254; austerity, 335
Tambe, Moropant, 275
Tanit (goddess), 110
Tasso, Torquato: *Jerusalem Delivered*, 149, 248, 256

Tatya Tope (pseud.), 287, 289, 291, 293–4

Taylor, Lieutenant (of Jhansi), 283

Telemachus, 288

Tennyson, Alfred, 1st Baron; *Boädicea*, 273, 289, 326

Teresa, Queen of Portugal, 160

Terry, Ellen, 300

Tertullian, 204

Tetricus, Gallic Emperor, 123n

Thatcher, Margaret: as Boadicea, 4, 321–2; and Falklands War, 4, 7, 11, 315–17, 320–1, 328–9; as honorary man, 7, 33, 209, 318; voice, 60, 314–15; denies debt to Women's Movement, 209; and Russian threat, 306, 315; premiership, 313–14, 318–19; as 'iron lady', 315–16; femininity, 317–21; disdains Women's Liberation, 319; antagonism to, 330; supposed 'bossiness', 331

Theodoric the Goth, 270–1

Thomson, James, 230, 324

Thornton, Deputy-Collector (Jhansi), 284

Thornycroft, Thomas: statue of Boadicea, 272, 297–8, 335

Thurloe, John, 313

Tiflis (Tbilisi), 172

Tilbury: Elizabeth I at, 213, 220–5, 227, 249, 252

Tilsit: Louise meets Napoleon at, 267–9

Titus, Roman Emperor, 109

Tocqueville, Alexis de, 7

Toledo, 191

Tomboy Syndrome: in Warrior Queens, 12–13, 331; Camilla exemplifies, 20, 22; in Matilda, 135; and Caterina Sforza, 197; in Rani of Jhansi, 275

Tomyris, Queen of the Massagetae, 30–1, 330

Tondelli, Leone, 149–50

torcs (Celtic), 49–50, 59

Toro, 191–2

Torqueri of Bouillon, 23

Trebellius Pollio, 114–16

Treece, Henry: *Red Queen, White Queen*, 304

Trevelyan, G. O., 288

Trevelyan, Marie: *Britain's Greatness Foretold*, 299

Trieu Au, 237

Trinovantes (tribe): submit to Caesar, 44; origins, 48; and Iceni, 50; and Roman rule, 64; and Camulodunum, 65, 73; rising, 69, 78

Trung Nhi, 237

Trung Trac, 237

Tubman, Harriet, 9

Turab Ali, 286

Turks *see* Seljuk Turks

Turner, Sir James, 225

Tz'u-Hsi, Empress of China, 297–8

Ubaldini, Petruccio, 5, 54, 217; *Le vite delle Donne illustri* and 'Le Vite e i Fatti di sei Donne Illustri', 218

Ubaldo da Carpineti, 147

Ulm, Battle of, 1805, 261

Urban II, Pope (*earlier* Odo of Champaigne), 143, 146–7

Urraca, Queen of Aragon and León-Castile, 160

Urushadze, Venera, 180

Vaballathus Athenodorus, 117, 119–20, 126

Valerian, Roman Emperor, 113–14

Vedriani, Ludovico, 135

Vega, Garcilaso de la, 195

Veleda (prophetess), 72

Vellocatus, Consort of Cartimandua, 54

Venus Aphacitis (oracle), 121

Venutius, Consort of Cartimandua, 53–5

Vercingetorix, 83, 87, 101

Vergil, Polydore: *Anglica Historica*, 216

Verne, Jules, 295

Verrio, Antonio, 25

Verulamium (St Albans), 81, 90–1, 94

Viaggio (Venetian minister), 190

Victor, Pope, 146

Victoria, Queen: Boadicea as, 5, 299; dismisses failure, 11; Agnes Strickland dedicates book to, 159; John Knox and, 204n; abhors Women's Rights, 209, 319; and Shame Syndrome, 228; biography of Louise dedicated to, 270; accession, 273; attitude to war, 273; and Rani of Jhansi, 276; and Begum of Bhopal, 277; and Indian Mutiny, 282, 288–9; death, 297; letter from Empress Tz'u-Hsi, 297–8; imperialism, 298–9

Victorinus, Gallic Emperor, 123n

Vietnam, 237

Vigée Le Brun, Madame, 254, 257–8

Virgil: *Aeneid*, 20–1, 42, 116

Visconti-Sforza, Bianca, 197

Vitruvia (or Victoria), 123

Vives, Joannes Ludovicus, 187

Vivian, Katharine, 180n

Voada (daughter of Boadicea), 217

Voadicia (daughter of Boadicea), 217

Voltaire, François Arouet de: and Catherine the Great, 10–11, 250, 255–6, 265; *Semiramis*, 29

Voracity Syndrome (sexual): in Warrior Queens, 11–12, 27, 34, 334; in Medb, 16; in Cleopatra, 39; and Cartimandua, 54; and Matilda, 135; and Tamara, 168; and Caterina Sforza, 197, 199–200, 334; and Rani of Jhansi, 290

Voss, Sophie Marie, Countess von, 258, 260, 268–9

Walpole, Horace, 234

Warner, Marina, 304

Warrior Queens: defined, 8–10; supposed sexual licence, 11, 334–5; characteristics and syndromes, 11–13, 331–2, 335; as war goddesses, 17; and matriarchal society, 17–18; voices, 60; and modern political women leaders, 305–6; feminist principles and unbecoming conduct, 326–30; and exercise of authority, 331; uniforms, 331; and motherhood, 332–3; and transcendent patriotism, 333–4

Watts, Isaac, 234

Welf v of Bavaria (Countess Matilda's second husband), 135, 146

Wheeler, Sir Mortimer, 66, 91

White Ship, 152

Wilcox, Toyah, 304

William I (the Conqueror), King of England, 135, 145, 152, 155

William II (Rufus), King of England, 155

William III (of Orange), King of England, Scotland and Ireland, 24, 229

William, King of Prussia, 271

William, Prince (son of Henry 1 of England), 152

William Clito, 155

William of Malmesbury, *see* Malmesbury, William of

Wilson, Robert, 248–9

Winchilsea, Daniel Finch, 6th Earl of, 234

Woman's Own (magazine), 322

Worms, Council of, 1076, 141, 143; Concordat of, 1122, 147

Xerxes, Persian King, 31–4, 205

Ximenes, Cardinal (Francisco de Cisneros), 184

Xiphilinus of Trapezus, 55–6

Yarfe (Moorish champion), 195

Young, Hugo and Sloman, Anne: *The Thatcher Phenomenon*, 318

Young, Janet, Baroness, 319

Zabdas, Palmyran General, 117, 122

Zabibi, Queen, 110

Zagal, El, 193–4

Zainab (sister of Zebbâ), 127

Zamora, 191–2

Zebbâ (al-Zabbà; az-Zabbà; legendary figure), 127

Zenobia, Queen of Palmyra: as Warrior Queen, 10, 106, 115, 177, 240; voice, 60; captivity, 101, 124–6, 160; compared to Boadicea, 107–8, 128; life and background, 107–12; described, 114–15; 'chastity', 115–16, 127, 334; reign, 117–20; conquests, 117–19; declares independence from Rome, 118; consults oracles, 121; war with Aurelian, 122–4; seeks Persian help, 124; retirement in Rome, 125–6, 332; and legend, 127

Zenobius, Bishop of Florence, 126

Zosimus, 113, 115, 122, 125